THE CIRCLE OF SECURITY INTERVENTION

The Circle of Security Intervention

Enhancing Attachment in Early Parent–Child Relationships

Bert Powell, Glen Cooper,
Kent Hoffman, and Bob Marvin

Foreword by
Charles H. Zeanah, Jr.

THE GUILFORD PRESS
New York   London

© 2014 The Guilford Press
A Division of Guilford Publications, Inc.
72 Spring Street, New York, NY 10012

www.guilford.com

Printed in the United States of America

This book is printed on acid-free paper.

Last digit is print number: 9 8 7 6 5 4 3 2 1

The authors have checked with sources believed to be reliable in their efforts to provide
information that is complete and generally in accord with the standards of practice that
are accepted at the time of publication. However, in view of the possibility of human error
or changes in behavioral, mental health, or medical sciences, neither the authors, nor the
editor and publisher, nor any other party who has been involved in the preparation or
publication of this work warrants that the information contained herein is in every respect
accurate or complete, and they are not responsible for any errors or omissions or the
results obtained from the use of such information. Readers are encouraged to confirm the
information contained in this book with other sources.

Library of Congress Cataloging-in-Publication Data

Powell, Bert, 1948–
  The circle of security intervention : enhancing attachment in early parent–child
relationships / by Bert Powell, Glen Cooper, Kent Hoffman, and Bob Marvin.
    pages cm
  Includes bibliographical references and index.
  ISBN 978-1-59385-314-3 (hard cover : alk. paper)
  1. Attachment behavior in children.   2. Parent and child.   I. Title.
  BF723.A75P69 2014
  155.4′192—dc23

                                                                        2013022255

The name Circle of Security and the Circle of Security graphic are trademarked.

*To the individuals and families
we have worked with through the years:
By opening your lives and sharing
your most intimate stories,
you became our most important teachers.*

About the Authors

Bert Powell, Glen Cooper, and Kent Hoffman have been in clinical practice together in Spokane, Washington, for more than 30 years. They have worked as a team to translate complex clinical insights and developmental research into straightforward and accessible protocols for use with individuals and families. Since the early 1990s, they have focused specifically on applying object relations and attachment theory to clinical practice, a shared vision that led to the creation of the Circle of Security (COS).

The three partners have served as consultants to university- and city-funded research projects involving COS protocols for a wide range of clients, including Head Start families, at-risk infants, street-dependent teenage parents, and incarcerated mothers. They have each received the Washington Governor's Award for Innovation in Child Abuse Prevention. They have coauthored numerous peer-reviewed journal articles and book chapters, many along with Bob Marvin, who served as principal investigator on the initial COS project, participated in the development of COS, and continues to be involved in implementing a COS model around the world.

In 2013, all four authors received the Bowlby–Ainsworth Award from the New York Attachment Consortium for the development and implementation of the Circle of Security Attachment Intervention. Cooper, Hoffman, and Powell formed Circle of Security International to provide training on COS early intervention, attachment theory, assessment, and differential diagnosis. In response to the need for a scalable COS model, they developed Circle of Security Parenting® (COS-P), an 8-week DVD protocol for use by clinicians and parent educators with groups, dyads, and individuals that has been translated into multiple languages. This protocol can be learned in a 4-day training program, now available throughout the world.

Bert Powell, MA, began his clinical work as an outpatient family therapist in a community mental health center. During training in family therapy at the Philadelphia Child Guidance Clinic in 1970, Mr. Powell became aware of the gap between cutting-edge treatment and intervention as practiced at the community level and has devoted much of his career to closing that gap by receiving and then offering training and supervision. He is certified in psychoanalytic psychotherapy from The Masterson Institute of New York and is an Adjunct Assistant Professor in the Graduate School of Counseling Psychology at Gonzaga University in Spokane, Washington. Mr. Powell has a private practice and serves as an International Advisor to the editorial board of the *Journal of Attachment and Human Development.*

Glen Cooper, MA, is a licensed Marriage and Family Therapist in private practice. He has extensive training in object relations and family therapy and holds a certificate of Advanced Training in Infant Mental Health Assessment from Tulane University School of Medicine. Mr. Cooper's commitment to social justice steered him to work with homeless men, sexually abused children, and preschoolers from low-income backgrounds, and his work with Head Start teachers led to the development of COS in the classroom. Early in his career, Mr. Cooper worked part-time so as to share in the day-to-day experience of parenting, including serving as a treatment foster parent. He considers being home with children a vital foundation for his clinical work.

Kent Hoffman, RelD, is a member of the Adjunct Faculty in the Department of Psychology at Gonzaga University. He spent the first decade of his career working with psychiatric patients in prison settings, individuals with terminal cancer, survivors of sexual abuse, and homeless persons on the streets of Los Angeles. In the late-1980s, while receiving certification in psychoanalytic psychotherapy through The Masterson Institute of New York, Dr. Hoffman designed treatment protocols for parents and young children. Since that time, he has focused on building the COS model, working with street-dependent teenage parents at a homeless shelter, and adult psychoanalytic psychotherapy. He is also exploring how object relations and attachment theory can inform our spiritual identity and practice.

Bob Marvin, PhD, is Professor Emeritus in the School of Medicine at the University of Virginia and the founder and director of the Mary Ainsworth Attachment Clinic in Charlottesville. Dr. Marvin was an undergraduate student and research assistant with Mary Ainsworth at the Johns Hopkins University. Throughout his career, he has conducted basic and clinical research, direct clinical work, and program development in the field of attachment across a wide range of ages and populations, and has also been involved in developing a number of attachment-related assessment procedures.

Foreword

Attachment theory and research have been of enormous interest to mental health practitioners for more than three decades. By linking certain behaviors in young children to specific motivations, the theory is clinically satisfying on at least two levels. First, it derives from and gives meaning to how infant behaviors are organized, that is, in the service of gaining proximity to attachment figures to feel more secure. Second, it suggests that behaviors derive from and inform mental representations that guide an individual's experience of and responses to the attachment figure and later to others. These representations, or what Bowlby called internal working models, are metaphors for complex processes by which we perceive, interpret, and respond to others in intimate relationships. The simultaneous attention that attachment theory gives to observable behavior and to the deeper meanings of those behaviors was uniquely appealing to many who were drawn to the richness of psychodynamic theories but impatient with their derivation from adult remembrances. Here was a theory that postulated that one could observe the behavior of young children and make meaningful inferences about the motivations, feeling states, and social rules of children as they interacted with important adults in their lives. Further, one could track these developmentally.

Research that was derived from attachment theory, such as the pioneering work of Mary Ainsworth and her colleagues (Ainsworth, Blehar, Waters, & Wall, 1978) on secure, avoidant, and resistant attachment, and later that of Mary Main and her colleagues on disorganized attachment (Main & Solomon, 1990) and the Adult Attachment Interview (Main, Kaplan, & Cassidy, 1985), further bolstered practitioners' excitement that cherished clinical constructs, like transference and the compulsion to repeat, might be understood and even tested in paradigms that were anchored in observable behaviors. In the 1980s, as research on adult and infant attachment exploded, it seemed that we were close to deriving practical treatment prescriptions directly from this work.

But that didn't happen. In presentation after presentation and article after article, nothing seemed to scratch the itch of the question "What does this research mean for clinical treatment of children and adults?" Practitioners were drawn to the work, excited by its appropriately complex focus on relationship approaches for relationship problems, but still unsure of exactly what could be applied and how. Late in his career, Bowlby (1988) wrote *A Secure Base: Clinical Applications of Attachment Theory*, but even that book fell well short of a roadmap. Books by others preceded and followed this one by Bowlby, each more or less successful in translating rich and meaningful developmental research into practical clinical applications, but none really adequately answered the question of how one might apply this knowledge about infant and adult attachment in the clinical setting. A number of interventions were attachment compatible, or attachment derived, but none seemed to fully embody attachment theory and research. In my view, the Circle of Security (COS) is an approach that has changed the game. Derived from attachment research and Masterson's object relations theory, this intervention translates attachment research more meaningfully and more directly than anything we have seen before.

What first struck me, on learning about the COS approach, was the remarkable way it made abstract ideas tangible and real for parents of young children. For years, I had given professional talks stating that a young child's secure base and safe haven behaviors—the venturing out to explore and returning to the caregiver for care—could be readily observed anywhere that young children were interacting with their caregivers. And yet I had not taken the logical next step of explaining these attachment behaviors in the context of interactions clearly and straightforwardly to the parents with whom I worked. By taking attachment theory seriously, even literally, the COS has made it so much more accessible than it ever had been.

Another strength of the COS is its creative approach in engaging parents. It goes beyond the typical video review of interactions, which has become mainstream, and also offers voluminous visual aids, handouts, "shark music," "beautiful tapes," and other approaches that resonate with caregivers and amplify their understanding of their relationships with their children. Repeatedly, I have witnessed the power of some of these efforts to make the attachment story more accessible and captivating than it otherwise would have been. Not all of the specific approaches are for everyone—practitioners or clients—but the emphasis on translating it to make it accessible to parents makes the COS compelling and important in a wide variety of applications.

What really hooked me, however, is the COS emphasis on core sensitivities. What these add to the equation is twofold: first, a deeper understanding of intergenerational transmission of attachment by explicating how differing internal experiences may underlie similar-appearing interactions and imply different meanings; and, second, a far more sophisticated approach to psychotherapy than we have yet seen from an attachment perspective, including implications for tailoring strategic approaches based on our understanding of core sensitivities. Adding sensitivities to attachment theory begs for operationalizing and standardizing their assessment, of course. Doing so will enhance not only the therapeutic promise of the COS but also our understanding of developmental processes.

This book makes the case for COS—clearly and eloquently—as a conceptual model, as a method of parent education, and as a psychotherapeutic technique. My hope is that it will inspire research that evaluates its efficacy, defines its range, and documents its promise.

CHARLES H. ZEANAH, JR., MD
Tulane University School of Medicine
New Orleans, Louisiana

REFERENCES

Ainsworth, M. D. S., Blehar, M. C., Waters, E., & Wall, S. (1978). *Patterns of attachment: A psychological study of the Strange Situation*. Hillsdale, NJ: Erlbaum.

Bowlby, J. (1988). *A secure base: Clinical applications of attachment theory*. London: Routledge.

Main, M., Kaplan, N., & Cassidy, J. (1985). Security in infancy, childhood and adulthood: A move to the level of representation. In I. Bretherton & E. Waters (Eds.), Growing points in attachment theory and research. *Monographs of the Society for Research in Child Development, 50*(Serial No. 209), 66–104.

Main, M., & Solomon, J. (1990). Procedures for identifying infants as disorganized/disoriented during the Ainsworth Strange Situation. In M. Greenburg, D. Cicchetti, & E. M. Cummings (Eds.), *Attachment in the preschool years: Theory, research, and intervention* (pp. 121–160). Chicago: University of Chicago Press.

Preface

In the fields of social and emotional development, attachment
theory is the most visible and empirically grounded conceptual
framework.
—JUDE CASSIDY AND PHILLIP SHAVER (2008)

More than 40 years ago, John Bowlby wrote, "Intimate attachments to other human beings are the hub around which a person's life
revolves." A mere 5 years ago, Cassidy and Shaver made the statement
above in the preface to the second edition of the *Handbook of Attachment:
Theory, Research, and Clinical Applications,* calling attachment theory
"one of the broadest, most profound, and most creative lines of research in
20th-century (and now 21st-century) psychology" (2008, p. xi). Intuitively,
few would dispute the importance of a parent or other primary caregiver
to very young children. Yet the endowments that accrue from our earliest close relationships have continued to be debated: Do we need parents
solely to ensure our survival until we can take care of ourselves? Somehow,
despite ever-mounting research evidence that secure attachment is so much
more beneficial, efforts to transform theory into practice seemed to get
derailed. Behavioral approaches to healthy psychological development pre-
vailed for several decades, thanks largely to the fact that it seemed much
easier to measure behavior than intimate attachment or a person's internal
working models. Not surprisingly, then, the holders of the funding purse
strings tended to favor behavioral research. All this behavioral research
paid off, too: It was, and is, relatively easy to apply in clinical settings, as
any parent who has ever been handed a star chart or taught to use time-out
and incentives can attest. And these time-honored techniques of behavior management work, at least for managing behavior, as any credentialed

teacher, social worker, or family therapist can confirm. *But when it comes to healthy child development, managing behavior is not where the work ends. It is where it begins.*

Is a child whose behavior is better managed a child whose well-being is all it could be? Do skills and self-control lead inexorably to optimal psychological development and success throughout childhood? Can incentives and reinforcement inoculate a child against unhealthy family dynamics and compensate for weak parent–child bonds? Even if they appear to have resolved a child's behavioral and emotional problems, do they keep the adult the child becomes from perpetuating a cycle of disturbances that often persists from generation to generation?

To oversimplify, we human beings are more than the sum of our behavior. As attachment theory proposes, we are creatures with an innate connection to each other through which we feel experienced and understood. We are so dependent from the moment of birth on a loving attachment that all the food and shelter the planet can provide cannot ensure that we will thrive in the absence of a close relationship.

In the years since Bowlby originated his watershed theory, we have been fortunate to acquire data that support our intuitive thinking. Researchers have clearly demonstrated that attachment plays not only a pivotal role in children's psychological development and well-being, but also a key role in the emotional health of adults throughout the lifespan. And in helping to shape adults, attachment helps determine what kind of parents they will be and, therefore, affects their own children's psychological development.

> Over a decade ago, Sroufe (1989) boldly declared that most clinical disturbances in the first three years of life, although poignantly expressed as child behavioral problems, are more usefully conceptualized as relationship disturbances. In keeping with this emphasis, the infant–parent relationship is emerging as the target of most intervention and prevention efforts in infant mental health. (Zeanah, Larrieu, Heller, & Valliere, 2000, p. 222)

Sroufe made that radical statement more than 20 years ago, and yet in most child care centers today the predominant focus is still on managing children's behavior, with little emphasis on children's relationship needs. Through the work and dedication of hundreds of developmental researchers from around the world, attachment theory has arrived in the 21st century as a reliable, valid, and richly detailed resource for clinicians working in the field of early intervention with caregivers and children. But to date, most mental health professionals and child care workers have, at best, a passing familiarity with attachment theory and the vital role that attachment plays in all of our lives.

After about a decade of impromptu hallway meetings, e-mails, late-night conferences, and shared clinical experiences, we came to the inescapable conclusion that it was time to close the gap between attachment research and clinical practice. The Circle of Security (COS) intervention described in this book is our attempt to do that by showing:

- How most behavioral and emotional problems in very young children can be traced to problems with attachment to their primary caregivers.
- How those caregivers can be taught to enhance the attachments that facilitate healthy child development and endow children with the capacity to form secure attachments with their own children as adults.
- How children who feel like they have security in relationships can become more robust at exploring their world.

Although caregivers have an almost universal desire to do the best they can for their children, how they actually interact with their children is, at least partially, based on the unconscious representations, beliefs, procedures, and strategies they develop through their *own* experience of being parented. *The COS approach assumes that the ability to help caregivers change their problematic patterns of interaction is enhanced by awareness of and reflection on the internal processes that guide those interactions.*

In the spirit of making attachment theory more accessible, we undertook the project of creating a one-page graphic to illustrate the salient features of secure attachment, which we call the Circle of Security, and it became the cornerstone of our intervention.

Through a federal Head Start research grant, we integrated the COS graphic into an early intervention treatment protocol. This COS protocol is a 20-session group model in which parents meet weekly to review edited videos of themselves and their children.

We have published three studies on the research implications of the COS protocol. The first summarized the results of the original Head Start study testing whether the COS group intervention (Hoffman, Marvin, Powell, & Cooper, 2006) would prove effective in reducing attachment disorganization and insecurity. The results showed a significant decrease in both disorganized (60 to 25%) and insecure (80 to 46%) attachment from pre- to postintervention. It is this intervention model that is described throughout the book (Hoffman et al. 2006).

The second summarized the results of a study with irritable newborns and their economically stressed mothers in a randomized controlled trial of the COS Home Visiting Intervention (Cooper, Hoffman, & Powell, 2000). The results indicated that for dyads significantly at risk of insecure infant attachment (e.g., a dismissing/avoidant mother with a highly irritable infant), the intervention significantly reduced the risk of insecure attachment (Cassidy, Woodhouse, Sherman, Stupica, & Lejuez, 2011).

The third summarized the use of the COS model focusing on infants (Cooper, Hoffman, & Powell, 2000) within a jail diversion program. The results indicated that the dyads receiving treatment showed a rate of security at the end of the program that was significantly higher (70%) than rates typically observed in samples of high-risk mothers and were in keeping with rates typical of low-risk middle-class samples (Cassidy et al., 2010).

The success of the original COS group protocol has spawned a variety of adaptations. In Spokane, Washington, the COS treatment approach is the cornerstone of the Children's Ark (a day treatment program for parents and children involved with Child Protective Services). It is also the central approach used with street-dependent teen mothers and fathers at a local homeless shelter. It is used in an Early Head Start home visiting program, a Head Start project to enhance relationships between teachers and children in the classroom, and a middle school and high school program for students with behavior problems who have not been successful in mainstream schools. A communitywide effort to coordinate assessment, treatment, and court-related services for young children has incorporated the COS approach. In addition, several Spokane social service agencies are using the COS treatment approach to work with infants, toddlers, school-age children, and adolescents.

In Virginia and in Norway, the COS approach is being applied to working with foster and adoptive parents on a state- and nationwide basis, respectively. In both places, it is also being applied to integrating and coordinating the care of children and parents during and after inpatient treatment at residential treatment centers. In Norway, the COS Parenting intervention is being used throughout the country. In Ontario, the COS approach is being used by a specialized evaluation and treatment center to train members of and consult with other centers and agencies throughout the province. In Japan, it is being used in parent–child treatment, and in Germany, it is part of a research project that uses the protocol with mothers diagnosed with significant mental health disorders.

In Maryland, the COS approach has been used in a home visiting program, and it is also the heart of a community residential program that allows mothers who are incarcerated to live with their babies. In Australia, the approach is used in parent–child treatment and parent education, and there are several projects integrating the Circle into child care facilities. The COS is part of college curricula in attachment theory and has found its way into conferences in England, Ireland, France, Italy, Portugal, Germany, Israel, Australia, Canada, South Africa, Norway, New Zealand, Sweden, Denmark, Japan, Spain, and throughout the United States.

As the pressure grows in our society for early intervention for children, the idea of infant attachment has become increasingly popular among policymakers and professionals in the field. The COS approach has gained such wide support because it makes attachment theory more user friendly: it shows us in an intuitively clear manner how to build a critically important foundation for the development parent of healthy, happy, and well-adjusted children.

Predictably, however, as "attachment" becomes a buzzword, misinformation and confusion abound. Therefore, this book begins, in Part I, with a chapter reviewing the details of attachment theory, including core terminology and concepts. Considering all that is required to transform caregiving practices, the COS treatment approach entails a great deal of complexity, despite the apparent simplicity of the COS graphic. The rest of Part I discusses the child's needs on the Circle, the caregiver's responses on the Circle, what the child needs for healthy psychological development, how attachment patterns are formed as the child and caregiver interact, and how a cycle of insecure attachment and disrupted psychological development can be broken using the COS intervention. Part II describes the COS protocol in detail, including various modalities by which the approach can be delivered, and Part III provides three detailed case examples.

In brief, Figure P.1 illustrates how COS interventions work.

Whether facing the inevitable shortcomings of their caregivers or dealing with serious childhood abuse or neglect, children create behavioral strategies to maintain enough proximity to their caregiver to survive. These

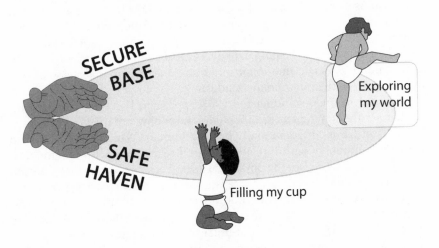

FIGURE P.1. Circle of Security: Parent attending to the child's needs. Copyright 1998 by Cooper, Hoffman, Marvin, and Powell.

strategies are based on their instincts regarding what is close enough but not too close, when it is time to approach and when it is time to withdraw, and what triggers a caregiver's acceptance versus what triggers rejection. They are developed in the preverbal stage, when children are so vulnerable that staying connected is a matter of life or death. It is not surprising, then, that even in adulthood making fundamental changes in these unconscious, nonverbal, life-saving strategies is a complicated undertaking.

The COS treatment approach brings into consciousness these core relationship strategies, which are often hidden within the complexity of human interactions and emotions. However, even when caregivers achieve this awareness, they face the difficult task of acting in opposition to what feels like a life-preserving tactic. It is like walking under a ladder, spilling salt, or breaking a mirror. Even if you don't believe the superstition and you know you are safe, your body may respond with alertness. When adults do not heed their childhood protective attachment strategies, they receive a subtle emotional warning not to step outside of these previously learned strategies. The COS addresses this process of alarm and defense because it has a profound effect on relationship and caregiving capacities.

Once the strategies and the defenses that maintain those strategies are acknowledged, the COS helps caregivers observe the cost, to themselves and their children, of sustaining the old problematic beliefs and behaviors. When caregivers have both awareness and motivation, they can best choose to maintain or change their patterns of interaction.

By enhancing caregivers' capacity to choose patterns of interactions that meet their children's attachment needs, the COS helps develop secure relationships essentially through the use of the COS graphic to guide video reviews and reflective dialogue with caregivers. Since children's essential capacities develop best in the context of secure attachment, the COS can be seen as an approach to helping caregivers create a healthy environment for their children's social, emotional, physical, and cognitive development— and, ultimately, their autonomy as adults.

Critical to understanding the COS approach, however, is the premise that secure attachment to others and autonomy are *together* the warp and weft of being an emotionally healthy human. What children need to develop is autonomy within relatedness *and* relatedness within autonomy. Based on the workings of the physical world, it seems obvious that a person is either with others or alone. There is, of course, no such clear dichotomy. Individuals, even when they are not in the presence of others, are not discrete entities. The internalized sense of being with others is inextricably woven into people's experiences of life, even when they are alone.

Autonomy is developed when children carry inside them a sense that their caregivers are concerned, interested, and available when needed. When children lack this type of connection, the effort to be totally self-sufficient is an act of desperation rather than genuine autonomy. Genuine autonomy is achieved from within a secure attachment. Self-sufficiency is not a sign of emotional strength or psychological health, or even a genuine option. The core of human consciousness is the potential for rapport of the self with another's mind. "The infant experiences being experienced" (Beebe et al., 2010, p. 14). This is true at the beginning of a person's life and is true to the end; being human requires the experience of being experienced and understood as well as feeling safe enough to be oneself and explore.

For these reasons, the study of infant attachment is not only professionally enriching but a profoundly personal experience. What drives the science of attachment is the fact that through our first attachments, for better or for worse, we learn about the world. What makes the science personally compelling is that it is a love story. It is not just any love story; rather, it is the story of the hope, fulfillment, and heartbreak of our first love.

The study of attachment brings our shared story to life with uncompromising honesty and a sense of immediacy partly because so much of the learning is based on observing interactions between caregiver and child through videos. Watching the ancient process of human attachment unfold in family after family can be uplifting. It can also be difficult to bear, yet impossible to turn away from, because the experience of our own history is reactivated by watching the intimate interactions. Sometimes it is painful to watch babies receiving the kindness that we longed for but went without. Other times, it breaks our hearts to see babies facing our greatest pains and worst fears. At its best, the study of infant attachment opens our hearts to the needs of children. We hope that it will become your love story as it has become ours.

Acknowledgments

The writing of this book included almost a decade of starts and stops, beginnings and near decisions to step away from the endeavor completely. Throughout the process, Seymour Weingarten, Kitty Moore, and Rochelle Serwator at The Guilford Press believed in the book, stood behind us, and encouraged its completion. To make sure this happened, they provided the guidance and remarkable skill of Christine Benton, a writer and editor of exceptional talent. While we are experienced in using video to illustrate clinical examples for teaching attachment and object relations theory, we needed Chris's wise counsel and artful writing expertise to help bring our approach to the printed page. We are grateful to her in ways we cannot begin to express. Working closely with Chris and Kitty in these past 3 years has simply been a pleasure.

It goes without saying that John Bowlby's and Mary Ainsworth's fingerprints are on every page of this book. In addition, we want to express ongoing appreciation to the countless attachment and child development researchers upon whose shoulders we stand.

We are incredibly thankful to Jude Cassidy for her scientific rigor, ongoing guidance, unwavering commitment to the COS, and, most important, her friendship, all of which have made this work possible.

We are deeply grateful to Dave Erb for planting the seeds of the COS graphic with his dock-and-boat metaphor. His capacity for Being-With continues to serve as a model for our work.

We are also indebted to James Masterson and Ralph Klein, who introduced us to a systematic understanding of intrapsychic structure, which became the blueprint for the COS core sensitivities. We also thank Ralph for his clinical supervision, where he modeled the relational wisdom at the heart of object relations theory, and for seeing beyond people's defenses and pathology to their intrinsic worth.

We will always be thankful to Susan McDonough, whose pioneering work with video intervention offered the initial inspiration for the COS model.

We are indebted to Sandra Powell, whose unwavering concern for families has inspired so much of what our work has become. Her dedication and commitment to quality treatment for hard-to-reach parents, infants, and children have consistently helped guide us through the years.

We want to thank Charles Zeanah for his help and unyielding encouragement for us to overcome our writing block and get this material published. His belief in the importance of COS inspired us to go the distance.

We would also like to thank the many colleagues, teachers, and mentors who have taught and inspired us throughout our clinical careers: Susie Amundson, Katherine Bair, Kathryn Barnard, Beatrice Beebe, Lisa Berlin, Neil Boris, Mary Dozier, Karla Clark, Robert Emde, Milton Erickson, Linda Gilkerson, Douglas Goldsmith, Mary Clare Heffron, Andrea Karfgin, Frank Kimper, Roger Kobak, Julie Larrieu, Karlen Lyons-Ruth, Salvador Minuchin, Susan McDonough, David Olds, David Oppenheim, Allan Schore, Phillip Shaver, Daniel Siegel, Bill Silvers, Arietta Slade, Susan Spieker, Alan Sroufe, Howard Steele, Miriam Steele, Daniel Stern, Susan Woodhouse, and Yair Ziv.

Our thanks go to the Spokane Research Affiliates who volunteered their time and expertise in the early development and implementation of COS research: Steve Balberg, Pam Barnes, Jennifer Backlund, Mary Brandt, Monica Becket, Polly Carlson, Judy Cooke, Mary Davis, Lisa Estelle, Patsy Etter, Beth Fergin, Jean Fredrickson, Devon Greyerbiehl, Sandra Higman, Diane Hermanson, Sarah Hesslink, Lisa Koch, Suzanne Kolbe, Molly Kretchmar-Hendricks, Clare Lucas, Elizabeth Mann, Janet Mann, Sandy Powell, Beth Raleigh, Michael Roberts, Harry Rosenkrantz, Jennifer Sparr, Katie Wisenor, and Nancy Worsham.

We are especially grateful to the staff, parents, and children at Bancroft School, Spokane Head Start/Early Head Start, Volunteers of America–Crosswalk of Spokane, and Janet and Paul Mann at The Children's Ark for being the original testing grounds for the COS protocol. We also want to thank Dave Tanner and Megan Schuyler Kennedy at North by Northwest Productions and Dan Baumgarten at Community-Minded Enterprises for their help and support.

We are also grateful to our many colleagues, in addition to those already mentioned, who continue to expand and develop the use of COS around the world: Gizem Arikan, Erin Atkinson, Michelle Ball, Neil Boris, Ida Brandtzæg, Kevin Burns, Mike Chewning, Joe Coyne, Robyn Dolby, Matthew J. Dykas, Jane Doyle, Clare Gates, Penny Free, Per Götberg, Carlos Guerrero, Deborah Harris, Mary Hood, Anna Huber, Jo Hussey, Stine Lier, Cami Maianu, Francesca Manaresi, Soledad Martinez, Pia Risholm Mothander, Megumi Kitagawa, Tim Page, Italia Parletta, Jenny Peters, Elizabeth Puddy, Deidre Quinlan, Brigitte Ramsauer, Kate Dent Rennie, Cindy Roberts, Ando Satoko, Avi Sagi-Schwartz, Charlie Slaughter, Stig Torsteinson, Sally Watson, David Willis, Danette Wallersheim, and Caroline Zanetti.

We are grateful every day for the important contributions of Gretchen Cook, Kaaren Goeller Bloom, and Mary Davies at Circle of Security International. Without their commitment, consistency, and kindness, our ability to offer this intervention would truly not be possible. We are also deeply appreciative of Jim Sheehan's vision in founding the Community Building in Spokane. His generosity in providing office and lab space for Circle of Security International, and the support of the community that he is so instrumental in sustaining, makes it possible for us to continue to develop COS and support our many colleagues and agencies in Spokane who are working in early intervention.

We give heartfelt thanks to all of the parents who participated in the initial COS research. It is our hope to honor their courage and contribution to the development of the COS through the retelling of their experience in this book. We trust that their willingness to share their stories will contribute to the security of children in future generations.

Finally, we offer our immense and ongoing gratitude to our own families for their continuing encouragement and steadfast presence during the writing of this book and throughout our lives. Sandy, Chelsea, and Travis; Christine, Erin, Sara, Scott, Benjamin, and Zachary; Kim and Kai; and Cherri—you make up our most intimate Circles of Security, and your caring and commitment are the reasons we could even begin to consider a career based on security and love.

Authors' Note

USE OF CIRCLE OF SECURITY® TRADEMARKED MATERIAL

We are pleased that you have found your way to this introduction to our work. It is our hope that this material will continue to be shared and used with parents and professionals around the globe. For free Circle of Security® downloads and other information, go to *www.circleofsecurity.com*. We ask only that you follow the parameters regarding the sharing of this material described on the Handouts page under the Resources tab.

We hope the information in this book will provide not only an introduction to our work but also an organizational framework that will enhance your own. However, we are aware that the written word is not a substitute for training and supervision, and we do not imply or endorse the notion that reading this material will adequately prepare you to provide Circle of Security® interventions.

It is extremely important to us to maintain the fidelity of the Circle of Security® protocols. To this end, the name Circle of Security and the graphic are trademarked. To request permission to use the name Circle of Security® in any promotional material or for research and direct service grants, please go to our website. Thank you for your help in protecting the fidelity of Circle of Security® and for your work on behalf of children and families.

GENDER-SPECIFIC PRONOUNS

Primary caregivers are both female and male, and attachment is an amazingly gender-neutral phenomenon. Therefore, we have chosen to alternate between masculine and feminine pronouns when describing caregivers. In the same spirit, we have used both "parent" and "caregiver" to honor the contribution of the many caregivers who are not birth parents.

CASE STUDIES

The examples in the book are taken from case material, but all identifying information has been changed to protect families' privacy.

Contents

PART III. CASE EXAMPLES

PART I

ATTACHMENT IN EARLY CAREGIVING RELATIONSHIPS

1

Hidden in Plain Sight

The Critical Importance
of Secure Attachment

If you set out to describe a baby, you will find you are describing
a baby and *someone*.
—DONALD W. WINNICOTT (1964/1987)

You think because you understand one you will also
comprehend two, because one and one make two. But to truly
understand two, you must first comprehend "and."
—SUFI WISDOM SAYING

A dark-haired woman, perhaps age 25, sits on a couch with her
legs crossed, watching her 3-year-old daughter play with a stacking toy
about 15 feet away. She has just returned to the room after an absence
of a few brief minutes, and seeing her daughter methodically loading the
different-shaped rings onto the post, she immediately starts issuing quiet,
matter-of-fact instructions, interspersed with questions: "What color is
that one?" and "What shape is the blue one?" and even "Where is the
hexagon?"

The little girl scrambles around on the rug, following her mother's
lead, but she doesn't turn around to face her. After a few minutes she picks
up a doctor's kit, takes it over to her mother, and tries to climb up on her
lap. Mom gently nudges the little girl back toward the floor, saying "You
haven't stacked all the rings yet. Look at that one . . . and that one!" Her
daughter dutifully returns to the stacking toy and adds another ring. Then
she picks up the doctor's kit and goes back to her mother. This time she
makes it onto her lap, where she examines her ear until Mom again points

3

out that she hasn't finished reassembling all the pieces of the stacking toy. The little girl ignores her prompt and tries to capture her mother's interest as she uses the toy stethoscope to listen to her heart. The mother doesn't look at the little girl but out at the rug and scattered toy parts. Finally the little girl slides down her mother's legs and returns to the toy, where she turns her back on Mom again and finishes putting the rings on the rod where they belong.

Casual observation would label this a typical interaction between an average young mother and preschool child. But this was not a spontaneous moment in the lives of a woman and her daughter. Laura and Ashley had just participated in Mary Ainsworth's widely lauded "Strange Situation" research protocol, designed to reveal attachment patterns between young children and their caregivers. This articulate young woman, clearly devoted to her daughter, had sought help because she wanted more "parenting tips." Although she believed she was already an "excellent mother," she thought it could not hurt to find out more from those who knew "everything about parenting." Laura joined a Circle of Security (COS) group led by one of us, and 12 weeks into the 20-week intervention she watched the video of the interaction just described. She had seen this clip before, at the beginning of the program, and said it showed her how cute her daughter was and allowed her to see details she didn't usually see. This time, watching the video was bringing her slowly to tears. As her face crumpled and she looked down at her lap, she said, "I wasted all that time pushing her away when all she wanted to do was cuddle with me."

What Laura was seeing was what had been invisible to her in the past: the all-important "and" between her and her little girl. Encoded in this unremarkable mother–daughter exchange were remarkable truths about the critical role of primary caregiver relationships in children's psychological development. Yet due to the "mind-blindness" that blocks us from seeing what we cannot tolerate (Shanker, 2004), Laura could not perceive those truths while interacting with her little girl. She could not see that there are moments to provide comfort and moments to encourage exploration—and that children's needs shift between them hundreds of times in a single day. She could not see that parents are often more comfortable meeting one need than the other. She did not know that parents' comfort or discomfort in answering their children's needs is strongly influenced by how their own childhood needs were met or unmet. And she could not see that even very young children learn what makes their caregivers uncomfortable and will use a confounding range of behaviors (what we call "miscues") to hide their need for those things in an attempt to maintain their connection with the caregiver.

The COS intervention and the graphic designed around it are intended to help caregivers increase their awareness of their children's needs and whether their own responses meet those needs. With increased awareness parents can expand their moment-to-moment parenting choices where needed. In this shift from mind-blindness to seeing what is hidden in plain sight lies the potential to break the stranglehold of problematic attachment patterns, passed from one generation to the next, that can compromise healthy relationships throughout a child's lifespan.

THE EVOLUTION OF THE CIRCLE OF SECURITY: A PERFECT STORM

The development of the COS is a story of four clinicians finding themselves happily at the confluence of "atmospheric conditions" that created the perfect storm. First there was emerging clarity that early intervention for children was necessary and viable. Concurrently, the importance of relationships in human health and development was becoming better established, and the internal world of infants and adults was being revealed. Meanwhile, extensive research was establishing the foundational role of attachment in all of the above.

The Need for Early Intervention

- *The field of infant mental health gained weight and maturity from advocacy organizations like Zero to Three and the interest of psychiatrists and continued to grow throughout the 1980s and 1990s* (J. Cassidy, personal communication, May 13, 2011).

- *The field of developmental psychopathology emerged.* During the mid-1980s scientists started to make a conscious effort to ask "What can normal development tell us about psychopathology, and what can psychopathology tell us about development?" (C. H. Zeanah, personal communication, May 17, 2011).

While these developments were brewing everywhere from the lab to the living room, we saw the need to focus on early intervention every day in our work with adults who demonstrated how much happens early that continues to impact individuals in later life. Observing parents acting out the pain from their childhood in a manner that inflicted pain on their children confirmed the centrality of early childhood experience. This held true in everything we had seen since the 1970s in counseling homeless adults, with foster parenting, and in family and individual therapy settings. And the rapidly growing field of infant mental health was now showing without a doubt that the mental health of the youngest children, even infants, was observable and measurable and therefore had potential to be a target for intervention and prevention. But *how* to intervene early? Exactly *how* could we keep the developing mind of the youngest children on an adaptive track to prevent adult problems from germinating?

The Need for Early Intervention to Focus on Relationships

The infant–parent relationship is emerging as the target of most intervention and prevention efforts in infant mental health.
   —CHARLES H. ZEANAH, JULIE A. LARRIEU, SHERYL S. HELLER,
      AND JEAN VALLIERE (2000, p. 222)

Our clinical experience also confirmed the primary tenet of family therapy that a person's behavior problems are rooted in the context of family relationships. This was especially clear when children were removed from chaotic families and placed in high-quality foster homes. The children would blossom, and their problematic behavior would diminish to the point that child protective services would assume the children's problems were solved and send them back to their chaotic families. The problematic behaviors would quickly reemerge.

The framework of family therapy provided many answers. But there were gaps in this therapeutic perspective. Although Salvador Minuchin stated that history is always present in the moment (Minuchin, 1980), and as early as the 1950s Murray Bowen began to explore the influence families of origin have on current relationships, the family therapy field in general paid little attention to internal experience separate from context.

The Need for Early Intervention to Focus on Internal Working Models

• *Selma Fraiberg's landmark 1975 paper "Ghosts in the Nursery" looked at the transgenerational effects of trauma on infants and 30 years later gave rise to Alicia Lieberman's counterpart "Angels in the Nursery," which explored the beneficial effects of good parent–child relationships.*

- *Following the work of many other developmental scientists such as Louis Sander, Daniel Stern, starting with his 1985 book* The Interpersonal World of the Infant, *suggested that caregiving relationships could alter the course of a child's development and future ability to form healthy, adaptive relationships.* No longer was a child's developmental fate viewed as sealed by key events that shaped personality according to old "red thread" and developmental arrest psychoanalytic ideas.

- *The Adult Attachment Interview (AAI) became a critical technological breakthrough that offered a standardized tool for looking at parents' working models (Main & Goldwyn, 1984; George, Kaplan, & Main, 1984).* The principles and information generated by the AAI were of great interest to clinicians because they made it possible for the internal working models of adults to be studied and coded (C. H. Zeanah, personal communication, May 17, 2011).

- *In an article published in 1985 entitled "Security in Infancy, Childhood, and Adulthood," Main, Kaplan, and Cassidy reported that the AAI coding categories for parents were strongly associated with the corresponding attachment categories for their children.* This represented a "major turning point for the direction of the field" (Hesse, 1999, p. 395). Attachment theory shifted the primary focus from the child's or the caregiver's behavior to incorporating the quality of attachment-oriented representations in the mind of the parent and the way these representations predicted the child's attachment behaviors (Main, Kaplan, & Cassidy, 1985).

It was clear from both research and our clinical work that parents were carrying personality traits from one situation to another, which suggested that there was more at play than their current context. It was also clear that when a child was "acting out," the explanation was rarely, according to the popular perspective of the day, a simple matter of behavioral reinforcement. It wasn't just that Dad gives his son what he wants when Junior screams loudly enough, and therefore Junior screams loudly all the time. Children's behaviors seemed to be more than immediate statements about the quality of the interactional family system in which they lived, and they did not appear to be meaningless reflexes that had been shaped by rewards and punishments as the behaviorists believed. Rather, children's behavior is guided by instincts. In effect, behavior is a way children communicate their innate needs. Problem behaviors seemed to emerge when parents chronically failed to meet those needs.

In clinical practice we witnessed children exhibiting clear needs for comfort that were ignored by loving mothers, who nonetheless had the best interests of their children as their top priority. We also watched parents insist on cuddling children who were eagerly reaching out to explore their surroundings. In spite of their best intentions, parents still were not meeting the needs of their children. It was as if we were seeing an invisible puppeteer manipulating the behaviors in every interaction between struggling parents and children.

The desire to understand this "man behind the curtain" and incorporate that understanding into an early intervention led three of us to pursue additional psychoanalytical training. It began when one of us brought James Masterson to Spokane in 1985 to present a workshop for the Spokane Community Mental Health Center's 200-person staff and the professional community. What we learned resonated so strongly with our clinical observations that in 1986 two of us began studying in a distance training program run by the Masterson Institute and received postgraduate certification in psychoanalytic psychotherapy.

Masterson's view of developmental object relations theory gave us hope that psychoanalysis would provide a key to early intervention. But psychoanalysis was still rooted in "red thread" and developmental-arrest theories that did not mesh with our observation that parental dysfunction has its roots in infancy and that the conditions supporting the dysfunction tend to be stable throughout childhood and into adulthood. The idea of personality developing throughout childhood in response to persistent themes offered more explanatory power than the idea of personality being the product of a single event that changed everything thereafter or the product of what had happened at a particular critical age.

During a weeklong seminar in 1989, which turned out to be an important stepping stone in the development of the COS, Daniel Stern answered repeated questions about his view of the theory of developmental arrest with the same answer: that it was a constrictive and limited view of infant development that failed to fully consider the validity of the child's internal experience at a very young age. During our training with the Masterson Institute, another perspective solidified our interest in the importance of internal experience, that of attachment theory.

The Need to Intervene in Attachments

• *Twenty years after Mary Ainsworth discovered the patterns of attachment she named secure, anxious–avoidant, and anxious–ambivalent,*

Mary Main and Judith Solomon added a disorganized/disoriented attachment classification (Main & Solomon, 1986, 1990). This addition brought attachment theory one large step closer to the clinical world, where it could make a difference to children who had been mistreated or whose parents were struggling with mental illness and other significant problems (Solomon & George, 2011; C. H. Zeanah, personal communication, May 17, 2011).

• *In 1989, we were introduced to the work of Susan McDonough, who uses video technology with difficult-to-engage families.* Her highly successful brief psychotherapy model employing video review with parents to support positive interactions with their children opened our thinking to the validity of creating a personalized video-based approach.

• *Filming became a less expensive process.* It might seem strange that a technological advance driven mainly by its entertainment value could pave the way for a clinical leap forward. But the fact that VCRs quickly gained favor with consumers forced the development of cheaper equipment and facilitated observational research (J. Cassidy, personal communication, May 13, 2011).

• *In 1990, Robert Karen's* Atlantic *article called "Becoming Attached" translated the dry concepts of child development into tangible concepts expressed in everyday language.* The expanded book version published 4 years later (1994) captivated readers with its history of attachment theory presented in an engaging nonfiction form, complete with heated debates, rivalries, and eureka moments of discovery. For the first time, attachment theory became known to a large segment of the general public.

• *In 1993, the three of us in Spokane were introduced to Jude Cassidy, an attachment theorist and researcher who would become our most influential resource and guide as we ventured further into understanding attachment theory.* Through her guidance in weekly phone conversations for the first 2 years and with consistent contact to this day, the theory and science of attachment came into focus for us.

Attachment theory supplies an overarching structure to our understanding of the need to intervene early with both family relationships and internal working models. It brought specificity into our understanding of the importance and function of relationships. It confirmed our sense that behavior is instinctual rather than reflexive and thus has meaning, that children are responding to persistent themes rather than to specific events or developmental arrests, and that their behavioral responses are goal-directed adaptations designed to maintain attachment. This attachment instinct was never captured more poignantly than by Judith Viorst (1986) in *Necessary Losses,* where she told the painful yet true story of a baby who was severely burned:

> A young boy lies in a hospital bed. He is frightened and in pain. Burns cover 40 percent of his small body. Someone has doused him with alcohol and then, unimaginably, has set him on fire.
>
> He cries for his mother.
>
> His mother has set him on fire.
>
> It doesn't seem to matter what kind of mother a child has lost, or how perilous it may be to dwell in her presence. It doesn't matter whether she hurts or hugs. Separation from mother is worse than being in her arms when the bombs are exploding. Separation from mother is sometimes worse than being with her when she is the bomb.
>
> For the presence of mother—our mother—stands for safety. Fear of her loss is the earliest terror we know. (p. 22)

In this agonizing story, Viorst is summarizing, from a slightly different angle, the fundamental theme from attachment theory upon which the COS work is founded. Relationship—with a primary caregiver in our earliest months and years—isn't merely important; it is an emotional requirement. Finding a way to stay in relationship—be it considered positive or negative, secure or insecure—isn't a convenient "add-on," chosen if it feels suitable or expedient and disregarded if not. Whether from the work of Harry Harlow (with monkeys who preferred a cloth "mother" to the metal one that provided food), John Bowlby, and Mary Ainsworth or the horrifying description of the child and parent Viorst presents, relationship emerges as an emotional necessity every bit as critical as oxygen is physically.

Attachment theory did not, however, merely confirm the importance of that bond. It also provided a framework, exactly as John Bowlby had envisioned, for intervening early in the lives of children. Attachments help children create what he called internal working models of themselves and the people in their closest relationships. Secure attachments would carry children along a healthy developmental path and into adulthood. With secure internal working models, they could thrive in relationship and form the same secure bonds with their own children. It might very well help break the cycle of psychological challenges that are often perpetuated across generations.

A BRIEF HISTORY OF ATTACHMENT THEORY

As early as 1940, based on his volunteer work with maladapted children, John Bowlby was promulgating a revolutionary view that children's relationships with their caregivers played an important role in mental health. Bowlby's theory departed sharply from Freudian theories that children are motivated intrapsychically by two primary drives, sex and aggression, and the struggle to resolve the Oedipus complex. In 1944 Bowlby published a study called "Forty-Four Juvenile Thieves." In that study he reported that the most disturbed delinquents in his sample all had a significant history of separation from their mothers. Findings such as these launched Bowlby on a lifelong inquiry into the nature of children's attachment to their primary caregivers.

So radical were Bowlby's ideas that when he began his work on attachment, he found that "of papers written for European or American journals between 1920 and 1940, only twenty-seven of them looked at the correlation between maternal care and mental health" (Blum, 2002). Since then thousands of papers have been written on attachment, starting with Bowlby's own widely read *Maternal Care and Mental Health,* first published by the World Health Organization in 1951 (a monograph that sold 400,000 copies!). There he made the groundbreaking, empirically based statement that for a child to be mentally healthy "the infant and young child should experience a warm, intimate, and continuous relationship with his mother (or permanent mother substitute) in which both find satisfaction and enjoyment" (Bowlby & Ainsworth, 1951, p. 11; Bretherton, 1992).

This idea was opposed by child care experts of the mid-20th century, such as physicians, psychoanalysts, and social learning theorists. From a medical perspective, an emerging understanding of the necessity of hygiene led Luther Emmett Holt (1855–1924), the premier pediatrician of his time, to suggest that adults should avoid contact with children, even affectionate touch and especially kissing. From a child psychology perspective, Dr. John B. Watson (1878–1985), the father of American behaviorism, suggested that hugging and coddling infants would harm psychological health and that children could be ruined for life by "overhandling" for even a few days. He went on to say that "mother love is a dangerous instrument" (Blum, 2002, p. 37). In Freud's view, continuing to rely on a parent was a sign of being overly dependent.

Enter Mary Ainsworth, who happened to answer an ad seeking a researcher to work with John Bowlby in investigating how separation from the mother in early childhood affected the development of a child's personality. Ainsworth brought to the job her own interest in the importance of secure dependence on parents to a child's developing autonomy, as well as impressive experience with methodology. She worked with Bowlby during the 1950s while Bowlby set about building a theory regarding the importance of a child's attachment to his or her primary caregiver. While Ainsworth largely agreed with the direction of Bowlby's thinking, she had doubts about how ethology (such as theories about imprinting) could explain a child's need for his or her mother. In another happy accident, she gained the opportunity to seek empirical evidence for the relevance of ethological concepts (along with those from developmental psychology and other fields from which Bowlby was drawing) when she and her husband relocated to Uganda in 1953. Observing mothers and babies in naturalistic settings, she found herself gathering data that eventually supported a theory that had not yet been formulated and would not be presented to the world until 5 years later. Ainsworth's observations led her to classify infants as securely attached, insecurely attached, or unattached, but she also noticed a correlation that became the foundation of the COS intervention: *The most securely attached infants—those who were generally content, easily soothed when upset, and willing to explore when with their mothers—had mothers who were most sensitive to the infants' signals about what they needed.*

John Bowlby spent the next decade writing his influential trilogy of books on attachment, loss, and separation, building a foundation for attachment theory that "would spawn one of the broadest, most profound, and most creative lines of research in the 20th century (and now the 21st century)" (Cassidy & Shaver, 2008, p. xi). Meanwhile, Mary Ainsworth undertook another major naturalistic study of mothers and babies in Baltimore, where she recruited expectant mothers and then observed the mother–child bonds until just past the baby's first birthday. Bob Marvin, then an undergraduate, worked on this project. By the beginning of the 1970s, Ainsworth had also devised the groundbreaking research instrument called the Strange Situation, which is a key vehicle through which COS videos of mother–child interactions are made. The Strange Situation, described more fully in Part II of this book, allows researchers to observe the nature of attachment between a caregiver and baby or young child via brief separations and reunions. When Ainsworth applied it in her Baltimore study, she found that separations generally triggered anticipated reactions from the children (distress, less exploratory play). What surprised her, however, was the reactions of some of the children upon their mothers' return. Some children—even though they had shown that they wanted their mother when she was out of the room—did not exhibit relief and joy when she came back. Some acted aggressively toward her, hitting or kicking her. Others turned their back or otherwise showed disinterest. Even more exciting to Ainsworth was that these reactions correlated with more discordant mother–child relationships in the same dyads at home.

From this work Ainsworth derived more specific attachment classifications: secure (distressed during separation, readily comforted upon reunion, and soon ready to resume active exploration), ambivalent/resistant insecure (the hitters), and avoidant insecure (the cool customers).[1] So compelling was the Strange Situation as a research method and so revelatory were these attachment classifications that the entire direction of the new field of attachment theory seemed to take a detour toward research and away from the clinical application that Bowlby favored, and even from what could be learned in naturalistic settings such as in Ainsworth's Uganda and Baltimore studies.

By the 1980s, thousands of studies of attachment via the Strange Situation had cemented the validity of attachment classifications and their behavioral manifestation in caregiver–child interactions, and they had begun to inspire further studies attempting to find correlations between attachment problems and emotional problems displayed by children as they matured. Attachment theory thus gained more and more credence in the broader field of developmental psychology. Still, the focus was almost exclusively on research, even though Bowlby himself returned during the 1980s to his earlier priority of developing attachment theory as an intervention, exploring how it could be applied in psychotherapy. It took the development of the other "atmospheric conditions" previously enumerated to build excitement about the viability of early intervention—and, in turn, to lay the groundwork for the conceptualization of the COS.

As a result of this confluence of events, by the early 1990s the implications of attachment theory were being explored in ever-widening circles— from different cultural perspectives; between other dyads (two adults, siblings, father and child); longitudinally; in links to the development of psychopathology; and, of greatest relevance to the eventual development of the COS, transgenerationally.

---

[1] Various labels have been used to describe these attachment patterns over the years. As noted earlier in this chapter, a fourth classification—disorganized—was later proposed by Mary Main and embraced by Mary Ainsworth. These patterns will be discussed in full in Chapter 4.

THE GATHERING "CLOUDS" FORM A CIRCLE

Attachment theory crystallizes the fact that children have essential needs not just for food and shelter but for emotional warmth, comfort, self-esteem, and the development of autonomy and a sense that the world of people is a positive place. Attachment theory confirms that it is not one moment or one problem that lays the foundation for later psychological health or the lack thereof; it is the transgenerational transmission of a caregiver's state of mind through 10,000 events each day that the child adapts to and builds a strategy to address. In other words, to understand a child, one must understand a parent and a child. The quality of the attachment between the primary caregiver and the child serves as the "and" that can help us comprehend "two" and thus help "one."

Attachment theory clarifies that avoid/approach strategies in adults are rooted in their upbringing. It shows how easily those avoid/approach strategies in parents become entangled with their growing child's needs to move closer for comfort and safety and to confidently move away to explore the world. How those procedurally ingrained strategies surface in a caregiver's behavior and influence the caregiver's response to a child's needs for closeness or exploration illuminates why well-intentioned parents often give children what they don't need. Attachment theory shows how easily we can be fooled by a young child's miscues when a child believes that what he really needs will be intolerable to the parent.

A shared desire to understand the context that shaped and organized the symptoms with which families were struggling—the essential focus of family therapy—was the initial drive for the work that would produce the COS. We were convinced of the powerful role that attachment patterns play in shaping families and determining the emotional health of the child. But how could we make abstract, sophisticated attachment theory and research accessible so that it could be applied in clinical settings to help the parents who were dealing with overwhelming problems?

After a decade of evolving quietly, the COS was suddenly launched after a phone call in 1998. The three of us in Spokane—Bert Powell, Glen Cooper, and Kent Hoffman—had been consulting with our local Head Start program for years. We had begun to introduce ideas that we were developing with Bob Marvin from the University of Virginia about applying attachment theory to practice. The Spokane Head Start director's administrative assistant came across a U.S. Department of Health and Human Services (USDHHS) University–Head Start Partnership Grant application.

She went to the director, Patt Earley, and said, "Isn't this what we are doing, and if so, why aren't we being funded for it?" The director brought us the grant application and asked the same question. We then called Bob and asked if the University of Virginia was interested in being a university partner with Spokane Head Start. Through the process of writing the grant application, the COS intervention took shape, and when the grant was received it underwent the first research trial. The COS has continued to evolve at a frantic pace ever since.

Our fundamental goal was and is to intervene early so as to prevent adult problems from taking root in early childhood, by changing the quality of the caregiver–child relationship. The medium for making a difference in this relationship is making a change in parents. But we know from the research on adult attachment that working with parents' state of mind with regard to attachment is more important than just changing parents' behavior, because a change in behavior may not change parents' underlying relationship strategies. As attachment theory reveals, a change in parents leads to a change in children because children are intensely motivated to adapt, for better or worse, to parents' relationship strategies in an attempt to maintain the connection so important to their security, growth, and survival. We knew that in order for parents to change, we needed to address the defenses that, according to psychoanalytic concepts, were likely behind parents' difficulties in meeting the needs of their children. And we knew we could use videos of the dyads in the Strange Situation to engage parents in reflective dialogue about their own strategies, especially patterns of interacting with their child that neither fulfilled the child's needs nor served the parents' goals to do their best for their children.

The optimal route to a change in parents' state of mind was reflective dialogue within the therapeutic relationship, the process by which the client experiences with the therapist what the therapist hopes the child will experience with the client. Every aspect of the COS is based on the contention that the nature of the relationship is a change agent—or, as Jeree Pawl has said so aptly, "Do unto others as you would have others do unto others" (Pawl & St. John, 1998). Family therapy emphasized the importance of parallel process in which therapists provided for the parents what the parents needed to give to their child to create the desired change. From Donald Winnicott's "holding environment" to Heinz Kohut's emphasis on empathy, mirroring, and "transmuting internalizations," psychoanalysis postulated that if the client does not feel the presence and genuine concern of the clinician, nothing seems to change. All of us had seen these truths borne out in long- and shorter-term therapies well before we started working with very young children and their parents.

We now had the medium for early intervention (the parents' positive intentionality), a tool to help parents see what was usually hidden in plain sight (video), an instrument to help us understand a parent's state of mind and attachment struggles (a modification of the AAI and the Strange Situation), and a conduit for facilitating difficult but desired change (a relationship with a concerned and supportive therapist). What we lacked was a way to show parents—including very young, disadvantaged, undereducated parents—what their children need from them. What we needed was a map of children's attachment needs.

The COS graphic is what we arrived at (see Figure 1.1). It took us more than 10 years to get to this diagram, through frequent discussion, consultation with experts in attachment and object relations theory, and much drafting and redrafting in response to what we continually learned in clinical practice. The graphic crystallized in our designing and redesigning so that ultimately it was a simple representation of the reciprocal relationship between the safe haven and secure base needs of children.

The intervention we proposed studying in the USDHHS University–Head Start Partnership Grant involved showing caregivers carefully chosen and edited videos of their interactions with their children in the Strange Situation and encouraging them to:

- Increase their sensitivity and appropriate responsiveness to the child's signals relevant to the child's moving away to explore and moving back for comfort and soothing.
- Increase their ability to reflect on their own and the child's behavior, thoughts, and feelings regarding their attachment–caregiving interactions.
- Reflect on experiences in their own histories that affect their current caregiving patterns.

In November 1998 the four of us began work together, with training in conducting the Strange Situation provided by Bob Marvin, and by January of 1999 we had recruited and assessed 18 parents to begin three 20-week group interventions involving weekly 75-minute meetings with a psychotherapist to review the edited videos of interactions recorded during a preintervention assessment. The therapist led psychoeducational and therapeutic discussions aimed at helping the parents achieve the preceding

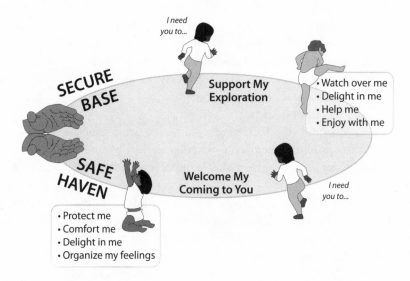

FIGURE 1.1. Circle of Security: Parent attending to the child's needs. Copyright 1998 by Cooper, Hoffman, Marvin, and Powell.

three goals, and at the end of the 20 weeks parent–child interactions were recorded again to show parents what had changed in their relationship with the child through the intervention. The attachment patterns were scored and the data analyzed following the 3-year grant period with 75 dyads.

HOW THE CIRCLE OF SECURITY PROMOTES ATTACHMENT

The study funded by our Head Start research grant was able to show that attachment between primary caregivers and children could be improved with an intervention. When we began the research, we had hoped to find that dyads scored as disorganized, the most problematic type of attachment, would be able to move to insecure (avoidant and ambivalent), but we were amazed to see many families had moved all the way to secure. Once all 75 participating dyads had been scored at the end of the study, only 25% of the dyads were classified as disorganized, compared to 60% preintervention. Only 46% of the dyads were classified insecure, as opposed to 80% before the 20-week program. But what did these outcomes mean for the future of these families?

It would not be an exaggeration to say that in our view these outcomes are at the heart of meeting the needs of growing children. We're defined by security whether we have it or not. Intimate connections hold the key to healthy development, adult self-confidence, fulfilling love, and much, much more. Attachment ranks as a basic necessity for infants along with food and water. Until this fact is fully appreciated, it is difficult to even begin to intervene on behalf of infants.

To put it simply, the COS promotes secure attachment between children and their primary caregivers—whether they be parents, grandparents, foster parents, or someone else who is number one on the child's list of go-to adults—by targeting the caregivers. Attachment is plastic. Even parents from the most insecure, threatening backgrounds can "earn" security—through secure relationships formed later in life, through the self-reflection processes that create new internal working models and override childhood insecurity. The same plasticity accrues to their children: when parents change the way they respond to their child's needs for care and confidence, a child whose attachment to the parent was insecure or even disorganized can be transformed.

The caregiver is the key, and we believe the COS is effective because it taps the innate desire of parents to do their best for their children. The COS intervention is not about telling bad parents that they are parenting badly. It is a celebration of parents. It is an opportunity for beleaguered, overwhelmed, perplexed parents, especially those fighting the odds of undereducation, poverty, abuse or neglect, lack of social support, even marginalization, to become the parents they wish they had had. We have seen the highest-risk parents with the fewest resources—15-year-old homeless mothers, mothers who are incarcerated, parents with histories of drug abuse, domestic violence, physical and sexual abuse, child protection services involvement, and so forth—exhibit positive intentionality toward their children when they become parents. Perhaps they are still looking for that face that babies seek from the moment of birth and are hoping to find it as a reflection of themselves in their own baby's eyes.

Most of all, the success of the COS flows from the parents' capacity for reflective functioning, the ability to reflect on their experience and the experience of their children. Parents' narratives about their experiences need to be coherent enough so they can develop the reflective functioning necessary to observe and come to understand their interactions with their child through the lens of attachment behaviors. They need to be able, with psychoeducation, therapist counseling, and the support of other caregivers in the group, to understand not only their child's cues but also the child's miscues. We have been amazed at parents' courageous willingness to see where they do not meet their child's needs as well as where they do. COS has not only helped them finally see what is hidden in plain sight but is able to change their reflective capacity so they can see their interactions with their child and their child's overarching need and love for them as they never have before.

The COS intervention seems to get through to the majority of participants mainly because it taps an innate longing that is as natural and irresistible for parents as it is for the babies who depend on them. When the stage is set adroitly, with video clips chosen carefully to highlight what parents do right as well as one thing—what we call the "linchpin"—that they are doing "wrong" in responding to their child's needs, the videos seem to reach parents through their deep love for and desire to do right by their child. The intervention focuses not on techniques, as is still prevalent in many approaches, but on state of mind.

What makes a difference is parents making an empathic shift toward their children and gaining a deep understanding of the immutable bond between parent and child. For parents who may have learned not to expect love and acceptance, the COS reveals that in every interaction their child is saying to them, "You are so beautiful to me." Once they truly understand the profound depth of their child's love and need for them, how to behave almost seems to follow naturally.

WHY IS THE CIRCLE OF SECURITY INTERVENTION SO IMPORTANT?

What's done to children, they will do to society.
　　—ATTRIBUTED TO KARL MENNINGER

Secure attachment in early childhood does not simply improve the odds of intimate connections and gratifying friendships in adulthood, although evidence is mounting that it does do that. But the benefits of secure attachment hardly end there. Beginning in the 1990s, one group of researchers came up with a model to help explain early behavior problems that included quality of attachment relationships among four risk factors (Greenberg, Speltz, & DeKlyen, 1993; Greenberg, Speltz, DeKlyen, & Jones, 2001). While a single domain of the four factors generally did not predict the development of disorders among children, when two domains were analyzed, secure attachment was shown to be protective in the presence of high infant negativity, whereas insecure attachment did predict later behavioral problems. When using the two domains of insecure attachment and high-risk parenting combined with a third domain of either multiproblem family ecology or high infant negativity, the probability of predicting high problem behavior in the child increased (Keller, Spieker, & Gilchrist, 2005). (See Box 1.1.)

Although insecure attachment has not been seen to clearly predict later disorders, especially in the absence of problems in other domains that affect the child's life, disorganized attachment is predictive of problems. According to van IJzendoorn, Schuengel, and Bakermans-Kranenburg (1999), disorganized attachment is associated with psychopathological outcomes such as:

- Increased problems with aggression in school-age children.
- Difficulty calming after stressful events.
- Elevated risk of dissociative symptoms in adolescence.
- Difficulties in emotion regulation.
- Academic problems.
- Lower self-esteem.
- Rejection by peers.

Even insecure attachment during infancy can lead to poorly controlled behavior, anger, and poor relationships with peers by the preschool years and later (Carlson & Sroufe, 1995; Sroufe, Egeland, Carlson, & Collins, 2005).

On the protective side, the attachment behavioral system—whereby a child does what is needed to initiate or maintain closeness with the caregiver—has been described as a kind of psychological immune system in its role of buffering the effects of psychological stressors (Lyons-Ruth et al., 1998). Fifty years of research has shown that children who are more securely attached:

- Enjoy more happiness with their parents.
- Feel less anger at their parents.
- Get along better with friends.
- Have stronger friendships.
- Are able to solve problems with friends.
- Have better relationships with brothers and sisters.
- Have higher self-esteem.
- Know that most problems will have an answer.
- Trust that good things will come their way.

BOX 1.1. ATTACHMENT THROUGHOUT HISTORY

Anecdotally people have been drawing connections between the quality of early attachment with caregivers and subsequent development—and even survival—perhaps since the beginning of recorded history:

Roman emperor Frederick II, attempting to discover during the 13th century whether children not taught another language would naturally speak the language God taught to Adam and Eve, instructed caregivers for a group of infants to take care of them but not speak or gesture. According to a monk who chronicled the experiment, "But he laboured in vain, for the children could not live without clappings of the hands, and gestures, and gladness of countenance, and blandishments" (Coulton, 1906).

Deborah Blum, in her book *Love at Goon Park* (2002), cites several studies showing that, even with good hygiene and care, foundlings deprived of attachment to a primary caregiver died at an alarming rate: 30% of the children in 10 foundling homes in 1931, and 23 out of 88 in a foundling home in 1945, compared to no deaths among children who had access to their mothers by attending a large, chaotic nursery school for children whose mothers were in prison.

In 1952, James Robertson, in conjunction with John Bowlby, filmed a 2-year-old who was in the hospital for 10 days with a herniated navel, whose parents visited roughly every other day for half an hour (as was typical in that era). The child was filmed every morning at the same time, and the film showed that, deprived of maternal care, the child went from bubbly and sparkly to angry, wetting the bed, throwing toys, and finally becoming despondent. Over the 10-day hospital stay the child just wilted. This film changed hospital policy all over England, allowing parents much more "visiting time" with their sick children.

- Trust the people they love.
- Know how to be kind to those around them.

Through watching video clips and learning about attachment theory in group sessions during the COS intervention, Laura could eventually see that Ashley's attempt to get on her lap was not only an expression of her daughter's need for comfort after the separation but also a question about whether she would be available to her little girl when she needed her. She could see that she tended to offer her daughter teaching and encouragement to explore regardless of what Ashley needed because that was what Laura was comfortable providing. She could see that her daughter's turning her back to her—and even attempting to "bribe" her into cuddling by bringing along an educational toy—was Ashley's way of trying desperately to give her mother what she thought *she* needed so that she would stay with her. Eventually, Laura was able to pull together the pieces of her childhood attachment to her own parents to understand how those patterns had been playing out—again, hidden in plain sight—in the way she interacted with her daughter.

At the end of the 20-week COS intervention, 3-year-old Ashley was assessed via the Strange Situation again and scored secure. She was now able to use her mom as a safe haven when she was upset and as a secure base from which to explore. When asked what was most rewarding and most difficult about participating in the intervention, Laura said the most rewarding thing was knowing how much Ashley needed her even if she acted so independent. The most difficult was seeing herself push her daughter away. In response to friends and family who asked her what she had gotten out of the COS, she said, "It's very eye-opening, but this is not something you can explain. You can't explain how to read a look on your kid's face or a rise in her voice or her body language. You can't explain how to read those things to someone."

2

The Circle of Security

Understanding a Child's Needs
for a Safe Haven and a
Secure Base for Exploration

Piglet sidled up to Pooh from behind. "Pooh!" he whispered.
 "Yes, Piglet?"
 "Nothing," said Piglet, taking Pooh's paw. "I just wanted to be
sure of you."
 —A. A. MILNE, WINNIE THE POOH

Figure 2.1, which is at the center of our work with families in the COS intervention program and was introduced in Chapter 1, is a roadmap intended to show parents the way to a secure attachment with their young child. It reduces to fundamental terms a profound truth about child development: having a primary caregiver who consistently provides both comfort (a safe haven) and encouragement (a secure base from which to explore) optimizes a child's chance of growing into an adult who can rely on both self and others and successfully navigate the world.

The simple nature of the COS diagram is not intended as a statement about the intellectual powers of parents. To the contrary, the parents we work with have exhibited the capacity for stunning insight into the parent–child bond. Parents like Laura, introduced in Chapter 1, who lack trust in themselves and their ability to fulfill their role in their child's life, seem able to put the power of attachment into words and actions by using the COS as both a starting point and a home base to return to in uncertainty. It took us nearly a decade to find a way to summarize the essence of security in an

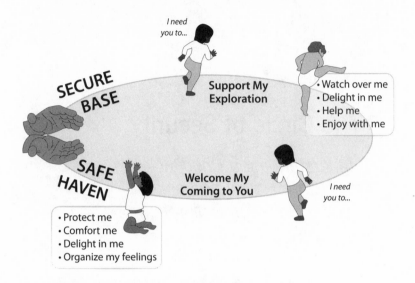

FIGURE 2.1. Circle of Security: Parent attending to the child's needs. Copyright 1998 by Cooper, Hoffman, Marvin, and Powell.

image that was immediately recognizable for parents. Our goal was to offer an icon that would be both scientifically valid and intuitively understandable.

The Circle diagram simplifies the complexity of attachment theory for parents; therapeutically, it is a way to reach parents who are having difficulty decoding their children's behavior as an expression of their fundamental needs. For parents who enjoyed a secure attachment when they were young, no map may be necessary; a child's fundamental needs for safety and confidence seem obvious. But parents who lacked a healthy attachment as children seem to be somewhat blinded by a veil stitched of their own unmet needs—a state of mind in which their children's basic need for security seems unacceptable, even threatening.

Every parent misinterprets a child's needs sometimes: a baby cries for warmth and Mom feeds him; an infant wails in hunger and Dad rocks him. But when parents have learned in the cradle that they can't trust someone to be there for them, that certain needs may be intolerable, then messages of those particular needs sent by their own young child are likely to be lost in translation. Lost, too, then is the child's chance of having that need met. Desperate now, the child encrypts the original message of need into a strategy of compliance to protect himself from parental disapproval or withdrawal, hoping this miscue will keep him close enough to a protective parent to feel connected and safe enough to survive. Parents typically accept the miscue, and a way of interacting develops that leads to the child's ever-deepening need remaining unfulfilled. Instead of a bond of trust and mutual caring, a widening breach forms between the caregiver and child, as if the language of behavior and empathy were carved on a Rosetta stone missing key phrases.

As this chapter explains, a healthy attachment bond equips children throughout their life with a deep instinctual understanding of how important a parent or other primary caregiver is to a child so that as adults they grasp not only how precious they are to their own children but also how capable they are of providing what their child needs. The COS depicts parents as strong, warm hands ready, willing, and able to hold their child. This vivid picture of parents as the hands on the Circle evokes the innate knowledge of how essential they are and how effective they can be as parents. In the process it defuses the defensiveness and self-blame that can stand in the way of parents' learning to speak the language of attachment again. The power of that holding environment, or what we have come to call a state of Being-With (see Chapter 3), is the very essence of the COS. If the hands are not available to be with the child, there is no Circle.

CARE SEEKING, CAREGIVING, AND EXPLORATION

Being-With requires an understanding, either implicitly known or learned later in life, of basic attachment theory. Maintaining enough proximity to avoid becoming easy prey and at the same time developing the skills that will be needed as an adult is a difficult task. Yet this balancing act defines the primal goal for all newborn children. Reaching it involves a reciprocal relationship among three attachment systems that Bowlby clarified and that are encapsulated in the COS:

- Care seeking (attachment): the instinct to seek proximity to a specific person who will comfort, protect, and/or organize one's feelings.
- Caregiving (bonding): the instinct to monitor a specific person and to comfort, protect, and/or organize that person's feelings when necessary.
- Exploration: the instinct to follow one's innate curiosity and desire for mastery when it feels safe to do so.

Children become securely attached when their primary caregiver recognizes when they need the comfort and protection of a safe haven and when they need the encouragement and confidence of a secure base. Very young children alternate between these two fundamental needs dozens, even hundreds, of times a day. They move between the two fluidly, often without warning. The COS diagram is a circle to convey to parents that children usually move from one set of needs into the other with no traffic-signal switch to indicate that they need something different from what was called for a minute ago. They go round and round, dabbling in discovery and then running back for comfort or protection. They fill their cups with renewed confidence and then dart off again. Thus, as we have previously noted, their rapidly shifting needs are hidden in plain sight, and therefore parents whose own needs went unmet need a roadmap.

The function of attachment behavior: comfort and protection.
The function of exploratory behavior: learning and mastery.

The relationship between attachment behaviors and exploratory behaviors is one of reciprocal inhibition. Imagine a seesaw, with attachment behaviors on one end and exploratory behaviors on the other. When a child feels unsafe or overwhelmed by incomprehensible emotions, attachment behaviors activate and exploration terminates. When the seesaw tips so that attachment behaviors go up, the exploratory behaviors go down. Once the child feels safe enough, attachment behaviors stop and exploratory behaviors engage, so the seesaw tips the other way. (See Figure 2.2.)

Of course, very young children have no grasp of a concept like reciprocal inhibition and often do not themselves understand why, in the middle of playing, they suddenly feel the need for comfort and safety. Maybe their caregiver has become unavailable without warning, which can mean something as seemingly unthreatening as getting a phone call (see Box 2.1). This separation nonetheless activates the child's attachment system, and at that point the only thing the child is interested in is doing whatever it takes to reestablish the connection with the caregiver. Think of preschoolers banging on the bathroom door just closed by Dad. Or a toddler who begins tugging on Mom's pants the minute she starts to talk to a neighbor when Mom and the toddler are in the front yard. When children cry out, they are making the statement that they need to know their attachment figure is available when needed so they can once again feel protected from some indefinable fear evoked by feeling momentarily disconnected. What baffles (and aggravates) parents is that when children seeking reconnection finally

Activation of Exploration

Activation of Attachment

FIGURE 2.2. Activation of exploration (top) and activation of attachment (bottom). Copyright 1996 by Cooper, Hoffman, and Powell.

get a caregiver's attention, they often can't answer the question "What do you want?" because the accurate answer would be "According to Bowlby, my instinct to maintain proximity to a specific trusted caregiver activated my attachment system when you appeared unavailable and triggered an attachment behavior (e.g., crying). Thank you for once again being that trusted available caregiver."

The youngest children are in no position to articulate *or* control these alternating needs. Fortunately for our species, children have a built-in facilitator of their inexorable march toward developing the skills to be responsive caregivers themselves someday. Let's call her Mom. It's Mom's job to meet the child and figure out what the child needs—protection, comfort, delight, help with organizing feelings—to terminate the attachment activation so the child can explore. Once the child is exploring, the job shifts: it's now the caregiver's task to watch over the child, to help when needed, to enjoy and take delight in the child's exploration.

How adept the caregiver is at recognizing and meeting these needs

---

**BOX 2.1. WHY THE MOMENTARY UNAVAILABILITY
OF AN ATTACHMENT FIGURE HURTS SO MUCH**

Daphne was speechless when her older sister, Vicky, hung up on her upon hearing the news that their middle sister, not Vicky, was going to accompany Daphne to take a first look at wedding gowns. Stan was confused by how devastated he felt when his mentor said he didn't have time to talk about the fact that Stan had just been fired without warning. Toshiko had stopped speaking to her best friend, who was so preoccupied with taking care of her aging mother that "she just doesn't have time for me these days."

Based on this information alone, many people would say that Vicky, Stan, and Toshiko were overreacting at the very least, even behaving irrationally. They might accuse Vicky of being jealous, Stan of being needy, and Toshiko of being selfish—in the same way that parents sometimes think their young children's intense reactions to their brief unavailability (to take a phone call, answer an important e-mail, even go to the bathroom) are signs of their being "spoiled," "babyish," or "temperamental." Many of us can recall a moment when, like Stan, we surprised even ourselves with the intensity of our reaction to the inaccessibility of someone to whom we have a close bond, over something that any reasonable adult would deem minor.

The fact is, emotions associated with attachment and the unavailability of the caregiver can be far more intense than the situation rationally calls for due to their survival/protective origin. But it is more than protection from a predator that is involved in attachments. So many capacities needed to survive and develop competence involve connection to others that it is not surprising when unavailability of the *most* important other evokes feelings with the intensity associated with life-and-death matters. Vicky felt bereft because she had often served as a substitute mother for Daphne and wanted to be able to delight in her joy at her upcoming marriage. Hurt and stunned by the rejection of his employer, Stan wasn't demanding that his mentor drop everything for him, but at this moment he needed the confidence and encouragement of this person who had provided it so often in the past, more than he ever had. Toshiko did not form close friendships easily. It had taken her years to trust someone enough to view her as a "best friend," and even though she knew it was neither rational nor fair to act slighted when her friend was under such duress, she could not help feeling personally abandoned when her friend was rarely able to spend more than a few minutes on the phone or go out for a leisurely lunch.

Understanding that this kind of unavailability can feel like such a threat to survival can help parents make an empathic shift toward meeting their child's needs around the Circle.

---

plays a large role in determining the fluidity of the relationship between attachment behaviors and exploratory behaviors and, ultimately, the child's developmental trajectory to adulthood. Being a sensitive, insightful parent is no mean feat, however. Many intelligent, well-meaning parents misinterpret the scenario in which a child seeks a response but then cannot articulate what he wanted from Mom as "My child just wants attention." When the misinterpretation is a pattern, it has consequences that we discuss in Chapter 4. The blinders that keep many parents from seeing that in fact "My child needs connection" are discussed in Chapter 5.

When it proceeds smoothly, the interplay among attachment, exploratory, and caregiving behaviors allows for both protection and skill development and provides a greater evolutionary advantage than any one class of behavior could offer independently. The hallmark of the parent who reads and meets needs adroitly—a parent of a securely attached child—is a relative degree of calm comfort with closeness *and* separation. For a securely attached child, the shortest distance between two points is a straight line. That is, the path of direct communication on the part of both parent and child is well developed. If the child has a need for either closeness or separation from the caregiver, that need is allowed to be expressed openly. Hurts can be hurts, wants can be wants, angers and joys and requests can be just what they are—nothing more and nothing less. Whether the child needs physical connection or time alone, she knows that the caregiver is likely to be available and responsive to the full continuum of requests in the direction of either closeness or distance.

Hence, in highly secure dyads, there is a sense of ease, an atmosphere of spontaneity and delight between parent and child. There is also a wealth of face-to-face contact and physical holding. A key trait of these parents is their capacity to feel free in the expression of both deep pleasure with their children and genuine anger. This directness and clarity of emotion becomes a cornerstone for communication.

When the child reaches an age for locomotion, these parents support and encourage the need for exploration with their new capacity for physical separation. Children's confidence that they can move away from the caregiver is predicated on their confidence that the caregiver will be available when needed. This feedback loop builds the children's self-assurance about following their innate curiosity and desire for mastery and trust in the availability of their caregiver.

In the Strange Situation Procedure (SSP), these children will explore the environment while periodically checking back in with their caregiver. Each time the child goes out to explore and finds that the caregiver is still available, the child becomes more willing and able to engage in further exploration. During the SSP parents are asked to leave the room for a brief separation. When the parent returns, the securely attached child is adept at turning to the caregiver for comfort and help with organizing his feelings about the separation. This trust in a responsive and accepting caregiver at the moment of reunion is, by no means, a given for all children. However, in the case of a securely attached child, this capacity upon return is the norm. Such a child mirrors the parent's comfort with proximity and differentiation, with the genuine expression of need for both closeness and separation from the caregiver.

READING THE CIRCLE OF SECURITY ROADMAP

Figure 2.1 is designed to teach caregivers and professionals that, whenever possible, caregivers need to follow their child's need and, whenever necessary, take charge. The top half of the Circle represents a child's needs when exploring: "Watch over me," "Delight in me," "Help me," and "Enjoy with me." The bottom half represents a child's needs when attachment behaviors are activated: "Protect me," "Comfort me," "Delight in me," and "Organize my feelings." As we have explained, caregivers not only have to fulfill these needs but also have to be alert for transitional needs from attachment behaviors to exploratory behaviors ("Support My Exploration") and from exploratory behaviors to attachment behaviors ("Welcome My Coming to You"). Children determine whether it is safe to explore the world based on an immediate signal such as a smile or nod from the caregiver, but they also factor in what they have learned from the caregiver's reaction to their desire to explore in the past. Caregivers' discomfort with separation can teach children to be ambivalent about terminating their attachment needs and activating exploration. Likewise a child who gets tired, hungry, frightened, injured, or otherwise upset while exploring will look for a sign—an empathic look, outstretched arms—from the caregiver of being welcomed back in but will also decide whether to seek comfort based on whether the caregiver has been comfortable giving it in the past. The caregiver's discomfort with physical or emotional closeness can teach children to avoid seeking comfort when needed.

Most of the needs on the Circle require little explanation. However, there are a few issues that need clarification. The difference between "Delight in me" and "Enjoy with me" on the top half of the Circle is that "Enjoy with me" refers to the process of shared positive emotion while engaging in mutual exploration, such as playing a game together. "Delight in me" refers to taking joy *in* a child for who the child is rather than enjoying an activity *with* a child. Delight is also on the bottom half of the Circle. We included it to emphasize how important delight is in general and also suggest that the ability to delight in children when their attachment behaviors are activated is different from delighting in them when their exploratory behaviors are activated. "Help me" refers to providing scaffolding (see Box 3.5 on page 54) during exploration. We tell parents to give their children just enough help so that they can do it by themselves.

The concept of "Organize my feelings" versus "Comfort me" on the bottom half of the Circle can also be confusing. "Comfort me" refers to responding when children are in distress (e.g., when they have fallen down and scraped their knee). "Organize my feelings" is about helping children when their feelings don't make sense to them. Sometimes children need help organizing an internal experience that is overwhelming. Most parents understand that their children may need help managing their external world or their behavior, but for many parents the idea that children also need help learning how to manage their emotional world is new. Children may need help with their internal experience when they are tired, hungry, disappointed, startled, sad, frustrated, and so forth. Whatever the cause, children need their parents' help because, developmentally, they are not yet equipped to do it alone. It is through the repeated process of parents helping their children recognize, name, assign meaning to, and deal with internal experiences that children become competent in managing feelings both by themselves and in relationship.

How therapists can learn to recognize whether parents are meeting or not meeting certain needs around the Circle is discussed in depth in Part II, which focuses on treatment.

Bigger, Stronger, Wiser, and Kind

In performing this role—as the hands on the Circle—parents receiving the COS intervention are encouraged to always be bigger, stronger, wiser, and kind. "Bigger, stronger, wiser, and kind" began as a catchphrase to give parents something they could hold on to and remember. Bigger, stronger, and wiser were all terms used by Bowlby to describe the role of parents (Bowlby, 1988). We were also influenced by Baumrind's work on high expectations and high affection (Baumrind, 1967). We wanted to speak to parents who struggle with taking charge as well as those who struggle with affection. Over time the catchphrase caught on with parents. We were very excited when a mom in one of the groups reported that while sitting in the back of a bus, she saw another group mom struggling with her 2-year-old in the front. The child was running wild, much to the displeasure of the other passengers and the driver. Suddenly Mom jumped up and blurted out loud, "Wait a minute. I am bigger, stronger, wiser, and kind." She quickly took charge, and her child responded by sitting quietly on her lap. We continue to hear stories of parents using this phrase as a mantra.

Through countless discussions with parents, it became clear that many of them did not have a role model for bigger, stronger, wiser, and kind. Many reported experiences of parents who acted bigger and stronger without being kind, and others talked about parents who acted kind without being bigger and stronger. Some talked about having one too-kind parent and one too-strong parent or parents who flip-flopped between the two extremes. There are problems with all of these configurations, which we will discuss in Chapter 7. Finding examples of parents who have the wisdom to balance bigger/stronger with kind turns out to be rather difficult. We also found we needed to clarify that bigger and stronger were employed not just for setting limits. Tenderly holding a frightened child is as much a part of being bigger and stronger as is laying down the law.

To help clarify that children need a sense of a bigger, stronger, wiser, and kind parent at all times, even when the child is asleep or at preschool, we added, "Always be." To further elaborate on the role, we added, "Whenever possible, follow your child's need." We clarify that we are not talking about the child's want or whim but about the needs on the Circle. We also want parents to know that there are times that they cannot follow their child's need. For example, the child may be playing happily on the top of the Circle in a "Watch over me" moment, but it is time to go to child care. The parent is still bigger, stronger, wiser, and kind even when overriding the child's need.

To further counter our fear that this formula would be mistaken as a motto for permissive parenting, we added, "Whenever necessary, take charge" (see Figure 2.3). Sometimes parents need to take charge because it is time to go to child care, but often the child simply needs to know that the parent *can* take charge. Children need to know that someone is in charge and will keep them safe. When parents are unwilling to take that role, children are left in a vulnerable position. From the child's point of view, if the parent is not strong enough to get a 3-year-old to bed, the parent is not strong enough. That parent certainly will not offer much protection from the things that go bump in the night.

Children often try to tell their parents they need reassurance from them in the form of taking charge by pushing the limits. If the parent reads the child's pushing as the child needing more freedom or more choices, bedlam ensues. It is as if the child is asking, "Is it safe: are you in charge?"

**Always: be Bigger, Stronger, Wiser, and Kind
Whenever possible: follow my child's need
Whenever necessary: take charge**

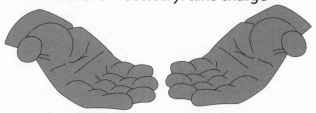

FIGURE 2.3. Hands. Copyright 1998 by Cooper, Hoffman, Marvin, and Powell.

and the parent refuses to answer the question but offers the child another toy or another cookie. The more the parent refuses to answer, the more loudly the child asks.

It is important to remember that sometimes children push limits by negotiating for something (e.g., one more story before bedtime). If the child negotiates in an age-appropriate manner and accepts the agreement (e.g., the parent reads one more story and then the child is relatively cooperative about going to bed), the child is not asking whether the parent is in charge. However, if no settlement is acceptable, it is important to consider whether the child needs reassurance that the parent is in charge.

The parent who is able—most of the time—to meet these various needs in a young child as they arise is creating the COS for the child, a profound gift that will last a lifetime. A child who is scored as securely attached to the primary caregiver in the Strange Situation can express whatever needs he or she has without worry of driving the caregiver away and ending up alone. Such a child, interacting with a parent or other primary caregiver, might look like this, although it's important to know that perfection is never feasible or desirable:

> Pablo, at 2½, is at the playground with his father. In the span of a mere 10 minutes the little boy travels between the top and bottom of the Circle at least a dozen times. He starts out on his father's lap, where Dad sits on a bench. As he looks around the playground with interest, his father holds him gently and watches his face. When Pablo's eyes light up upon seeing the sandbox, Dad smiles and says softly, "That looks pretty neat,

huh?" Pablo looks up at his father as if to ask if it's OK to go to the sandbox, and Dad smiles again and nods, then lets the little boy slip to the ground, where he runs off to the sandbox. When he gets there, he turns back to Dad as if to see if he's still there. Dad's eyes haven't left his son, and he smiles encouragingly and nods again. Pablo turns to the sandbox and climbs in. He crawls through the sand to another little boy who has a dump truck and some shovels. As he starts to reach for one of the toys, the other child squeals in protest and pulls the toy back. Pablo looks slightly alarmed and runs back to Dad.

Dad waits until Pablo reaches the bench and then reaches out his arms, but he doesn't pick Pablo up until Pablo reaches his arms toward his father. Then Dad scoops him up, gives him a big hug, and says, "You didn't like it when he wouldn't let you play. Was that a little scary? We should have brought some trucks. Next time, OK? Maybe he'll share with you for a minute." Dad then walks back to the sandbox hand in hand with his son and asks the little boy's mother if Pablo can play with her son. She agrees, and she hands Pablo one of the trucks in the toy bag she has brought along. Pablo warily and silently starts to push the truck around, but he hasn't let go of his father's hand, so his dad sits on the edge of the sandbox, occasionally murmuring "Neat truck" and "Wow, you've really got it moving in that sand," until Pablo lets go, then stays there until his little boy has glanced back at him a few times and finally smiles at Dad. Dad returns to the bench, where he continues to watch his son and smiles, nods, or makes an encouraging remark whenever Pablo looks back as if to ask whether he can be sure of his dad.

Pablo shows that he can cue his needs for comfort or reassurance directly, perhaps because he knows from experience that he'll get what he needs from his father. Pablo's dad helps him make the transition from the bottom of the Circle to the top by being calm and softly encouraging—bigger, stronger, wiser, and kind—when his son shows interest in the sandbox, a new environment for him. He shows delight in what his son is doing. When Pablo looks back to make sure Dad is there, his father already has his eyes on him, reinforcing his role as bigger and stronger. When Pablo is upset by the minor "rejection" of the other boy, his father welcomes him back to his lap and helps him organize his feelings but waits for Pablo to accept being picked up rather than rushing to his side and removing him from the sandbox—a good example of not only bigger and stronger but also wiser. Dad takes charge when his son needs help negotiating playing with the other child, but he takes his time reading his son's cues and has a way of translating the cues into a reasonably accurate way of knowing and anticipating his son's needs before offering either a safe haven or a secure base. This implies a strong capacity for reflective functioning (see Box 2.2).

BOX 2.2. REFLECTIVE FUNCTIONING

The capacity to view yourself and others as separate beings, each with his or her own mind, is referred to by many names, such as "mindsight" (Siegel, 1999), mind-mindedness (Meins et al., 2002), reflective-function (Fonagy, Steele, & Steele, 1991), or mentalization (Fonagy, Gergely, Jurist, & Target, 2002) and theory of mind (Premack & Woodruff, 1978). Each term emphasizes certain aspects of developing the reflective consciousness needed to have emotionally secure relationships. We will use the term "reflective functioning" to mean the capacity to perceive and understand oneself and others in terms of psychological states that include feelings, beliefs, intentions, and desires. Reflective functioning develops when the caregiver not only communicates a reasonably accurate perspective of what the child may be seeing or feeling but also uses language that says the caregiver appreciates how separate minds function.

No one can truly know what another is seeing, thinking, feeling, or interpreting at any given moment. We can be good at guessing, using the cues others give us, but still we never know for sure until we get confirmation. "I think" says "I am a separate mind and can only guess what you may be feeling." Through guessing and participating in confirming the accuracy or inaccuracy of the guess, our separate minds can connect and have a mutual experience of being together. The guessing can get so accurate that it can be experienced as true, but with adequate reflective functioning the caregiver does not lose sight of the fact that the infant is a separate being. There will also inevitably be moments when this feeling of truth is simply not accurate.

What happens when the caregiver is routinely inaccurate in offering a perspective, repeatedly insists that his or her perspective is always right, or keeps saying he or she knows what is in the infant's mind better than the infant ever can? Essentially the infant learns not to trust his or her own perspective and comes to believe there is no difference between "you" and "me." In the end, the infant's capacity to take another's perspective will be compromised, which can lead to problems with empathy, and affect the quality of friendships and intimacy. This can also have an effect on the capacity to focus on the self and organize internal experience with language that is personally meaningful.

This is a very simple, and very familiar, scene, but it illustrates how interactions with a caregiver that create the Circle might look in one specific context. The Circle can be created with many types of interactions that might look quite different for different dyads engaged in different kinds of interactions. For this reason therapists must be scrupulous in relying on "seeing" (astutely observing behavior) versus "guessing" (inferring based on preconceived notions) when making any assessment of the security of a child's attachment.

SEEING VERSUS GUESSING

The brain is such an effective learning machine that it can be very difficult to see past the associations the mind has already formed and stored in memory. As a result, what we observe is usually based on our preestablished conclusions. This is true of therapists, no matter how well trained, and it is certainly true of parents. The representations formed via our early attachment bonds, for better or worse, strongly influence the attitudes that inform our own parenting. It takes a lot more discipline to base our conclusions on what we actually observe—to release the stranglehold of preconceived notions—than to simply see what we have already concluded. Yet all parents have innate wisdom and a desire for their children to be secure. Most parents, even those severely challenged by major life stressors and unsupportive upbringing, can be motivated to do what is called for to see beyond the veil of their own poor attachment history.

To draw conclusions from actual observations, parents need an underlying structure to organize those observations—the roadmap we call the COS. All human behavior has meaning, and the Circle is designed to open parents' eyes to that meaning, to show them that underneath all "negative behavior" in their child is a legitimate need. The goal of the COS is to facilitate the shift from "What does this child want from me?" to "Oh, I see what she needs!" Via the Circle parents can not only come to understand their child's affect but also track and regulate their own cognitive and affective response to their child's affect—what we call hearing their "shark music," or the legacy of their own childhood attachment, discussed in Chapter 5. The capacity the COS intervention develops to help caregivers make this shift is reflective functioning (see Box 2.2).

How this impressive transformation takes place is not entirely clear. Through reconsolidation, therapists' soothing of clients during the COS intervention sessions may add new pages to parents' long-term attachment-related memories, enabling them to do the self-soothing outside therapy they never learned with their own parents. A form of security priming whereby parents are exposed repeatedly and intensively in sessions to concepts and images of secure attachment behaviors, in addition to soothing music and clips intended to soften their defenses (softening clips), may retrofit parents' internal working models in a way that opens the door for new behavior toward their own children (Gillath, Selcuk, & Shaver, 2008). These processes are just beginning to be studied, however, and their effectiveness and potency are far from certain.

What we do know is that the COS seems to elicit change by creating a holding environment that makes parents feel safe and secure enough to see what they have been mind-blind to in the past. Just as the goal of the intervention is to help parents develop the capacity of Being-With their child all around the Circle, no matter what the child's needs or emotions, the therapist's task is to Be-With the parents as the parents undertake the often distressing work of confronting ghosts from the past that are intruding on their ability to care for their children in the present.

When the therapist succeeds in creating this holding environment, and in great measure as a direct product of the courage and commitment of the parents, the COS results in the majority of children being scored as securely attached. The critical power of Being-With is discussed in the next chapter.

3

Being-With

*Meeting the Child's Needs
through Relationship*

I am here and you are worth it.
—JUDE CASSIDY

Being-With, a deceptively simple term, represents a profound need that, when answered, paves the way for a lifetime of satisfying relationships, for mastery of a raft of developmental tasks and adult competencies, for trust and self-regulation and even physical health. Being-With, when it is a need unmet, becomes "Being-Without," leaving a child bereft not only of an essential human bond at this formative stage of life but of the uninhibited ability to thrive in future relationships and as an (autonomous) adult. It is by Being-With the child that the parent provides responsive caregiving and has the greatest hope of meeting the child's needs around the Circle. And it is by Being-With the parents that the therapist is able to elicit change.

THE EXPERIENCE OF BEING-WITH

Being-With starts with this fundamental fact of human life: to be human is to be in relationship. Children arrive in this world with an innate need to "Be-With" a caregiver who will provide protection, comfort, and necessary interaction. In study after study around the globe research findings remain consistent: a child will respond with trust and delight to a caregiver who provides sensitive and careful attention. And a child will respond with protest, despair, and eventual detachment when such attention is not available. **At the heart of developing a secure attachment is the child's knowledge that her caregiver is** *emotionally available* **to Be-With her when needed.**

Being-With means knowing someone is emotionally available
all the way around the Circle.

What British pediatrician and psychoanalyst Donald Winnicott called a "holding environment" is any caregiving relationship that engenders a genuine and safe experience of belonging—a relationship characterized by Being-With. Belonging in an attachment sense means having an "other" who is available to understand and empathically regulate the often difficult and confusing experiences of the child's emerging sense of self. In the countless experiences of being soothed, comforted, sensitively stimulated, and calmed, it is as if the child repeatedly calls out and the consistent response is "You can be sure of me."

Being-With means being known.

It also means that the child's needs are acceptable. They may not always be met—no parent can be or should be perfect in this role. But in a holding environment the majority of the child's accumulated experiences affirm that the child's needs are normal and can be shared and understood even—or especially—when the child herself doesn't understand them and finds those needs painful and difficult to tolerate.

Being-With means the child's needs are accepted.

Children are born with the potential to feel—and express—the full range of emotions. Not all of these emotions are comfortable. Most of them are not manageable for the very young infant. They can easily be overwhelming before a child learns to regulate them. In a holding environment the caregiver demonstrates that all human emotion—anger, sadness, fear, joy, shame, curiosity, and so forth—is normal and acceptable. Being-With a baby who has not yet developed the capacity to regulate emotion means *resonating with and being attuned to* the child's emotional experience—all the way around the Circle, as described later in this chapter (Stern, 1985). It means *empathizing* with those feelings. (If we could hear what the baby needs, it would be something like "Having someone here *with me* in this difficult feeling allows me a way out of feeling bad.") It means *staying with* the baby until the baby's arousal subsides. ("Please let me know that you get what I'm feeling and that you will wait here *with me* until things change.") It means *responding* to the need that the emotion expresses, whether the need is for warmth, comfort, food, sleep, encouragement, or something else.

When a child is very young, Being-With means managing
and regulating those emotions—organizing feelings—for the baby.

Being-With a child in her emotional experience is more than an airy metaphor. Recent research has revealed the existence of so-called mirror neurons, defined as neurons in the brain of one individual that respond to the firing of neurons in the brain of another individual. "When we perceive another's emotions, automatically, unconsciously, that [emotional] state is created inside us," say Daniel Siegel and Mary Hartzell (2004, p. 65). When Mom smiles at her baby in delight, the same neurons that fire in her brain fire in her child's, eliciting the same experience. Scientists speculate that it is through the firing of these neurons that infants begin to learn about emotions and begin to view them as acceptable parts of their experience. Aptly, V. S. Ramachandran (TED talk in November 2009), a pioneer in this field, has called them "empathy neurons." Daniel Goleman has called this capacity "neural Wi-Fi" (Goleman, 2006, p. 41).

The effect of mirror neurons in the experience of Being-With is palpable in the following encounter between a mother and her baby:

Four-month-old Chelsea, sitting directly across from Denise, her mother, yawns and closes her eyes. As Denise stares into the face of her child with gentle, kind eyes, she matches the tempo of the yawn with her voice and says "Oh yes" in rhythm with the infant's nodding head. Chelsea finishes the yawn, looks around, and you can hear her breathing. Denise says, "Such a long afternoon, such a long afternoon" in time with her daughter's breathing. Chelsea looks at Mom; Mom looks at her baby, smiles, and says, "Are you my darling?" Chelsea looks into her mother's eyes and slowly begins to smile with a look that would melt any parent. In response Denise's smile spreads to her whole face as her eyes sparkle with delight. Chelsea's smile then turns to mutual shared delight.

Quickly the positive emotions crescendo, and Chelsea looks away. Research has shown that when an infant looks away at a moment like this the infant is overstimulated and is trying to calm (downregulate). If the infant is allowed to do this, she will quickly downregulate and return to interacting with the caregiver. Denise accepts her child's going away for a moment and maintains a positive emotional availability for her child to return to interacting with her. Chelsea looks around for a few moments, turns back to her mother, and begins to smile. Denise smiles back, and another interactive crescendo of positive emotion and mutual delight takes place. When the intensity becomes too much for Chelsea, the baby looks away for a few moments and calms slightly while her mother waits patiently. Then Chelsea returns once more to the positive interaction.

What we can see in this interaction is all the elements of Being-With described so far: attunement, resonance, acceptance, holding, contingent responding to the child's need. This scene depicts the beginning of an infant learning to regulate her emotions both with her mother and on her own. It also highlights the role of empathy in this relationship—and, by extension, others.

Empathy is a capacity essential for the development and maintenance of successfully intimate relationships. Without empathy, emotional experiences are not sharable and understandable. Without receiving empathy, how can you learn about your own emotional states? Without having empathy, how can you ever get to know the people you care about? Empathy is mirror neurons in action. It's the resonance of another's experience within our own experience. With empathy comes the essential experience of feeling guilt if you have hurt another. When you feel bad that you have hurt someone you care about, you are primed to repair the relationship, which maintains relationship security. (The essential concept of "rupture and repair" is described more fully in Chapters 6 and 11.)

Being on the receiving end of empathy is how children learn to develop their own capacity to have empathy for themselves and for others. Empathy has both an emotional component—nurtured in a holding environment—and a cognitive component, where the child learns from the parent's Being-With how to take the perspective of another person (see Box 3.1).

THE DEVELOPMENTAL BENEFITS OF BEING-WITH

Much of what happens during Being-With is implicit and nonverbal. During every interaction, a baby who has not yet developed speech is nonetheless learning about people and relationships, about emotions and needs,

---

BOX 3.1. CAN A CHILD BENEFIT FROM BEING-WITH ANY ADULT?

Definitely. Empathy, acceptance, and the other benefits of a holding environment are a good thing even on a part-time, temporary basis. Teachers, babysitters, coaches, big brothers and sisters, and others who are part of a child's life will all enhance the child's self-esteem and mastery by attuning to the child in these critical ways. It also gives children an idea of what is possible in a relationship and thus the motivation to look for security in future relationships. In fact, when speaking with caretaking professionals (child care, education, etc.) we often say that offering a genuine Being-With option for a high-risk child may make a significant difference in that child's life trajectory. Having access to a single "North Star" (or Southern Cross) person may be essential for some children: "Oh, I see, there really is a coherent theme hidden behind all the chaos. I don't know how to find it on a regular basis yet, but because of you I will keep looking until I do." It may take years or decades, but having access to one person who activates the Being-With paradigm can be of huge benefit to a child.

Part-time/temporary Being-With is not, however, sufficient to create the attachment bond that is critical to the child's healthy development, fulfilling future relationships, and personal competence. Attachment is driven by care seeking— the instinct to seek comfort from a *specific* person to help the child organize his feelings. Children will show attachment behavior to a stranger if they are in a challenging situation, but that does not make it an attachment *relationship*.

In the first 7 months of life, children accept care and comfort from any willing and able provider. Grandma and Grandpa will come to visit and be received happily when the baby is 6 months old, but a month later (stranger or separation anxiety starts at around that age) when Grandma or Grandpa tries to pick up the baby, the baby screams. At about 7 months, children develop a preference for their primary caregiver and start developing primary attachments. They develop a hierarchy: maybe Mom, Dad, Grandma, and then the babysitter. They will go to these people in order when in need. But anyone who is not on the list will not be readily accepted.

An infant's access to many caregivers may eventually put another person on the list, but it is difficult to say how long the list of caregivers will be in total: four or five or maybe six, but fewer than 100? As Mary Ainsworth discovered in Uganda (see Chapter 1), neighbors can become attachment figures when they are all participating. In American society, children probably have fewer attachment figures.

Should we take a page from the countries where, as Hillary Clinton said, "it takes a village to raise a child"? Possibly. In terms of survival and consistency of security, common sense says there is some advantage to having some "spares."

---

about how to communicate and what types of responses to expect from others. Interactions with the primary caregiver are particularly important, because here is where the baby is paying very close attention: here is the baby's "go-to person," the infant's greatest potential source of comfort, acceptance, and approval (C. H. Zeanah, personal communication, 2004). In Being-With a young child as we've described, a parent is sending messages, both verbal and nonverbal, that the baby is OK (even if uncomfortable), that in fact the baby is delightful, that Mom or Dad understands the awful feeling of need unfulfilled, and that with the parent's help the baby will not become overwhelmed and drown in a sea of emotion.

Being-With is beneficial not just to the child, however. Providing a true holding environment requires parents to have a degree of self-acceptance. Without it, the parent cannot truly meet the child's needs around the Circle. Take "Delight in me" as an example. The parent who feels (nonconsciously) wholly imperfect may tend to idealize the child, offering rigid, limited, and limiting adoration rather than the delight that emanates from accepting herself and thus demonstrating to the child that the child is acceptable too. The baby is, in part, picking up the parent's sense of self, which enhances a sense of connectedness and a feeling of security in the caregiver.

The "conversation" between Denise and 4-month-old Chelsea re-created earlier illustrates a mother creating a holding environment, building a secure attachment with her daughter, and in the process helping Chelsea form procedural, implicit memories about how intimate relationships work (see Box 3.2 and also Chapter 5 for a discussion of implicit/explicit information processing in the brain, the "unthought known," and procedural memory). This implicit relational knowing (Lyons-Ruth, 1998) will become part of Chelsea's interpersonal repertoire in the same way that knowing how to ride a bike becomes part of a child's long-term physical repertoire and reading a book part of the child's cognitive repertoire: Chelsea will know how to relate to important others in her life, step by step, because of what she learned implicitly from her mother before she was old enough to put it into words. Due to its implicit nature, Chelsea won't necessarily recognize that she became a giving, trusting, confident intimate partner and parent because of her mother's Being-With her as an infant, since one of the qualities of procedural memory is that it feels like something you know rather than something you are remembering. Yet this procedural memory will fuel her expectations for all relationships as she grows up. This is, in part, what Salvador Minuchin meant when he said that history is always present in the moment: We don't need to ask adults about their history; all we have to do is observe their pattern of behavior in intimate relationships, and it will reveal their history—that is, their implicit relational knowing (Minuchin, 1980).

The formation of these memories and the relationship expectations

---

**BOX 3.2. THE BRAIN ORGANIZES INFORMATION
INTO TWO MEMORY SYSTEMS: IMPLICIT AND EXPLICIT**

The implicit memory system is formed in infancy prior to the development of language and therefore is not semantically organized. Yet information continues to be stored and retrieved in an implicit form after the baby acquires language and throughout life, such as the procedural information needed to ride a bicycle. The key to implicit information is that it does not require conscious awareness to retrieve and use it; it has an intuitive quality that says "This is just how things work." Karlen Lyons-Ruth and the Boston Process of Change Group coined the term "implicit relational knowing" for nonsymbolically coded information about how to do things with others (Lyons-Ruth, 1998). How we negotiate our attachment needs is learned prior to the development of language and is encoded in our minds as implicit relational knowing.

    The explicit memory system is language-based and stores information such as facts and autobiographical memory. Episodic memory is an example of a specific autobiographical memory that has enough detail to allow the listener to travel back in time and have a clear mental picture of what actually happened, as opposed to a generalized description representing more than one event.

---

that flow from them starts with learning emotional regulation through Being-With.

Learning to Manage Emotions: Coregulation and Self-Regulation

Attachment, which refers to a special relationship between infant and caregiver that evolves over the first year of life and beyond, is inherently an emotional construct. Not only does it imply an "affective bond" between parent and infant, it also is properly characterized in terms of the regulation of infant emotion. In fact, it is the apex of dyadic emotional regulation, a culmination of all development in the first year and a harbinger of the self-regulating that is to come.

—L. ALAN SROUFE (1995, p. 172)

As humans, we must learn a way to manage our emotions: to find comfort when we're sad, to allow feelings to grow when we're happy and feel good, and when angry to find ways to calm, organize a perspective, and make decisions about productive self-assertion. In other words, we need to be able to manage our internal experience if we are to have any way of choosing appropriate external behavior. It is difficult to imagine having a successful intimate relationship and being productive at work—two criteria often considered essential for success in life—without being able to both inhibit the impulse to attack when angered and cultivate the joyful moments.

Within the primary caregiving relationship in the first year of life, infants begin to learn how to manage emotions. The caregiver initially manages much of the infant's early experience, following and joining a baby in her emotions without trying to push her into a different feeling, soothing a baby in distress, being with an overstimulated baby as she turns away—all part of the interaction Denise had with Chelsea. As the child grows in age and feeling states grow more complex, the child and the caregiver begin to work together to mutually regulate emotions. This is part of what Winnicott meant by "holding environment" (Winnicott, 1965b, p. 47): the caregiver intentionally *holds* the emotions of the child, while responding verbally and nonverbally, to give the child some relational space to build the all-important capacity of holding and regulating emotions on his own.

Through the coregulation of emotions, the child learns self-regulation.

Self-Reliance, Not Self-Sufficiency

There is now widespread agreement that the brain is a self-organizing system, but there is perhaps less of an appreciation of the fact that the self-organization of the developing brain occurs in the context of a relationship with another self, another brain. This other self, the primary caregiver, acts as an external psychobiological regulator of the "experience-dependent" growth of the infant's nervous system, whose components are rapidly organizing, disorganizing, and reorganizing in the brain growth spurt of the first two years of life.
—ALLAN N. SCHORE (1996, p. 60)

The capacity to regulate one's own emotions *is* all-important (see Box 3.3). But if this statement conjures up a picture of a steely Lone Ranger type dampening his anger and fear so as to vanquish the bad guys singlehandedly before riding off (alone) into the sunset, think again. Contrary to many cultural beliefs, self-regulation in itself is not the ultimate goal. Rather, the desired goal is to be able to coregulate and self-regulate depending on what serves you best in each situation throughout life.

Using only one capacity exclusively does not lead to optimal development. Think of adults who, when upset, go off alone until they can compose themselves, believing that to reach out to others makes them far too vulnerable. Soothing by seeking isolation from important relationships

---

BOX 3.3. BEHAVIOR MODIFICATION VERSUS BEING-WITH

Carl, age 15, is in a behavior intervention classroom because of his long history of aggressive acting out. His teacher is trying to help him learn to master a math problem, and, while he struggles, one of his classmates makes faces at him and laughs at his efforts. Carl blows up and throws a book at the classmate while yelling obscenities. Carl cannot seem to calm down, so his teacher has little recourse but to remove Carl from the classroom to the familiar time-out room, where it is hoped he will de-escalate. The teacher wants to help Carl choose a different behavior when he is upset. Even though choosing more productive behavior is a significant part of Carl's problem, it is not the core issue.

The book *From Neurons to Neighborhoods,* published by the National Research Council Institute of Medicine (National Academy Press) as a summary of what we knew and didn't know about childhood development as of the year 2000, stated, "The capacity for self-regulation is a *prerequisite* for the critical task of learning to comply with both external and internalized standards of conduct" (Shonkoff & Phillips, 2000, p. 113). In other words, we must learn to manage our internal experience before we can competently manage our external behavior. If we are flooded with emotions and experience what we refer to as unregulated affect, our ability to choose productive behaviors diminishes rapidly.

Unfortunately, being isolated in time-out is not likely to teach Carl how to regulate his emotions so that he can make intentional choices of behavior. Nor is fear. Perhaps if Carl was in prison and the classmate was a murderer, his fear would be so great that he would be able to inhibit the desire to throw something. But to be a productive member of society Carl obviously does not need to live in overwhelming fear. He needs less fear, not more. You cannot cure deficits in the capacity to emotionally regulate with fear, which unfortunately is tried all the time by well-meaning people who think that if the threat is great enough children like Carl will change their behavior. Behavioral intervention classrooms remain full of students like Carl, who still don't know how to manage their emotions.

The process of learning to regulate emotion seems complex when described in words: First, Carl needs to know and have language for the fact that he is upset and perhaps hurt by his classmate's antics. To do this he needs to pause and inhibit his impulse to throw something long enough to hold and identify his emotional experience. From a brain perspective, he needs to move from a primitive limbic response to using his prefrontal cortex to mediate and organize his experience. To pause and inhibit requires enough self-soothing that his emotions subside to a point where he can reflect on what is happening. If he cannot self-soothe, then he needs to reach out to a trusted other like the teacher to help him calm down. Implied in this process is that Carl has a reflective self that can internally talk himself through this difficult process and organize a useful perspective. Once he has some understanding and language for what is happening to him internally, he can choose how to negotiate with the classmate.

Complex in words and profound in impact, this implicit relational knowing seems to blossom with the natural ease of a wildflower in a holding environment,

(continued)

BOX 3.3. (*continued*)

through everyday, mundane interactions between parent and child. If he had had the benefit of Being-With, Carl would likely have been soothed by his mother (or other caregiver) when very young, then helped to soothe himself along with his mother, and then been able to soothe himself when called on. But he also would have known when to tap each capacity, such as reaching out to his teacher in the scenario just depicted.

Many would argue that managing emotions is a behavior and as such can be taught explicitly, as through behavior modification (incentives, removal of privileges, etc.). We would argue that it is more than behavior; it is about the quality of a child's relationship with himself and the quality of his relationship with significant others. Allan Schore, who has successfully integrated attachment theory and brain research, speaks of the importance of shared delight in the first months of the child's life in terms of the effect it has on the developing brain and on setting the stage for competent emotional regulation. Schore states that the mutual sharing of positive emotions prepares the child for the more difficult management of negative emotions as the child develops. An article in *Developmental Psychology* (Feldman, Greenbaum, & Yirmiya, 1999) found that the more synchrony of emotion between the caregiver and the infant in the first year of life, the more the child complied with parental demands and delayed acts upon request at age 2. In other words, children who have more emotional connection in the first year of life are more available and responsive to their parents' directions as they develop.

We can see this benefit in all kinds of settings. In day care for infants in East Germany, even when influenced by prescriptions to favor group-oriented behavior management, babies had more secure attachments to caregivers who showed empathy (Ahnert, Lamb, & Seltenheim, 2000).

The ability to regulate emotion *leads to* the ability to regulate behavior.

---

significantly interferes with the development of intimacy and limits the individual's ability to integrate complex emotional experiences.

And what about those who, because they cannot self-regulate, constantly seek the care of others? Getting stuck in a coregulation rut interferes with the development of autonomy and self-determination. The result is a life less rich than it could be, a life with very limited choices.

The truth, we believe, is that there is really no such thing as autonomy, at least not in the way the word is usually understood.[1] Even when we are alone we are influenced by internal representations of others. The destination of a child's healthy developmental path is not self-sufficiency—none of

---

[1] *Webster's* defines autonomy as independence and freedom of will and defines independence as freedom from the influence of others. At its core the word "autonomy" is misunderstood.

us is "sufficient" unto ourselves—but rather the capacity for self-reliance when appropriate. One of the most important functions of Being-With is to provide an environment in which a child learns both self-regulation and coregulation *and* develops an implicit knowledge of when it is best to choose which strategy. Within the COS protocol, this balance is described as "autonomy-within-relatedness" and "relatedness-within-autonomy" (Hoffman, 1997, p. 31). Ultimately, the experience of being able to share a broad range of emotions with your attachment figures promotes security of attachment. Correspondingly, the freedom to experience the full range of emotions without fear of losing coherency is a key component to an internal sense of security.

> *Autonomy-within-relatedness: Be with me so I can do it myself.*
> *Relatedness-within-autonomy: Keep the "me" and "you" in "us."*

Imagine a toddler going to his mother, tugging on her sleeve, and when he gets her attention saying, "I need you to watch me so I can do this all by myself." The mother chuckles inwardly and then watches her son build a Lego tower. This interaction is what is depicted in the top half of the COS. Perhaps you, too, smiled at the child's apparent self-contradiction: How can the child do it "all by myself" and need someone to be part of the doing? Because autonomy is achieved only within relationship, Winnicott called it "the experience of being alone while someone else is present" (1965a, p. 30). This being alone in the presence of someone else is a pattern that continues throughout life. Adults do not achieve individuation from their parents by walking away and never needing them again but rather by using their parents as a secure base from which to explore. Autonomy is not a negation of needing others but a capacity that arises from that need being met.

In fact, the experience of being known mentioned earlier means the self is never completely separated from the relationship. It is as if the child is saying "I am me, but I am not only me" and "You are you, but you are not only you." The center of gravity for a child's developing identity is at first within the parent. Although it gradually moves toward differentiation, it never reaches complete separation. The "I" that is being formed is really an experience of autonomy-*within*-relatedness . . . a uniqueness-*within*-belonging . . . a paradoxical wholeness of individuality and connection.

The idea that the healthy self develops only in relation to important others was expanded by Heinz Kohut as a variation of object relations theory (Kohut, 1977). When Kohut first described our need to rely on others, he did so in the context of narcissism, in which the therapist seeks to provide the necessary but missing empathy to the malformed self of a person lacking self-esteem. This approach implied to some that continuing to try to have personal needs met as an adult was a sign of pathology. Yet within healthy psychological development, access to empathy from key caregivers always plays the essential role of mirroring the child's worth as a precursor to later self-reliance. Kohut was clear that the need for this connection does not expire upon maturation. Indeed he believed that the emotionally healthy adult continues to require the empathic support of significant others throughout the lifespan. He was equally clear that this was in no way a sign of psychopathology.

Great Expectations—of Others and Themselves

- In addition to a capacity for self-regulation, Being-With (via attachment security and early supportive care) fosters a basic sense of social connection and positive expectations concerning oneself and others (Sroufe et al., 2005).
- The best way to promote independence and competence in children is to provide secure attachments for them: "experiences of sensitive, responsive care; consistent availability of parents for comforting, support and nurturance; and later encouragement and guidance predicted measures of competence at every age" (Sroufe et al., 2005, pp. 268–269).
- Teens with secure attachment histories have been seen to be more competent in peer relationships, from effective negotiation and skilled interactions to strong leadership (Sroufe et al., 2005, p. 181).

These are just a few of the gifts that Being-With bestows on children raised with secure attachments. The relationship with a primary caregiver gives birth to lasting expectations about others, the self, and relationships by forming internal working models or representations of the self and others in the child's mind that will accompany the child as she grows (see Box 3.4). With a secure attachment, the child will behave as if those close to her can be trusted to help in times of need. She will allow herself to be vulnerable and to rely on others in a way that makes deep intimacy possible. And she will hold herself to the same standards, responding with empathy and comfort when someone she cares about is in distress. This is, after all, the way human beings behave toward each other. This learned trust will then

---

BOX 3.4. EMOTION AND INTERNAL WORKING MODELS

A number of object relations theorists, including Otto Kernberg, believe that sorting experiences into positive and negative emotional states—what we could call informally "feeling ok" and "feeling upset"—is the infant's first level of brain organization. The goal of this primitive organization is to maximize what feels good and minimize what feels bad.

As the infant develops, emotions become linked to internal representations associated with that particular affective state memory—or, as Daniel Stern puts it, to representations that are internalized and become generalized (1985, p. 97). As adults we choose how to behave based in part on how we expect others to react to our having a certain feeling (other representations or object representations) and how we think about ourselves for feeling that way (self-representations). This process of linking feeling with representation is taking place all the time, although we may not be aware of it. These emotional states and representations of others and the self form basic building blocks for understanding experience.

Developing infants need a way to make sense of and organize all these different building blocks so they can learn to maximize experiences that have a positive emotional tone and minimize experiences that have a negative emotional tone. This is why a child who learns to expect comfort from a caregiver will seek out intimate relationships in the future—they are associated with "feeling OK" (or even "feeling great"). A child whose caregiver also encourages and supports exploration will, likewise, grow up being outgoing, an avid learner, one who welcomes growth—another pursuit that perpetuates "feeling okay." Internal working models of primary caregivers inform children's choices as they grow because they represent the promise of "feeling OK" or "feeling upset." (See Chapter 4 for further discussion of the concept of splitting.)

---

have the chance to translate into a broader faith in the human species, an attitude that the world is generally a safe place—safe enough to explore and to relish.

Because Mom or Dad has accepted and also delighted in who she is, the same child will believe she is worthy and competent. Her expectations of herself will include the ability to be courageous, accomplished, and successful. (The securely attached teens who were more skillful in peer relationships also tended to have higher math and reading scores in high school, even when controlled for IQ (Sroufe et al., 2005). Interestingly, the finding of recent research concerning infants is that when children are provided with a secure and consistent holding environment they are less likely to cling and be overly dependent later in life. Children whose needs are met and responded to adequately in their early years relax and build a sense of confidence that life is safe and that relationship can be trusted. This might be considered a kind of "confidence-at-the-core." Developmental theorists conclude that when children can trust in the availability and sensitivity of their primary caregivers, this trust is gradually incorporated into their growing sense of self. Securely attached children hold the safe haven and secure base offered by their caregivers at the core of the developing self, where the resulting confidence and sense of safe connection are deeply internalized and thus available in much of what they experience for the rest of their lives.

Being-With an Infant around the Circle

The COS intervention and the SSP can be used effectively only with children 12 months old and older. Yet during the first year of life, infants are learning the basic rhythm of how and when to rely on their caregiver and how and when to rely on their own internal resources to manage a wide variety of experiences. Therefore meeting the baby on the top and the bottom of the Circle is just as important as meeting an older child's needs. As noted earlier in this chapter, Being-With an infant is often largely about emotional regulation—regulating the baby's emotions for her and then helping the baby learn self-regulation through coregulation. This emphasis on emotional regulation is illustrated in the infant Circle depicted in Figure 3.1. How parents can plant the roots of a secure attachment by Being-With their infant is important in many settings where the COS can be a significant preventive tool, such as in our work with incarcerated pregnant mothers in a program called Tamar's Children (Cassidy et al., 2010).

When the Baby Is Asking for Autonomy-within-Relatedness: When Feeling OK

• *Delight in me as I explore.* Delighting in an infant as she explores her world is a very powerful message. Delight is about the infant as she ventures out and not about the parent's pride in the infant's accomplishing developmental goals that the caregiver has in mind. Self-esteem—the sum of an individual's self-representations—involves a sense that someone delighted in you for who you are, for your being, in addition to feeling good about what you do and accomplish.

• *Watch over me as I turn to new sights, sounds, and touches.* When infants feel calm, their natural curiosity about the world emerges and they want to use their caregiver as a secure base to explore. Their exploration is often expressed in their gaze as they turn to new sights, sounds, and touches. Often all the infant needs is for the caregiver to watch over him

FIGURE 3.1. Creating the Circle of Security by accepting and matching all my feelings (anger, sadness, fear, joy, shame, and curiosity). Copyright 2002 by Cassidy, Cooper, Hoffman, Marvin, and Powell, with thanks to Beatrice Beebe.

as he explores and to remain available for interaction upon the infant's cues. Having their caregiver support exploration helps children develop their own sense of interest, which leads to mastery and competency in later years.

  • *Look at the world through my eyes and talk to me about it.* When infants are exploring their world with their eyes, they have not developed a way of organizing information that matches the complexity of what they experience. An infant's grasp of how minds work is enhanced when the caregiver takes the infant's perspective and talks about what the baby may be seeing, hearing, or feeling while also acknowledging that the caregiver can only guess what is happening inside the infant's brain. This means saying not "You are angry at me" but "I think you are angry at me." Adding the word "think" is critical: even if the caregiver's guess is accurate, making a guess instead of a statement emphasizes the fact that the infant is a separate being. This helps the infant develop the ability to take another's perspective, as well as the ability to focus on the self and organize internal experience with language that is personally meaningful.

• *Wait when I look away so I don't get too wound up.* As depicted between Chelsea and Denise earlier in the chapter, even with positive emotion an infant can have too much of a good thing. A common example is a child who is tickled until the laughter turns into dysregulation and becomes painful. When a baby turns away from the caregiver, the infant is trying to calm himself, and he needs the caregiver to wait and allow him to manage. Once the excitement moderates, the infant will turn back to the caregiver for further interaction. This capacity to turn away, self-calm, and then reengage is innate and is part of the early foundation the infant is building on to develop the all-important ability for competent self-regulation.

When the Baby Is Asking for Autonomy-within-Relatedness: When Feeling Upset

• *Give me just enough help when I get frustrated so that I can do it.* Sometimes a baby will get frustrated with a task but show a desire to figure it out by staying focused on the task and not cueing the caregiver for help. For instance, before a baby is fully able to sit up on his own a parent might support his body while the baby explores. In the exploration the baby reaches for a toy close enough for him to grasp. Rather than get the toy for him, the parent lets him struggle for a while to grasp the toy and have the experience of self-mastery (see Box 3.5). In all likelihood, the infant is attempting something that is at the edge of his developmental ability. This is a difficult moment for any caregiver: Do you wait and let the infant struggle or do you help? If you help, do you do it for the child or try to help him figure it out so he can do it? There is no simple answer to these questions. If the caregiver cannot stand for the infant to be frustrated and always jumps in and takes over, the infant will not learn to manage and use frustration as part of learning new skills, which will limit the child's learning potential. If the caregiver rarely comes to the child's aid, the infant will constantly be faced with the need to learn material that is developmentally

---

BOX 3.5. SCAFFOLDING

Scaffolding is a learning process that has to do with the gap between what children can do on their own and what they still require assistance doing. Ideally caregivers will help an infant or young child organize a task so that success is within the child's developmental grasp while supporting the infant in struggling with what he or she is capable of doing. This caregiving skill is called "scaffolding" and is an important teaching tool. Ten-month-old Ally was doing her best to take her first steps. As she stood on her own facing her father, he kept saying "You can do it! Yes, you can!" Dad's smile matched Ally's as she tried once again to stand and then venture forth. Noticing that her balance wasn't quite up to the task, her father reached out, offering a hand for her to grab. Holding on, yet all but unaware that he was helping, she marched forward five steps before falling. The look of triumph in her eyes as she greeted her father's enthusiastic grin seemed to say it all: "See what I can do all on my own!"

When the child is allowed to struggle and learn the aspects of the task that he doesn't know how to do, *with* the parent's help as needed, the child develops a sense of mastery and confidence while also experiencing the support of the parent (autonomy-within-relatedness). There is no blueprint for appropriate scaffolding in every circumstance, because all parents struggle with knowing exactly how much help to give. The caregiver who provides too little help puts the child in a situation where she is trying to do something that may be beyond her developmental capacity. Providing too much help diminishes the child's efforts and takes over by doing the task for the child. Neither of these helps build confidence.

---

over his head and will not think of others as a resource for learning, which will diminish his capacity to learn from others.

• *Wait when I look away so I can practice using myself to calm down.* Sometimes an infant will suddenly turn away and limit contact for a few moments while using the caregiver for comfort, as described in the interaction between Chelsea and Denise earlier in the chapter. Research has shown that just before the infant turns away she is experiencing increased arousal and after turning away the arousal drops. As discussed above, when parents interpret this turning away as rejection, they deny the child the opportunity to learn to self-soothe.

When the Baby Is Asking for Relatedness-within-Autonomy: When Feeling OK

Infants have a constant rhythm of reaching out to their caregiver for closeness and contact. They cue their need with many behaviors, such as crying, fussing, reaching out, moving closer, gazing with their eyes, and cooing. All these cues signal the caregiver that the infant wants the caregiver to be closer. If the price of connection is the loss of autonomy, however, the infant's development will suffer.

• *Delight in me as I fall in love with your face.* Infants like to look into their caregiver's face and experience a safe haven in their relationship with their caregiver while feeling delight. This is part of falling in love. Gazing into a parent's face and eyes while showing happiness, curiosity, and glee is the beginning of knowing that very positive emotions can be shared with intimate others and so be sustained. Mutual delight with a parent is a core process in the capacity for developing intimacy with a romantic partner as an adult.

• *Show me you get it by matching my emotions with your voice, face, and touch.* Daniel Stern (1995) has given the name "feeling-shape" to the intensity, duration, rhythm, contour, and quality of a given emotional experience. Seeing and feeling that a caregiver shares an emotion in all these dimensions enhances and expands the infant's connection with both the caregiver and his own positive internal state. Joy, happiness, delight, and other positive feelings lose their power to make life rewarding if they are not sharable.

When the Baby Is Asking for Relatedness-within-Autonomy: When Feeling Upset

• *Comfort me.* An infant's ability to use her caregiver for comfort is facilitated by the caregiver displaying a feeling-shape similar to the infant's while simultaneously exhibiting emotional stability. The caregiver shows the infant a similar feeling-shape by matching the infant's feeling with his or her face, with vocal rhythm, with voice and body tempo, and with quality of touch. But it can be difficult not to go too far in trying to convey an empathic connection. The caregiver needs to find a way to Be-With the infant's feeling state while making it clear that the distress is the infant's and the caregiver is only resonating with the infant's experience. The parent must remain "bigger, stronger, wiser, and kind" in this sharing of experience, and to do so requires the parent to regulate any internal distress of her own evoked by her baby's feelings.

• *Organize my feelings by accepting, sharing, and naming them.* When the caregiver accepts, shares, and names the infant's feelings, emotional organization and coregulation are made possible. The first step is for the caregiver to accept the baby's feeling. The parent does not have to like it, but it is important to accept it. Not every emotion the infant has needs to be coregulated perfectly, but the child needs to know that the caregiver is often able to accept and share the baby's feelings. Once the feelings are accepted and shared, naming them helps the infant learn to have language to organize what is happening to him (see Box 3.6).

WHEN CIRCLE NEEDS GO UNMET

We cannot emphasize enough that the goal is not to be a perfect parent or other primary caregiver. The goal is to be a "good enough" parent—one who meets the child or baby's needs often enough for the child to feel free to express those needs, because they will probably be met, and because they will be viewed as normal and acceptable. As we will describe in the next chapter, rupture and repair—the parent *not* meeting the child's needs and possibly not even tolerating the expression of that need at a given moment, and then admitting the slip—is just as important as the pattern of reliability the parent manifests. A child who comes to understand that even when a parent is not perfect, the "good" parent returns and repairs, builds not only a secure attachment but very strong self-acceptance and acceptance of others as well.

It is the pattern that's key to secure attachment. As explained in Chapter 4, a child who finds over and over that certain needs are neither met nor tolerated cannot travel smoothly around the Circle because it is incomplete, resulting in insecure or disorganized attachment.

BOX 3.6. A VOCABULARY FOR EMOTION

Many adults have difficulty answering when asked how they are feeling. Without language to organize emotional experience, finding and communicating a coherent perspective becomes difficult if not impossible. Having accurate language to describe emotion helps children and adults develop a stronger capacity for self-regulation.

4

Limited Circles

Insecurity and the Power of Adaptation

At every moment, behind the most efficient seeming adult exterior, the whole world of the person's childhood is being carefully held like a glass of water bulging above the brim.
—TED HUGHES (1986, IN REID, 2008)

Little Colin, 14 months old, sits on the carpeted floor, one leg bent under him, crying softly as he holds on to an activity-center toy with one hand. He stares at the closed door of the room and briefly increases the vocal volume, seemingly trying to get the attention of his absent mother. Soon his mother calls "Hello" from the hallway as she opens the door. Walking into the room, Sarah says, "Hi . . . Hi . . . ," and Colin's crying quickly ratchets down to a few final breathy protests as he looks at his mother and the tears stop flowing. Just as quickly, Colin turns away from his mother and starts fingering the activity center as Sarah passes him by on the way to the couch, where she sits down and immediately turns her attention toward the toy.

Colin looks up at her for 2 seconds and then immediately turns toward the toy again. The two never make eye contact; both are looking at the toy. Sarah's voice turns playful, and she reaches down to operate parts of the toy along with Colin, saying "Whoa . . . whoa . . . this is a fun toy, isn't it?" Colin coos once, as if in agreement, but still doesn't look at his mom.

What's wrong with this picture? It would appear that nothing is wrong: Mom is back, her baby seems calm, and now the two are playing quietly side by side. The reality, as revealed by the Strange Situation Procedure (SSP), however, shows a different picture. The video clip just described was recorded during the SSP, which was staged to examine the attachment bond between Sarah and her toddler son. The SSP, designed as a research tool, has proven very effective at helping developmental psychologists understand attachment patterns of large groups of dyads and predict outcomes. The COS intervention uses this assessment to help us see the strengths and struggles between a particular child and caregiver for the purpose of designing a specific treatment plan for intervention that will help the two enhance their security.

If Sarah and Colin were securely attached, we would expect to see Colin demonstrate positive expectations of his mother when the two were reunited: The baby would probably keep crying upon his mother's return and reach up to her to be picked up and held. (While this is the prevalent response to separation of a securely attached infant from 12 to 18 months, other responses, including a limited signaling of distress, are also possible.)

He might have looked into his mother's face to be sure his mother understood the anguish he had felt upon their separation and could help Colin manage that emotional pain until it subsided. After he calmed down, he might have smiled and seemed happy to see his mother, then snuggled with his mom and kept close contact for a brief time until he felt comforted and safe. Then he probably would have shown interest in the toy he was playing with or one of the other toys scattered on the carpet or stowed nearby in a netted bin. Maybe he would have pointed to a toy and looked at it, turning again to his mother for some signal that his mother found it intriguing too, that it was safe to go investigate its possibilities and that Mom was willing to give him permission to leave the sanctuary of her lap and go off to explore. When he started playing with the toy, he might have occasionally looked to his mother to see if Sarah was watching. He would have smiled or cooed or engaged in the kind of full-body expression of wriggling joy that only the youngest children can exhibit.

For her part, Sarah would have shown that she was attuned to what Colin needed and wanted from moment to moment. She would have looked into her son's eyes to see how upset he was upon their reunion. She would have picked him up when reached for, held him for as long as her child was clinging or still showing signs of distress, and started to loosen her hold as soon as Colin appeared to settle and then show signs of restlessness and wanderlust. Overall, Sarah would have shown a willingness to follow Colin's lead as much as she could, letting the baby decide when to explore but actively taking charge to comfort her child when the little boy was clearly upset about the separation.

That is not the picture that can be seen in this video clip. Of course, the description just offered is overgeneralized, painted in broad strokes that do not do justice to the chaotic, unscripted moments of real life. Many, many interactions between a caregiver and child who are securely attached are not nearly that pretty. Parents are distracted or tired and do not shift from their other adult concerns to meeting their child's needs with the precision of a programmable nanny. Children are hungry or cold or tired, and even when Mom is there with food, a blanket, or a lullaby, they fuss and fret and start out expressing anger at the very person most likely to answer their need. Mom may heave a deep sigh at her 2-year-old while she picks her up to hold her close. The 2-year-old might have to try two or three times to get Mom to look at the block tower she's building—but she keeps trying because she trusts her effort will be rewarded. In addition, a whole host of interfering events, environmental circumstances, and personality traits can make a secure attachment appear at first glance to be insecure—and vice versa. What matters ultimately is what Susan Woodhouse calls "getting the job done in the end" (personal communication, 2009)—the child using the parent as a secure base and a safe haven even if there are difficult moments along the way.

Secure reunions between child and caregiver
are typically marked by a calm of connection.

The danger in expecting perfection in caregiver–child interactions or in trying to assess an attachment by glancing at a snapshot cannot be overstated. This is why investigators trained in performing the Strange Situation view hundreds of hours of examples and learn to observe with the scrutiny of a microbiologist armed with a microscope. Because they have only one chance to record a dyad when performing the Strange Situation for research purposes, a well-executed assessment is critical. In our work with caregivers and children, we use a modified Strange Situation to look at parent–child interactions, the Circle of Security Interview (COSI) to get access to parents' perceptions, and our interaction with parents in group to assess strengths and struggles and figure out how best to help caregivers become effective hands on the Circle.

With the understanding that all of these varied types of input might be needed to arrive at any accurate conclusions about the video clip of Sarah and Colin—or any single video clip of a caregiver and child—and despite appearances that all is well, this boy can be said to have an insecure attachment. In the Strange Situation (more details on the procedure can be found in Part II of this book), a child is left in a room with toys and a stranger, who sits by quietly, having been instructed to respond to the child after the caregiver exits. The caregiver stays away for only a very brief time, but it is perfectly normal for the child to exhibit distress over the separation, as Colin does.

In the research protocol, the dyad's attachment bond is evaluated mainly on the basis of what happens when the caregiver and child are reunited. As just noted, a securely attached child can be expected generally to be relieved and pleased to see the caregiver return and to show that he expects to be comforted to ease his distress. Colin does stop crying when his mother reenters; in fact he shows remarkable self-control and stops crying almost instantly. Yet instead of crawling toward his mother or extending his arms to be picked up, he acts as if he wants to go back to playing with the toy.

We know from research that Colin is still very upset, because even securely attached children, who are capable of being soothed upon reunion, have an elevated heart rate for about a minute after the caregiver returns (Sroufe & Waters, 1977). In addition, infants and young children are dependent upon regulation of their physiological response to fearful stimuli within the hypothalamic–pituitary–adrenal (HPA) system. This HPA axis regulates the body's level of the stress hormone cortisol. Increasing evidence shows that the regulation of a child's stress response is directly correlated to the child's capacity to use a caregiver as a resource (Lyons-Ruth, 2007). Yet Colin exhibits the stoicism of an old soldier and continues to play with the toy as if he is all business. If we could look into Colin's mind, we might see that, consciously or not, he is trying not to show his great need for his mother because he senses that doing so might make Sarah uncomfortable and thus drive her away. Colin hides his need for comfort in an attempt to stay close enough to a protective adult to survive and avoid feeling abandoned and unprotected (Main, 1981).

This sense of abandonment, of utter aloneness, is one of the internal anxieties described by Donald Winnicott as "primitive agonies." Winnicott categorized the primitive agonies as "not going on being," "having no orientation," "having no relation to the body," "complete isolation because of there being no means of communication," "going to pieces," and "falling forever" (1974). The mirror opposite of our primal need to be attached, this terror associated with abandonment is a particular form of pain that the developing mind of a child cannot sustain for more than a few moments. The experience of "Being-Without," of being disconnected from his or her source of belonging, occurs when the relational needs of a child go unmet.

Abandonment is abandonment is abandonment.

Primitive agonies seem to be a given for every one of us. Themes of "falling forever," "not going on being," "complete isolation," "going to pieces," and so forth are the stuff of the nightmares, nursery rhymes, fears, and fairy tales to which all children (and adults) can relate. Although the attachment goal for parents and children is to establish internalized trust and relatedness, the reality is that experiencing the agonies associated with the lack of parental attunement to the highly sensitive and specific needs of young children is inevitable. All parents fail. It is never a matter of *whether* caregiver failures will happen. It is more an issue of *how often* and *to what degree of intensity* these moments of actual and perceived abandonment occur.

The reality of secure attachment is that parents serve
as the hands on the Circle by being BIGGER, STRONGER,
WISER, AND KIND OFTEN ENOUGH.

This is why interactions even in dyads who are securely attached do not always look pretty—or even secure. Needing your caregiver and experiencing "Being-Without" is so distressing for children that they can easily develop defensive strategies to protect themselves, and when individual circumstances raise the threat of abandonment even slightly, the child may very well react in a way that makes the relationship look insecure. And this is why those in a position to evaluate attachment bonds in individuals must take care not to overgeneralize based on little observable evidence.

According to the COS model, the instinct for attachment is not just a simple desire for intimacy. If it were, then disappointing connections would be just that: disappointing but manageable. But when Being-With is recognized as the fundamentally essential aspect of relationship that it is, it becomes clear that Being-Without leads to painfully dysregulated emotional states that threaten our experience of survival. This, we believe, is why nonsecure attachment can lead to systemic dysfunction, lifelong relationship dissatisfaction, struggles with both intimacy and self-activation, and even, in extreme cases, personality disorders. It is why we consider it so important to help parents consistently recognize and repair the inevitable breaks in the Circle that are part of childhood.

LIMITED CIRCLES

When caregivers provide at least adequate support and respond appropriately often enough to the needs outlined on the COS, children develop a secure attachment (Cassidy et al., 2011). How much support is adequate and how often is enough is still being studied, but what is known is that only 50 to 60% of children are securely attached, according to the Strange Situation research data (Cassidy, 2008).

When a pattern emerges in which parents consistently do not respond to specific needs on the Circle (top, bottom, or hands), the Circle can be said to be limited, as if an arc had been cut out of it, leaving a gap, resulting in attachment that is not secure. (It's important to note, however, that minor sporadic ruptures occur over and over during a normal day: a parent snaps at a fussy child in frustration or ignores a demanding one out of exhaustion. If these ruptures do not form a pattern and if they are repaired appropriately most of the time, they can actually make the relationship stronger, as noted in Chapter 3.) **However, at the heart of developing an insecure attachment is the child's knowledge that his caregiver is *emotionally unavailable* to meet specific needs on the Circle.** This might mean that instead of the caregiver helping the child regulate whatever emotions a need raises, the caregiver in essence says, "Don't have this feeling. Don't have this need." For infants, emotional states in which they must Be-Without a caregiver are increasingly experienced as distressing and will be defended against.

As shown in the Circle graphic (Figure 1.1 on page 17) the child's needs have to be met on both the bottom and the top half of the Circle—both when the child needs comfort and when the child needs support for exploration. That children are constantly moving from needing a safe haven to needing a secure base for exploration is, in fact, why the graphic is circular. Yet some parents, because of their own state of mind, which is often largely a product of their upbringing and their attachment history with their own caregiver during childhood (see Chapter 5), have trouble meeting these needs, usually more on one part of the Circle than the other.

In Circle language, children who do not turn to their caregiver as a safe haven when upset are having trouble on the bottom half of the Circle. As mentioned in Box 4.1, attachment theorists call this an "avoidant attachment." You can think about this as children avoiding activating the parent's caregiving system because they know that doing so makes the parent uncomfortable. Children who have trouble separating from their caregiver to explore are having trouble on the top half of the Circle. This is called an "ambivalent attachment." You can think about this as children being ambivalent about activating their exploratory system because that makes their caregiver uncomfortable.

Avoidant Attachments

When we talk to parents and other primary caregivers about insecure attachments, we show them graphics that we call Circles of Limited Security (or "limited Circles"; see Figures 4.1 and 4.2).

According to Mary Ainsworth's original scheme, Colin would be

---

BOX 4.1. CHILD RESPONDING TO THE PARENT'S NEEDS

When a child's requests for help with needs on the Circle that are consistently met with parental distress and a negative response, the child will stop trying to get this need met directly by the caregiver and learn to put the parent's emotional stability first. We call this shift "responding to the parent's needs" because the infant or toddler is being pressured to take care of the parent. For example, when the caregiver is uncomfortable with separation and so responds negatively to the child's desire to explore, sending the message that the child shouldn't have the feelings associated with curiosity, mastery, or autonomy, the child learns to inhibit exploration and instead overfocuses on needing proximity to the caregiver as a way to maintain that vital connection. Over time this pattern becomes associated with the type of insecure attachment called an "ambivalent attachment." In the same way, a caregiver who is uncomfortable with providing comfort as a safe haven—one who communicates that the child shouldn't have the feelings associated with needing safety and closeness—will discourage care-seeking behavior in the child, resulting in what is called "avoidant attachment." Both types of attachment are insecure, and in both cases the child has limited opportunity to experience closeness or separation and has a distorted sense that the purpose of emotional regulation is to protect the parent.

These attachment patterns obviously cause children difficulty, but when a caregiver consciously or unconsciously abdicates his or her role as the bigger, stronger, wiser, and kind parent, the child is in a profoundly frightening situation. The parent may relinquish his or her role by becoming childlike (and thus the child's peer), by demanding that the child act like an adult who doesn't need a parent (and thus become the parent's peer), or by turning the adult role over to the child and demanding to be taken care of. In all of these scenarios, the primary caregiver is no longer a protective adult, which leaves the child extremely vulnerable and afraid with no one to turn to. Both role distortions and role reversal can lead to the most serious pattern of attachment: "disorganized attachment." All three types of nonsecure attachment are discussed later in this chapter.

described as having an avoidant attachment to his mother. Note that we did not say that Colin, based on his behavior in the Strange Situation, is an avoidant *child*. It is not accurate to say a child is avoidant because the avoidance does not reside in the parent or in the child, but in the relationship. Avoidance is not the same as being shy or reserved, which are temperaments that do reside in the child. Children who are shy or reserved may have a secure attachment to their primary caregiver. Furthermore, children may have an avoidant relationship with one caregiver and a secure or ambivalent relation with another.

An attachment classification describes
the relationship, not the individual.

During the SSP reunion, the child's attachment is activated, but both parent and child in an avoidant dyad act like nothing has happened. This miscuing on the part of the child is self-protective in two important ways: "Masking of negative affect simultaneously protects the infant from the rejection that often results from her attempts to seek contact as well as from the painful fear of alienating the attachment figure on whom she depends for survival" (Cassidy, 1994, p. 235). Such a child goes over and gives the parent a toy, and the interaction is all about the toy, as it was between

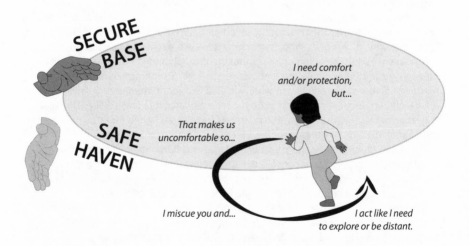

FIGURE 4.1. Limited bottom of the Circle: Child miscuing—responding to caregiver's needs. Copyright 1999 by Cooper, Hoffman, Marvin, and Powell.

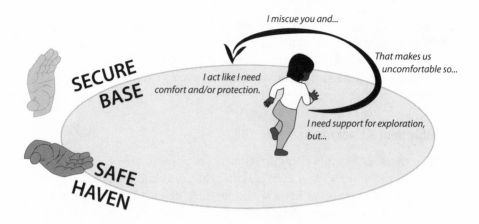

I miscue you and...

SECURE BASE

I act like I need comfort and/or protection.

That makes us uncomfortable so...

I need support for exploration, but...

SAFE HAVEN

FIGURE 4.2. Limited top of the Circle: Child miscuing—responding to caregiver's needs. Copyright 1999 by Cooper, Hoffman, Marvin, and Powell.

Sarah and Colin. Most avoidant dyads turn everything into a task instead of an emotional encounter. If toys are not the focus, we might see a mother ignore the child or undertake some caregiving "business" like picking lint off her baby's pants instead of making eye contact, touching, and engaging.

We can see all of these behaviors in the mere minute that passes between Sarah and Colin in the video clip described earlier. Colin cries while his mother is out of the room but then cuts off his weeping within 4 seconds of Sarah's return. (Many children with avoidant attachments and even some with secure attachments will not even seem visibly distressed while the parent is absent.) He turns immediately to the toy and spends the great proportion of their time in the Strange Situation fiddling with the activity center, even though it's evident to most observers that there is no joy or even true interest in his play. Assuming that Colin's behavior correlates with research evidence, his heart rate was elevated through the entire reunion with his mother even though he didn't show overt signs of distress (Sroufe & Waters, 1977).

If this relationship stays avoidant, Colin is likely to grow up to become overly reliant on himself and dismissing of relationships in an impossible attempt to be self-sufficient. But true autonomy may elude him. Avoidant attachment in infancy is associated with externalizing problems (e.g., aggression and hostility), conduct disorders, and pathology in general (Sroufe et al., 2005). This is not to say the majority of children in avoidant relationships will suffer from these disorders, but rather children with a history of avoidant attachment are more likely to have these problems. Adults with an avoidant attachment style (referred to as a dismissing state of mind with regard to attachment) tend to hide their feelings, deny painful emotions, and dismiss painful memories or events (Mikulincer & Florian, 1998).

Ambivalent Attachments

When we describe ambivalent attachments to parents and other caregivers, we show them in Figure 4.2, explaining that the child seeks proximity to the caregiver when upset but does not become calm. The child often seeks to be put down before feeling comforted but then wants to be picked up again.

> In a video clip from a Strange Situation, 18-month-old Dwayne stands facing the door from which his father exited the room, crying for his dad's return. When Jamar comes back in, he picks Dwayne up and carries him to a chair, where he lifts him to his shoulder. Dwayne does not reach up to embrace his father. Jamar rocks his son in the chair and says somewhat defensively "I had to talk to someone," then, as Dwayne continues to cry, he repeats that statement more sympathetically and starts saying "It's OK, it's OK" as he rocks his son. Jamar bends down as if ready to place his son on the floor, but Dwayne reaches up to encircle his neck again. Thirty seconds later, Dwayne is still crying, and Jamar is still cradling him and patting his back.
>
> The stranger, who was sitting quietly on a couch at the other side of the room, quietly gets up and leaves. Dwayne seems interested in this development, following her with his eyes; he has stopped crying. As the door closes behind the stranger, Dwayne turns back toward Jamar and starts crying again. Jamar says, "What happened? What happened?" He then picks up a puppet and pushes it into Dwayne's face, saying "Why are you crying?" in a gruff voice as if it's coming from the puppet.
>
> Dwayne reaches out and points toward the couch. He is still crying, though it is beginning to sound slightly forced. Jamar says, "Oh, OK, go play with it; go play with it" as he puts him down. Dwayne walks over to the couch, where he picks up a toy mallet with his back to his father. Jamar chuckles, sounding uncomfortable, and says, "It's OK." Immediately Dwayne puts down the toy, turns around, starts crying again, and comes back to wrap his arms around his father's knees. Jamar picks him up again and starts rocking his son, patting his back, and saying "It's OK" all over again.
>
> Dwayne stays on his father's lap until he finally quiets. Jamar then

puts him down, and the little boy starts playing with one of the toys spread out on the floor. Jamar watches him silently for about 15 seconds and then reaches down to the floor and lifts up a pacifier, asking Dwayne, who is not looking at him, if he wants it. Dwayne dutifully puts down the toy and waddles over to his dad to get his pacifier and sticks it into his mouth.

Dwayne is scored as ambivalently attached to his father, Jamar. The term "ambivalent attachment" refers to the pattern of children asking to be put down while they are still visibly upset and their heart rate is still elevated (Sroufe & Waters, 1977) and then asking to be picked up again. The ambivalence Dwayne experiences consists of both wanting to explore and wanting his caregiver to be available, but fearing that exploration will make his caregiver unavailable. Trying to resolve this quandary leads to holding on and pushing away. This kind of up and down behavior may be seen with any child who is frustrated or overly tired, but it is a sign of ambivalent attachment when it regularly prolongs attachment behaviors and disrupts exploration.

As you can see from their interaction, Jamar hardly ever seems to follow his son's lead, and when he takes charge it is at inopportune moments in inappropriate ways. For example, when Dwayne stops crying as he watches the stranger leave, his dad pushes a puppet into his face and demands, "Why are you crying?" This is not a comforting gesture. Soon after that, Dwayne gets down and settles into playing with the toys, and Jamar says, "It's OK" at a time when his son is showing no sign of needing comfort or reassurance. This seems to trigger him, and he turns around, starts crying, and returns to Jamar's lap. When, at the end of the episode, he gets down to play again and his father asks him, out of the blue, "Do you want your pacifier?" he instantly goes over to get it. When Jamar was shown this video in group and asked why he thought Dwayne might need his pacifier, his answer was revealing of the underlying process. He said, "I felt alone."

Ambivalent attachment seems to come from several underlying causes. From what we saw in the SSP, we would refer to Jamar as an "I need you to need me" parent. In this case the parent and child were working together to maintain proximity via activation of the attachment system. "The parent may realize, at an unconscious level," explains Jude Cassidy, "that prolonged negative emotionality keeps the child embroiled with her and prevents the child from moving away to explore the environment" (Cassidy, 1994, p. 243). Mary Ainsworth's original formulation was that ambivalent attachment comes from parents being inconsistently available, with the children using attachment behaviors to keep the caregiver available. We also see ambivalent attachment in dyads where the parents are preoccupied with the child's safety even when no danger is present, and so they keep their child close. This "the world is too dangerous" view is closely related to the "my child is too precious" view that causes parents to hover over their child.

We also have worked with several mothers who were quite dismissing but whose children had an ambivalent attachment. As we learned more about the violence in their homes and neighborhoods, we concurred with them that their world really was so dangerous that they needed to keep their children very close. The issue in treatment was to deal with the parents' dismissing state of mind (George et al., 1984) so they could shift from a "Stay close but don't need me" strategy to closely monitoring their children in the context of a secure relationship.

Just as with avoidance, people with a history of ambivalent attachment have problematic outcomes. However, ambivalent attachment is associated with internalizing as opposed to externalizing problems, specifically anxiety disorders (Sroufe et al., 2005). In adulthood ambivalent attachment strategies are associated with more passive and emotionally focused coping strategies that include increased emotionality and limited assertion.

INSECURITY ON ONE HALF OF THE CIRCLE AFFECTS THE OTHER

Although avoidance and ambivalence are each seen as struggles mainly with one half of the Circle, in reality these caregivers struggle on both the top and the bottom. Although Jamar clearly struggles with letting his child leave his side to explore, he also struggles with the bottom, because Dwayne does not calm down while on his father's lap. Jamar's pushing the puppet into his son's face and having the puppet demand to know why the little boy is crying is, again, not a skillfully comforting gesture. This child keeps his attachment system overactivated; he seeks comfort that should make him calm but then resists calming because on a preverbal level he understands his father's discomfort with his feeling calm enough to go explore.

The ambivalent child is chronically upset but vacillates between wanting to be put down and wanting to be held. The parent may feel very successful at "meeting the needs" without being aware of how the unrecognized requirement that the child remain close is actually disruptive to a sense of genuine closeness (relatedness-within-autonomy) as well as genuine exploration (autonomy-within-relatedness).

Children in ambivalent relationships are stuck: They do not learn competent affect regulation because the minute they feel calm they want to explore, but that sends a mental warning that this behavior might be threatening to Mom or Dad and they should continue to act like they need comfort. Sadly, the fact that both their exploration and affect regulation are hindered means that the development of the self is hindered as well. Unless their attachment strategy changes, this can consign them to a life of chronically overfocusing on others.

Likewise, the avoidant child keeps attachment behaviors underactivated, but this does not mean that dyads in avoidant relationships have no problems with the top half of the Circle. Bottom-half discomfort seeps into top-half activities as a feeling that the secure base for exploration is not truly there because comfort and connection will not be allowed when needed. Thus, with no secure base it may not be safe enough to really explore. This can rob a child's exploration of the color and richness imparted by the sense, even when alone, of a caregiver who is Being-With the child. The play of a child whose parent is not watching over him with delight, joyfully participating when invited, can seem lackluster, as in the case of Colin, or forced, as with Ashley (see Chapter 1). Playing alone becomes playing while lonely.

Clearly, a parent's struggle with either separation or closeness affects competency in caregiving on both halves of the Circle.

ADAPTATIONS: AVOIDANT AND AMBIVALENT STRATEGIES IN THE SERVICE OF ATTACHMENT

If necessity is the mother of invention, then there is no one more inventive than a child at risk of experiencing Being-Without. Separation from a parent or other primary caregiver is felt as a type of free fall that robs a young child of the relatedness that provides structure to the developing self. It shatters the holding environment that makes emotional experience less overwhelming to an infant. It threatens to make the child feel like an outcast and isolated, as if the safety net of being understood, accepted, and valued in a cruel world had been whisked away. And this is all in addition to the practical matter of being torn from the protective arms of an adult who can keep the predators at bay and ensure the child's survival until he can take care of himself.

No wonder Colin learned not to cry for comfort in front of his mother. No wonder Dwayne learned to interrupt his venturing out to play whenever his father beckoned. Both children had learned to recognize their caregivers' discomfort, a discomfort that may be displayed in flashes of nervousness, anger, sadness, and so forth lasting only a micro-moment but signaling that the caregiver is unable to remain present. Both children then sent their parents signals that they would "cooperate in helping maintain the parent's own state of mind in relation to attachment," according to Jude Cassidy. In avoidant attachments (such as that of Colin with Sarah) those signals manifest as "minimizing of negative affect [signaling] that the infant will not seek caregiving that would interfere with the parent's dismissal of attachment," whereas "the heightened negative emotionality of the ambivalent infant signals to the parent that the infant needs her and thus helps maintain a state of mind in which attachment is emphasized" (Cassidy, 1994, p. 248).

Sarah was uncomfortable on the bottom half of the Circle. She didn't reach out for her son to offer physical comfort upon their reunion. She didn't look into her son's eyes to see how distressed the little boy was about their separation. Even at the tender age of 14 months, Colin had learned to perceive his mother's discomfort and head it off, changing his own behavior so that his mother stayed relatively happy and comfortable, and therefore would be more likely to meet his needs.

Jamar was uncomfortable on the top half of the Circle. He cued his son that he needed him to be upset when he had already gone out to play, saying "It's OK" and signaling him that he should come back to be comforted. When he was actively involved with a toy, Jamar interrupted and offered his son his pacifier even though he had shown no signs of being fussy or needing anything from his father on the bottom of the Circle. Dwayne had learned that his being away from his father often made him anxious, and so he obligingly kept returning to ask him to fill up his cup. Dwayne was helping his father regulate his emotions instead of the other way around.

Colin knows that if he continues to cry in front of his mother, things will be worse, so he pretends to explore. Dwayne knows if he keeps playing by himself, his father will get upset, so he pretends to need his arms wrapped around him. Young children trying to survive and grow are the most creatively adaptable creatures on the planet.

Why would such young children be so intensely focused on maintaining both physical and emotional connection to their caregivers? What anxiety do they carry that seems to compel them to give up legitimate needs on the part of the Circle that their caregivers are unable to respond to? How is it that Being-With—even when compromised—is preferable to the experience of Being-Without? The answer to this question lies in part with a concept called "splitting."

Good Face, Bad Face

Current infant research is focusing on how babies establish "patterns of expectation" in their first year of life (Beebe, Knoblauch, Rustin, & Sorter, 2005). Researchers reviewing parent–infant interactions can discern that infants are paying moment-to-moment attention to their caregivers, tracking the minute details offered by the caregiver, such as tone and inflection of voice, pacing of conversation, quality of eye contact (gaze acceptance vs. gaze aversion), facial gestures, openness to touch, acceptance of distress. Thus they are learning to anticipate specific patterns that support a growing experience of predictability. The work of Beatrice Beebe and her colleagues has concluded that it is possible to predict infant attachment at 1 year based on the study of observable patterns of dyadic coordination between parent and infant at 4 months (Beebe et al., 2005).

Through repeated interactions children form two discrete representations of their caregiver. One is of the good caregiver (the tender and caring one that feeds you when you are hungry, wraps you up when you are cold, basically meets your needs in a sensitive manner), and the other is of the bad caregiver (the harsh or impatient one who tries to feed you when you are cold or wraps you up when you are hungry and is basically misattuned to your needs). The baby doesn't know that these are two representations of the same person. Infants have no idea that this "bad" parent has been awakened six times that night and has to get up early for work. When we are tired, frustrated, and hurried, we naturally react differently than when we are rested and have the whole day to spend with the baby.

To keep the good caregiver representation from being contaminated by the bad caregiver representation, the infant, via a concept called "splitting," sees the caregiver as two people. When the good caregiver is present, the bad one doesn't exist, and vice versa. A primal goal of all developing infants is to keep the good caregiver present and thus the bad caregiver absent. The attachment strategies seen in children who are avoidantly or ambivalently attached are intended to keep the good caregiver around as often as possible.

In healthy development, children first organize their experience of the caregiver into good and bad representations. Over time they begin to see that the good and bad caregivers are one person who is sometimes good and sometimes bad. If things go well, eventually children realize that their parent is neither all good nor all bad, but everything in between.

This developmental realization "may be likened to the difference between a B movie and an A movie; in the former the characters are all clearly good or evil, they are one dimensional; the characters in an A movie are more complicated, they have depth, they suffer from internal conflicts and their characters have good and bad aspects" (Lichtenberg & Slap, 1973, p. 779). We all continue to use splitting throughout our lives (e.g., in sports, politics, and war, or when there are tensions between religious or racial groups, people often subtly or not so subtly categorize others as bad or good, depending on which side they are on). Also, the strategies used early on to manage the good/bad caregiver can become part of our procedural memory about relationships and thus affect our current life.

It is important to note that when the representation of the bad parent emerges, children believe that it is because they are bad. This allows them to have hope that there is a good parent out there, and if they do just the right thing they'll get the good parent back. If they believed they were good, they would have to conclude that the parent was bad, and then all hope would be lost. Ronald Fairbairn called this the "moral defense" and stated:

> It is better to be a sinner in a world ruled by God than to live in a world ruled by the Devil. A sinner in a world ruled by God may be bad; but there is always a certain sense of security to be derived from the fact that the world around is good—God's in His Heaven—All's right with the world! And in any case there is always hope of redemption. In a world ruled by the Devil the individual may escape the badness of being a sinner; but he is bad because the world around him is bad. Further, he can have no sense of security and no hope of redemption. The only prospect is one of death and destruction. (1952, pp. 66–67)

We prefer to call it the "universal defense," believing the reference to morality is confusing, and clinically the defense seems to be universally used to manage painful experiences derived from trusted caregivers.

Miscues: Attending to the Caregiver's Needs

When children directly or indirectly make their need known to their caregiver, we call it a "cue." When children hide their need from their caregiver, we call it a "miscue." When Colin acted interested in the activity center at a time when we know he must have been distressed and in need of comfort, he was miscuing his mother in the hope that answering Sarah's need would keep Sarah close. If Colin had continued crying and reached up to his mother when Sarah reentered the room, he would have been "cuing" his

true need. Sometimes securely attached children also use "indirect cues," such as wearing an angry expression, or looking sad, or crossing their arms and pouting—they do want comfort, but right now they are irate about the separation. If offered the comfort they want, they will calm and accept cuddling from their caregiver. As adults, we all use miscues as well. When greeted on the street and asked how we are, even if we are having a horrible day, we may smile and say, "Fine, and you?"

Although we said above that Dwayne and Colin pretend to need what they believe their caregiver will find tolerable, it is important to understand that they are not making conscious decisions to deliver miscues. The awareness that their caregiver is uncomfortable with one half of the Circle and the strategies they hit upon to keep the caregiver close are part of procedural memory, or implicit relational knowing (see Chapter 3). In infants these perceptions and behaviors are formulated at a preverbal stage, and they percolate under the surface of consciousness as children get older. As Chapter 5 will explain, in fact, this procedural disguising of their own need carries forward into adulthood and is often translated into relational behavior that leads to acting in a dismissing or preoccupied manner with partners and their own children—without any conscious awareness on the part of the adults. (This is why the COS protocol can be so powerfully transformative: it gives parents a chance to see with their own eyes the internal working models that are driving their caregiving.) Over time the discomfort of separation or the discomfort with closeness can be internalized and then passed on to the next generation as a feeling that the secure base for exploration or the safe haven for comfort is not truly there because connection and support was not allowed when needed. These adults may say that this is just who they are, but in reality it is who they have learned to be. Some babies are more temperamentally outgoing while others are more reserved, but temperament does not predict attachment. We are born looking for a face, and turning away from the face that is more important to us than any other is learned behavior.

Miscues are outward manifestations of the defenses that everyone has against being hurt and alone. The insecurely attached child has a very tough job, having to keep one eye on his own needs and one on his parent's needs. Imagine how difficult it is to manage the pain of being all of 12 months old and having to deny yourself the comfort of your mother's arms because if you ask for it you will likely experience rejection and Being-Without. Imagine the frustration of denying your legitimate need to explore and follow your curiosity.

Secure attachment does not inoculate us against hurt and isolation so thoroughly that we can drop all our defenses and leave them behind forever. Remember, when we are being threatened or attacked, defenses are strength. Security can provide us with a sense of safety that can allow us to reflect on our present situation and thus be more accurate about when to use our defenses. If you are jousting, a suit of armor is a benefit, but if you want to go for a swim after the match, the suit of armor becomes a serious liability.

Unfortunately, the nature of miscues makes them difficult to identify because they are designed to show us what we want to see and disguise what we don't want to see. Parents need a great deal of support and courage to decode their own and their child's miscues and embrace the very needs they are trying to protect themselves from.

DISORGANIZED ATTACHMENT: THE WILD CARD

Nikki, at 13 months old, is once again crying for her mother, Alexis, at the door. It's the second separation and reunion during the SSP, and Nikki seems bereft without her mother's presence. Only 70 seconds into the separation, it is clear that her distress is so significant that Alexis is asked to return to her child early. As is required within the standard protocol, Alexis knocks gently on the door and calls out her daughter's name. Still distraught, upon hearing her name called, Nikki stands and immediately begins running in a direction opposite of where her mother would be entering. Now 20 steps away from the door, Nikki pauses for 4 seconds, frozen in place. Trying to decide her next move, Nikki turns toward Alexis, then away, then toward, then away. Again she pauses. Now 30 seconds into the reunion, Nikki brings her hand to her mouth and gradually begins to move toward her mother's waiting presence.

Attachment bonds cannot be classified accurately until a child is 12 months old. Nikki is old enough to be seen as demonstrating a third type of attachment bond, called "disorganized attachment." As attachment researchers accumulated more and more videos of caregivers and children, a small percentage could not be classified as secure, avoidant, or ambivalent. It wasn't until enough of these videos were compiled that a pattern was detected. The underlying commonality is that these children seem to be seeking and fearing their caregiver at the same time. Like Nikki, they exhibit a confusing jumble of behaviors, often crying while the caregiver is absent but then running away when the caregiver returns or then suddenly turning toward the caregiver, freezing, and when the caregiver approaches, turning around with hands to face and walking backward toward the caregiver. Disorganized attachments seem to be relationships founded on the management of fear (Main & Hesse, 1990; Solomon & George, 1999). However, we caution that disorganization is extremely difficult to identify accurately, and harm can come to children who are assigned these labels by people who are not properly trained.

As discussed throughout this chapter, adaptive strategies that are employed when secure attachment is not available are all aimed at managing fear. But in the case of ambivalence and avoidance, the fear is solvable: Secure infants of course reach out to their caregiver when frightened; that is their solution. Avoidant infants defensively turn their attention away from the possibility of being rejected by their caregiver in times of need and focus on exploration. Ambivalent infants maintain connection to a protective caregiver by exaggerating their attachment behavior.

Disorganized attachment, in contrast, precludes a coherent response (Cassidy & Mohr, 2001). Children have a four-million-year-old instinct to run away from what frightens them and a four-million-year-old instinct to run toward their caregiver when they are frightened. When what is frightening them is the caregiver, they are stuck, caught in a bind of wanting to go toward and go away at the same time.

Some caregivers of disorganized children are frightening (hostile and intrusive). Others are frightened themselves (helpless and withdrawn). Either one leaves the child feeling abandoned in times of need (see Box 4.2).

Circle of Disorganization:
I need you, but you are so frightened or frightening that I have no one to turn to and I don't know what to do.

The Circle of Disorganization (Figure 4.3) is used to depict disorganized attachment to professionals but is not presented to caregivers because it does not contribute enough clarity to the process to offset the risk of evoking a defensive response. Notice that the hands are removed from the Circle and that specific needs are not listed. The child is simply saying, "I need you." When children feel abandoned, their overriding need is connection. The starkness of the Circle of Disorganization is meant to illustrate the desolate nature of disorganized attachment.

The absence of the hands represents the fact that the caregiver lacks the capacity to balance bigger, stronger, wiser, and kind. When "bigger"

BOX 4.2. THE ROLE OF FEAR IN ATTACHMENT

- Secure children fear danger.
- Avoidant children fear closeness.
- Ambivalent children fear separation.
- Disorganized children fear their caregiver.

---

and "stronger" are expressed without the wisdom of kindness the child experiences the caregiver as mean. When "kind" is expressed without the wisdom of "bigger" and "stronger," the child experiences the caregiver as weak. And when bigger, stronger, wiser, and kind are missing altogether, the child experiences the caregiver as gone.[1] Manifestations of mean, weak, and gone can take different shapes. Meanness is most obvious when it is loud or violent, but it can even be laughing at, mocking, and berating an infant. Weakness might appear in a caregiver who does not set limits or take charge, asks permission from the child at inappropriate times, or turns to the child and says, "What should I do now? I don't know what to do." Drug and alcohol abuse, depression, anxiety, significant mental illness, and focus on a new romantic partner are a few examples of what leads to a parent being gone.

> *Disorganized attachment is the irresolvable paradox that occurs when the parent is both the source of the child's fear and the haven for the child's safety. This paradox leaves a child feeling chronically afraid, on the verge of losing emotional and behavioral control, and a diminished capacity to see adults as a resource.*

Living in Fear

Infants and young toddlers with disorganized attachments are afraid to move toward and afraid to run away from the caregiver. When these children are reunited with their caregiver in the SSP, these contradictory impulses can take the form of odd movements, as mentioned above, such as walking backward toward the caregiver, turning in a circle, putting hands to face, cringing, flapping, freezing, and so on. At about their third

---

[1] At first we used "mean and weak" for the absence of "hands." Our colleagues in Norway, Stig Torsteinson and Ida Brandtzæg, suggested that we were not acknowledging the absent/unavailable parent and thus suggested that we add "gone" (see Box 4.3).

FIGURE 4.3. Limited hands: Child's response to living with fear. Copyright 1999 by Cooper, Hoffman, Marvin, and Powell.

birthday, these children become exceptionally controlling of their caregiver (Solomon & George, 2008). This role reversal takes two forms: controlling punitive or controlling caregiving. Using these "strategies of desperation" (Cassidy & Mohr, 2001), the child takes control of the interaction in a hostile or punitive manner (controlling punitive) or takes control of the relationship and tries to entertain, direct, organize, or reassure the parent (controlling caregiving). Often children switch back and forth between the two.

An Example of Controlling Punitive

Jamie is about to turn 3. During the second reunion in the SSP Jamie does not turn to her mom and starts to play with the toys aggressively, using

---

BOX 4.3. PRECURSORS OF DISORGANIZED ATTACHMENT

- Maltreatment of the child
- Abuse
- Neglect
- Substance abuse by the parent
- Frightening behavior by the parent
- Parent's unresolved loss or trauma

Note: Based on van IJzendoorn et al. (1999).

one doll to hit another doll. Mom appears uncomfortable and tries to direct Jamie's attention to another toy. Jamie suddenly picks up a doll and throws it at her mother. Mom says softly, "Hey, don't do that. Please let's just play and we'll get your favorite ice cream on the way home." Jamie then tells her mother what toys she should play with, and her mother complies with an overbright tone: "OK, I will play with the dollhouse." Jamie continues to use the doll to hit other toys.

An Example of Controlling Caregiving

Four-year-old Darla has been waiting for her mother's return during the separation phase of the SSP. Over the past few minutes, Darla's play has diminished and she has found her way toward the door where her mother had exited. As her mother returns, Darla looks closely into her mother's almost expressionless face. As they make eye contact, Darla quickly focuses on a doll and lifts it toward her mother. "Wanna play?" she calls with a voice almost shrill with excitement. Her mother quietly nods in apparent agreement. Darla then moves quickly toward her mother, animating her gestures as if attempting to awaken her from a very noticeable depression. Taking a doctor kit to her mom, Darla exclaims, "Come closer. Something's wrong. Let me see your arm."

Whatever the exact behavioral manifestation, these behaviors serve to help the child manage fear. The freezing and stilling during the reunions with disorganized infants can be viewed as precursors to dissociative process ("protodissociative experiences" [Sroufe et al., 2005, p. 248] or "states that become traits" [Perry, Pollard, Blakley, Baker, & Vigilante, 1995]). Eventually dissociation and other primitive defenses become a part of the child's repertoire of coping mechanisms and will evolve into part of the personality. Once these defenses become part of a child's coping repertoire, it takes only minor emotional disruptions to evoke the full-blown defensive state, like a classmate making a face at you when you are trying to do your work.

Current research is focusing on how children who live in these chronic states of emotional dysregulation are subjected to prolonged activation of their brain's stress response system. This "toxic stress" response can occur when a child experiences strong, frequent, and/or prolonged adversity—such as physical or emotional abuse, chronic neglect, caregiver substance abuse or mental illness, exposure to violence, and/or the accumulated burdens of family economic hardship—without adequate adult support. "Studies indicate that such stress responses can have an adverse impact on brain architecture. In the extreme, such as in cases of severe, chronic abuse, toxic stress may result in the development of a smaller brain. Less extreme exposure to toxic stress can change the stress system so that it responds at lower thresholds to events that might not be stressful to others, thereby increasing the risk of stress-related physical and mental illness" (Shonkoff et al., 2005, p. 1).

It can be difficult to grasp why a child would still seek proximity to a dangerous or ineffectual caregiver. But in the context of the child's attachment needs it becomes clear that a very young child simply has no choice. In Chapter 1 we quoted Judith Viorst describing a young burn victim who cries out for his mother despite the fact that his mother is the one who has set him on fire. This story depicts the paradoxical bond of disorganized attachment. As the words of Judith Viorst make painfully clear, a young child will hold tenaciously to the caregiver even when that person is harsh and abusive, because to give up such a connection is to fall into intolerable chaos. For the still developing self of a child, traumatic separation from the primary source of emotional refuge is the greatest pain possible.

Disorganized attachments are seen in about 15% of low-risk samples. But as the parents' challenges mount, so does the incidence of disorganization: 34% in families of low socioeconomic status, 43% with mothers who abuse alcohol or drugs, and 77% with abusive or negligent parents, according to a meta-analysis of 80 studies representing 6,282 parent–child dyads of which 1,285 were categorized as disorganized (van IJzendoorn et al., 1999). "In the original COS Spokane study of low SES parents, the percentage of disorganized attachment of children in the pretest was 60%" (Hoffman, Marvin, Cooper, & Powell, 2006).

As mentioned above, disorganization begets other problems later in development: In the University of Minnesota's longitudinal study it was concluded that "chronic vigilance, apprehension, and worry about needs being met take a toll. . . . Being disorganized and disoriented cuts one off from vital experiences originating inside and outside the self" (Sroufe et al., 2005). "For individuals with histories of extremely harsh or particularly chaotic caregiving contexts (disorganized attachment relationships), the process of regulation, the consolidation or integration of self across behavioral states and acquisition of control over states, may be disrupted" (Sroufe, Carlson, Levy, & Egeland, 1999, p. 10) (see Box 4.4).

THE PATH TO SECURE ATTACHMENT

Fortunately for parents and children like Sarah and Colin, Jamar and Dwayne, there are ways to change relationships so that attachment can become secure. The COS intervention has been designed for the therapist to Be-With the caregivers to provide a secure base from which they can make the necessary changes and a safe haven from which they can take comfort and feel protected. But the foundation of successful intervention is something that the parents bring to the process. Parents like Vicki (whom we discuss in Chapter 5) usually have a number of challenges. Besides problematic attachment bonds from their own childhood, they may struggle with low socioeconomic status, fractured adult relationships, and isolation. Yet they have a quality that is essential to success in the COS intervention: positive intentionality to function as a caring parent for their child. It is essential that the therapist believe in and honor the parent's positive intentionality, or the intervention is doomed to failure before it starts.

The next step is to use the Circle to help caregivers see and understand their child's needs. Parents of infants can learn about their babies' need to have their feelings organized by using the COS graphic as a map. To make use of this map, parents must learn to stand back and watch themselves and their children. COS is designed to build those observational skills. The final step is to invite the caregivers into a reflective dialogue about what they are doing and not yet doing to meet their child's needs. By coming to understand their children's needs around the Circle, their own needs, and how they interacted based on those needs, Jamar, Sarah, and Alexis were able to attune to their children, help them manage their emotions, and feel secure that they would Be-With their children—at least often enough and well enough to get the job done. At the end of the COS intervention, all of these dyads' attachments were scored secure in the 12-month Ainsworth Strange Situation.

Using the COS to attune to their child's needs is a courageous endeavor for parents. Most have lived their whole lives with their defenses as a shield that can be both impenetrable and invisible—particularly to them. To look unflinchingly at needs in their child that cause them such great discomfort means putting down the defenses they feel are vital to their survival. Although it may not be dangerous to respond to their child's needs, it can be profoundly frightening.

We have found, virtually without exception, that even highly traumatized parents have a deep positive intentionality and wisdom. This positive intentionality may be distorted, but it can be seen even in what they deny their children: If, in their own childhood, expressing distress led to rejection, ridicule, or abuse, then teaching their child to avoid such expression is actually a loving act.

**BOX 4.4. DEVELOPMENTAL OUTCOMES
FOR DISORGANIZED ATTACHMENT IN EARLY CHILDHOOD**

- Increased problems with aggression in school-age children
- Difficulty calming after stressful events
- Elevated risk of dissociative symptoms in adolescence
- Higher scores on suggestibility
- Difficulties in emotion regulation
- Lower reflective function
- Academic problems
- Lower self-esteem
- Rejection by peers

Note: Based on van IJzendoorn et al. (1999).

That is how it was with Laura, whom we discussed in Chapter 1. Laura and her daughter, Ashley, came to a COS group with an avoidant attachment. Extremely uncomfortable with her daughter's needs for closeness because of the abandonment and rejection she had suffered as a child, Laura had set out to make herself the best teacher a parent had ever been. Learning is what had worked for her growing up, and she could establish a connection with her daughter that protected both of them from attachment-related emotions. Yet as we worked together it became clearer and clearer that Laura's pursuit of didactic interactions with Ashley was like eating cotton candy to ease hunger: never satisfying.

Facing her own longing for connection with Ashley was a great risk for Laura. Even the thought of it set off alarms that were hard for her to ignore. But her powerful intention to have a secure and intimate attachment with her daughter gave Laura the courage needed to be able to see and override the fears that arose in her whenever she or Ashley felt the need for closeness. We call the alarms set off by such fears "shark music."

5

Shark Music

How State of Mind Shapes Caregiving

> We do unto others as we're done to.
> —SELMA FRAIBERG (1980)

Chrissy, 5 months old, is looking at the wall with flat affect. Vicki, her 19-year-old mother, says, "What are you looking at?" with a disapproving tone. Chrissy looks away from the wall but does not make eye contact with her mom as she turns her head to her mother's gaze from left to right. She looks around the room, stares at the ceiling, rapidly kicks her feet, shakes her arms, and has a distant, detached look. Vicki looks upset as she says to Chrissy in an aggressive tone, "What's the trouble? What's wrong? *What is the matter with you?*" Now Chrissy is becoming more agitated, looks more distressed, and emits a soft, mournful cry. Vicki sits up, looks angry, and calls her name in a harsh tone: "Chrissy, Chrissy, little angel, what's wrong?" Then, much louder than before, "Stop it!" Now Chrissy is much more distressed and cries louder while kicking and shaking her arms. Vicki looks very uncomfortable but then laughs as Chrissy's cry intensifies. As the interaction progresses, Vicki continues to demand in an angry tone that Chrissy stop fussing, interspersed with moments of uncomfortable laughter when she does not. Throughout the interaction, Chrissy slowly dysregulates. Finally little Chrissy is crying and flailing her arms and legs, and Vicki is so upset that she mocks Chrissy by barking at her.

When Laura's 3-year-old daughter, Ashley, tries several times to cuddle with her mother during the reunion part of the Strange Situation, Laura gently but persistently steers her back to completing her "work" with an educational toy. While nudging her down to the floor where the toy lies, she looks not at the little girl but at the pieces of the toy that lie unassembled on the carpet.

When 18-month-old Dwayne becomes absorbed in playing with a toy mallet during the Strange Situation reunion, his back to his father, Jamar squirms, seems to force a laugh, and then says, "It's OK." A few minutes later his son starts examining another toy, and suddenly Jamar reaches down to the floor, picks up a dropped pacifier, and asks Dwayne, "Do you want your pacifier?"

These last two scenes were described in the preceding chapters, but they are worth looking at again, along with the interaction between Chrissy and Vicki, to focus on the question "Why would these three parents give their children what seems to be the opposite of what the children were asking for?" Ashley wants comfort; her mother offers her teaching. Dwayne wants to explore; his father tries to draw the child back in to him. Chrissy wants help regulating her emotions; her mother asks Chrissy to help regulate her own. Why would Laura, Jamar, and Vicki not follow their children's lead and meet their children's needs?

To help parents make sense of why they are acting against their children's best interest, we show them a video clip of the Oregon coast with music from Pachelbel's Canon playing in the background. As the camera follows the path down to the beach, it is easy to think that this would be a good place to go for a swim or let the children wade in the water. Then we show the same video clip with music that quotes the cello baseline from the movie *Jaws*. Suddenly the response to this previously tranquil scene is transformed into a terrifying sense of impending doom. We tell parents that the background music that plays in our heads determines which needs on the COS feel safe and which feel dangerous. The moments captured in the parents' clips are examples of children's needs causing each of these parents to hear what one of the parents in our original research study described as "shark music." For obvious reasons, we've chosen to call it shark music in every group since then.

None of these parents lacked the desire to do right by his or her child. In fact all of them had participated in the Strange Situation precisely because they wanted to form a secure attachment with their young child and become the best parents they could be. They just did not know how, largely because the parenting they themselves received had not taught them.

What their own caregivers did teach them—in some way or another—was that certain needs around the Circle were precarious to express: asking for them to be met resulted in driving the caregiver away, physically, emotionally, and/or mentally. The distance that resulted left the child vulnerable, with her survival at risk, or at the very least left the child subject to the isolation of Being-Without. It left the child, now grown into an adult, afraid of being devoured by sharks that no longer exist.

Simply watching a video clip like those just described will not reveal the shape or color of the dangers that Laura, Jamar, or Vicki internalized as children. But we use a tool called the Circle of Security Interview (COSI) to reveal parents' state of mind, particularly their perceptions about caregivers and caregiving, to fill in some of the gaps in our understanding of what is going on between each parent and child. The Ainsworth system of assessing attachment did not look closely at the caregivers. Classifying attachment was about the child, and scoring systems focused on the child's behavior. As family therapists, however, we intuitively wanted to look at the caregiver as well, as part of assessing the whole relationship. Bob Marvin introduced the Classification System for Parental Caregiving Patterns in the Preschool Strange Situation (Britner, Marvin, & Pianta, 2005) into our work together, giving us a systematic way to look at what the parents were doing and ultimately to be able to discern the steps in the intricate attachment dance.

By looking at both child and caregiving behavior during the SSP, we could develop a more clinically useful understanding about how dyads like Laura and Ashley negotiated the needs around the Circle together. And between the intake interview (see Chapter 7) and the COSI (see Chapter 10) we discovered that Laura's parents, preoccupied by drugs and other problems, were often not there for her when she needed a safe haven. Laura found that academic achievement seemed to be her best hope to get what she needed. Determined to do better for her daughter, she had overcome substance abuse problems of her own but was unaware that, in turning herself into mother-as-teacher, she was imposing her insecure strategy on her daughter. She was blind to the fact that she was denying Ashley comfort. Comfort seeking had not worked out well for her as a child, and focusing on learning had been a life saver. All she knew was that she was functioning as a clean and sober parent who was offering Ashley the same chance to achieve that she believed had served her so well in her own childhood times of need.

This is an important point to recognize, which we alluded to at the end of Chapter 4: Parents who appear to be callously ignoring their young child's needs around the Circle are often actually attempting to protect them, consciously or not. Imagine that as a child you were slapped every time you cried. You quickly taught yourself not to cry—to avoid being hit, certainly, but perhaps even more urgently to avoid being bad and angering your caregiver, on whom your life depended. Either way, crying invoked shark-infested waters. Certainly, as a loving parent, you would teach your child to stay out of shark-infested waters even if that came at a high cost to your child.

It is also important to remember that a child will find a way to remain connected to a parent who is not acting in the child's best interests. The idea that the little boy in Judith Viorst's horrific tale would cry for his mother after she has set him on fire defies logic *unless* we give credit where credit is due—to a child's inexorable drive to remain attached to a caregiver. That caregiver, despite conclusive evidence to the contrary, is, after all, the child's best hope of avoiding Being-Without.

PROCEDURAL MEMORY: THE MAN BEHIND THE CURTAIN

What happens when children attempt to get their needs for attachment met with strategies of despair? Their attempts, failures, and relative successes become woven into procedural memory and stitch together the child's internal working models of parents and relationships. The endurance of internal working models and procedural memories and their power to affect the next generation is difficult to overstate. If we didn't appreciate their force, it would be easy to label Jamar as selfishly overprotective of Dwayne. It would seem natural to accuse Vicki of being cruel to the baby who needs comfort from her mother. Yet Jamar's procedural memories of his own upbringing may be telling him that children who stray too far from their mother are punished by withdrawal. Vicki's childhood may have taught her that expressing distress leads to Mom's quick exit. Laura wasn't coldly withholding affection from her little girl but trying to shield her from the danger of exposing a need for comfort by leading her to deny the need itself.

Unfortunately, parents usually have no idea that procedural memories are at work in their parenting. When parents act from a procedural memory, it doesn't feel like they are remembering something. This is why the phenomenon has also been called the "unthought known" (Bollas, 1987). Because the psychological defense mechanisms kick in at a procedural level, the parent does not have a narrative to describe what is happening. For example, if a child expresses a basic need for comfort, and the parent's early experience of needing comfort was rejection, then the parent's response will be influenced by his unconscious procedure for avoiding rejection by denying the need for comfort. In addition, activation of this procedural memory will evoke undefined distress in him. To protect himself from this distressing feeling state and the child from the dangers of seeking comfort the parent immediately shifts into defense. The child soon learns that unless she avoids seeking comfort her parent will become distressed and defensive and thus less available. When parents are guided by their defenses against past pain rather than by an accurate evaluation of the current situation, their children can pay a very great price.

We accumulate implicit memories of all kinds of procedures throughout life, and not just preverbally. Riding a bicycle is an obvious example. It would be impossible to write out the instructions for riding a bike and have someone who has never ridden a bike use them successfully. We could tell a thousand stories about bike-riding episodes without giving a would-be cyclist a clue about how to duplicate the bike-riding procedure. How to ride a bike is learned and then stored as procedural memory, which imbues it with some peculiar characteristics.

One is that it just feels like something we do naturally, without thought, like how close we stand to someone we are talking to, how often and how long we look into a person's eyes, when we do and do not touch a person during an interaction. When and how we show anger, how we calm ourselves when anxious (jiggling our feet, rocking back and forth, stroking our head, playing with our hair, reaching out to a trusted other?), and many other "automatic" behaviors are procedural in nature. This can make behaviors based in procedural memory feel as if they are simply "truth," not something that has been learned. This characteristic serves us well in that there are some procedures we never forget. That's why the comment "It's like riding a bicycle" is so often tossed off when someone expresses doubt about being able to do something not done for a long time, whether it's going back to school (even educational pursuits involve some nonverbal procedures) or returning to dating or sexual activity after being widowed for a decade. The downside, however, is that it can be really difficult to unlearn something stored in procedural memory. (Try going through the steps of your daily bathing ritual in a different order if you need proof.)

Operating on procedural memories does not feel like remembering anything. It just feels like the way things should be—as if this is the natural and only way to do something—"the way God intended it." For this reason, procedural memories about relationships are almost never questioned. The result is that parents—Laura, Jamar, Vicki, and the rest of us—usually embark on parenting without a clue that a puppeteer born of their own childhood is pulling the strings that make them one type of caregiver or another.

State of Mind

When what you see, hear, touch, smell, and taste . . .
When everything you think . . .
When every emotion you have . . .
When everything you have ever perceived, thought, or felt . . .
leads to the same conclusion . . .
IT'S TIME TO QUESTION IT!

Children create the puppeteer from events experienced before they were capable of forming autobiographical memory. But parents have language now and can make the procedural explicit (i.e., the unconscious can be made conscious). This is what the COS strives to do: It makes what is learned about our most important relationships explicit so that we can recognize our defenses and choose whether or not to allow them to hold sway over our caregiving and our other intimate relationships.

SHARK MUSIC: AN ALARM RUNG BY PROCEDURAL MEMORY

When the video clips described at the beginning of this chapter were made, these parents were completely unaware that their child needed something different from what they were offering. They also had no idea what was blinding them to their child's true needs. They did not know that deep-seated memories from their own early childhood were issuing a warning that they were getting dangerously close to unregulated affect—feelings of being all alone, overwhelmed by emotional states that they could not manage on their own and that no one had helped them manage when very young. In fact, they did not even know on a conscious level that they were hearing and responding to this warning.

We found "shark music" a perfect name for these warnings because shark music says to parents "Back away from here, now!" as stridently as the theme from *Jaws* said a great white shark was on its way. All parents, including those whose attachment to their own caregivers was secure and whose attachment to their children is secure, are more comfortable on one part of the Circle (top, bottom, or hands) than the others. But for some parents, one part of the Circle in particular represents the gaping jaws of a great white shark of Hollywood proportions. In the scene depicted above, Laura's eagerness to push Ashley back to the task at hand rather than letting the little girl sit on her lap and receive comfort indicated discomfort with the bottom half of the Circle. For Jamar, shark music started playing when Dwayne began to go out on the top half of the Circle. At only 5 months of age, Chrissy's precise needs are difficult to identify from observing her agitation, but her distress apparently arouses such distress in Vicki that she commands the baby to feel better so that *she* can feel better.

Because shark music plays at a preconscious level, a parent's discomfort cannot always be observed easily in the parent's outward behavior. Without the information gathered through the rest of the intervention, Laura, for instance, would probably just appear to be competent and calm in the interaction described above.

DEFENSES REVEALED

The COS intervention borrows heavily from James Masterson in defining problems as the compulsive use of psychological defenses in relationship with others and with the self even when the current situation is sufficiently safe to render them unnecessary and, in fact, they actually interfere with positive outcomes. All humans need defense mechanisms for protection. The more insecure our early attachments are and the more traumas we have to contend with during development, the more intense and powerful the defense needs to be for us to survive. Trauma of such intensity that it gets blocked, or trauma experienced so early that it predates the developmental capacity for creating autobiographical (or episodic) memory, is processed as implicit rather than verbal information. It becomes part of the amygdala's library of things associated with danger (see Box 5.3), which has long-term effects on the procedural management of fear. Big trauma begets big defenses to protect the self—dissociation, numbing, profound emotional detachment, isolation, and the chronic acting-out of aggression, to name a few.

A basic assumption in the COS is that current relationship needs
(Circle needs) in the self or in others can evoke fear
that is instantly met with self-protection.

Because we are vulnerable beings with procedural memory and herculean self-preservation instincts, we all develop defenses. The goal of the COS intervention is therefore not to remove caregivers' defenses—an unrealistic and unhealthy aim—as much as it is to reveal them so parents can have a choice about when to use their defenses. Without conscious awareness, before participating in a COS group, Laura continued to defend herself against the pain of childhood neglect by denying the importance of closeness and comfort and focusing on achievement. Common sense might suggest that if being denied comfort as a child had caused Laura pain, the obvious way to spare her daughter the same would be to give her comfort when she needs it. That is exactly what Laura would do *if only she understood that her shark music was making her afraid of something that was safe (i.e., comforting her daughter).*

You know it's shark music when your child's need requires a response that is safe but feels dangerous: You suddenly feel uncomfortable—lonely, unsafe, rejected, abandoned, angry, controlled.

This is a key to reestablishing the COS. Caregivers seldom know they are hearing shark music until it is made conscious for them. The COS intervention accomplishes this via two routes:

1. COS is designed to make the procedural memory verbal, beginning with the simple step of giving shark music a name. When the limbic system is activated, using a word to describe the feeling (affect labeling) diminishes the response of the amygdala (a part of the brain that alerts us to danger) and other areas of the limbic system and increases activity in the prefrontal cortex, which regulates negative affect (Lieberman et al., 2007). Over and over we have seen a whole new vista open up for parents once they can put a name—shark music—to the previously ineffable discomfort they have felt when faced with certain needs in their child. The way we talk to parents about this is to say that wisdom is not found in the feeling brain (limbic system) or the thinking brain (prefrontal cortex) but in the dialogue between the two.

2. The COS protocol uses video, which allows parents to see themselves interacting with their child at a distance. The camera is like an electronic observing ego whose observations, in the form of video, can be shared, discussed, and watched as many times as needed. With no pressure to do or be something for the child right then and there, they have the

chance to see the child's needs without quite the same filter of procedural memory. And a light goes on when parents can observe their own behavior from the outside. Many of our clients have watched video clips of themselves and their child and said, "That [the child] would be me, and I'm my mother, doing exactly what she did to me."

The apple doesn't fall far from the tree. Eliminating parents'
self-protective strategies is about as easy as reversing gravity.

Seeing themselves react to their children's needs in ways that are both harmful to their children and unplanned, previously unrecognized, and unintended is a shocking eye opener. Realizing that procedural memory is pulling their strings is a hugely liberating revelation. With practice parents can begin to hear the shark music that was once inaudible. At the very least this capacity slows down the cascade of events that leaves a child's needs unmet. Procedural memories are slowed down enough that parents might just be able to have a moment to reflect and then offer their child or themselves access to a part of the Circle that they had not experienced as safe (see Box 5.1). While not reversing gravity, the Circle opens new doors for parents.

HOW STATE OF MIND SHAPES CAREGIVING

"State of mind" refers to how an individual integrates thoughts and feelings about relationships, as well as to the processes that support or exclude relationship-based information from the individual's thinking.
—CAROL GEORGE AND JUDITH SOLOMON (2008, p. 841)

The shark music video clip is our way of introducing parents and other caregivers to state of mind, an overarching concept utilized throughout attachment research. State of mind regarding attachment is primarily a way of tracking the internal working model that we each carry regarding self and significant others. As we have discussed, an individual's internal working model starts to take shape in infancy, and each person imposes this model on relationships throughout childhood and adolescence and into adulthood. State of mind can be thought of as a lens through which we each look at close relationships. It's a way of seeing the world that allows us to think we know unquestionably the way things are. We cannot think beyond our state of mind until we stand back and see that relationships are larger than our current perception.

BOX 5.1. INTRODUCING SHARK MUSIC GENTLY

As we discuss in detail in Part II, revealing parents' defenses to offer them different choices in caregiving must be done delicately, with the therapist creating a safe haven and a secure base for exploring what have often been painful themes throughout the parent's life. This is why we choose video clips very carefully so that we initially reveal what we consider to be *underutilized strengths*. As we are inviting parents to recognize that they struggle somewhere on the Circle, instead of initially showing them the full struggle that will be shown later (if they appear to have the capacity to accept an intervention), we focus on a few moments in which they show modest signs of having some capability on the part of the Circle they primarily stay away from. This is more hopeful than showing failure. It also offers the support of a holding environment while parents muster the necessary courage to watch themselves being less than they want to be for their child. Even at the distance afforded by watching a video, seeing themselves react to their shark music can bring up shark music for parents during the intervention. To create safety and to avoid triggering parents' self-protection, we also take great care to support parents' exploration rather than overinterpret what we are seeing in the SSP videos. By teaching parents to make accurate behavioral descriptions before making inferences, we try to pique their curiosity: "What were you feeling when you did . . . ?" and "What do you think Johnny was trying to tell when he did . . . ?" The critical difference between seeing and guessing was introduced in Chapter 2 and is discussed as a treatment principle in Chapter 11.

A secure state of mind is marked by autonomy-within-relatedness and relatedness-within-autonomy, as defined in Chapter 3. That is, parents with a secure state of mind value Being-With yet also clearly perceive the line between the other or the relationship and the autonomous self. A secure state of mind with regard to attachment has been shown to lead to positive relationships throughout a child's developmental path, from competence in friendships to high-quality romantic relationships to a well-honed ability to regulate emotions even during difficult interactions with spouses (Miga, Hare, Allen, & Manning, 2010). Exactly how insecure and disorganized attachment states of mind affect later relationships and ultimately an individual's own ability to provide secure caregiving with a child takes a long time to study, but we do know that parents' state of mind predicts the attachment of the child 75% of the time (van IJzendoorn, 1995). As Alan Schore has stated, "In an early history of traumatic attachment the developing infant/toddler is too frequently exposed to a massively misattuning primary caregiver who triggers and does not repair long-lasting intensely dysregulated states. These negative states reflect severe biochemical alterations in the rapidly maturing right brain, and because they occur during the brain growth spurt, the effect of ambient cumulative trauma is enduring. In the infant brain, states become traits (Perry et al., 1995), and so the effects of early relational trauma as well as the defenses against such trauma are embedded into the core structure of the evolving personality." (Schore, 2002, p. 18). Recent studies of the effects of toxic stress show that early trauma can even change the physical architecture of the brain (Polan & Hofer, 2008), and adverse childhood experience can lead to a wide array of medical problems in adulthood (Felitti et al., 1998). Likewise, a large meta-analysis of the validity of the Adult Attachment Interview (AAI) found that among mothers and their biological babies the strongest predictor of secure or insecure infant attachment to date (1995) was the caregiver's state of mind (van IJzendoorn, 1995).

Yet we don't yet fully understand how attachment styles are transmitted. The parent's state of mind should result in caregiving behaviors that in turn result in child attachment strategies. And in fact state of mind does predict child attachment. However, caregiving behavior only modestly predicts attachment (van IJzendoorn, 1995). The caregiver's state of mind seems to find its way into the procedural/implicit state of mind of the child. This is why we can predict a child's attachment strategy at 1 year of age based on the caregiver's state of mind. How state of mind gets translated into child attachment behavior is, however, a matter for ongoing study (see Box 5.2).

Also, apparently, the apple sometimes *does* fall far from the tree— about 25% of the time. How do parents who had disorganized attachments as children avoid continuing the "tradition" of disorganized attachment with their own children? Alan Sroufe has said that "change, as well as continuity, in individual development is coherent and lawful" (Sroufe et al., 2005, p. 19) and that "salient experiences, especially experiences in important relationships, can have a transforming influence on the person" (Sroufe et al., 2005, p. 220). He found that alternative supportive relationships, therapy of 6 months or longer, and a supportive spouse stood out as factors that helped parents not pass on abuse to their child. So when the apple falls far from the tree, there is a relational reason. (See more on "earned security" at the end of this chapter.)

Carol George and Judith Solomon call the root of an ability to overcome an insecure or disorganized attachment "representational flexibility," components of which include coherence, mind-mindedness, and reflective functioning:

Coherence is the underlying sense of order that comes when behavior

---

BOX 5.2. BEING-WITHOUT

Formation of defensive structures and transmission of insecure or disorganized attachment does not always result from overt maltreatment by a caregiver. Sometimes Being-Without becomes a family legacy that has been passed down through many generations. Imagine that every time Ann arrives at day care to pick up her 2-year-old, Carrie, the little girl turns away and starts playing with the nearest toy. Ann feels confused: Part of her is proud that her daughter is so independent and "grown up." But all the other kids are clamoring to be picked up by Mom or Dad or toddling over to them as fast as their little feet can take them. Why does she feel so nervous when she thinks about going over to pick Carrie up?

When interviewed Ann could reveal that Carrie had been a colicky baby and that she quickly came to dread hearing her daughter cry and fuss and did everything she could to distract her with infant toys, but that is not the whole story. If we could reach into Ann's history, we might find that Ann was uncomfortable with Carrie's need to be rocked because her own mother always bristled when Ann needed comfort as a young child. Ann's mother had that defensive reaction because her father had experienced a traumatic response to his own childhood bids for comfort. Ann's grandfather had learned to avoid physical and emotional closeness and so chose a wife who didn't make many demands for closeness. Ann's mother therefore grew up in a family in which both parents were emotionally unavailable, and she came to associate a need for comfort with withdrawal. Therefore, when, as a child, Ann made bids for comfort, those bids were met with anxiety and withdrawal from her mother. Now Ann is trying to understand the origin of the shark music that she is passing on to a fourth generation, her own daughter, Carrie. There is no abuse, and no identifiable trauma, yet the procedural information of Being-Without is passed along like a family curse.

---

and emotions form a unified whole that has meaning rather than seeming to be contradictory, meaningless, or random. For example, a statement that shows a coherent understanding of one's past might be "While I in no way approve of what my father did to me, I'm beginning to understand that he wasn't able to make sense of being a dad. With his history, how could he? It just makes me sad for both of us."

Mind-mindedness is "the proclivity to treat one's infant as an individual with a mind, capable of intentional behavior." This capacity enhances the ability to be aware that others have minds that are separate from your own mind: "I have a mind and you have a mind and they aren't the same. Even so, I can make sense of how you think the way you do and honor how I can think the way I do" (Meins et al., 2002, p. 1716).

Reflective functioning or mentalization is the capacity "to envision mental states in self and other" (Fonagy et al., 2002, p. 23)—to stand back and recognize your own particular point of view or state of mind as well as that of another and how your feelings affect your behaviors, which, in turn, affect the feelings and behaviors of others. It includes mind-mindedness with the additional skill set of keeping each person's state of mind fully in perspective.

The COS intervention can be viewed as a way to draw on parents' innate capacity for representational flexibility to widen the gap between problematic childhood attachment and adult caregiving.

Researchers have been looking at how childhood attachment translates into adult caregiving styles from many different angles and have found a variety of biological and environmental contributing factors. The path from early childhood through adolescence and into adulthood is lined with developmental tasks that are achieved or not depending on the events along an individual's journey and how those are integrated into the person's caregiving representations (internal working models). At every step in this journey any individual has the chance to turn insecure or disorganized attachment into security. Perhaps the most compelling opportunity comes with the birth of a baby. The innate desire to provide caregiving that promotes secure attachment in one's own child creates a golden opportunity to develop a secure state of mind with regard to attachment. We have taken advantage of this learning capacity to capitalize on such opportunities through the COS intervention.

At the core of our work is the recognition that it is the caregiver's state of mind that is being communicated to the child, regardless of the behaviors that the parent uses to achieve the goals of caregiving. Various parenting experts will advocate the benefits of different discipline techniques, diets, breast-feeding versus bottle feeding, co-sleeping versus separate sleeping, time-ins versus time-outs, free play versus the use of flash cards or classical music to enhance IQ, and so on. These issues are important, and parents need to make their best decision about all of them, but the overarching concern is caregivers' state of mind regarding the top, bottom, and hands of the Circle. A disorganized or insecure state of mind can turn any parenting approach into unintended consequences with significant problems for the child, and a secure state of mind covers a multitude of sins. Our protocol is designed to give caregivers access to recognizing and reflecting on their particular state of mind. ("Where do I struggle on the Circle: top, bottom, or hands?")

State of mind is a complicated subject, and actual caregiving behaviors are the product of complicated interactions among different behavioral systems (George & Solomon, 2008). Shark music is our way of introducing parents to state of mind (specifically insecure and disorganized states of mind) without ever calling it that. It's a street-level approach to the real issues that we all face in intimate relationships (parents, children, spouses, associates). Rather than lecture on state of mind, we simply offer parents a cross-modal experience that can give them a different perspective on the subtle role that self-protection plays in relationships.

The Circle offers parents a quick, no-nonsense, nonpejorative way of tracking where they are currently struggling. Once parents know what they want to do—such as let the child explore or pick up the child—they can get interested in what is stopping them from doing it. One parent we worked with was saying to herself "Pick up my child, pick up my child" as she prepared to enter the room where her toddler was, and then went right into the room, stepped over her, and sat down. Suddenly the power of shark music was very clear to her.

SHARK MUSIC AROUND THE CIRCLE OF SECURITY

When we are trying to help parents hear their shark music, we ask them questions about observable behavior that indicates certain states of mind (George et al., 1984):

- Preoccupied: "Have you ever known people who can't rely on their own capacity in a time of difficulty and can only turn to and rely on others?"
- Dismissing: "Have you ever known people who can rely only on themselves in a time of difficulty and can't turn to others for support?"
- Unresolved/disorganized: "Do you know people who can't be bigger, stronger, wiser, and kind but instead move to being mean or weak or gone?"

These questions normalize the commonality of these themes while giving people the opportunity to turn themselves in. As noted earlier, parents generally struggle mostly on either the top or bottom half of the Circle or with functioning as the hands on the Circle. Each state of mind sends a particular message to the young child, which then generally (but not always) becomes translated into a certain type of attachment seen in the child. The fact that the youngest of children can hear the shark music that their care-givers are deaf to is a phenomenon that only underscores the strength of the yearning to Be-With that accompanies all children into this world.

Infants and young children are remarkably sensitive to their need to be in relationship and ingenious in establishing whatever strategy is neces-sary to stay in relationship. The youngest infants are capable of finding the means to stay connected only by making very primitive mental connections. As noted in Chapter 4, sometimes every parent is the "good parent"—the parent who soothes a frightened baby and feeds a hungry one—and some-times every parent is the bad parent, the one who is too tired to pick up a crying baby or simply misinterprets the baby's crying and doesn't offer what the baby needs. The baby is incapable of integrating these two par-ents into one and so uses "splitting" to pursue the good and avoid the bad (see Box 5.3). As the baby gets older and her cognitive capacities increase, she begins to understand cause and effect. But we can see even 4-month-olds in split-screen videos act defensively, miscuing before they understand cause and effect because their defenses are procedural. This is how miscues, described in Chapter 4, come into being: A child who wants closeness and comfort but has sensed repeatedly that Dad gets anxious when that need is expressed acts like he wants to explore instead of cuddle. Dad is comfort-able with that behavior, and Dad's comfort leads to Dad's staying nearby.

The child's behavior is highly adaptive; it keeps the parent as close as possible, even if the parent isn't all that effective in meeting the child's needs. As we said earlier, the parent is still the best bet the child has. But because it works, that state of mind becomes a trait (Perry et al., 1995) noted), the faulty attachment is preserved, and the child takes the corre-sponding state of mind out into the world, where it informs his future rela-tionships and his own caregiving behavior once he has a family.

With state of mind being the psychological version of a dominant trait, it is clear that the time to modify a problematic attachment is when a child is very young. Otherwise the misleading messages of shark music can have far-reaching effects. Picture Dwayne at age 19, dropping out of college after the first quarter of his freshman year. Although the university was only 30 miles away from his home, he found that without constantly checking in with his father and a few hometown friends he'd had since elementary school, he didn't know what to do with himself, from which clubs to join to what to wear and which dining hall to go to for meals. Imagine Ashley at age 25. She graduated summa cum laude from an Ivy League college, where she started dating Steve in her sophomore year. The two moved in together

---

BOX 5.3. THE HIJACKED AMYGDALA

Adults who are ambushed by shark music behave in ways that turn them into the "bad parent" when a second ago they were the "good parent." Daniel Goleman (1995) has called this being hijacked by the amygdala. The amygdala's job is to scan the environment for anything associated with danger, and when the association is made, it puts the body on high alert. Adverse childhood experiences are stored in the amygdala library of things associated with danger. Some parents have a vast collection in their amygdala library and others a relatively small collection. These amygdala hijackings, shark music, can contribute to splitting. Once parents can recognize that a rupture involves the parent's stepping off the Circle (from either the top or bottom or with both hands), they can learn to repair ruptures when they occur. As they begin to recognize these shifts from good to bad and acknowledge them to their child—"Mommy just got mad, because . . ."—the child is offered a parent living within a state of coherence. This acknowledgment helps young children begin to integrate the "good" and "bad" parents, building a sense of coherence so that they *can* grow up with an understanding that everyone is capable of both types of behavior and no one is good or bad all the time. This perspective lays the groundwork for realistic expectations about relationships and the ability to negotiate within relationships in the future.

---

when they got their first jobs after college, and everything was fine until Ashley got laid off 6 months later. Devastated, she retreated into a 20-hour-a-day Internet search for a job where "they'll really appreciate what I have to offer." After weeks of reassurances that the layoff had nothing to do with her qualifications or job performance, and daily failed attempts to get Ashley to go out and have some fun with friends, Steve finally moved out. The woman he thought he was likely to marry had sent him the message loud and clear that she just didn't need him.

Happily for all three of the children depicted at the beginning of this chapter, their attachment with their parents was scored secure following the 20-week COS intervention. Without that shift, Dwayne might have ended up without the degree or college experience he really wanted, Ashley could have ended up a bitter, lonely woman, and Chrissy might have ended up in prison, right where Vicki started when she was pregnant with her. These outcomes are not meant to imply that a child's destiny is sealed by the earliest attachment bonds. But an insecure or disorganized attachment orchestrated by a caregiver's shark music has great potential to make navigating relationships, and therefore the rest of life, challenging.

It's difficult to form the relationships that will serve us well when shark music is telling us that something that is safe is dangerous. Being able to differentiate between safe and dangerous is an essential skill in raising children, and it's essential in friendships and romance too. Each of the three types of state-of-mind struggles around the Circle misdirects parents about what is safe and what is dangerous.

Bottom-Oriented Struggles

Bottom-oriented struggles tend to involve problems with vulnerability related to emotional comfort. In a parent this is described as a "dismissing" state of mind (George et al., 1984). The caregiver encourages independence at the cost of either close physical and/or emotional contact and is considered "dismissing" of attachment. Such parents tend to be uncomfortable with direct communication about and expression of need (Main, 1981; Ainsworth, Blehar, Waters, & Wall, 1978). As difficult as it is to imagine, these parents find a crying child dangerous in the sense of shark music: when their child cries, they see themselves in the child and fear the same emotional free fall they experienced themselves when expressing similar needs as children and/or the face of the punitive or withdrawing parent. Now they are often efficient at the tasks of practical care*taking*, while being dismissing of emotional care*giving* opportunities (Britner et al., 2005).

Over time, the child of such a parent finds a way to deny direct expression of want or need for the caregiver, and the attachment between the child and parent is likely to be defined as avoidant. Such a child expects his attachment needs to be dismissed, so it is not surprising that in the Strange Situation he shows little distress when the parent is absent and tends to act like he does not need the parent upon reunion. To avoid the pain of rejection associated with reaching out to the caregiver, this child begins to build a pattern of creating distance and prioritizing exploration and/or achievement. Not coincidentally, it is exploration and achievement that a parent of an avoidant child tends to emphasize as important.

The dismissing caregiver tends to focus on the child's performance or self-sufficiency, choosing either as a defensive priority over the intimacy needs on the bottom half of the Circle that all children require.

Susan, for example, appears to be more interested in what 3-year-old William does than in who he is. When he cries in frustration because he can't make a toy work the way he wants it to, she says things like "You're smarter than that" and "Just keep trying—you'll get it"—and stays where she is seated across the room. To another adult on hand, she might add, "I was just like that when I was his age, and my mother made me keep at it till I got it right. It's how I've gotten where I am today," without recognizing the irony in that latter sentence.

Interestingly, it's not that dismissing parents don't want their children around. In many cases their behavior says, rather, "Stay close, but don't need me." A parent who appears to be delivering this message to a distressed child may seem to have a shadow. The child is right there, perhaps self-regulating quietly with toys, but does not seem to need the parent to participate or provide comfort. The child senses that the parent's proximity is contingent upon approval but also that bids for coregulation of distress will go unanswered and so may seem to have a "Whatever" or "Why try?" attitude.

Some dismissing parents try to push their child to perform tasks the child simply is not developmentally able to do yet.

Darryl talks a lot about how "independent" 2-year-old Sadie is, proudly pointing out that she didn't "need me at all" during separations in the SSP. From our observations, Sadie played with the toys robotically, rhythmically banging a hammer into a peg on a pegboard, even after the peg was all the way in the hole. She showed no recognition of having achieved the task and no satisfaction in it. When her father returned to the room, she looked up at him briefly and then looked away quickly, as if afraid to betray her sadness at his absence, and Darryl just said "Hi" and breezed on by to the couch as if Sadie were an adult.

Top-Oriented Struggles

Top-oriented struggles tend to involve problems with physical or emotional separation. In a parent this is described as a "preoccupied" state of mind; the parent is preoccupied with the attachment relationship. If in our childhood we experienced a sense of safety and support for separation and exploration, then our children's innate desire to explore will tend to evoke nonthreatening music. If, on the other hand, our history of exploration and individuation is associated with aggression, abandonment, or threats of aggression or abandonment, then our children's need for separation—being on the top half of the Circle—may evoke shark music.

Children raised within this context of caregiving face the frustration of both wanting to explore and needing to keep their attachment system activated, which is why their attachment to their caregiver is often scored ambivalent/resistant. They alternate between clinging and attempting to separate (Cassidy & Berlin, 1994). Remember Dwayne? He didn't reach up to his father when he was on his lap during the Strange Situation reunion, but he returned to his father when Jamar said "It's OK" while he was playing because he inferred that Dad was really saying "It's not OK, and you need your father."

Not coincidentally, the primary caregivers of children like Dwayne present something of a moving target when it comes to attachment behavior. Rather than communicate directly, these parents send mixed signals, offering a distorted closeness that is either intrusive or tending toward enmeshment or fusion. Jamar illustrated this when he shoved a puppet into Dwayne's face and made a barking noise when he had just been going through the motions of trying to comfort him. This strategy attempts to keep the child's attachment activated. For Jamar, shark music says that a child's individuation in one form or another is dangerous (even though intellectually he would agree that the goal of childhood is to grow up).

The caregiving behavior system outlined by Britner and colleagues (2005) clarified that preoccupied caregivers (with ambivalently attached children) emphasize the "intimacy and specialness" of the relationship and become overly involved with the child, often to the point of infantilizing the child to keep the child available to the parent (Cassidy & Berlin, 1994). In some dyads, this "intimacy and specialness" seems relatively difficult to see because it is the enmeshed conflict that is most apparent. One father we worked with when looking at a video clip of himself walking hunched over his toddling child exclaimed, "I look like a vulture, I am vulturing my child." Although the child was in no danger, he felt she was so special that she could not survive without him attending to her every step.

Louis constantly describes little Samantha as "precious" and demonstrates with his protective actions how firmly he holds to this description. He barely lets Samantha leave his side, driven by the same shark music that made Jamar ask Dwayne if he wanted his pacifier when he was happily playing with his back to his father. This "too precious child" view is sometimes known as the "Shirley Temple syndrome."

When Louis has to leave the room for the first SSP separation, he backs out of the room uttering reassurance after reassurance: "I'll be right back, baby . . . Don't worry; Daddy won't leave you for long . . . You'll be fine, sweetie." Naturally Samantha was very upset about the initial separation, breaking into a wail the minute her father started talking about leaving. However, upon his return the little girl gave mixed signals concerning reconnection—as Dwayne did with Jamar. She cried, demanded attention, and when Louis went over to her and focused exclusively on her, she got angry and threw a tantrum. For these parents, their usefulness depends on the child's not being able to handle many developmental tasks without the parents' help. On some level such children know that Mom or Dad is actually standing in the way of their growing up, which certainly makes it understandable that they sometimes act frustrated and angry around their parents.

Sometimes parents want their child to cling to them, but they are uncomfortable with the child's distress. They can be alternately available (usually in the direction of intrusiveness) and ignoring of or embarrassed about the child's needs and requests. Hence, the ambivalence on the part of the children is an accurate reflection of the context in which they find themselves. In Louis's case, Samantha's crying and demands upon reunion seemed to make him squirm, as he chuckled sheepishly and said with a slightly rough tickle of his daughter, "Hey, baby, it wasn't so terrible, was it?" But then, when Samantha threw herself to the floor and started kicking and screaming, Louis said, "I'll bet you really missed me while I was gone" with a slight tone of satisfaction. He seemed uncomfortable with Samantha's dependence but then appeared to try to prolong it. Parents within this category have a hard time being in charge and establishing the hierarchy necessary for the child to feel secure within a context of known rules and limitations. So once again, the child adapts in whatever way possible, molding to the expectations of the caregiver: "If clinging, resistance, drama, and worry are what you need for me to stay connected, then that is what you are going to get."

Melody is preoccupied with Tiffany's needs throughout the day. In the little girl's first preschool, where the parents were invited to stay with the child during class for as long as they needed to make the child comfortable there, Melody was the only parent still in the room by Thanksgiving. Tiffany does cry when her mother proposes leaving her, but Tiffany doesn't seem sure she should be upset, looking up at her mother with a questioning look on her face as the tears start to flow. Tiffany looks remarkably like her mother, and Melody tends to dress her in the same colors she herself favors. She beams when strangers remark with amazement that the two look "exactly alike!" To Melody, Tiffany is exquisitely sensitive and fragile and needs her mother by her side to ensure that her unique little girl has all her needs met. When the clown that Melody hired for her daughter's fourth birthday party dared to ask for payment in front of Tiffany before leaving, Melody refused and insisted she would mail a check because Tiffany started to pout.

Not all parents in ambivalent dyads are preoccupied with their "perfect" child, but the ones that are tend to feel always on the edge of being applauded or criticized. If you were watching Melody, you might begin to recognize that she is acting as though a hidden television camera were monitoring her every deed as a parent. It may seem that she feels compelled to put on a presentation for an ever-present audience that is either pleased or displeased with her functioning as a parent. Such parents are often rather overbright, with an implied "Am I not a remarkable parent?" sense about themselves.

Both Louis and Melody might be viewed by other parents as "overprotective." Louis in particular might defend his keeping his daughter so close with a statement like "It's a dangerous world." He doesn't really mean there are criminals and hazards everywhere, though. This explanation for keeping a child close is a ruse to avoid revealing how strong the caregiver's shark music really is. What feels really dangerous to Louis is what separating from Samantha will do to *him*.

Hands-Oriented Struggles

Hands-oriented struggles tend toward problems with taking charge at a basic organizational level (the executive role in the relationship). When the parents are called upon by the child or by circumstance to organize the child's experience, these parents become dysregulated by the self-activation required and defensively manage by acting "mean, weak, or gone" rather than bigger, stronger, wiser, and kind. This often implies a disorganized or disturbed state of mind. These parents are often profoundly distressed—depressed, neglectful, and/or abusive. Parents in this category often are found to have had an unresolved loss of a primary caregiver in their history and/or an experience of unresolved trauma. The amygdala is intended to alert us to anything that is a sign of danger. Parents with a history of abuse have an amygdala library—things that signal danger—that is huge and therefore probably exaggerated. One client of ours became severely dysregulated—even dissociated—just by the sound of people clinking glasses as in a toast, because his parents repeatedly got drunk and then violent when he was a child. For most of these parents the relationship itself with their own primary caregiver likely was so frightening or left them so unprotected and unsupported that simply being called on to give care to a child of their own may set off alarms worthy of the apocalypse. The lack of resolution to a sense of internalized relational chaos tends to leave something of a black hole where caregiving responses might be expected to exist. How else can one react to the feeling of falling into that black hole?

The result for the child is an experience of disorientation and chaos when attachment-related needs are shared with such a caregiver. In some significant way children experience these caregivers as either frightening or frightened. Because the caregiver is experienced as unpredictable, the child is continually unsure about the options for attachment. When the potential source of comfort is as likely to also be a source of danger and disorientation, a child is unable to formulate a consistent strategy for relationship. This leads to the kind of confused, incoherent behavior upon reunion in the Strange Situation that we described in Chapter 4.

One of the most interesting—and potentially heartbreaking—aspects of disorganized attachment is that free fall leaves one with no sense of what is safe and what is dangerous. Instead of finding certain safe situations dangerous, as with dismissing and preoccupied parents, disorganized/disturbed parents often find dangerous situations safe. It's as if the absence of the hands on the Circle leaves it to spin out of control, like a plate being balanced on a stick instead of a planet on a stable axis. The top of the Circle becomes confused with the bottom, and neither parent nor child knows which way is up.

Not surprisingly, then, children raised in this context may take excessive risks, have difficulty knowing whom to trust, and seem self-destructive or lacking in common sense. As they grow up, they form unholy alliances, perhaps because, as Freud noted, they keep seeing what they expect to see in people once they have come to understand relationships as chaotic, untrustworthy, and even frightening. Because they spent their early childhood running to and from their caregiver, whom they both needed and feared, they may exhibit the same confusion in their choices of adult relationships.

The disorganized parent may not mean to frighten the child (though some do), but because she has a black hole where caregiving behaviors should be, she does not know how *not* to frighten the child. Leaving a young child unsupervised during episodes of major mental illness, getting drunk and passing out, or completely ignoring a child's needs in favor of a partner's may all seem like normal or at least unavoidable behaviors. Even if the parent does not find these behaviors acceptable, she may not be able to control her actions enough to let her child's needs govern her behavior. The mere fact of the child's presence may start shark music playing—we have heard parents say to a toddler or even an infant who is just gazing at the parent "Stop glaring at me"—and as a result the parent becomes either mean or gone.

Role reversal, in which the parent abdicates his function as caregiver and takes on a childlike role and in response the child fills the void by taking on a parent role, was discussed in Chapter 4 and is associated with disorganized attachments. Disorganized parents who are acting weak or childlike may be hearing shark music whenever they are in a position in which they must take charge.

> Danielle grew up continually on the lookout for her father's explosive rage. Most of it was focused on her mother, but several times a week she would become his designated target. Now a young mother with a 2-year-old child, she finds herself unable to take a stand. When Missy refuses to cooperate, Danielle begins by asking her daughter to be "a grown-up." As her daughter's upset escalates, Danielle begins to bribe her with what she hopes will be compelling options. "If you pick up the toys, you can have a treat on the way home." Finally, as Missy spins into a tantrum, Danielle pleads: "Honey, you can't be this way. Mommy needs you to be nice to her. Mommy wants you to be nice."

When disorganization is manifested as weak hands on the Circle, even a very young child may find himself in the position of having to take care of a parent instead of being cared for. As noted in Chapter 4, by their third birthday, these children become controlling in either a punitive or a caregiving way.

Different Ways to Cut the Pie

When we look at caregivers and children through the lens of attachment, we sometimes feel as if we're looking through a prism. To state the obvious, relationships are complicated. Parents bring to their caregiving their entire history of receiving care as children. Even the toddlers we see have already developed procedural memory and internal working models of caregivers. This "backstory" enters into all the behaviors we see around the Circle, and that makes it difficult to organize a discussion of attachment around a single system of categorization. To complicate matters, we cannot simply look at parents on one hand and then at children on the other, but we always have to try to understand the "and" that holds them together. So we've looked at the four basic attachment styles—secure, insecure avoidant, insecure ambivalent, and disorganized—and how children who qualify for each attachment category tend to behave (Chapter 4). In this chapter we have looked at the state of mind that informs parents' caregiving behaviors when needs come up on the top of the Circle, at the bottom of the Circle, and with the hands on the Circle. In Part II we discuss child and parent behaviors in much more detail, and how we assess them so as to plan the best possible approach to applying the COS intervention. In Chapters 7 and 8 we show how we observe and evaluate attachment based on the interactions seen in our assessment procedure, which is a modified SSP that we film and then review. In Chapters 9 and 10 we talk about "core sensitivities" that parents develop depending on their attachment history with their own parents and show how our COSI reveals which sensitivities are likely behind the caregiving behaviors of the parents that we saw in our videos. Each of these perspectives—each way to slice up the pie, or Circle—fills in the picture of the attachment in each relationship and how we can help each dyad become securely attached.

UPDATING STATE OF MIND: EARNED SECURITY

History builds up inertia.
    —DANIEL STERN (1985, p. 113)

State of mind is a somewhat paradoxical concept. On one hand it seems to be quite stable over time, even stubborn, for many of the reasons discussed in this chapter. Sometimes that's simply because a child is cared for by the same parent or other adult over at least 18 years of life. The caregiver continues to have the same limitations and to behave toward the child in the same ways. Meanwhile, because the brain is always attempting to integrate various inputs to achieve homeostasis of internal working models, it seems to favor new information that confirms the old state of mind. Yet state of mind can also be revised. In fact Bowlby defined health as the ability to update old internal working models with more current ones. As noted earlier in this chapter, security can be developed (or "earned") long past childhood, not just for those with insecure attachments but also for those with disorganized attachments. Shark music volume can certainly be turned down once reflection is introduced into the procedural chain of reaction. The key for clinicians and researchers attempting to help parents and children improve their attachment bond and thereby improve the quality of relationships and life for both is to intervene in a way that gives caregivers a choice about when to use defenses without dishonoring their historical need for the armor they wear.

6

Completing the Circle

Loud music is usually considered a threat to our hearing.
Shark music can damage our vision.

Whenever parents hear shark music, their awareness of the nature and meaning of a young child's emotional and relationship needs is obscured. Shark music makes it difficult for parents to perceive the intricate dance between their own perceptions, thoughts, emotions, and behaviors and those of their child. With time and repetition, shark music blocks conscious awareness of the very emotions aroused by their child's needs and focuses caregivers' attention instead on diversionary tactics and escape routes to protect themselves from sharks that no longer exist. As a result the interactions between a caregiver and young child can begin to look disjointed, stilted, labored, or disconnected—as if neither parent nor child is responding to the actual person in front of him or her.

While all the parents we have worked with (secure, insecure, and disorganized) identify with having shark music, it has been our experience that the greater the degree of insecurity, the more prevalent the experience of shark music. In one study, adults who had an insecure state of mind on the AAI showed heightened amygdala activation in response to the sound of a crying baby compared to adults with a secure state of mind. The insecure adults also tended to experience more irritation when they heard the crying. "Amygdala hyperactivity might be one of the mechanisms underlying the experience of negative emotions during exposure to infant crying in insecure individuals and might explain why insecure parents respond inconsistently to infant signals or reject their infants' attachment behavior"

(Riem, Bakermans-Kranenburg, van IJzendoorn, Out, & Rombouts, 2012, p. 533).

The ultimate goal of the COS intervention is to give parents the opportunity to make choices in their caregiving that will create a secure attachment between them and their child. For parents who are already struggling in their relationship with their child, new choices become possible only with a new perspective on the caregiving landscape. The COS intervention is intended to provide that perspective, shifting away from "mindblindness" and illuminating so much about parent–child attachments that is hidden in plain sight. By managing their shark music, parents can begin to see that the "and" between their child and themselves is all important to the child (and, arguably, to the parent; see Box 6.1). In addition, parents become aware that even very young children are acutely sensitive to a parent's relational discomfort because it might presage parental unavailability. Children will go to heroic lengths to prevent that type of separation. Parents also learn that their state of mind regarding relationships has deep roots in childhood and that this state of mind guides their caregiving of their own child. As long as this influence is unrecognized and unarticulated, it is not under the caregiver's control.

Whenever parents hear shark music and utilize defenses intended to protect themselves and their child, a chain of events is taking place just outside of conscious awareness. Many parents carry within themselves an amygdala library stocked with shelf upon shelf of memories associated with genuine needs on the Circle that trigger feelings of apprehension, distress, and fear. As described earlier, one of the main functions of the amygdala is that it constantly scans for signs of danger to protect us from harm, and this part of the brain performs its job brilliantly. Unfortunately those associations are akin to reference works packed with outdated information. Maybe reaching out for comfort or encouragement had a painful outcome for the parent during childhood, but the amygdala has overgeneralized and now sees the same threat in the needs expressed by her child. So, when the amygdala sets off shark music—even when the reading it has gotten is a "false positive"—this parent now experiences the same emotional and physiological response experienced as a child. In this way the learned defensive response the adult utilized to manage those emotions since childhood comes to the rescue. The adult may feel less anxious. The child, however, likely does not, despite all miscuing appearances to the contrary. Negative consequences then accrue to the child, whose needs go unmet and who is starting to build an impressive amygdala library of his own. The adult is learning nothing new about regulating affect or recognizing a false

---

BOX 6.1. BENEFITS OF COS FOR PARENTS

1. Less conflict and perceived struggle with their child.
2. Greater sense of empowerment or efficacy in meeting their child's needs ("I really can have a positive impact on how my child feels and acts").
3. Greater sense of coherence when reflecting about the relationship ("When it comes to raising my child, things really do make sense").
4. Increased experience of comfort, ease, and positive feeling in parenting.
5. Less negative attributions regarding their child's motivations.
6. Increased sense of connection with their child.
7. Greater sense of how close relationships function (with significant others, parents, siblings, coworkers, etc.).

---

positive. As to the relationship, the attachment suffers, intimacy is elusive, and there's not much joy to benefit either child or parent.

It takes a lot more time to read the description of that sequence of events than it takes for the events to actually unfold. In fact the whole process happens so fast that it hardly seems like a sequence, and this is one of the main reasons an adult can seem so inextricably in the thrall of shark music. Before he realizes what he is doing or why, a father can find himself turning away from his crying toddler or a mother can suddenly be interrupting a game her son is clearly relishing to pull him back to her side. The COS intervention is designed to illuminate this rapid-fire sequence of events. Awareness of what is happening opens up a tiny window during which the caregiver has a chance to opt for the road not usually taken.

How the intervention accomplishes that, and does so in a way that gives parents new options in caregiving and better attachments with their children, will be discussed later in this chapter and in full detail in Part II. But first it is important to know why parents seem so willing and able to make changes that initially may seem radical, threatening, and extremely effortful. The odds have been stacked so high against many of the parents and other primary caregivers we have worked with that the transformations we have seen seem almost miraculous.

For example, Emily, a young mother of two, is now a successful nurse technician in a nearby community. But 7 years ago she was a teenager pregnant with her first child and living in the back of her brother's car. Having come from a home where her father had been both sexually and emotionally abusive and her mother had been drug involved throughout Emily's childhood, Emily had chosen to live on the streets as a way to escape the combination of "too much" and "not enough" that had defined her early years.

"Getting pregnant," she would later say, "is probably why I'm still alive. If it weren't for Latisha, I likely would have overdosed and been dead by now. But having that little girl made all the difference for me." In part, what Emily is trying to say is that finding herself pregnant was the wake-up call that offered her another path in life. In a way that is so common for many of the parents we work with, suddenly staring the responsibilities of parenthood directly in the eye wakes up a commitment to "do something for my baby that wasn't done for me."

In Emily's case, she found her way to a local shelter where COS was being utilized. Over a period of several years Emily took full advantage of how COS was being offered: through an initial group using video review, then through a long-term "open" COS group where parents attend weekly sessions to discuss the issues that arise in the raising of their children—all within the context of the COS paradigm. The combination of what Bowlby called a parent's "preprogramming" (Bowlby, 1988, p. 3) to be a good parent and a coherent model for making sense of our most common needs offered Emily the roadmap she needed to make sense of a highly disorganized childhood. "I liked what I learned here. I liked that things no longer seemed crazy in the way they always had. I liked that I could love my baby and know what she needed. I liked that I could feel sad for how those needs weren't ever recognized by my parents. I have two beautiful children, and I know what I'm doing. I like that."

On top of those socioeconomic and psychosocial obstacles is the fact that mental representations of relationships—state of mind—have an enormous influence on the parent's caregiving. The Adult Attachment Interview (George, Kaplan & Main, 1984) has been shown to predict attachment between the adult interviewed and the adult's child with 75 percent accuracy (Fonagy, Steele, & Steele, 1991; van IJzendoorn et al., 1999). This implies a chain forged of the strongest steel. To break it, and make new choices possible, parents need access to the "unthought known" (procedural memory) that directly influences their interactions with their children.

POSITIVE INTENTIONALITY

[Selma Fraiberg] once characterized the psychotherapy of a mother with her infant as a little bit "like having God on your side."
—ROBERT EMDE (1987, p. xix)

Mustering the courage to look a shark in the face requires a powerful motivator. Implied in Fraiberg's statement is the fact that all parents have it, in the form of a built-in desire to do the best they can for their baby. As powerful as the child's innate care-seeking system is, a parent's innate care-giving system is every bit as formidable: within our hardwiring to seek a secure attachment is the corresponding preprogramming to provide secure caregiving. The reciprocal pull of care seeking and caregiving has been acknowledged throughout history, in literature as well as science. We each have within us, as Robert Frost said, the "irresistible desire to be irresistibly desired." The love of a newborn baby for his or her mother is the first such irresistible desire a human being experiences, and when babies grow up, the birth of their own child sparks the irresistible desire to desire irresistibly.

Yet the unthought known can get in the way. A mother who has just given birth is handed her minutes-old infant, takes one look at his screwed-up face, and says, "Oh, you're just like your no-good father"—mental representation at its most flagrant. Overriding the mother's instinct to look at her baby, see someone beautiful, and yield to her baby's irresistible desire is the imprint of a disorganized attachment from childhood, which has been imposed on her relationship with the baby's father and is now instantly being passed on to her new child. This mother might have been able to feel the irresistible desire to love and be loved by her baby if it were not for the defenses that have served as her relationship armature for decades. These defenses are very powerful: "Flexibility and balance are undermined when defensive processes distort and exclude information and feelings to the extent that the parent is not able to detect and integrate the signals associated with caregiving, attachment, and other behavioral systems. This results in exclusion, confusion, or breakdown" (George & Solomon, 2008, p. 841).

In other words, shark music can be so loud that we can't see straight.

One of the greatest gifts of human nature, however, is the fact that even adults who have had the most traumatic childhood relationships do not seem to lose the instinct to protect their own child (Fraiberg, 1980). The mother just described could very well harbor a deep desire to protect her new baby. What she may lack thanks to her problematic background is the ability to apply the four-million-year-old wisdom that would guide her in providing secure caregiving. The COS was created to show parents the effects that their defensive caregiving is having on their child. This revelation taps the deep well of protectiveness that parents possess and provides motivation for change. We use that motivation to gently reveal to parents how they might override their costly defenses when their shark music inevitably sounds its dire warnings.

We all have the instinct to provide care for our children by comforting, monitoring, and protecting them and/or organizing their feelings when necessary. We can all unearth that instinct even if it means digging through layers of defenses laid down in childhood. This is the core power that the COS taps. Even when parents have intellectual, behavioral, or other problems and may not get much out of insight-oriented therapies or didactic parent education, they can access their built-in desire to protect and care for their child (George & Solomon, 2008, p. 850). This is one salient area in which COS diverges from behavioral approaches. It is not whether a mother or child behaves "correctly" that is the underlying force of change. It is tapping into a mother's strong instinct to protect, care for, and respond to her child—and the child's instinct to seek that protection and care—that has the potential to transform an insecure or disorganized attachment into a secure one.

A baby can be fed without love, but lovelessness as impersonal management cannot succeed in producing a new autonomous human child.
                                        —DONALD W. WINNICOTT (1971, p. 127)

REFLECTIVE FUNCTIONING AND THE FLEXIBILITY OF STATE OF MIND

In the old working model, especially when emotions arouse the shrill warning of shark music, a parent may identify with and act out scripts from her childhood experience rather than responding to what is real in this moment with this child. Shark music can blind the parent to the reality that her child is a separate being acting on thoughts and feelings of his own. Instead it's as if the parent is suddenly watching a movie based on her own childhood, driving her to act out or identify with the child role, her own parent's role, or the wished-for fantasy that isn't grounded in what her child needs (Lieberman, Padrón, Van Horn, & Harris, 2005). This static view limits the parent's choices of how to respond to the child—it even limits the parent's perception of what need the child is trying to convey—because, after all, the movie never changes.

How do parents see what is really happening with the child right in front of them? If it is shark music that distorts or limits their vision, as we have been suggesting, then the easy answer might seem to be to turn that music off altogether. Yet that is not possible. However, although painful memories are painful, they are not events that are currently in progress.

What we can do is help parents recognize what triggers shark music and invite them into reflective dialogue. Over time they may be able to turn down the volume so that shark music hums along in the background without forcing a behavioral reaction. What we offer parents is the chance to organize with language what has been implicit and procedural, thus offering a new perspective on the shark music trigger for what it is: a memory rather than a threatening event. As one woman diagnosed with posttraumatic stress disorder said, "I still hear the music. I just don't believe there are sharks anymore."

Arriving at that destination can take time, depending on the nature of the individual's childhood experience, though we've begun to see remarkable shifts even in the 8-week COS-Parenting model. We believe this progress can be attributed not only to the seemingly boundless courage and devotion to their children that participant after participant displays, but also to their four-million-year-old wisdom that our central focus on creating a strong holding environment allows to emerge. The creation of a therapeutic holding environment is discussed in detail in Chapter 11, but the aspect of it that is important here is that we do not try to tear down defenses that have been used for years. Rather, we help parents come to understand the nature of their defense. We don't perceive our task to be the removal of either the defensive process or the pain that first gave rise to those defenses. Our primary goal is to offer parents access to some of the holding environment they have been missing, a modest awareness of their early childhood pain, a way of seeing their learned patterns of response to that pain, and then to offer the opportunity to choose, at least some of the time, to act from outside the defense.

First we call parents' positive intentionality to the fore by showing them video clips of moments in which their child is clearly in need. We then offer reflective dialogue to facilitate a more empathic understanding of their child's need. When parents move to empathy for their children, it activates their caregiving system and makes them more willing to bear the discomfort of the process for the sake of their child. Once they see the legitimacy of the need, we show them a combination of videos, some in which they are struggling with meeting this particular need and some in which they are able to meet this particular need. The proposition we are making is that their child needs them in ways that make them uncomfortable, they have the capacity to meet these needs, as evidenced in the video (we call this an "underutilized strength"), sometimes they meet the particular need, and sometimes they turn away from it because they hear shark music. Through a gradual process of watching themselves with their child on video and gaining the support of the other parents in the group and the therapist, parents can find a way to manage their shark music and help their child create a more secure attachment.

Now that their shark music can be identified by name, when it manifests itself they can make a conscious choice: They can either continue to be frightened by sharks that no longer exist and miss the child's needs and cues or stand back and say "There's my shark music" and go on to meet the need. At these new choice points parents can respond to their child's needs (in spite of the discomfort it causes them) or protect themselves from the pain by overriding their child's need (limiting or avoiding a response). What becomes known and organized with words through the COS intervention is that they can choose to pay now or pay later. If they protect themselves from the immediate discomfort, their child's need will go unmet, and over time the child will begin to express that need in a distorted manner, causing both parent and child difficulty.

> *All parents hear shark music with some of their child's needs.*
> *The parents of secure children recognize their shark music.*
> *Often (not always) they choose to find a way to meet*
> *their child's need in spite of the temporary pain it causes them.*

State of mind can, indeed, be changed. But it takes time for parents to begin to interact with their child in a way that promotes secure attachment and to learn from experience the benefits of doing so. That is the process by which internal working models are changed and the urgency of parents' defenses may eventually change too, some languishing from disuse and some becoming less strident in their demand to be heeded.

If we were to conceptualize this transformation from the point of view of a neuropsychologist, we might say the COS is helping parents and children create new neural pathways. Another way to conceptualize this change is to think of it as helping parents see again what is hidden in plain sight: that focusing on the "and" supports security more than attempts to fix the "me" or the "you."

As noted in Chapter 5, internal working models need to be flexible enough to allow data from current relationships and contexts to update perceptions of self and other. A core facet of this flexibility hinges on reflective functioning. By engaging in reflective dialogue the COS protocol is designed to develop parents' reflective functioning, which leads toward more secure outcomes. The specific nature of reflective dialogue is explained in Part II of this book.

Reflective Functioning

Despite the predictability of infant–parent attachment based on the state of mind of the parent, no one really knows how the adult's childhood attachment and then consequent state of mind is transferred to the parent–child attachment in the next generation. This gap in our understanding naturally makes it difficult to come up with a "cure" for intergenerational transmission of insecure and disorganized attachment. There is growing consensus, however, that reflective functioning is a critical fulcrum.

Our working definition for reflective functioning is "the psychological capacity for understanding one's own mental states, thoughts, feelings, and intentions as well as those of the other"—in this case those of the care-seeking child. Reflective functioning makes it possible for parents to recognize what needs to change—especially in the self. As already explained, unless we manage shark music, it limits that capacity, sometimes sharply.

Secure parents can (1) stand back and see what they are doing (and not yet doing) for their children (reflective functioning); (2) admit where they struggle and, for the sake of their children (positive intentionality), work to find another way. Reflective functioning, in fact, consistently emerges as a cornerstone capacity within the state of mind of those who are able to support secure attachment (Fonagy, Steele, Steele, & Target, 1997).

Reflective functioning: The ability to shift from focusing on what my child is doing (whining) and how it makes me feel (frustrated) to what I am doing and how it makes my child feel.

If reflective functioning can allow parents to understand their shark music, then it may be the key to breaking the transgenerational cycle of poor parent–child attachments. Fonagy et al.'s (1991) groundbreaking prospective study showed that pregnant mothers' state of mind predicted their attachment with their child a year after birth with very high accuracy (75%). If reflective functioning can be improved, then state of mind becomes open to change—and so does the subsequent parent–child attachment pattern.

Significantly, Fonagy, Steele, Steele, Higgitt, & Target (1994) found that at-risk parents with high reflective functioning were very likely to have children with secure attachments. We have found that almost any capacity for reflective functioning made parents viable candidates for the COS intervention. In fact, we tend to see parents with the lowest reflective functioning making the largest gains in reflective function (Huber, 2012). Occasionally parents have such low reflective functioning that they are disruptive of group process, and so individual therapy is indicated. The COS protocol is designed to increase reflective functioning with the goal of facilitating secure attachment. This potential is based on one of Bowlby's original ideas: that health constitutes being able to update the model based on current experience. The goal is to have internal working models that are stable enough to assist in navigating the world but flexible enough to respond to the vicissitudes of daily life, and adaptable enough to update when the old model is no longer accurate.

In other words, reflective functioning incorporates a number of different mental functions described by others using various terms, such as mentalization, metacognitive monitoring, mind-mindedness, and theory of mind, among many others. An important capacity undergirding all of these is coherence. "Secure attachment is marked by coherent stories that convince and hang together, where detail and overall plot are congruent, and where the teller is not so detached that the affect is absent, is not dissociated from the content of the story, nor is so overwhelmed that feelings flow formlessly into every crevice of the dialogue. Insecure attachment, by contrast, is characterized either by stories that are overelaborated and enmeshed . . . or by dismissive, poorly fleshed out accounts" (Holmes, 1999, p. 58).

This translates as the ability to maintain coherent, cooperative discourse while simultaneously remembering attachment-related events. This is one of the most powerful predictors of secure attachment. The implication for psychotherapeutic interventions is that in reflective dialogue with the therapist, the patient can integrate distorted or defended-against experiences into a more organized sense of self, softening defenses and enhancing regulation of affect and even behavioral self-control (Slade, 2008, p. 775). This is exactly what the COS is designed to do (see Box 6.2).

HOW THE CIRCLE OF SECURITY INTERVENTION TAPS POSITIVE INTENTIONALITY AND INCREASES REFLECTIVE FUNCTIONING

Figure 6.1 shows how the COS intervenes in the psychological cascade of events following a young child's expression of need to alter the parent's

---

BOX 6.2. CHOICE POINTS AND THE RUPTURED CIRCLE

When a child gets difficult—frustrated, demanding, upset, out of control—a parent may feel frustrated, powerless, lost, angry, or afraid. All the parent may see in that little face is rage or rejection or demands that make no sense. If the parent steps off the Circle in that moment, a rupture is created in the relationship. If the child is being difficult and the parent remains available and able to Be-With, it is an "Organize my feelings" moment. Ruptures are inevitable; all parents get off course some of the time. But reflective functioning and new experiences of Being-With through therapy can create a choice point where none existed before. The parent can learn to reflect and respond based on a new understanding: "When my child gets really difficult, what my child is really saying is 'I need you.'"

The measure of the repair—the response the parent chooses to get back to being the hands on the Circle—is whether the relationship is stronger after the repair than it was before the rupture. If the parent does not acknowledge the rupture in any way or recognize how the rupture must have felt for the child or use it to create new possibilities the next time a triggering event emerges, but rather sweeps the whole experience under the rug, it is an unfortunate waste of an important opportunity. Imagine a 2-year-old sitting on the floor of the living room while her father is sitting nearby, reading. The child starts to fuss and whimper, getting no response from the father, who simply seems to clutch his newspaper a little more tightly, holding it up higher to block his view of his daughter. Soon she ratchets up her cry for help, quickly breaking into full-blown distress. Dad gets up and abruptly stomps out of the room. The little girl, left alone, tries desperately to quiet herself but keeps whimpering. Her father walks back into the room with a bright smile on his face and says "How's my girl? You're OK, right?" Even if he goes over to his daughter and picks her up, the little girl has no idea why her father walked away from her in her time of need and no idea of what her father expects from her now. With repetition of this scenario she builds a belief that Dad doesn't like crying, and so she tries to stifle it as often as she can. Her father learns nothing about what his child's cues mean and continues to step outside the Circle when she expresses need. Her attachment with her father will eventually be scored as avoidant, and the relationship will be compromised. Imagine how the outcome would be different if the father had recognized how he had taken his hands off the Circle and returned to his daughter with the commitment to repair his rupture, talking to her about what had just happened and clarifying his commitment to finding new ways to be available when she feels distressed.

---

defenses and promote secure attachment. When the child's affect evokes an organized and regulated emotional response in the parent, "good enough" parenting and secure attachment are promoted. But if the infant's affect triggers unregulated affect in the parent, it also tends to trigger cognitive responses that impart negative attributions regarding the child's

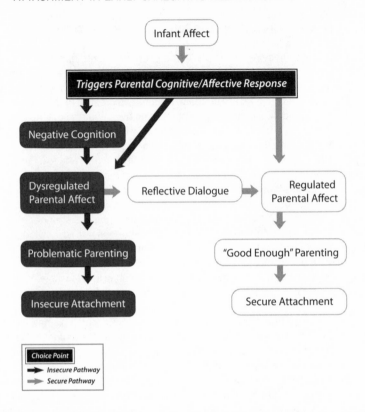

FIGURE 6.1. Emotion regulation. Copyright 2009 by Cassidy, Cooper, Hoffman, and Powell.

motivations; this pathway leads to problematic parenting and insecure attachment. COS intervention focuses on engaging the parent in reflective dialogue about his unregulated affect with the goal of helping the parent organize and reflect on his affective and cognitive response, which then opens the pathway to "good enough" parenting. Throughout this process COS capitalizes first on parents' positive intentionality and then on their capacity for reflective functioning.

When children's expression of need instantly triggers alerts of danger and portents of doom, caregivers tend to move into defense rather than opening up to cognitive transformation and affective change. Parents hearing the blare of their shark music are in the clutches of an amygdala gone wild and may see fight, flight, or freeze as the only avenues available to them. For this reason the therapist begins the 20-week intervention by focusing on the parents' positive intentionality, hidden strengths, and role as the beloved center of their child's universe. The therapist's goal is to start to soften defenses by creating a sense that parents are safe and secure within the group. Once the group has been established as something of a safe haven, the parents can also use the group as a secure base from which to explore a defensive (insecure or disorganized) interaction chosen as the linchpin of treatment for each of them. Through reflective dialogue among the parent, the rest of the group, and the therapist, each caregiver is nudged gently toward an understanding of the negative consequences of using such defenses. When all goes well, the parents realize that their deep desire to protect and care for their child is not being manifested in their caregiving behavior: instead dysregulated emotion raised by painful procedural memories leads to problematic defensive parenting and creates nonsecure attachment. They also have a chance to see that by regulating their affect they can override the action tendency of the feeling and choose to meet their child's need often enough to be a "good enough" parent for their child to have a secure attachment.

Although we do not fully understand the mechanism by which its transformative power operates, video clearly plays a crucial role in parents' ability to change their caregiving behavior. Something about seeing recordings of themselves and others breathes life into the concepts. Also, video facilitates the delivery of a respectful competency message showing both strengths and struggles. The tacit statement that parents can handle the truth about their struggles both normalizes them and gives parents confidence that they have what their child needs and can learn to give it often enough for a secure attachment to blossom.

The COS offers a path to creating a secure parent–child attachment through the following steps.

1. *Accepting, honoring, and utilizing parents' positive intentionality.* A facilitator who doesn't have or loses a sense of the parents' positive intentions can no longer be the hands holding the group. Facilitators can get flooded with negative attributions of the parent, which imbues them with a sense of helplessness, hopelessness, and powerlessness. It is as if the facilitator becomes the disorganized child, acting controlling punitive, controlling caregiving, or alternating between the two. In our work with parents—including those who were incarcerated, referred by child protection, had drug and alcohol histories, were homeless, were still teenagers, and so on—we were unable to find positive intentionality only a handful of

times. There may be other factors that rendered them unable to parent, but the positive intentionality was virtually always there.

2. *Providing a roadmap.* This is the COS graphic (Figure 1.1, page 17). It depicts in simple terms the three systems involved in parent–child attachment: the attachment system (the bottom half of the Circle, where the child asks for the comfort of a safe haven); the exploratory system (the top half of the Circle, where the child asks for a secure base from which to go off into the world and acquire knowledge, competence, and self-confidence); and the caregiving system (the hands on the Circle, where the parent is bigger, stronger, wiser, and kind, following the child's need whenever possible and taking charge when necessary). This map helps parents understand their child's needs, how the child shifts back and forth between them over and over all day, and how the parent helps support the child's need for protection and encourages the child's growth toward independence. It shows parents that what their state of mind often tells them are shark-infested waters are actually legitimate needs that can safely be met.

3. *Increasing parental observational and inferential skills.* By allowing them to see their interactions with their children (or the interactions on film through the lens of the COS needs), the intervention increases parents' observational skills regarding their child's needs on the Circle. Once they have a clear behavioral description, they are well prepared to use the Circle to make accurate inferences about the meaning of both their own and their child's behavior. The safety and acceptance of the group gives them distance from the shark music that influenced their behavior at the time the scene was recorded. Some parents instantly recognize that their behavior mimics that of their own caregiver. In a group setting, parents have the benefit of other parents' input and of seeing other parents struggle with their own shark music, normalizing the ruptures of the Circle that might otherwise lead to shame and defense.

4. *Engaging in reflective dialogue.* What parents learn by watching video clips of their child with them in the Strange Situation, and talking about these insights with the therapist and other parents, sets in motion a critical shift. What was once hidden in plain sight, implicit relational knowing, is now available and open for discussion. With their innate positive intentionality rising to meet the challenge, they begin to understand that their internal working models are not set in stone and that they can have a better relationship with their child—and usher their child more adroitly to adulthood—if they make choices different from the ones that their own

childhood ingrained. In the process their former shark music loses some of its power to cause distress and parents improve their ability to regulate the emotions that have been driving the behavior that creates insecurity and disorganization in attachments.

5. *The final step.* The final step on the path is to continue to enjoy, maintain, and enhance the ever-deepening relationship with their child.

Figure 6.2 is a handout we give to parents to help them understand how central reflection and dialogue based on caregiver state of mind are to security for their child.

THE PATH TO SECURE ATTACHMENT

In Part I of this book we have focused on basic attachment theory, the importance of secure attachment, the relationship needs that must be met to create secure attachment, and the power of Being-With in meeting those needs. We have also looked at adaptations to secure attachment (avoidance, ambivalence, and disorganization), the role of the caregiver's state of mind in attachment, and an outline of the path to secure attachment. In Part II, we will use this background to explore the specifics of the COS assessment and intervention.

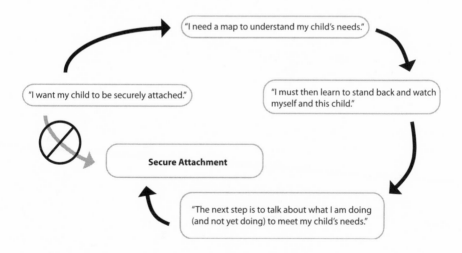

FIGURE 6.2. The path to secure attachment. Copyright 2004 by Cooper, Hoffman, and Powell.

As a preface to the nuts and bolts of the COS intervention, we want to acknowledge that it continues to be a remarkable privilege to work with high-risk parents who come to this intervention with histories of profound abuse, neglect, family disorganization, and significant limitations in parenting skills. Our experience over the years has led to the common understanding that the parents themselves guide us in how to be of assistance. They are the ones who have taught us that their first and most urgent need has little to do with the transmission of information. When a parent is feeling overwhelmed by shark music, handouts about the developmental phases are not likely to be effective. Over the years parents have taught us, again and again, "Begin where I am; don't begin with where you think I need to be. If I'm lost in my shark music, I need to find a way to make sense of my shark music. You need to learn about me before I can learn from you. Let me know I'm safe here with you. Let me know you care. And then address the pain. When I am ready to explore, be with me on the top of the Circle as I learn new ways to respond to my baby."

PART II

THE CIRCLE OF SECURITY INTERVENTION

7

Observing the Relationship

You've got to be very careful if you don't know where you're
going, because you might not get there.

—Yogi Berra

Caregiver–child dyads come to the COS intervention through
various routes with a wide range of presenting problems. Whether the
need has been noticed by a staff member at Early Head Start, at a neonatal
clinic serving at-risk mothers, via child protection services, by a private
practitioner, or through another route, the first question for COS treatment is how the family is struggling with the "and" in their relationship.

INTAKE: THE TRUE BEGINNING OF TREATMENT

The COS treatment truly begins with the initial contact, whether that is a
phone call, a face-to-face interview, a text message, or a casual conversation with a parent who is only considering involvement in COS. As with
any intervention, intake provides an important opportunity to screen for
factors that could thwart the therapeutic process or warrant a different
kind of treatment. If the therapist is using the COS group format for intervention, screening the participants is necessary to ensure a safe working
group with the highest possible potential for positive outcomes (see Box
7.1 for guidelines). But whatever else, internally or externally, is troubling
the parent or child individually—whatever is happening with the "me" or
"you"—the COS intake must focus primarily on that "and." This involves

establishing the centrality of relationship in the following two senses that were emphasized in Part I:

- Reframing the presenting behavioral struggles as an opportunity to support the relationship.
- Positioning the therapist as the hands that hold the caregiver.

Framing the Problem as a Relationship Issue

Even when the practitioner understands that the problem is relational, parents who are having problems with a young child almost always see the problem as residing in the child. They may frame this perspective in a protective manner—"He is just too sensitive"—or a punitive manner: "He is being a brat, and he needs to shape up." In the COS approach, one of the therapist's first and most important tasks is to start shifting parents toward viewing behavior as part of an interactive sequence of communication. When parents look at behavior as relational, they can begin to understand that it is the child's way of trying to tell the caregiver what he needs; suddenly, behavior has meaning and does not pop up out of the blue or occur in a vacuum. When interventions focus simply on extinguishing the behavior, they inadvertently cut off the child's ability to communicate rather than meeting the child's legitimate need.

Picture a parent who states that the problem is that his child cries too much. The therapist then shows interest in this problem by asking several specifically relational questions, such as: When your child cries, what do you do? When she cries, does she come to you? When she cries, do you go to her? How do you try to soothe her? What does she do? When does the soothing work? When does soothing not work? What's it like for you to soothe her? What is it like for you when your child doesn't soothe? What do you imagine it is like for her when you try to be soothing? In conveying an interest in how the parent and child interact, these questions imply both a relational context and meaning for the problems and the potential solutions.

Therapists can take this reframing a step further by crafting some questions in a "when . . . then" form: When your child does behavior A, what (behavior B) do you do? When you do B, how does your child respond? Such questions fill in the blanks and paint a picture of interaction, helping to track the process of relationship. Notably, they do not point a finger of blame at the parent as an alternative to blaming the child. However, parents often see the problem as residing in the child precisely because they are afraid the problem may have something to do with them, so the therapist must be sensitive to how or even whether such questions are asked, to avoid triggering

---

**BOX 7.1. CAREGIVERS WHO ARE NOT GOOD CANDIDATES
FOR THE COS GROUP INTERVENTION**

Some caregivers' defenses compromise the safety and coherence needed for the COS group therapy process, and these are best seen using an individual model (see Chapter 12). Caregivers who are not considered a good match for group work include the following people.

- Those who are using drugs and alcohol with no commitment to actively seek concurrent treatment.
- Those who have acute mental health problems such as significant depression (such problems can, but do not always, take center stage in a way that makes parents unavailable for COS at the current time).
- Those who demonstrate rigid and pervasive negativity toward the child with no signs of willingness to reflect on the self.
- Those who live within a context of domestic violence and choose to prioritize a dangerous partner over the needs of the child with no willingness to reconsider this choice.
- Those who are acting out narcissistic issues by devaluing others or incessantly elevating themselves.
- Those who manage their affect by flooding the group process with nonrelevant conversation.

---

defensiveness. It might help to reassure parents that you are interested in how they struggle and how they are successful with the problem.

In the same spirit of understanding what is happening for the family, acknowledging relationship strengths along with struggles will fortify the holding environment. It is best to acknowledge only general strengths, such as parents' deep commitment to their child, at this stage and not try to get into specifics until the intervention is under way. Before a clear understanding of the relationship is established, it is easy to inadvertently encourage the parent to focus on strengths that the parent overuses to avoid key struggles on the Circle—as in the case of a parent who is reasonably competent in promoting exploration but also uses it as a way to avoid the bottom of the Circle.

*Lasting change results from parents developing or enhancing
relationship capacities rather than learning techniques
to manage their children's behaviors.*

The Therapist as the Hands

If parents are to be receptive to a new view of their child's behavior, the therapist needs to meet the parents where they are and Be-With them throughout the process. Although therapists may feel some pressure to have diagnostic and informational forms filled out and even to develop a justifiable diagnosis during the initial meeting, all this gathering of information at the beginning can get in the way of creating an atmosphere of genuine interest—one about which a parent might think "I feel less alone because someone seems to be here with me in this feeling of being so alone." With parents with multiple risk factors in particular, a goal for the first session may be as simple as to have them feel heard, hopeful, and safe enough to want to have a second meeting.

Responsiveness to the parent should trump solicitation of information
throughout the COS intervention, but especially in the first visit.

Setting a Preliminary Relational Goal

The initial goals can be quite useful in negotiating the foundation for treatment. The fact that parents are participating in the intake suggests a desire to have a better relationship with their child. Now is the time to introduce video recording as the first step in understanding more about how their child interacts with them and to emphasize that the video will be used for parents to watch and learn new ways to help their child. Using the video to see how parents struggle and how they are successful in meeting their child's needs and managing stressful emotions is at the core of the intervention the parent is about to undergo.

This initial contact also provides the beginnings of the therapeutic contract that will help guide the treatment process. It helps to have the procedures of therapy—assessment and video review—make sense for the parents in terms of their goals. Over time, the contract will become more sophisticated and focused as the therapist and the parent form a safe haven/secure base relationship. The therapeutic contract is not a series of symptom-oriented checkmarks but a dynamic process that evolves over time as the parent experiences a sense of safety unfolding from the therapist's interest, care, and concern.

THE CIRCLE OF SECURITY ASSESSMENT PROCEDURE

The COS assessment of parent–child interaction is designed to develop a clear picture of the quality of attachment between parents and children for the purpose of directing clinicians' interventions. (The COS assessment

---

**BOX 7.2. THE ROLE OF THE COS ASSESSMENT
IN CHILD PROTECTION AND CUSTODY CASES**

The COS assessment can be used as *one component* in a comprehensive treatment plan for child protective services or custody disputes. However, it is never to be used alone to make determinations about child placements; many other factors must be taken into account. The COS assessment facilitates development of clear, coherent treatment plans that have measurable goals. Where placement depends on undergoing some form of intervention, it is essential to have measurable goals to determine whether the intervention was successful rather than depending on attendance or therapist subjective impressions as a measure of the therapeutic outcome.

An evaluation for the courts based on a clearly delineated treatment plan and at least 3 months of intervention will likely give a reasonable indication of a parent's capacity to reflect and respond to a clear and systematic approach that addresses the struggles inherent in the relationship. It has been our experience that an evaluation based on this level of assessment and response during treatment more clearly indicates the parent's capacity for success in caregiving.

---

can also be used in child protection and custody cases; see Box 7.2.) More specifically, the goal is to identify a "linchpin" struggle as the focus of treatment. The linchpin (defined in *Merriam-Webster's 11th Collegiate Dictionary* as a locking pin "that serves to hold together parts or elements that exist or function as a unit") represents what is keeping problematic parent–child interactions the way they are, and as such it clarifies what needs to change in the parent–child relationship to establish a secure attachment and promote healthy child development.

As noted in Part I, during the interactional assessment we are looking specifically for momentary strengths on the part of the Circle (top, bottom, or hands) where a parent and child struggle the most—*underutilized strengths*. For example, with parents who dismiss the importance of intimate connection, we're looking for instances in which the parent meets the child's needs on the bottom of the Circle. It's important, however, to avoid reinforcing strength in the parent that is being overused to the point that it becomes a weakness in terms of attachment style. If the COS assessment reveals that a child is avoidant, then congratulating the parent on promoting exploration or success on the top of the Circle only encourages the parent to keep using the defensive tactic of keeping her child at arm's length and will not contribute to forming a secure attachment.

As explained later in this chapter, we look at both the child's and the parent's behavior during the COS assessment. Even more important, however, is that we consider the sequence of the interaction: the parent's response to the child's behavior, the child's response to the parent's behavior, the child's response to the parent's response to the child's response, and so on. When you observe parent–child interaction, it is important to train your mind to think in terms of "When the parent does A, the child does B, and then the parent does C"—the same construct used in the initial questions posed during intake. The sequencing reveals what is hidden in plain sight: repetitive patterns of interaction that represent a strategy for negotiating a particular need. After seeing several sequences (typically we look for at least three) of a similar interaction in different forms—for instance, parental intrusiveness as seen when the child is absorbed in a toy and the parent suggests another toy, the child moves away to explore a different part of the room and the parent calls the child back, the child engages with the stranger and the parent inserts herself into the interaction—the therapist can begin to place the interaction on the menu of potential strengths or struggles. Discerning significant repetitive patterns in the dyad that can represent either secure or insecure relational strategies is a skill that requires more training and experience than can be offered in a book. We hope this material can help begin to lay the foundation of understanding that supports ongoing learning.

Attachment does not exist in the parent or the child,
just as music is not contained in the fiddle or the bow
but rather in the interaction between the two.

The COS interactional assessment procedure is a modified Strange Situation. The Strange Situation was developed in the late 1960s and became the core research tool for attachment theory. It has been performed thousands of times, on every continent except Antarctica, and was a key element in launching attachment theory into the stellar line of research it has become (Cassidy & Shaver, 2008, p. xi).

During the 1960s there was great pressure to use controlled laboratory procedures to understand child development and psychology. As Bronfenbrenner famously said, "it can be said that much of contemporary developmental psychology is the science of the strange behavior of children in strange situations with strange adults for the briefest possible periods of time" (1977, p. 513). The beauty of the SSP is that it capitalized on the strangeness of the laboratory to make it an asset rather than a confounding factor. Putting a young child in a strange situation without an attachment figure activates the attachment behavioral system. When the parent returns, we see, in real time, the child's strategy of attachment with the parent and the parent's strategy of providing caregiving to the child. The structure takes the guesswork out of knowing whether the child's attachment system is activated (whether the child is on the bottom of the Circle), as opposed to videos or observations in the family's home and in office settings without the SSP that leave us less confident about where the child is on the Circle.

For these reasons the SSP, or any number of other, similarly structured protocols, is well worth using if at all possible, yet the SSP does require a fairly sophisticated setup—a playroom equipped with toys and seating, with a large clear area on the floor for playing, a camera/observation room with a one-way window into the playroom, and a camera attached to a microphone in the playroom. Fortunately, it is eminently possible to replicate the same structured–unstructured paradigm with less rigid requirements for clinical purposes (although this would be unsuitable for research uses). Those in private practice without the requisite space and equipment may find both available at a nearby university clinic or child mental health center. Even a sole practitioner with a video camera could achieve many of the essential elements by recording a dyad at play in the office with the parent exiting and returning to establish the required separations and reunions. In this variation the therapist functions as both camera person and "stranger." Likewise, we have seen home visitation videos yield enough attachment-related information for us to make a COS assessment based on them.

The SSP

The SSP involves brief separations of parent and child, followed by reunions, which are captured by hidden cameras. The protocol is described in detail in Ainsworth and colleagues' *Patterns of Attachment* (1978); here we provide an overview, covering both the Ainsworth baby system and the Cassidy-Marvin (1992) preschool system, and a summary of the segments (see Box 7.3). To conduct this procedure for research purposes, training and adherence to the manuals for both systems is required, but to gather clinical material for intervention there is more latitude. For example, it's possible to do without the stranger and still get a relatively good picture of the attachment strategies used by the parent and child.

The procedure begins with the parent and child entering the room. The parent is then left alone with the child for 3 minutes of free play with the toys provided. At the end of that episode, a person who is a stranger to the child enters the room and in the baby system sits quietly for a minute

---

BOX 7.3. SUMMARY OF THE COS
ASSESSMENT PROCEDURE

1. Caregiver and child come into the room
2. Free play   3 minutes
3. Stranger joins   3 minutes
4. Separation and stranger remains   3 minutes
5. Reunion and stranger leaves   3 minutes
6. Separation and child alone   3 minutes
7. Stranger returns   3 minutes
8. Reunion and stranger leaves   3 minutes

End of SSP

- Reading   4 minutes
- Cleanup   3 minutes

---

before conversing with the parent and then engaging with the child. In the preschool system, the stranger engages with the parent for a minute and then engages with the child. At the end of that episode, the parent exits the room, and after the separation the stranger is left to respond to the child.

After 3 minutes (or less if the child is overly distressed) the parent returns. The parent is instructed to greet and/or comfort the child and then help the child return to play. It is in this episode that we first see the dyad negotiate the child's attachment needs. During this reunion episode the stranger leaves. At the end of 3 minutes the parent leaves the child alone in the room. After the child has been alone in the room for 3 minutes or less, the stranger returns and responds to the child.

After another 3 minutes, or less if necessary, the parent returns and again we get to see how the dyad negotiates the attachment. The stranger exits unobtrusively. This again creates an amazing opportunity to watch the parent and child in their attachment/caregiving dance. At the end of 3 minutes, the Strange Situation is over. A tremendous amount is learned about the dyad in just over 20 minutes.

We added two episodes to the SSP—reading and cleanup—both for diagnostic purposes and to give us additional opportunities to get video clips of positive interactions that we could use to show parents' strengths. At the end of the SSP, books are brought in and the parent is asked to sit on the couch and read to the child for 3 to 4 minutes. This episode often requires the parent to take charge in the transition from play to reading and do so in a way that makes it possible for the two of them to enjoy the activity. This helps us see how well the parent can take charge of a transition (vs. following the child's needs) and also how well the two engage in "enjoy with me" on the top of the Circle. The episode also requires physical proximity. For dyads that avoid proximity, this often shows their underused capacity (a "strength") and at other times highlights their struggle with closeness.

Cleanup more often displays the parent's strengths or struggles in taking charge. It is important to keep in mind the child's developmental capacity to take on the task and to observe whether the parent has developmentally appropriate expectations of the child. We like to let this task run until the parent and child are successful (typically 3 to 4 minutes), but occasionally, especially with older children, it becomes clear that they won't complete the task, and you must find a graceful way to end the session.

Scoring the SSP for research purposes focuses on the child's behavior in all the episodes, especially the two reunions. For COS purposes we are interested in assessing how the dyad negotiates the child's need for exploration (top), need for attachment (bottom), and the presence of a protective/in-charge other in the form of both a safe haven and a secure base (hands). Hopefully, we can capture video examples of each of the domains to show the parent's strengths and struggles in the relationship.

After the modified Strange Situation, the parent is given some time to orient the child to the child care provided. Then the parent is taken into an interview room for the Circle of Security Interview (COSI). The COSI takes about an hour to complete and will be discussed in Chapters 9 and 10.

LOOKING FOR THE LINCHPIN

The central question in the interactional assessment is: If you could change one interactional pattern in the dyad, what pattern would that be? With at-risk dyads it is easy to come up with a long list of problems, so it's a challenge to select one pattern with the greatest likelihood of significantly increasing the security of that parent and child. The question is, will changing the process on the top of the Circle, the bottom of the Circle, or the hands on the Circle make the largest shift toward security for this family? This pattern will be a defensive process that holds the family's dysfunctional attachment "dance" or strategy together. The linchpin should be something that helps parent and child defend against emotional closeness (dismissing/avoidant attachment) or separation (preoccupied/ambivalent attachment) or issues that involve taking charge and hierarchy (unresolved/disorganized) and the emotional distress triggered by the child's needs for a safe haven or a secure base.

Because the ultimate purpose of the assessment is to identify the linchpin struggle, not just name the particular attachment theme (as in the SSP used for research purposes), it is important to think of assessment conclusions as action tendencies rather than designations of static states. For example, the statement "This is an avoidant child" does not inform intervention, whereas "This child avoids expressing needs on the bottom of the Circle because such actions consistently lead to negative responses from the parent" focuses the intervention on the parent's response to the child's needs on the bottom of the Circle.

Seeing versus Guessing: Assessing Relationship via Behavior

The importance of the distinction between behavioral observations and inferences about the meaning of behavior, introduced in Chapter 2, cannot be overstated with regard to assessing parent–child interactions. Skipping over the behavioral observation (seeing) and leaping to inferences (guessing) not based on clear observational descriptions often tells us more about ourselves than about the relationship we're observing.

Seeing versus guessing is important as well because once you've decided that a family demonstrates a dismissing/avoidant attachment style, it becomes difficult to see signs that this is not an avoidant family unless you keep your eyes wide open and resist the urge to keep confirming your original conclusion. The tendency to make quick judgments is one of many reasons that interpreting dyads' behavior accurately requires rigorous training and extensive experience, as does scoring the SSP.

It is beyond the scope of this book to offer comprehensive training in parent–child assessment, and as noted earlier, training, supervision, and experience are all prerequisites for drawing accurate and insightful conclusions from what is learned during a COS assessment. This chapter is designed to be an introduction to the process and the dimensions to be considered in assessing parent–child interactions. Toward that end, we present the questions that we ask in assessing parent–child interactions. Even though it takes a lot of experience and supervision to draw accurate and well-calibrated conclusions from these questions, asking the right questions is a powerful first step.

The first factor to keep in mind as you move from seeing to guessing is that both parents' and children's behavior needs to be viewed as communicating clues to underlying needs that, if met, lead to a better outcome for the relationship. Secure dyads' behavior more often makes the underlying needs apparent. With insecure and disorganized dyads, behaviors often function to hide underlying needs.

It is often necessary to comprehend what a behavior
is hiding rather than what it is revealing.

To understand the parent–child relationship through behavior, we have to consider the context, intent, and function of the behavior to discern the need that the behavior is expressing or hiding.

The Context of Behavior

To use behavior to understand the relationship, it is essential that we know whether the child's exploratory system is activated or the child's attachment system is activated. In other words, is the child on the top or the bottom of the Circle? Looking only at the behavior, it is easy to be misled about where the child is on the Circle. This is because, as we discussed earlier, by the time they are 12 months old, we can see in the SSP that children have become very proficient at miscuing us about their needs.

For example, seeing a child playing with toys does not tell us whether the child is on top of the Circle actively exploring or on the bottom of the Circle miscuing to hide his need for comfort or protection. We need to know more about the context. First, is the child alone? If so, the child may be distracting himself with the toys to soothe himself while his caregiver is away. Miscuing is relational communication; there has to be someone there to miscue. When Mom is in the room, there may be some telltale signs in the quality of the child's play that help us determine whether the child is on the top or bottom of the Circle. When a child's exploratory system is activated, his play is more likely to be expansive and creative. When a child is miscuing, the play may be serving as self-soothing and thus will tend to be repetitive and constricted. This is a useful hint, but since the quality of exploration may vary from child to child, it cannot be used as a sole indicator of when the child is on the top or the bottom of the Circle. Seeing a behavior such as playing as part of the sequence of events offers us more information about where the child is on the Circle.

The Intent of Behavior

We often make assumptions about the intentions behind behaviors. For a behavior we judge to be negative, we typically assign a corresponding negative intention to the person engaged in the behavior, which will skew the assessment and severely impair our ability to help the dyad. It is easy, for example, to fall into the trap of assuming that a child is throwing a tantrum "just to get attention" or to manipulate the parent. Watching a parent micromanaging a child's play, it is common to assign a negative intention to the parent such as that the parent just wants a trophy child.

To accurately assess a relationship, it is imperative to assume that a child's behavior is an attempt to communicate legitimate needs and that underlying a parent's behavioral response is a positive intention to meet the child's needs. Approaching the parent with the underlying concept that her problematic caregiving behaviors are attempts to provide something of value to the child will make the parent feel safer with vulnerability. Helping a parent feel seen and appreciated facilitates intervention. Often this is more an attitude than something specific that the therapist says, though an example might be something like this: "I can see the minute you came back into the room you wanted to do something for your child because he was upset. As you offered him a toy, what kinds of thoughts and feelings were you having in that moment?"

Accurate interpretation of behavior also demands recognition of the power of cross-generational transmission to distort behavioral communication. Consider an oppositional/defiant child with a conflict-avoiding parent. The parent in this scenario may have grown up with a controlling or abusive caregiver and, in an attempt to avoid repeating that pattern, now avoids conflict, thus abdicating being bigger and stronger in the relationship. It is also not uncommon to see parents using conflict avoidance as the strategy they learned from their conflict-avoiding caregiver. Regardless of the origin of the behavior, the underlying intention is positive.

The child's response is to use oppositional and defiant behavior to communicate a need for safety. "Please show me that you can be bigger, stronger, wiser, and kind." The child needs to know that the parent is strong enough to take charge; otherwise the parent doesn't seem strong enough to provide protection. The child's intention is also positive.

However, the ensuing feedback loop quickly escalates: the child becomes increasingly demanding to see if the parent can provide protection, and the parent, rather than demonstrating an ability to take charge, becomes more compliant to avoid the conflict. This can result in such extreme and disturbing behavior on the part of the child that it is difficult to maintain the assumption that the intent of the child is both to ask the question "Are you strong enough to protect me?" and to evoke a more functional response from the parent.

When distorted behavioral communication is attributed to a negative intention on the part of the child, the resulting recommendation to the parent may be to respond in a punitive manner (e.g., ignore/shun the child when the child displays the behavior or use time-out and logical consequences with a negative state of mind) rather than meeting the child's underlying need. Of course, the misattuned, punitive response leads to further distortion of the parent and child's behavioral communication.

The Function of the Behavior

The function of behavior in the relationship is ideally related closely to the intention of the behavior. Miscues may hide a need to protect the child from the pain of exposing a need that has been unmet and simultaneously protecting the parent from the discomfort that is triggered by the child's expression of the need. Often, miscues unintentionally perform a specific function in maintaining the problem. For example, children who have an ambivalent attachment to their caregiver tend to act whiny and clingy. This behavior is exhausting for both the child and the parent. As noted in Chapter 4, Ainsworth's original formulation of ambivalent attachment was that it was the child's response to an inconsistent caregiver. The child's unconscious intention may be to keep the parent's caregiving system activated to assure the parent is attentive enough to protect the child. Yet the clingy behavior sometimes overwhelms the parent and sets up a runaway feedback loop of the parent pulling away, which makes the child cling harder. Understanding the unintended function of the behavior in the relationship as well as the intention will help shape treatment planning.

The Need behind the Behavior

If we accept the premise that behavior is a form of communication, then an integral part of any assessment is to understand what the behavior is communicating. Behaviors can simultaneously serve several functions. COS assumes that one function young children's behavior always serves is communicating needs on the Circle. For example, a child's immersion in exploratory behavior functions as a means of learning and enjoyment, but it simultaneously communicates to the parent that it is a "Watch Over Me" moment.

Sometimes children's behaviors accurately communicate a need and the parent responds sensitively. However, it is the behaviors that are unclear, problematic for the child or parent, or in some way costly to the child's development that we urgently need to decode. In essence, persistent misbehavior by the child is saying that the cost to the child of the parent knowing and reacting to the real need is greater than living with the pain that the misbehavior causes.

ASSESSING BEHAVIOR AROUND THE CIRCLE

One of the great gifts that attachment theory makes available to clinicians is specificity about children's relationship needs. The 10 needs represented in the COS are not intended to be all-inclusive of children's needs, but in terms of attachment, if caregivers can regularly meet these 10 needs they are providing good-enough parenting. The overarching question is "Does the child have enough confidence that he can get to a protective and emotionally supportive parent when needed to have the confidence to explore when it is safe to do so?"

Good enough parenting does not have to look pristine. The question that is at the heart of it is:

> *Does the job get done in the end—at least half the time?*
> —SUSAN WOODHOUSE (PERSONAL COMMUNICATION, 2012)

Does the child come in when stressed, calm, and then go out to explore? Even if it looks like some struggle is involved, if the job gets done more often than not there is a foundation of security.

On the top and bottom of the Circle, whether the job gets done is typically revealed by the child's cues or miscues (i.e., is the child showing or hiding her needs?). A parent may try to act as if she is available for the purpose of the assessment, but the child, through cues and miscues, will tell the story of the dyad's typical interactions on the bottom and top of the Circle.

The Child's Behavior on the Bottom of the Circle

Assessing the bottom half of the Circle—relatedness-within-autonomy—requires that you know the child's attachment system has been activated. By design the SSP assessment creates a bottom-half moment: we see how the child behaves after his attachment system is activated by separation from the parent, with and without a stranger present. We can thus assess whether the child cues a need for protection, comfort, delight, and/or help organizing feelings.

Cuing is sometimes manifested as the child seeking proximity, but, especially once children can speak, it may be verbal/emotional connection without physical proximity. Does the child approach the caregiver directly, engaging with the parent through touch and/or speech to elicit comfort? Children who reach up for their parents are showing that they expect to be picked up; those who make eye contact so that the parent can see the anguish caused by the separation are showing that they expect Mom or Dad to help them manage these feelings because the parent has done so fairly reliably in the past. Children use cuing to seek affection, delight, and a sense of being welcomed. Through cuing, children communicate their own needs, as opposed to acting in ways to take care of their parent's needs.

Children's miscues on the bottom of the Circle often mimic their exploratory behavior. Miscues that are consistent with avoidant attachment are avoiding or rejecting of care and distracting from the need. It is not uncommon for children with an avoidant attachment to appear absorbed in a toy even though their play is repetitive and flat. Also, children may direct the parent's attention to a toy and away from the need for comfort. An obvious and not uncommon example is a child looking at the returning parent and then abruptly looking and pointing to a toy across the room that the child has previously shown no interest in.

Children with ambivalent attachments may directly cue the caregiver about needing comfort, but to maintain the parent's caregiving system the soothing must fail. It is common to see the child want to be picked up and then demand to be put down before feeling comforted and then demand to be picked up again. Or you might see the child be upset, pouty, even have a tantrum—all with the nonconscious plan to maintain the involvement of the caregiver.

Sometimes children are very controlling of the parent during a reunion. It is as if the child is organizing the parent's distress as opposed to the parent helping to organize the child's. This is a crucial distinction and will be covered more thoroughly under role reversal later in this chapter.

The Child's Behavior on the Top of the Circle

Assessing the top half of the Circle—autonomy-within-relatedness—requires that you know the child's exploratory system is activated. As was stated earlier, sometimes children use toys to self-soothe or distract from their need; this is a miscue to hide a need for comfort rather than a cued need to explore. Looking at both the context and the robustness of the play helps determine whether the child's exploratory system is activated. *Expansive, imaginative play suggests exploration, and repetitive, impoverished play suggests the child's attachment system is activated.*

As with observing the child on the bottom of the Circle, the next step is to determine whether the child is cuing (i.e., showing a need to explore) or miscuing (hiding a need to explore). As indicated in Figure 7.1, cuing is direct, engaged, comfortable, calm, and shows positive expectations of the caregiver. So a child on Mom's lap pointing toward a toy and making eye contact is an example of a direct cue. If it is a safe and an appropriate time, a secure parent would support the child's exploration. Typically if a child is cuing so directly, the parent is willing and able to support the child. If the parent has a history of not supporting the child's exploration, you would not expect the child to continue to cue. The cue might be more indirect, however, such as looking at the toy and looking at the parent and then back at the toy. This is not necessarily an attempt to hide the need to explore.

Push–pull exploration—where the child approaches the toys, then returns to cling to the parent, becomes helpless, and then wants to return to the toys—is typically a miscue used by ambivalently attached children. Competent exploration is being sacrificed to keep the parent's caregiving system activated.

Miscues used by preschool children with disorganized attachments include being suddenly overbright, especially on reunion, overly compliant, "walking on eggshells," or overly focused on organizing or taking care of the caregiver. The child's goal is to protect, manage, or take care of the parent who is frightening or frightened in his primary role as hands on the circle. The miscues above are examples of the controlling caregiving pattern seen in disorganization and described in Chapter 4. Controlling punitive behavior in disorganized attachments includes argumentativeness, defiance, aggression, ignoring, rejection, and other attempts to chastise or punish the parent.

Earlier in this chapter we noted that the child's behavior reveals what is hidden in plain sight. However, to get the full picture, we also need to look at the sequence of the interaction, tracking the child's response to the parent's response to the child's response and so on. So the parent's caregiving behavior is important to observe during this assessment as well.

Caregiver Behavior: The Hands on the Circle

When assessing hands on the Circle, we are looking for evidence that the parent is providing effective caregiving by being bigger, stronger, wiser, and kind. Parents misattuning or pressuring when they need to follow children's lead is associated with problems on the top or bottom of the Circle. If the parent is clearly acting "mean, weak, or gone"—what we call "limited" hands on the Circle—the child's top or bottom needs are seriously compromised as well. However, despite problems on the top and bottom of the Circle, which we'll discuss later, mean, weak, or gone generally means the linchpin struggle has to be with the hands. Limited hands are revealed in the diagnostic Circle as either actual, or threats of, abandonment or aggression, shifting or competing attachment strategies, or dimensions of abdication—all of which point to disorganization.

We assess the quality of the caregiver's functioning as the hands by looking at the caregiver's ability both to follow the child when possible and to take charge when necessary. Numerous variations of following (attuning, misattuning, and pressuring) and taking charge (bigger, stronger, wiser, and kind, vs. mean, weak, or gone) can be seen in parents, and the distinctions can be subtle. We have struggled over the years with categorizing these behaviors in a way that will help therapists not only assess attachment but also couch the linchpin struggle in action terms as noted above. Keep in mind that dyadic interactions are very complex and do not fit easily into boxes or checklists. Figure 7.1 is intended to help organize thinking and offer signs to watch for that can help in the diagnostic process.

Since all of the categories are caregiving behaviors and thus hands, saying that the linchpin is hands can be confusing. When we say that the linchpin is "hands," we are specifically stating that the caregiver is "mean, weak, or gone," exhibiting the problematic affect and behavior associated with disorganized attachment.

Follow: Attuned, Misattuned, Pressuring

As explained earlier in this book, a key to secure attachment is to follow the child's needs whenever possible. Daniel Stern used the words "attunement," "misattunement," and "tuning." Tuning was used to describe "covert attempts to change the infant's behavior and experience" (Stern, 1985, p. 213). Successful following can be viewed as being "attuned." Inadvertently not following the child's needs—misreading them, making inaccurate, negative attributions, or just being tuned out—we call being "misattuned."

Child Behavior: Top Half Moments

Child Cueing: Direct, Engaged, Comfortable, Calm, Showing Positive Expectations of Caregiver

Child Miscuing: Clinging, Helpless, Overly Focused on the Caregiver, Over Bright, Walking on Egg Shells, Resistant/Argumentative, Controlling, Defiant, Aggressive, Ignoring, Rejecting, Overly Compliant, Flat

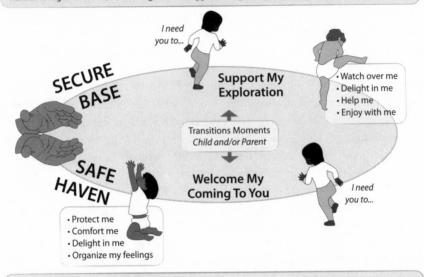

I need you to...

SECURE BASE

Support My Exploration

• Watch over me
• Delight in me
• Help me
• Enjoy with me

Transitions Moments
Child and/or Parent

SAFE HAVEN

Welcome My Coming To You

I need you to...

• Protect me
• Comfort me
• Delight in me
• Organize my feelings

Child Behavior: Bottom Half Moments

Child Cueing: Direct, Engaged, Showing Positive Expectations of Caregiver, Affectionate

Child Miscuing: Avoiding or Rejecting Care, Distracting from Need, Taking Care of the Caregiver, Controlling, Defiant, Resistant/Argumentative, Aggressive, Overly Compliant, Overly Bright, Vigilant, Flat

Caregiver Behavior ("Hands")   *Indicates possible marker for disorganization*

Follow

Attuned: Confident presence, Co-regulation of emotion

Misattuned: Flat/Going through the motions, Overbright, Anxious/hypervigilant, Distracted, Negative affect/attributions, Rejecting/Neglecting attachment

Pressuring: Pressure to achieve, Pressure to be self-sufficient, Pressure to stay involved with me, Pressure to top/bottom of Circle

Take Charge

Bigger, Stronger, Wiser, and Kind: Confident Presence/Expectation, Scaffolding/Co-Organizing

Mean, Weak, or Gone: *Aggression or threat of, *Abandonment or threat of, *Helplessness/fearful, *Dissociation, *Neglect, *Conflict avoidance

Role distortion (peer to peer): *Let's be little together, *Be an adult with me, *Be my companion, *Don't need me

Role reversal: *Parent controlled by: *Child's caregiving, *Child's aggression

Shifting/Competing Strategies

FIGURE 7.1. Circle of Security: Relationship assessment. Copyright 2007 by Cooper, Hoffman, Marvin, and Powell.

We use the word "pressure" to describe attempts to influence the child's behavior or experience because it is more evocative of this meaning when used alone. All parents do this. It becomes a problem when a predictable pattern emerges, causing specific needs on the Circle to go unmet.

Attuned

Ideally parents follow with a *confident presence and coregulation of emotion,* the style of following associated with true attunement and secure attachment.

CONFIDENT PRESENCE

In such cases, even though the child is leading, it is always clear that the parent is bigger, stronger, wiser, and kind. It is as if the parent reassures the child by saying, "Although I am giving you the freedom to take the lead, you can always be assured that since I am the one organizing this experience, you are safe, and I am still in charge." So if the child is taking the lead in pretend play and assigns the parent the role of playing a baby, it is the parent's confident presence that allows, in the play space, the parent and child to suspend reality enough to engage in the play without losing touch with the truth that the parent is still the parent.

This style of following provides the child with the safety and security to explore the role of taking the lead without feeling overwhelmed with the responsibility. The child can explore and develop his imagination and creativity because he is held in the safety of knowing that his parent is capable of keeping him safe. The parent's leadership is clear, expressed unobtrusively, and available when needed—in a way, hidden in plain sight.

Misattuned

When parents are misattuned in the sense that we use the term, they seem out of touch with their child's needs. This is especially problematic when the parent's empathy for the child's experience has been compromised because something about the child's need has triggered shark music and the parent can no longer have an accurate response to the child's need. Misattunement can take various forms.

FLAT/GOING THROUGH THE MOTIONS

One way that parents can be misattuned is to appear emotionally flat (lacking in enthusiasm, emotional connection, enjoyment, and delight), just going through the motions of following their child without contributing to the creativity or complexity of the play. These parents may appear bored or inattentive or may even seem to resent having to play with the child. They might appear to be unfamiliar with how to play with the child in a mutually satisfying way. You may notice a flat, nonresponsive facial expression and very slow, labored movements.

This type of caregiver behavior leaves the child feeling alone and unacknowledged or, worse, feeling like a burden to the parent. The parent's lack of emoting and flat face give very little information to the child and thus make it difficult for the child to develop relational and social competence. This style of following is sometimes seen in parents who are depressed, exhausted, or overwhelmed.

OVERBRIGHT

Sometimes a parent's discomfort over dealing with negative emotions—in herself and/or the child—is managed by presenting a bright and cheerful affect at all times. To the observer and the child, it is clear that the positive affect is not genuine.

Genuine positive affect tends to rise out of the situation, reach a peak, and then return to neutral in a very smooth manner. When people are overbright, they tend to turn the positive affect on and off like a light switch. You sense a pressure behind the brightness, and the smile appears forced and almost fake. Sometimes people use the weather person on a local news show as an example of unrelenting, bubbling, even syrupy cheerfulness despite the forecast.

It is important to note that an overbright affect is also often used to bring praise and a sense of excitement to everyday events that merely require a relaxed presence. Sometimes, but not always, the overemphasis in our culture on saying "good job" can be a form of this. An overbright affect is more problematic when it results in children's needs on the bottom of the Circle going unmet.

This disingenuous affect can be very confusing to children because they must either trust their own sense that something is wrong and distrust the parent's face and words or distrust themselves and accept the disingenuous affect as real. When a child is distraught, a parent being overbright is the antithesis of Being-With and leaves the child alone in her pain or feeling as though she needs to perform, do something special, or act happy to match the affect of her caregiver.

NEGATIVE AFFECT/ATTRIBUTIONS

We all carry positive and negative internal representations of ourselves and of others. Which representation of another person is in the forefront affects how we feel about that person. When we are upset or angry with someone, it is sometimes hard to remember the good things about that person. And when we are especially delighted with that person, it is sometimes hard to remember the bad things about him. This representation of the other as all good or all bad is usually fleeting, and in general we know that the other person is neither all good nor all bad, but everything in between.

However, if a parent reifies her negative representation of a child, it becomes the definition of the child's character or quality. This attribution of the child always carries with it the negative affect associated with that representation.

How does this look to the observer? It is unusual for parents to come out and directly reveal their negative attributions of their children, but it is difficult for them to hide their negative affect. Negative attributions/affect that the parents hold inside can bleed over into their interaction with their children. It may be seen as a dismissive or devaluing tone, harsh or jerky movements, rolling of eyes, or flashes of contempt in facial expressions. When one child in the SSP wanted to have all of the blocks, the parent huffed, pulled back, and said, "Well, I guess that's the way it is." She then tried to cover with a brittle laugh, but the affect was chilling. Even when the attribution is wildly inaccurate, it feels very believable to the parents. The more inaccurate parents' sense of the child is, the more distorted their response to the child is going to be.

Consequently, negative affect/attributions make it very hard for the parent to follow the child. In fact, following the child can feel dangerous or destructive because it supports the perceived negative character of the child. Statements like "That child is always up to no good" or "He always demands what he wants when he wants it" suggest that following the child would contribute to the problem.

Since a child's sense of self is highly dependent on how the child thinks his parent thinks of him, a parent's negative attributions/affect can create a very distorted sense of self in the child. It is beyond a young child's developmental capacity to realize the parent's attributions are inaccurate.

It is important to be aware of the parent's attributions; otherwise the intervention may not make any sense to the parents. For example, if a parent believes that the child is just trying to get her own way and you insist that the parent follow the child, the parent will likely resist your interventions for fear that they will reinforce the child's negative behavior.

ANXIOUS/HYPERVIGILANT

Sometimes parents' anxiety is so overwhelming that they can't focus and follow their children's exploration on the top of the Circle or proximity seeking on the bottom of the Circle (see the discussion of distracted behavior below). Other times their anxiety leads to a hypervigilant focus on the child that disrupts their ability to follow the child's lead. One parent we worked with was convinced that letting her child move away from her would inevitably lead to danger. She became an expert at restricting her child's locomotion to the point that the child was significantly delayed in gross motor development. Even though parents like this seem to be focused on their child, they are usually following their own fears rather than their children's needs. How do you tell the difference? Generally, if the parent's monitoring of the situation interferes with the child's needs, when there is clearly no danger to the child, you're seeing anxious or hypervigilant behavior. When parents are anxious and hypervigilant, their children's response can range from hiding their needs to help manage their parents' anxiety to feeling so frightened of the world that they cling to their parents.

DISTRACTED

Distraction can range from extreme cases of anxiety to more subtle forms, such as daydreaming or mild preoccupation. When parents are distracted, by definition, they are not following their children either on the top or the bottom of the Circle. A new job, a new love interest, financial worries, a death in the family, trouble at work or school, and so on can divert a parent's attention and make it difficult to follow the child. Distraction can take the form of the parent gazing off into the distance as if lost in a pleasant daydream or wringing his hands and seeming to be preoccupied with worries. A parent may appear distracted for a moment or appear distracted throughout the Strange Situation. In more severe forms of distraction, the parent might dissociate, which can occur in parents with a history of trauma who lose a coherent sense of self. In these cases the parent is truly gone, leaving no hands on the Circle, which has a much greater impact on the child and is associated with disorganization, which we discuss later.

Distraction has different implications depending on whether the parent is distracted while watching over the child's play or when the child is seeking care on the bottom of the Circle. Also noteworthy is whether the child can readily gain the parent's attention or is unable to do so. Along the continuum of "distracted," a parent's distraction when the child is not making a bid for interaction is less severe than when the child is making a bid for contact. At some point on this continuum the parent crosses the threshold to "gone."

When the parent is distracted, the child must decide whether to hold the connection to the parent or carry on without it. Children with avoidant attachments tend to miscue the parents, acting like they want to explore, like they don't really need anything from the parent. Children who are ambivalently attached will attempt to break through the distraction and gain access by clinging and whining.

REJECTING/NEGLECTING OF ATTACHMENT

Rejecting the child's bottom-half needs has a more active quality than neglecting. Rejection takes the form of rebuffs or snubbing, whereas neglecting is characterized by overlooking or disregarding the child's needs. Children's miscuing may develop in response to rejection, but over time miscues make it easier for the parent to simply neglect needs.

Rejecting and neglecting of the child's attachment needs often means the child's bid for comfort triggers feelings that threaten to flood the parent, and so the parent rejects or neglects the child's needs on the bottom of the Circle as a way to maintain the parent's emotional state.

It also may take the form of an earnest attempt to teach the child not to risk the vulnerability of making certain needs known. Parents may say that they don't want their child to be a crybaby and so they want to discourage the child from showing distress by rejecting/neglecting the need.

Pressuring

Parents who exhibit pressuring behavior are trying to lead where they should follow. Pressuring is an attempt to alter their child's behavior or emotions, generally in a direction that the parents find less distressing. The parent may appear to be joining in with the child's activity as if following the child's lead but then tries to steer the child's experience in a different direction. This is not necessarily a sign of insecurity unless it is a pattern, a typical one being the parent's turning an "enjoy with me" or "help me" moment in exploration into an opportunity to show the child how to play "better."

Pressuring can occur on either the top or the bottom of the Circle. Parents who pressure their child on the top of the Circle often want the child to achieve or to stay involved with the parent. Some parents introduce toy after toy, bringing in something new before the child has had an opportunity to fully explore one toy. This may indicate that the parent is uncomfortable and/or unfamiliar with how to play with the child, or it may be a way for the parent to stay central in the play. Other parents direct the child in the "proper" use of the toy (e.g. "That's the tow truck, not a race car. Don't race with it; use it to tow the racecars when they crash") rather than allowing the child's imagination and interest in exploration to unfold. Caregivers may also quiz their child about colors or names of objects. See below, under "Pressure to Achieve." The emphasis is clearly on performance rather than allowing the child to explore within a quiet sense of belonging.

Noticing where on the Circle a parent becomes pressuring can give you a good idea of what needs trigger the parent's shark music. You might find the linchpin struggle on the bottom of the Circle if a parent pressures the child not to be upset upon reunion in the SSP, on the top if the parent intrudes on play during "Watch over me" moments, and in the hands if the parent pressures the child to take care of the parent.

Seeing not only where on the Circle a parent becomes pressuring but also what specific outcome the parent is pressuring for can tell you a lot about the dyad's attachment and help you identify possible linchpin struggles.

PRESSURE TO ACHIEVE

Some parents overdefine their role as a teacher for their child, constantly looking for moments to teach even if such moments interfere with meeting the child's needs on the Circle. Clearly teaching is essential, but pressure to achieve is the overuse of this aspect of parenting as a defensive substitute for attuning to some or many of the child's needs all around the Circle. Besides instructing children in the proper use of a toy, parents may disrupt play to create a teaching moment (e.g., "My car is red. Before we race, tell me the color of the other cars"). Sometimes parents believe that pressuring their children to learn colors, numbers, and shapes is just what good parents do, and sometimes parents pressure their young child to achieve because they feel a strong need to be perfect parents with the perfect child or they harbor anxiety about their own history of achievement-related struggles in school, work, or with their parents while growing up. Children may react to pressure to achieve with compliance or defiance. Tracking the child's response may shed light on issues of hands. Knowing the parent's core sensitivity (see Chapter 9) can shed light on what pressure to achieve means to the parent and thus further inform treatment.

PRESSURE TO BE SELF-SUFFICIENT

Learning to rely on oneself is an important skill. But supporting self-reliance by following a child's lead is very different from pressuring children not to need a parent. You may see parents pressure a child to be self-sufficient on either the bottom or the top of the Circle.

When children are on the bottom of the Circle, pressuring them to be self-sufficient generally takes the form of pressuring them to manage their own feelings: "Big girls don't cry." Sometimes this pressure takes the form of neglecting or rejecting the child's needs ("I am not going to help you; you can do it yourself") or pushing the child to take on tasks that are above her developmental level ("You have to learn it sometime, so you might as well learn it now").

On the top of the Circle a parent may be pressuring the child to be self-sufficient as a way of maintaining the esteem that comes with having a "highly competent" child or protecting herself from being controlled by the child's need for her, a product of the parent's own core sensitivity (see Chapter 9).

It's important to discern when the parent's attachment history and the child's defensive strategies are driving the pressure to be self-sufficient and when expedience may be the prime mover: Sometimes parents want to be able to focus on other relationships or tasks (e.g., a new baby or a new boyfriend, schoolwork), and sometimes they are so overburdened by their lives that they need the child to be self-sufficient just to manage daily demands.

Believing that you are sufficient unto yourself is a hazardous delusion. Children know they are not self-sufficient, and feeling that they should be can lead to feeling inadequate and less able to rely on themselves or anyone else. Furthermore, acting self-sufficient rather than seeking help and advice from a competent adult can, especially in the teenage years, lead to disastrous consequences.

PRESSURE TO STAY INVOLVED WITH ME

On the top of the Circle, parents' pressure to stay central often comes in the form of inserting themselves into their children's play when what all that is needed is for the parent to watch over the child. Sometimes parents act this way because they feel unimportant or even abandoned if their child plays alone. Jamar demonstrated this when he offered his son, Dwayne, his pacifier while he was playing with his back to him. Dad later admitted that he "felt alone" (see Chapter 4). Some parents like Jamar try to reel their children back in to them on the top of the Circle to satisfy their longing for closeness without the discomfort of intimacy on the bottom of the Circle. The parent's intention to maintain connection with his child in this manner is often self-defeating, and the result is that the child pushes the parent away.

A parent's pressure for the child to stay involved on the bottom of the Circle can lead to an ambivalent attachment characterized by the parent needing the child to need her. The child may meet that need by acting like he wants to be close or needs comfort even when that child is ready to explore.

The parent's intention in pressuring the child to stay involved is to have a close relationship, yet such pressure not only functions to create an entangled but emotionally distant relationship but also can thwart the child's attempt to develop both a sense of autonomy and intimate connection.

PRESSURE TOWARD THE TOP OR BOTTOM OF THE CIRCLE

Sometimes parents pressure their child to be on one part of the Circle rather than the other because they are uncomfortable on one part of the Circle and want to steer their children away from needs expressed there. When parents do this effectively, they tell you where they hear shark music. A consistent pattern of steering a child away from either top or bottom is described as having only one hand on the Circle. This can be viewed as a hands moment, but it is associated with insecurity whereas removing both hands (see "Mean, Weak, or Gone") is associated with disorganization.

Parents who steer their child toward the top of the Circle may be uncomfortable with emotional issues, so they try to get the child into exploration and play. This promotes an avoidant attachment. Parents who steer their child toward the bottom of the Circle may be uncomfortable with separation, and this promotes ambivalent attachment.

Take Charge: Bigger, Stronger, Wiser, and Kind versus Mean, Weak, or Gone

Although we separate following from taking charge, taking charge is also taking the lead in organizing the child's experience by following the child's need. For instance, during a reunion, does the parent or the child take the responsibility to organize the relationship?

Children need a clear sense that someone is in charge because it is too scary to feel like they are on their own. To assess a caregiver's ability to take charge, you need to be able to observe the parent in a situation that requires him to assert his authority. Can the parent set necessary boundaries during a play episode where the child is pushing the limits?

What if no limit-setting opportunity arises? It probably will if the child doubts the parent's ability to take charge, because the child will try to evoke the parent's authority by acting out. It's when the child is confident in the caregiver's ability to be bigger, stronger, wiser, and kind that you may get no opportunity to confirm the parent's ability. And it does need to be confirmed, because a child's not testing the limits does not rule out a problem. For instance, children who are controlling caregiving overcomply, making it unnecessary for a parent to set limits. Children who control by intimidating a frightened parent may appear not to need the parent's expression of hierarchy (Cassidy & Marvin, 1992).

As noted earlier, the reading and cleanup episodes that we added to the Strange Situation typically provide "take charge" moments in case no opportunity arises in the SSP, but note that some children are very obedient during cleanup, which can either be the fearful compliance of a disorganized caregiving child or the cooperation of a securely attached child. Cooperative children who are securely attached often feel there is room for negotiation, not as peers but as one might negotiate with a boss. Overcompliance in disorganized children has a driven or compulsive feel, rather than that of a negotiated settlement.

In treatment we help parents determine whether a specific interaction is a "follow moment" or a "take charge" moment. In the assessment, it is important to note not only whether the parent is taking charge, but also whether the parent is taking charge in an appropriate manner—bigger, stronger, wiser, and kind—and at an appropriate time. It is important to remember that taking charge is not restricted to setting limits. Picking up a distressed child and offering comfort is as much taking charge as telling a child no. In fact, these two types of take-charge situations go hand in hand. It is hard for a child to feel protected and comforted by someone who has no authority over her, and having experience of her caretaker as somebody who provides comfort and protection makes it easier for a child to accept limits.

Bigger, Stronger, Wiser, and Kind
CONFIDENT PRESENCE/EXPECTATION; SCAFFOLDING/CO-ORGANIZING

When a parent is clear that he is in charge and confident that when he asserts his authority his child will respond positively, we say that the parent has a confident presence and expectation. Although it is not always possible, taking charge is most productive as a teaching moment when it includes scaffolding and co-organizing with the child. The more confident the parent is in his ability to take charge, the more likely he will employ scaffolding/co-organizing. For example, at the separation in the SSP, a father walked over to his son, who was playing on the floor, and said, "I need to go, but I'll be right back." The child protested, and the father knelt down and said, "I know you don't want me to go, but you'll be all right." His confidence that he would be able to leave allowed him to wait calmly for the child to respond rather than anxiously moving toward the door. The child, reassured by Dad's calm demeanor, said, "Will you play cars when you come back?" The father smiled and said, "Yes, you set them up so they're ready." Dad then walked quietly to the door, turned, and said, "You be all right?" He paused until his son nodded. Scaffolding the separation by offering confidence, connection, and reassurance (giving his son just enough help so he could manage by himself) and co-organizing by accepting his son's request to "play cars" and asking his son if he would be all right did not make the child happy to see his father leave, but it made it possible for him to manage the separation without undue stress.

Parents' confident presence/expectation can often be seen in their demeanor and confirmed by their child's response. Caregivers who feel confident in their authority as parents tend to be relaxed and efficient at taking charge. Children who feel confident in their parents' authority don't need to question it by being impossible but can negotiate in an age-appropriate manner. Even though the child might protest when a parent takes charge with an attitude of no-nonsense tenderness, the child will usually settle in to the limits and relax.

Having a parent who is comfortable and confident in taking charge
is a tremendous gift to a child, giving the child the confidence

*to go out and explore and confidence that the parent
can make the child safe and offer comfort when needed.*

Mean, Weak, or Gone

Sometimes parents are neither taking charge nor following their child but rather abdicating their authority and executive role—taking their hands off the Circle. Essentially, the child has been orphaned, with no adoptive parent in sight. This is associated with disorganized attachment. In such cases the child may act out to pressure the parent to at least be bigger and stronger, if not wiser, and kind. Or the child may take care of the parent, but either way the issue of taking charge dominates parent–child interactions. Once parents have instilled confidence in children regarding their ability and willingness to exert their authority appropriately, taking charge becomes a very small part of parenting. We often tell parents that taking charge is only 10% of parenting, but it is the first 10% because it is the foundation of the parent–child relationship. We also say that if that initial 10% is missing, the remaining 90% will feel as if it's all about maintaining control of a difficult or "impossible" child. This, of course, is where focusing on the child's problematic behavior is actually missing the deeper issue of the child's need to experience the safety that comes with a caregiver who can remain in charge in a kind yet firm way.

It is important to assess the nature of the abdication as well as what it means to the parent. This allows the therapist to meet the parent where the parent is and address the issue in a manner that is meaningful to the parent. Understanding the heart of the parent's struggle also supports the therapist's empathy. Even when a parent is inadequate and the therapist must act in the best interests of the child, it's essential to maintain empathy for the parent and to hold on to a sense of the parent's positive intentionality. Otherwise therapeutic efforts become punitive rather than helpful.

*AGGRESSION OR THREAT OF AGGRESSION[1]

Parents can use aggression and/or the threat of aggression to assert their authority over their children, but this is fear-based authority and is associated with disorganized attachment. The COS protocol describes this form of disorganizing caregiving with the word "mean."

---

[1] An asterisk indicates that this behavior is a possible marker for disorganization.

Assessing aggression or threat of aggression can be difficult because it is sometimes very subtle, especially in front of the therapist. Aggression can be as overt as physical violence but also as subtle as baring of teeth. For example, when parents pretend to be monsters and chase their children about, it can be good-natured fun or thinly veiled aggression. Even when parents think they are being playful, aggression is problematic when a child's attachment system is activated and she is seeking care and comfort; context is important. It's often in the child's response to such play that we are able to differentiate between the two. Threats that the parent has no intention to follow through on can nonetheless frighten children. Conversely, threats that are never spoken can also be frightening to children.

*ABANDONMENT OR THREAT OF ABANDONMENT

Attachment and abandonment are flip sides of the same coin. As discussed in Chapter 9, our innate need for attachment is matched with an innate fear of being abandoned. Both the threat of abandonment and actual abandonment as a means of taking charge are destructive to children and are associated with disorganized attachment. It is not uncommon to hear parents try to elicit their children's cooperation with statements such as "If you don't get in the car, I'm going to leave without you." It is less common, though sadly not unheard of, for parents to actually drive away.

Repeated experiences of the caregiver as having abandoned or being about to abandon the child are considered genuinely traumatic at the level that they can lead to disorganization.

Themes of abandonment may come up in play between the parent and child. At some level, hide and seek or peek-a-boo could be seen as abandonment, but when the child's exploratory system is activated, these are games of mastery. Children's response often offers a clue to whether something is a play theme or a threat. As with issues of aggression, children are most vulnerable to veiled threats of abandonment when their attachment system is activated.

*HELPLESS/FEARFUL

When parents feel helpless or frightened in the face of their children, they are not able to be either a secure base or a safe haven. Parents need not be fearless and all-powerful to provide security for their children, but they must feel bigger, stronger, wiser, and kind "enough." It is often the child's response to the parent that clarifies whether the parent has reached the standard of "good enough."

You may see helpless or fearful behavior—what COS describes as "weak"—at any point in the Strange Situation. Separations sometimes give an indication of a parent feeling helpless/fearful because they demand that the parent act in a way that the child will not like. Sometimes parents show their struggle during separation by abruptly leaving the room and other times by having long drawn-out partings. Either of these strategies can indicate that the parent feels helpless and/or fearful. Sometimes the parent will be so fearful of the child becoming angry that she tiptoes around the child's needs and appears overly accommodating. This can become especially evident in the cleanup.

Fear can also take the form of fearful compliance, which is a form of abdication at take-charge moments and also a form of misattunement during follow moments. In this category the child is given the lead because the parent is fearful of the child's response to the parent asserting authority. The parent may be afraid that the child will become aggressive or withdraw and withhold affection.

It is often the parent's demeanor that gives the first hint that the parent is following with fearful compliance. The parent may appear timid and halting in interactions with the child, requests may be stated as questions, and the parent may quickly withdraw suggestions that don't meet with the child's approval. The child may appear demanding or punitive, but sometimes the child simply ignores the parent. A clear example of this was seen with a 4-year-old boy who responded to a parent's timid suggestion by turning and looking at his mother with disdain and loudly saying, "That's stupid." Mom's response was to apologize. Of course, fearful compliance can be much more subtle and hard to detect.

Following in this manner deprives children of the safety and security needed to become competent in the role of taking the lead, developing their imagination, and following their creativity. The parent's fearful compliance may make the child feel very powerful but leave the child without a sense of control. It is much like an untrained person flying a 747 jetliner. Although the person would have a great deal of power, the lack of control would make the experience terrifying.

Following with fearful compliance also makes it very difficult for the child to feel confident in the parent's ability to meet his needs on the bottom of the Circle. Children in this type of relationship often look like they're on the top of the Circle, but there is an undertone of feeling afraid, on the verge of losing control, with no one to help them.

*DISSOCIATION

Dissociation is a much more profound form of being absent than distraction or daydreaming (discussed above). It is not uncommon to see dissociation in nonclinical populations, but it is experienced infrequently and in a very mild form. Arriving home from your daily commute and not remembering getting on or off the highway is an example of dissociation. Especially when there is a history of trauma, dissociation can be persistent and severe enough to cause problems in the parent–child relationship.

A parent's face becoming flat and expressionless, with eyes dull and unfocused, for a significant amount of time is cause for further investigation. This is an experience that young children don't have the words to report and parents are often very hesitant to report, so it can easily be overlooked. When prevalent within the relationship, dissociation is seen to be a mixture of "weak" and "gone" on the part of the parent.

*NEGLECT

Children experience a dramatic form of "gone" with caregivers who routinely neglect their responsibilities as parents, an experience that is very frightening to children. This is different from the parent specifically neglecting the child's attachment needs (discussed earlier). We are talking about the hands not being on the Circle to meet any needs.

The SSP does not necessarily bring parental neglect to the forefront, and so it is often necessary to make inferences based on the child's behavior and appearance as well as any history that is available.

Avoidant children try not to activate their parents' caregiving system because they have found that they get less of what they need then. However, they believe that in severe enough situations they can go to the parent. Children who have been disorganized by their parent's neglect have a limited sense of their parent as a resource. Children who have been seriously neglected show signs of fear and will struggle to maintain emotional congruence.

*CONFLICT AVOIDANCE

Conflict can be uncomfortable for everyone. All of us have had times when we have gone out of our way to avoid high-conflict situations. On the other hand, conflict is an inherent part of parenting. Parents who find conflict so uncomfortable that they abdicate their authority as parents are showing themselves to be "weak" in relationship to the child, creating a disorganized attachment. Setting limits, by its nature, is conflictual. If caregivers chronically avoid setting limits, it is quite likely that, in the time span of the Strange Situation, interactions will arise that require the parent either to deal with the conflict or to avoid it. However, it is possible that by the time children are 3 years old they can display a disorganized controlling caregiving attachment. In these cases, the child protects the parent from conflict by being overly compliant.

*ROLE DISTORTION (PEER TO PEER)

Originally we thought the only role problems involved role reversal, but over time we began to realize that there are sometimes distortions in the parent's and child's roles that are not role reversal.

*Let's Be Little Together. Sometimes the parent is not inviting the child to take over the parental role and at the same time is not taking on the parental role himself. The parent may seek to have a relationship in which both people can be children. In these dyads, the parent joins with the child by being silly and playful even when the situation calls on the parent to set limits. The parent tends not to take responsibility for the child's behavior, safety, and well-being. At times in the Strange Situation that require the parent to take charge, the parent may refuse or simply act out childlike incompetence.

The parent's insisting on being a child in the relationship leaves the child without a parent. This is another form of "weak" and as such is very frightening for the child and leads to disorganized attachment.

*Be an Adult with Me. Sometimes in peer-to-peer role distortion, the parent is inviting or pressuring the child to be an adult, which is yet another experience of being "gone." This is still not role reversal because the parent is also playing an adult role in the relationship. This tends to come in two variations as we will discuss below.

1. *Be my companion.* Parents may abdicate their role as the caregiver while maintaining a role as an adult. This pressures the child to come join the parent in the adult world. Sometimes what the adult pushes for is the child to be a companion or a confidant. In the Strange Situation this

becomes apparent because the caregiver doesn't set limits, provide nurturing or comfort, or support the child's play. If the child is overly compliant, at first glance the relationship may not seem troubled. But watching how parent and child negotiate the reunions makes it more apparent that their strategy is not driven by the child's needs.

Being a companion to a parent is very disorganizing for the child because, even though the parent maintains his position as an adult in the family, the child has no parent. If the child accepts the proposition, she becomes controlling caregiving.

One father talked about his father recruiting him to be a comrade in the fight against his mother. By accepting the role, he gained time and access to his father but essentially lost both parents. His father became a peer, and his mother became the enemy. This kind of triangulation is not uncommon but is very destructive.

2. *Don't need me.* Parents may promote peer-to-peer role distortion because they are uncomfortable with the child needing them. They are not looking for a partner or comrade, but rather pressure the child to be self-sufficient on both the top and the bottom of the Circle. Whether the situation requires the parent to follow the child or to take charge, the parent's hands are off the Circle, thus he is often being experienced as "gone" or a combination of "gone" and "mean." It is common for the parent to be very dismissing and/or devaluing of the child's needs. For example, on reunion during the SSP, a mother walked in and sat across the room from her daughter. Her daughter brought a toy over to her mother, and her mother frowned and said, "You play with it." The child was crestfallen but turned to go. The mother snapped, "Don't act like such a baby."

As with a peer-to-peer relationship of being a companion, this leads to disorganization. However, when the parent abdicates her role and makes it clear that she does not need the child and she does not want the child to need her, the child feels profoundly abandoned.

*ROLE REVERSAL

In some relationships the parent and child have traded roles. The parent may present as helpless or fearful, but there is also an element of pressuring the child to take charge. The parent may turn to the child when decisions are required and leave some of the adult social obligations, such as introductions in the Strange Situation, to the child. The parent may act childlike or may simply be passive. In either case, the parent is experienced as "weak."

By the time the child has reached the third birthday, signs of a disorganized controlling behavior—either caregiving or punitive or switching back and forth—are apparent. Although the intervention will focus on the hands either way, the distinction between caregiving and punitive can play a role in how the interventions are presented to the parent.

*Parent controlled by . . .

1. **Child's caregiving.* Controlling caregiving children act as caregivers to cope with the parent who is either frightening (mean) or frightened (weak). The child takes on the function of managing the parent's affect as well as physical needs. It is difficult to differentiate between controlling caregiving and appropriate cooperation and concern on the part of the child. With appropriate cooperation the child will, at times, negotiate for himself or protest the parent's decisions and the parent will respond with a confident presence.

Controlling caregiving is too bright and cute to be genuine. Smiles turn on and off abruptly rather than building to a peak and then diminishing in a smooth manner. Smiles and cuteness are focused on the parent, as is the play. The child may take the leadership in the play by bringing toys to the parent and working to keep the parent engaged and happy. Sometimes the child takes on other parental functions like instructing the parent or negotiating with the stranger.

2. **Child's aggression.* Controlling punitive behavior is much easier to spot than controlling caregiving. The child may be aggressive, coercive, demanding, and/or demeaning toward the parent. In one classic example, the child was demanding and directive of her mother, who moved from the parent chair to the floor to do as she was told with the toys. Within a minute the child sat in the parent's chair and directed the parent in the play. The role reversal was unmistakable. It is important to remember that role reversal does not mean the child takes the role of a bigger, stronger, wiser, and kind parent but rather an internally frightened and externally either mean or weak parent.

*SHIFTING/COMPETING STRATEGIES

In some dyads, you will see examples of more than one type of attachment during the Strange Situation. For example, in one reunion the child may display an ambivalent attachment and in the next reunion an avoidant attachment. Sometimes within the same reunion you may see two competing or shifting strategies. Such apparent contradictions do not necessarily indicate an error in observation but should raise a relational question: What is going on in this dyad's relationship that would make a child cast about for different strategies to get her needs met? Usually, a child's shifting strategies mirror the parent's shifting or competing caregiving strategies. In such cases the child hasn't been able to develop a coherent strategy to maintain proximity and get support for exploration. Perhaps the parent seems to be uncomfortable with closeness at some times and uncomfortable with separation at others, and the child can't predict when either type of discomfort will be activated. This is very frightening for a child and leads to the child becoming disorganized, so it is important for practitioners to look for the pattern—even when the pattern is chaotic.

Seeing versus Guessing Revisited

Space constraints demand that we limit descriptions of what you might observe during an interactional assessment, whether the setting is the Strange Situation or something less (or more) formal. Again, we cannot overemphasize the importance of looking for observable patterns rather than yielding to the mind's eagerness to use association, projections, transference, and bias associated with the view of colleagues to draw conclusions. Defining a dyad's attachment, identifying defensive strategies, and choosing a linchpin struggle as a treatment target all revolve around differential diagnosis, discussed in detail in the next chapter.

8

The Interactional Assessment

Differential Diagnosis and Identification of the Linchpin Struggle

"Would you tell me, please, which way I ought to go from here?"
"That depends a good deal on where you want to get to," said the Cat.
"I don't much care where—" said Alice.
"Then it doesn't matter which way you go," said the Cat.
—LEWIS CARROLL, *ALICE'S ADVENTURES IN WONDERLAND*

In the COS interactional assessment, Tanya fidgeted and looked uncomfortable when her son toddled off to play, but when Nick, seemingly trying to meet his mother's need for him to need her, came back seeking comfort, she acted exasperated. Ultimately this push–pull significantly restricted the 2-year-old's exploration. However, because he was able to maintain some distance and played independently in the last 20 seconds of the reunion episode, Nick was scored "secure with some ambivalence" rather than ambivalent.

Although it is somewhat unusual, our conclusions from the COS interactional assessment can be at odds with the scoring of the Strange Situation. For our treatment purposes, regardless of Nick's secure scoring, our COS assessment focused on this dyad's ambivalent process. Even within security, there can be significant problems that need to be addressed. At the time Tanya came to our clinic Nick was described as "fussy" and "always clinging." In his child care setting he was seen to be "excessively needy."

COS recognizes that security and insecurity fall along a continuum of behavior. The goal of our assessment is to support positive change rather than establish an attachment classification for research purposes. For this reason our task is to make an informed decision based on the calibration of strengths and struggles inherent within the Strange Situation coding without being focused on the demarcations built into that system. As with Tanya and Nick, it is possible to be scored "secure" and still have genuine struggles. Knowing where on the Circle difficulties exist offers a way to ascertain where the linchpin struggle is to be found. For this reason the skills needed to code Strange Situations are helpful but not sufficient for the COS assessment and treatment planning. In addition, as the clinician continues to interact with the family and the therapeutic relationship evolves, new information will likely become available that can modify treatment goals.

DRAWING CONCLUSIONS FROM THE CIRCLE OF SECURITY ASSESSMENT

As noted in Chapter 7, we have attempted to define key issues and suggest questions that need to be raised about what you see in a dyad's behavioral dance, but the information there and in this chapter is offered only as a way to clarify the fundamentals of the COS diagnostic system. It is crucial to exercise caution in drawing any conclusions from the interactional assessment, and conclusions must be based on adequate training and supervision.

The COS diagnostic system is based on the implied correlation between parent and child behavior, one that always includes a discernible constellation of interaction. For example, if a parent is following a child's play with a noticeable degree of fearful compliance that includes signs of role reversal, the observer can begin to assume that this particular dyad is behaving in a manner consistent with disorganized attachment. For the purpose of treatment, it would be helpful to begin zeroing in on a linchpin struggle based on hands, one in which the parent is asking the child to be in charge at huge cost to the child.

Conversely, an interactional dance can be "good enough" with very little need for change. Take, for example, a parent who follows her child while remaining in charge with a relatively confident presence all the way around the Circle, except that during times of emotional distress there is a modest push in the direction of keeping the child focused on play. While definitely secure and clearly "getting the job done" (Susan Woodhouse, personal communication, 2012), this mother might still be helped by having access to her nervousness when it comes to offering full support on the bottom of the Circle. As long as there is no implication of danger or pathology, knowing that her daughter would "welcome a bit more welcoming in" might be of real benefit to each of them.

In making a differential diagnosis of any dyad, when a mismatch is observed between the parent's and child's attachment/caregiving behavior, it is important to ascertain whether the cause may be associated with any of the following:

1. An organic issue such as ADHD or autism in the child.
2. A life event such as separation due to the parent's military deployment, recent illness, or divorce.
3. The child having recently been placed in protective foster care or adopted.
4. The child's current or recurring illness.
5. Additional confounding stressors that can be discovered either during the intake or during the course of treatment.

The COS Decision Tree

COS has developed a decision tree that helps in selecting the linchpin treatment focus. The goal is to identify the strengths and struggles for the top of the Circle, the bottom of the Circle, and the hands on the Circle (caregiving behaviors). Certain types of information tend to be revealed in particular episodes of the COS interactional assessment. These are listed in Box 8.1. While observers should be alert to information that comes out of all the episodes, these clues may be a good place to start or may help observers ferret out as much information as possible during second, third, and subsequent reviews of the video. The videos of each episode for a specific dyad are illustrated in the case example starting on page 170, which goes through the differential diagnosis process.

A tool that many clinicians find useful is the Circle of Security Assessment and Treatment Plan Organizer, shown in Form 8.1 on pages 182–184. After watching the video of the interactional assessment (probably several times), you should be able to fill out the information in item 1 and draw preliminary conclusions for items 6 and 7, as shown in Figure 8.1 (pages 180–181), a partially filled-in sample form, with answers highlighted by the shading in the form. The rest of the Treatment Plan Organizer is filled out during the state of mind assessment and treatment planning described in Chapters 9 and 10, when the information for items 6 and 7 is finalized.

This is the sequence that we follow in identifying the dyad's linchpin struggle during the SSP:

1. We look first for whether the parent is functioning as the hands on the Circle. If the parent is mean, weak, or gone, the child will be feeling unsafe, and struggles on the top or bottom of the Circle cannot be resolved adequately until a safe haven and secure base are established. In these cases, we have no choice but to focus on the "hands" as the linchpin struggle.

2. If the parent provides basic hands, then the next level of priority is the bottom of the Circle. The question "Can the child come to the parent and receive comfort?" is often the best place to start, and the answer is most often found in the dyad's interaction after the reunions. If the answer is no, then the linchpin struggle will be on the bottom of the Circle and the broad treatment goal will be to help the dyad so that the child can make use of the parent as a safe haven. Sometimes parents are intrusive on the top of the Circle in an attempt to experience closeness without the vulnerability of the bottom of the Circle. It is tempting to focus on the top of the Circle, but the problem is better resolved by first establishing the intimacy that comes from engaging on the bottom of the Circle, which allows the parent to support exploration.

3. If the child can use the parent as a safe haven, the last question is "Can the child use the parent as a secure base and explore on the top of the Circle?" With a top-of-the-Circle linchpin the focus is on the parent inhibiting the child's exploration and autonomy. You might see the child seeking and resisting comfort and be tempted to focus on teaching the parent to be more efficient at providing comfort. The child both seeks comfort and is not comforted because the parent both encourages seeking comfort and intensifies the child's distress—if the child calms, he or she will go out to explore and the parent will experience separation. If the underlying issue is that the parent is trying to avoid the separation intrinsic to the child's exploration, then focusing primarily on providing comfort would reinforce the ambivalent attachment.

*How much time is the child focused on the environment
and how much on the relationship with the parent?*

During the SSP a secure child's focus is balanced between the relationship with the parent and exploration of the environment. Avoidant children overfocus on exploring the environment at the expense of relationship, and ambivalent children overfocus on the relationship at the expense of exploring the environment. A bottom-of-the-Circle linchpin means that the treatment will focus on pseudo-autonomy at the expense of relationship (insecure avoidance), and a top-of-the-Circle linchpin means the treatment will focus on pseudo-closeness at the expense of autonomy (insecure ambivalence).

BOX 8.1. GUIDE FOR FINDING VIDEO CLIPS IN THE STRANGE SITUATION

As you watch videos of the COS interactional assessment, it helps to know that each episode tends to bring out certain aspects of the Circle. With the following guidelines in mind, you can often find video clips to use for processing with the parents. Throughout the procedure you may find "struggle with some success moments," which are short video clips in which the parent struggles with shark music and then finds a way to at least partially respond to the child's needs. For instance, the child wants to be close and the parent wants the child to go play with a particular toy. The parent first pressures the child to go play and then eventually sees what the child wants and lets the child come in, even for a moment, and be closer.

Celebration/resolution clips are brief moments of success in the linchpin struggle and are employed at the end of the video review to create a note of celebration for both the linchpin strength and the parent's often nonconscious wisdom and positive intentionality. For instance, if a parent's key issue is not taking charge, finding a moment, however brief, in which the parent does take charge constitutes a good celebration/resolution clip. Sometimes it can be hard to find a clear underutilized strength that is resolved precisely because these strengths are underused. In that case, the celebration/resolution video is simply a clip that shows something in the parent–child relationship that the group can celebrate.

Episodes 1 and 2: Enter and Play

- This episode will often have the best examples of top-of-the-Circle moments, so you may find "struggle with some success" clips.
- Find the rhythm of the child going out to explore and coming back in to touch base with the parent, which we call "Circle moments." It may happen the second they walk into the room. Sometimes the touching base is only a look at the parent to make sure the parent is there. We call them Circle moments (see Chapter 12 for how to use clips) because children already know about the Circle and we want to show parents that the Circle is already a part of their life.
- Some children are anxious in this episode. If so, how does the parent respond? The parent's response can indicate a strength or shark music.
- Is there support for exploration or pressure to achieve, pressure to be self-sufficient, or pressure to remain involved with the parent?

(continued)

BOX 8.1. (*continued*)

- How much does the parent lead versus follow the child in exploration? A positive sign is a balance between the two.
- For the "Name That Need" exercise in week 2 (see Chapter 12), you may find good:
  "Help me" moments.
  "Watch over me" moments.
  "Enjoy with me" moments.
  "Delight in me" moments.

(For definitions, see Chapter 2; see Chapter 12 for how to use these clips.)

Episode 3: Stranger Comes In 1

- How does the child manage the anxiety about a stranger coming into the room? Does the child withdraw, engage the stranger, go play alone, come to the parent, and bring a toy to the parent? Does the child use the parent as a secure base in negotiating a relationship with the stranger?
- How does the parent manage the stranger? Does the parent start to compete with the stranger for the child's attention? Does the parent use play with the child to manage his own feelings of anxiety, thus becoming less available to help the child?
- How can the clinician use video of this episode? It can be used to teach emotion regulation. If you can show the child was anxious, the parent can learn something about how the child self-regulates and how the parent coregulates the child's anxiety. The interaction can indicate a strength or shark music.
- This episode can also be used to teach the parent the importance of helping to organize the child's feelings. Does the parent help organize this moment by introducing herself and then the child to the stranger? Does she provide any structure at all or remain passive and let the stranger or the child initiate?
- For the "Name That Need" exercise in week 2, you may find good:
  "Protect me" moments.
  "Organize my feelings" moments.
  "Comfort me" moments.
  "Support my exploration" moments.

(For definitions, see Chapter 2; see Chapter 12 for how to use these clips.)

Episode 4: Separation 1

- How is the separation negotiated? Does the parent talk with the child about what is going to happen or just walk out without explanation? If the child protests, does the parent address the anxiety directly or distract?
- Does the child show need for the parent at the time of separation? If so, this episode can be used to show the child's need and perhaps as a softening moment.
- Does the child show that he missed the parent? He may show this by calling out for the parent, going to the door through which the parent left, crying,

(*continued*)

BOX 8.1. (*continued*)

looking lost, and so forth. If so, it can be used as a softening clip to show how much the parent is needed or missed.

- What is the child's play like while the parent is gone? The play is often less joyful than when the parent is present and thus can be used in a softening clip to show need and the use of toys for self-soothing and emotion regulation.
- You may find good:

   "Softening" clips: short clips that evoke the parent's caregiving. When the child is alone, he or she may look sad and call out for the parent. A clip such as this shows how important the parent is to the child and might be used to "soften" the parent's experience prior to being shown a more challenging clip. What is softening for one parent may not be softening for another; therefore, knowing the core sensitivity of the parent is important (see Chapter 9).

Episode 5: Reunion 1

- Does the child go to the parent, and is the parent available? If so, this is a "strength" moment; if not, this may be a "shark music" clip.
- With some dyads you may find a little more secure reunion in this episode than the next. If so, it may be used as a "struggle with some success" clip.
- Do the parent and child avoid each other?
- Do they manage to eventually connect? If so, it may be used as a "struggle with some success" clip.
- Do the parent and child resist comfort? If so, it may be a "shark music" clip (video clips that show a particular relationship struggle). Or if eventually the child settles and explores, the behavior may be used as a "struggle with some success" clip.
- Who organizes the reunion? If the child does, then this may be a "shark music" clip. If the parent tries to reclaim leadership, then it may be a "struggle with some success" clip.
- Is the child punitive or caregiving? If so, it may be a "shark music" clip.
- If the parent tries to reclaim the executive role, then it may be a "struggle with some success" clip.
- Are there multiple shifting strategies? If so, it may be a "shark music" clip.
- You may find good:

   "Comfort me" moments.
   "Shark music" clips.

Episode 6: Separation 2

- How do they negotiate separation? This separation tends to be more intense, and the child might protest being left alone more strongly this time. With ambivalent dyads this might be the linchpin struggle, and the separation does not happen. Sometimes parents will do things like acknowledge the child's feelings or softly touch the child to reassure, which might be used to show underutilized strengths.

(*continued*)

BOX 8.1. (*continued*)

- With the child alone you may find the best moments of the child showing a need for the parent for "softening" clips, especially in avoidant dyads. You can also use this to teach the parent about the child's capacity for emotion regulation and limits to that capacity.
- With some very avoidant dyads you may need to contrast play during this episode with play when the parent is there to make the point for a "softening" clip that the child is stressed and misses and needs the parent.
- With ambivalent dyads you may need to use the play to demonstrate both the child's competence in managing without the parent and the child's still needing the parent. Competence by the child does not mean the child does not need the parent.
- Some children manage their anxiety by becoming aggressive during the separation. You can use this to teach how anger can be a way to manage fear and distress (emotion regulation), which can begin to help the parent have a more empathic, less punitive stance toward the child's anger.
- You may find good:
    "Softening" clips.

Episode 7: Stranger Comes In 2

- When the stranger comes in, sometimes the child momentarily mistakes the door opening for the parent coming back and will indicate that she expected the parent by calling out "Mom" or "Dad" or looking disappointed when she learns it is not the parent. With some avoidant dyads this may be the only place where the child overtly reveals her need for the parent, which can be used as a "softening" clip.
- When the stranger is in the room, there may be moments when the child shows that he misses the parent, such as by asking the stranger about the parent.
- Some children who were upset will settle down more with the stranger than with the parent. Some parents will use this and say "See, I told you my child did not really need me; anyone will do." We tend not to use this material.
- You may find good:
    "Softening" clips.

Episode 8: Reunion 2

- Does the child go to the parent, and is the parent available? If so, this is a "strength" moment; if not, this may be a "shark music" clip.
- This episode tends to be the most intense reunion and often used for "shark music" clips with many dyads.
- May be used to contrast longing for the parent in the prior episode with avoidance in this episode for avoidant dyads.
- May be used for ambivalent dyads to explore the parent's need to be needed and his anxiety regarding his child's exploration.

(*continued*)

BOX 8.1. (*continued*)

- Controlling and/or caregiving may be most intense for disorganized dyads, and this behavior can be used to teach the parent that the child needs him and is negotiating this need through these behaviors.
- Some parents tend to be most stressed during this episode and may show frightened or frightening behavior that you may use for "shark music" clips.
- You may find good:
    "Shark music" clips.

Reading

- The reading episode can be used to find competencies not seen in other episodes.
- Is the reading used as a tool to relate? If so, it is a strength.
- Is the process of reading negotiated? If so, it is a strength.
- You can often find mutual enjoyment and delight for "celebration" clips.
- Sometimes the structure of reading brings out the best in the parent and thus also in the child.
- Sometimes the inability of the parent to negotiate the reading with the child shows shark music for parents who struggle with taking charge.
- Sometimes the parent's need for the child to perform comes out most strongly here and can be used as "shark music" clips.
- You may find good:
    "Enjoy with me" moments.
    "Delight in me" moments.
    "Organize my feelings" moments.
    "Shark music" clips.

Cleanup

- Can the parent take charge?
- Is the parent frightened of the child's emotions or behavior (often anger)? This can be a key "shark music" clip.
- Does the parent scare the child into obedience?
- Does the child take care of the parent and organize the cleanup for him or her?
- Track how the style of executive function is negotiated.
- Is the parent bigger, stronger, wiser, and kind?
- Does the parent beg and plead?
- Does the parent intimidate and threaten?
- Does the child have a voice?
- Do they actually negotiate?
- Does the job get done?
- You may find good:
    "Help me" moments.
    "Organize my feelings" moments.
    "Shark music" clips.

The following is an episode-by-episode analysis of a case that illustrates the differential thinking at the core of the COS interactional assessment.

Differential Diagnosis Following the COS Interactional Assessment

As noted earlier, the goal of the COS interactional assessment is to differentiate the behavior observed: Are the hands sufficient as evidenced in this part of the interaction, or are you seeing a secure, an avoidant, an ambivalent, or a disorganized attachment in action? Exactly what is the dyad struggling with around the Circle?

While the description that follows cannot fully substitute for viewing an assessment video, we have attempted to illustrate how observations can be gathered in each episode and how the accumulated information is integrated into a differential diagnosis.

It helps to start with a series of key questions:

1. Does the job of security get done? Remember the interaction does not have to be without struggle, and it does not have to be lovely; it just has to work for this child. When the child is distressed, does he or she go to the caregiver, receive comfort, and then return to exploration? That is, can the child's cup get filled? If yes, then you are observing a secure strategy. If no, then it is an insecure strategy.
2. Who organizes whom? If the parent is organizing the relationship, then the "hands" are on the Circle. If not, then this is more of a disorganized relationship.
3. Are bottom-half needs being cued and met?
4. Are top-half needs being cued and met?

Episodes 1 and 2: Enter and Play

A mother and her 3-year-old son enter the room. The child runs in first, looks around, and looks at Mom, and she smiles. He smiles back, runs to the toy box in the center of the room, and starts to take out toys. Mom follows him to the box, bends over, and says, "That looks like fun." He shows the puzzle box to her, she smiles, and she says, "It's a puzzle box." He tries to take it apart, and when he has some difficulty he looks at her. She smiles and asks, "Can you figure out how to take it apart?" He tries several times while she watches calmly, and finally when he is unsuccessful he selects the doctor kit to play with.

By now Mom has sat down in a chair and is quietly watching him. He takes the doctor kit to her and asks about the blood pressure gauge. She tells him it is for blood pressure and asks whether he can put it on his arm. He takes a minute to figure it out, and when he squeezes the bulb they look at each other and laugh for a moment. She then picks up the thermometer. He says, "What's that?" She hands it to him and says, "It is for taking your temperature."

A rhythm of coming to the mother during exploration is already evident. The child finds something and Mom comments; he explores it more, and if he gets stuck Mom tries to get him to figure it out. If he can't, he selects another toy and engages Mom about the toy.

- *Is there support for exploration?* Yes, Mom smiles as her son makes the decision to go out and explore. She has a positive attitude as he selects the toys he is interested in.

- *Is there "watch over me"?* Yes, Mom watches him as he starts to play with the puzzle box and the doctor kit.

- *Does Mom follow?* Yes, because of all the above.

- *Is there "enjoy with me"?* Yes, the mutual smiling as they engage in the toys.

- *Is there delight?* The smile was not intense enough, it did not linger long enough, and the moment was about the toy and not focused enough on each other to indicate delight.

- *Is there "help me"?* Yes, the little boy asks for help with the puzzle box and blood pressure gauge. When he needs help, Mom either waits, encourages him to figure it out, or tells him what it is. She does not show him how to do something but talks to him about it.
  - *Is this just good scaffolding, or is this pressure of some sort?*
    - *Is she pressuring him to achieve?* Maybe, but if so it seems that when he gave up she would not have liked it, and she did not show that.
    - *Does she want him to be self-sufficient?* Perhaps; all her comments seem to focus on him figuring it out.
    - *Does she pressure him to be involved?* Not really. There's way too much waiting and giving him space.

- *When they were looking at and smiling at each other, the mother was the one to get a toy and end that moment of connection. Does it mean anything?* We don't know yet, but it's always good to notice who begins and ends engagements.

- *Are there potential problems?* We don't know yet. Modest pressure to achieve or to figure it out can be appropriate scaffolding.

- *Does Mom break intense emotional encounters?* Again we don't know; seeing something once does not constitute a pattern.

Episode 3: Stranger Comes In 1

When the stranger enters, the little boy looks up at the stranger, looks at Mom briefly, and then focuses on his play but now with a more muted affect. As Mom and the stranger talk, he plays quietly for about 20 seconds and then takes the puzzle box to Mom and asks her about it. Mom turns and tells him how to take the box apart and then turns and talks more to the stranger. Her son plays at her feet with the puzzle. After a while the stranger tries to interact with the boy, and he modestly responds to her overtures. The stranger disengages and sits back in her chair so as not to interfere with the upcoming separation.

- *Did the child show any anxiety when stranger came in?* Yes, the muted affect and momentary disengagement.

- *Did he use his mother to manage his discomfort?* Yes, but indirectly. He miscued her as if it was a "help me" moment on the top of the Circle when he was seeking to be close to her because he was on the bottom of the Circle with a "protect me" moment.

- *Is this a problem?* We don't know this yet; children and even adults miscue often. The question to be answered is: Does this represent an overarching strategy to hide my experience when I am on the bottom of the Circle? So for now, we hold the question in mind.

Mom responded much the same way this time as in the other episode when he asked for help. She tried to give him information so that he could figure it out. What she does seems like a pattern, but we have to see what function this takes. The differential is scaffolding versus pressure to be self-sufficient.

Episode 4: Separation 1

Mother hears the knock that is her cue to leave, goes over to her son, and says she has to go for a minute and will be right back. He shows her the doctor kit and asks her about the rubber hammer. She says it is for checking reflexes and they can play with it when she gets back. She turns and heads for the door, and as she begins to exit her son appears uncomfortable and asks her if he can go too. She says she knows that he wants her to stay, he will be OK in the room, she will be right back, and he can play until she returns. She goes out and closes the door. He continues to play with the doctor kit but with flat affect and occasionally looking sadly at the door. The stranger tries to play with him but with modest success. He plays quietly for the remainder of the time.

• *Do they negotiate a separation?* Yes, the mother tells her son what is going to happen and tries to reassure him by saying she will be right back. He miscues with a "help me" moment using the doctor's kit. She answers his question and offers mild reassurance about her return. He looks uncomfortable and cues her that he wants to be with her. She acknowledges that he does not want her to go, reassures, tries to encourage his exploration, and leaves.

• *Does he show that his attachment is activated?* Yes, he says he wants to go with her and appears uncomfortable staying, then he shows a flat affect in play and, for the rest of the episode, a pattern of looking at the door through which his mother left.

• *How does he self-regulate when he is without his mother?* He distracts himself with exploration, which is a very common strategy for this situation. Sometimes the way a child tries to self-regulate becomes central to the case. For instance, some children become aggressive as a way to manage their distress. It is very helpful for parents to see this as it shifts their perception from a punitive or frightened stance of "This is an aggressive child" to an empathic stance of "This is a child who is afraid and managing fear with aggression."

Episode 5: Reunion 1

Mother enters and says hi. Her son turns to her, makes eye contact, and looks away. She asks what he is doing. He says, "Playing" as he turns away from her and picks up the rubber hammer. She sits down in the chair and smiles at him. He takes the hammer to her with somber affect, pauses for a few moments, and then places one hand on her leg. They talk about the hammer, and after a while they both smile briefly. After about a minute he goes over to the toy box and finds something else of interest.

The key question on reunion is: Does he or does he not seek proximity with her, use her to calm, and then move into exploration? If so, as here, it's an indication of security. If not, then what miscuing strategy do they use?

- *Is his looking away after initial eye contact a miscue?* Probably not; many children have a quick gaze aversion upon reunion even if they are secure. It is most likely a moment of self-regulation. You may notice that when you meet a friend you make eye contact, turn away, and then reengage.

- *Was taking her the toys a cue or miscue?* This is a more complex question. If toys are used to hide his need for comfort, it is a miscue. If toys are used to engage and receive comfort, then it is not a miscue even though it is less direct than reaching out without a toy. He sought proximity and showed his distress. A key moment was when he touched her, which indicates positive contact. He went from somber to more positive affect while close to her and then went out and explored. It was hard to tell who ended the mutual smile. Using only this reunion, he looks secure but somewhat reserved in his approach.

Episode 6: Separation 2

Mother hears her cue to leave, goes over to her son, and tells him she has to go and talk to the doctor for a minute. He immediately wants her to play with him. She says she must go but will play with him when she returns. She turns and walks toward the door, and as she does so he follows her. She turns to him, bends down, makes eye contact, and says she will be right back and he needs to stay here and play. He reluctantly agrees, and she leaves. He then does what he did in the first separation, which is play with toys with little positive affect for the rest of the separation. At one point he walks over to the door, tries the door knob, calls, "Mom," and when the door does not easily open he goes back to play.

This separation is much like the first one, except that by following her to the door he is protesting more strongly for her to stay. With the increased emotional intensity, the mother did not acknowledge his feelings the way she did in the first separation. Is this an indication that as the intensity of emotion increases she becomes less emotionally responsive? Hold that thought: it's another good question to ask of the second reunion. When the little boy went to the door, he was more clearly showing his distress and his wanting to find Mom.

Episode 7: Stranger Comes In 2

As the stranger begins to open the door, the boy is mildly startled, and before he can see who is entering he calls out "Mommy." Once he sees it is the stranger, he turns away and plays with the toys. The stranger tries to interact and play with him with modest success.

Calling out for Mommy before knowing who is at the door certainly indicates who is on the little boy's mind. His attachment system is activated, and he is waiting for his mother to return. This might be a good video clip to use to show the mother that his attachment was activated during the separation. It also shows that during this episode he is using toys to distract himself while waiting for her. The toys are fulfilling a different function than they do in exploration.

Episode 8: Reunion 2

Mother enters the room and says hi, and her son turns away and plays with the toy. She walks over to him and asks, "How are you doing?" He has his back to her and says something barely audible about the toy. She asks him if he likes the toy. He quietly says, "Yeah." Mother goes to a chair and sits down and watches him play. After about 15 seconds he comes over to her and shows her the toy with a sad expression. She tries to get him interested in the toy. He doesn't respond, and she tries several times, focusing on how interesting the toy is. He is subdued in his response, and then she says, "Oh, you are upset and need a hug." She holds out her arms, and he gets up onto her lap, snuggles in, and looks relieved. After a few moments she points at the toy and he smiles. He then gets off her lap and goes over to the toy box and looks inside.

• *Does he come to her and use her for comfort?* When he had his back to her and focused on the toy, it was clearly a miscue.

After a short time he does come to her, looking modestly unhappy, perhaps sad, and has a toy in hand. Is this a cue or miscue? The answer depends on whether he is using the toy to mask his distress or as a means to approach. His affect says this is a cue.

She focuses on the toy, trying to encourage him to have fun. Is she cuing or miscuing? She miscues him because his nonverbal signals are all about distress and she is trying to pressure him to be on the top of the Circle to explore.

He follows her interest in the toy, but it is clear his heart isn't in it, and she keeps trying to spark his interest. After a while she sees what she is doing is not working, and she shifts to the bottom of the Circle. When she invites him in, he responds by snuggling into her with his body and looks relieved.

After a few moments she points to the toy he has been holding, and he looks at the toy but does not play with it. She encourages him to engage with the toy. A few moments later he initiates getting off her lap to see what else is in the toy box.

• *Did the job get done? Was there any struggle? If so, what kind?* By now the observer should have several good questions that need answers. We prefer to come out of the first viewing of the SSP with good questions rather than answers. Now is the time to dig in and rewatch the video to find answers to the questions. You may need to watch some sections repeatedly and in slow motion to answer the questions. For instance, when the little boy was in his mother's lap in the second reunion, did he initiate getting down, or did she indicate it was time for him to get down? Did she wait until his cup was full, or did she say "Time to get down even if your cup is not quite full"? After reviewing the video in slow motion, it was clear that she was the one that initiated getting down to explore by directing his attention and pointing with her finger outward to a toy just a second before he turned and looked at the toy.

Reading

The reading episode goes well. Mom has her son choose a book, and they sit side by side on the couch. As she reads she also asks questions about the pictures in the book, and they talk about what he sees. They appear relaxed and enjoy the reading. Mom has no trouble organizing this activity in a way that is enjoyable and conversational.

Cleanup

The cleanup starts with the mother telling the boy it is time to clean up the toys, and he resists. He likes the reading and wants to do more. She acknowledges that he doesn't want to stop reading and it is time to pick up the toys and go. She uses a warm and firm tone, and after a little more resistance he starts to join her in placing the toys in the box. Mother tries to make a bit of a game of it, and by the time they end he is doing well.

What Is the Linchpin?

• *The first big question is: Do they get the job done?* Does the child seek her out for comfort, maintain contact until he is calmed enough, and then return to exploration? The answer is yes, but not without some struggle. It looks like this mother employs a more insecure strategy as his distress increases. She pushes him from the bottom of the Circle to the top of the Circle in the face of mounting evidence that he is still distressed and needs more comfort. Even though his persistence suggests that there is sufficient history of him getting some of what he needs, she ends the process before he indicates that his cup is full and that he is ready to explore.

• *Who organizes this relationship, mother or child?* There seems to be no evidence of the mother acting in a frightened or frightening manner. She is not mean, weak, or gone. Mom can take charge as a bigger, stronger, wiser, and kind parent, and, not surprisingly, her son is not controlling. The answer is that Mom is the one who organizes the relationship, and so the hands on the Circle are not the linchpin.

• *Does she support exploration?* They seem to do fairly well here. The only aspect that is potentially a problem is that this mother does pressure the boy to figure things out on his own. This may teach him to not come to her when he is stuck with a problem, and, especially in adolescence, that can be a serious issue.

There are a lot of strengths to acknowledge, but we still have to ask whether her continuing to pressure him to the top of the Circle when he needs help on the bottom of the Circle will make him gravitate toward miscuing and finding ways to hide his bottom-half needs. Does he get enough to keep insisting on a bottom-half response from her even when she hesitates to give him one? Which way will all this go? We don't know, but there is an obvious vulnerability in their security that could be impacted by life events, like another sibling, sickness, accident, entering school, and so forth.

The linchpin is on the bottom of the Circle. The treatment goal is to help the parent manage her own feelings (shark music) so she can welcome the child in and help organize the child's feelings.

Differential diagnosis can be straightforward or rather complex, depending on how obvious the struggles are. There can be contradictions, subtleties, and unanswered questions after repeated viewings of the assessment video. When stuck, it can be helpful to get together with a colleague who has a similar lens through which to observe video and share consultation. At the very least, it is important to admit that there is some question in the evaluation and not pretend that the answer is clear. Maintaining some semblance of humility when diagnosing through video assessment can protect the parents and children we serve from the risk of our potentially inadequate treatment assumptions. In our opinion it is better to keep wondering until we are relatively sure than to force certainty in the face of ongoing and unanswered questions.

*Therapists should serve as the stranger in the SSP at least once
to get an idea of what it is like to be "on the hot seat."*

Common Constellations of Parent–Child Behaviors in the Interactional Assessment

While we caution against guessing while observing the SSP instead of focusing on seeing, it is helpful to know that there are common constellations of parent–child behaviors that manifest during the assessment. The most common form of a hands struggle is the parent who seems afraid of the child, especially if the child is upset or angry. These relationships will usually have a significant amount of role reversal where the child is more in charge than the parent. It is also common for a parent to use intensity (facial gestures and voice) in a way that is experienced as threatening and frightening for the child.

The most common form of a top-half issue is the parent who needs to be needed and is threatened by the child's autonomy. This parent often alternates between being intrusive and unavailable. It is not uncommon for this parent to struggle as well with taking charge and trying to avoid the child's being upset while simultaneously feeling needed because the child is upset.

The most common form of a bottom-half struggle is the parent who becomes anxious when his child is upset and needs comfort, with the parent managing his anxiety by pressuring the child to stop being upset. Many children will have this figured out and will miscue by not showing their distress and need for soothing.

Remember three important caveats:

1. Rely on what you see and not on what you expect to see. When what you see does not fit neatly into one of these constellations, make the best diagnosis you can based on what you have seen, make the best choice of a linchpin struggle that you can arrive àt, and then be prepared to revise as treatment proceeds.

2. Remember that it's the sequence—the child's response to the parent as well as the parent's response to the child—that tells the tale, not an isolated action by the child or parent. For example, the parent's tone and mannerisms in response to the child leading the play as well as the tone and

mannerisms of the child as he or she leads often offer clues to the dyadic dance. If the child is either punitive or overly solicitous, it may suggest that the parent is following with fearful compliance (see Chapter 7) even if the parent's compliance is very subtle. Sometimes a child's bright and cheery demeanor may be compensating for the parent's restrained emotional engagement, which may not be readily apparent to the observer. You can begin to see this in the interactional assessment when you observe an overbright child and a parent with flat affect.

3. Finally, keep in mind that at the end of the assessment you may have several goals, but it is necessary to prioritize the linchpin. Having too many goals confuses the parent and can water down the impact of the intervention. Secondary goals may be incorporated as steps along the path to facilitate the linchpin. For instance, even if the dyad is role reversed and that is your linchpin, the process may shed light on how to support delight in a parent who shows limited positive affect. But if you don't keep a clear focus, it is less likely that you will be effective.

Creating a Story to Use in Treatment

The assessment is used to co-create a story with the parent during treatment. The story for the parent depicted in the differential diagnosis above goes something like this: My child needs me for comfort when upset. When my child needs comfort, there are times when he miscues me by acting like he wants to play, and after a while he cues me for comfort. When I respond to his need for comfort, there comes a point when I try to get him to explore before he is finished and he lets me know his cup is full and he is ready to explore. I do this as a way to manage my shark music about staying with him in his distress until he cues me he is ready to go.

The interactional assessment clarifies the plot—the dyad's defensive strategies around the Circle. The next important piece is to assess what is called the parent's core sensitivity, as described in the next two chapters. The core sensitivity guides us in co-creating the story in such a way that the parent can embrace his or her struggles rather than defending against them. When we misattune to parents' core sensitivity, rather than being on their side in an effort to help their children, we become the sharks they are defending against. When we have identified the parent's core sensitivity (see Chapter 9), we can come back and choose video clips that support a story that will unfold and be explored during treatment. Figure 8.1 is the treatment plan organizer with questions 1 and 6 completed using the data gathered so far.

FIGURE 8.1. Example of a Circle of Security Assessment and Treatment Plan Organizer with questions 1 and 6 completed.

1. **List the strengths and struggles on each part of the Circle.**
   - Hands
     - □ Follow: *Many examples of confident presence and coregulation of emotion.*
     - □ Misattune: *Some pressure to be on top of Circle when child is on bottom. Some pressure to be self-sufficient.*
     - □ Take charge: *Takes charge with confidence and without evoking fear.*
     - □ Abdicate: *No signs of abdicating. Mother organized the relationship.*
     - □ Shifting/competing strategies: *No signs.*

   - Top
     - □ Support for exploration: *Mom smiles as her son makes the decision to go out and explore. She has a positive attitude as he selects the toys he is interested in.*
     - □ Watch over me: *Mom watches him as he starts to play with the puzzle box and the doctor kit.*
     - □ Delight in me: *She seems to enjoy his exploration, but she is limited in expressing delight.*
     - □ Help me: *He asks for help with the puzzle box and blood pressure gauge.*
     - □ Enjoy with me: *The mutual smiling as they engage with the toys.*

   - Bottom
     - □ Welcome my coming to you: *In the first reunion when she smiles and he comes to her and in the second reunion when she holds out her arms and offers a hug.*
     - □ Protect me: *Only example of a "protect me" moment was when stranger came in but Mom did not read her child's anxiety at that moment and he did not directly cue her that he needed protection. So there is no clear example. (This is not unusual in the SSP.)*
     - □ Comfort me: *When he had his back to her and focused on the toy it was a miscue. Mom miscued him when she pressured him to go out to explore before his cup was full. When she held out her arms, he got up onto her lap and calmed, so she can provide comfort.*
     - □ Delight in me: *Closest to delight was the reading, but still limited.*
     - □ Organize my feelings: *When he was standing in front of her looking sad in the second reunion, she took charge and said you need a hug and brought him in, which helped him organize.*

FIGURE 8.1. (*continued*)

- Of the above struggles, which is the "linchpin struggle"? *Comfort me: Mom can provide comfort but overuses distraction to explore and rushes him to finish with comfort before he is ready. A secondary goal would be to help Mom express more delight.*

6. **What do you want this caregiver to learn? (Mini-story for shark music)**

    Create step-by-step learning goals. (You may need to do this twice with some complex dyads where you have two linchpin goals.) [This is the preliminary version without the additional information from the COSI.]

    - Learning Goal One (My child needs me for *X* on the Circle) "Linchpin Need": *My child needs me for comfort when upset.*

    - Learning Goal Two (When child needs *X* s/he miscues by doing *Y*) "Child Linchpin Miscue": *When my child needs comfort, there are times when he miscues me by acting like he wants to play.*

    - Learning Goal Three (When my child needs *X*, I miscue by doing *Z*) "Parental Linchpin Diversion": *When he needs comfort, I encourage his exploration. When I respond to his need for comfort, there comes a point when I try to get him to explore before he lets me know his cup is full and he is ready to explore.*

    - Learning Goal Four (I do *Z* as a way of managing my [name affect if possible]) "Shark Music": *I encourage exploration when he needs comfort as a way to manage my shark music. For now we don't know the nature of the shark music. We will need to look to the COSI for more detail.*

    - Learning Goal Five (I have the capacity to respond to need *X* and manage my shark music as exemplified by . . .) "Underused Linchpin Capacity": *When my child is upset and comes to me (reunion 2) I offer to pick him up and comfort him.*

7. **Choosing Video Clips** [This cannot be done without access to the video, so this part of the treatment plan will not be filled out here. The second reunion is the linchpin.]

Circle of Security Assessment and Treatment Plan Organizer

1. **List the strengths and struggles on each part of the Circle.**
   - Hands
     - ☐ Follow: _____
     - ☐ Misattune: _____
     - ☐ Take charge: _____
     - ☐ Abdicate: _____
     - ☐ Shifting/competing strategies: _____

   - Top
     - ☐ Support for exploration: _____
     - ☐ Watch over me: _____
     - ☐ Delight in me: _____
     - ☐ Help me: _____
     - ☐ Enjoy with me: _____

   - Bottom
     - ☐ Welcome my coming to you: _____
     - ☐ Protect me: _____
     - ☐ Comfort me: _____
     - ☐ Delight in me: _____
     - ☐ Organize my feelings: _____

   - Of the above struggles, which is the "linchpin struggle"? _____
     _____

2. **What is the sensitivity?** ❑ Esteem ❑ Safety ❑ Separation

   - How does the sensitivity inform an understanding of the linchpin struggle?
     _____
     _____

   - How might the sensitivity inform the presentation of the linchpin struggle?
     _____
     _____

Give examples of how to frame the issues or approach the caregiver regarding the linchpin struggle: _____

_____

_____

Give examples of how **not** to frame or approach the caregiver regarding the linchpin struggle: _____

_____

_____

3. **Rate reflective function.**
   A. Low: evasion and/or generalized statements to questions that ask for reflection
   B. Medium: a number of instances of reflective functioning
   C. High: reflective functioning is clear throughout the interview
   Comments: _____

   _____

4. **Rate empathy on two dimensions.**
   A. Rate perspective taking
      a. Low: lacks and/or evades perspective taking
      b. Medium: a number of instances of perspective taking
      c. High: perspective taking is clear throughout the interview
      Comments: _____

      _____

   B. Rate affective resonance
      a. Low: lacks resonance
      b. Medium: limited resonance with certain affective states
      c. High: capacity for resonance across broad range of affect
      Comments: _____

      _____

5. **Rate capacity to focus on the self.**
   A. Low: avoids or seems unable to focus on self
   B. Medium: limited focus on the self
   C. High: can focus on self when appropriate
   Comments: _____

   _____

6. **What do you want this caregiver to learn? (Mini-story for shark music)**
   Create step-by-step learning goals. (You may need to do this twice with some complex dyads where you have two linchpin goals.)

- Learning Goal One (My child needs me for *X* on the Circle) "Linchpin Need":

  _____

  _____

- Learning Goal Two (When child needs *X* s/he miscues by doing *Y*) "Child Linchpin Miscue": _____

  _____

- Learning Goal Three (When my child needs *X*, I miscue by doing *Z*) "Parental Linchpin Diversion": _____

  _____

- Learning Goal Four (I do *Z* as a way of managing my [name affect if possible]) "Shark Music": _____

  _____

- Learning Goal Five (I have the capacity to respond to need *X* and manage my shark music as exemplified by . . .) "Underused Linchpin Capacity":

  _____

  _____

7. **Choosing Video Clips (Put the in and out frame numbers).**

   Phase I

   - Softening/Caregiver activation (Phase I—Clip 1): _____

     _____

   - Underutilized capacity with Success (Phase I—Clip 2): _____

     _____

   - Linchpin/Shark Music minor (Phase I—Clip 3): _____

     _____

   - Celebration/Resolution moments (Phase I—Clip 4): _____

     _____

   Phase II

   - Softening/Caregiver activation (Phase II—Clip 1): _____

     _____

   - Linchpin/Shark Music major (Phase II—Clip 2): _____

     _____

   - Underutilized capacity with Success (Phase II—Clip 2): _____

     _____

   - Celebration/Resolution moments (Phase II—Clip 4): _____

     _____

9

Understanding State of Mind and Defensive Processes through Core Sensitivities

> Don't ever take a fence down until you know the reason it was put up.
>
> —G. K. Chesterton

When working with a parent, don't ever take down a fence, period. If a long-standing defense is to be relinquished, it is the caregivers' job to take down that fence, not ours to do it for them. Find a way to empathize with the pain that led to putting up the fence in the first place. Simply honor that pain and the wall that was built to block it. Help parents create a choice where there was none by seeing what is happening now and how their thoughts and feelings about the present are colored by what has happened throughout their life. Trust that, for the sake of their child, they will choose to respond in a new way, rather than continue protecting themselves in ways that are more about walls than relationship.

The COS interactional assessment video might show a mother averting her gaze when her toddler whimpers. We might see a father interrupting his young daughter's play to ask her to come give him a hug but then, when his daughter does need him for comfort, mildly scolding her for being a "daddy's girl" while she sits on his lap. These interactions around the Circle could help us identify a linchpin struggle and point to a need for the mother to offer comfort more frequently when cued by her son or for the father to hold back and let his daughter explore. But for the therapist to target these behaviors directly and ask the parents to simply shift to a new way of caregiving would be to ask them to knock down the fences that have been protecting them for years.

Advising the dismissing mother that hugging her 2-year-old son more often will nurture an intimate bond and thereby resolve the child's angry behavior might make logical sense. But it will fall on deaf ears if the mother hears it as asking her to give up a defense that has been shielding her from the danger that shark music heralds. As is true for many parents before intervention, the mother is not consciously trying to avoid a perceived danger. She feels uneasy and may react even more viscerally, interpreting the advice as flagrant insensitivity to an emotional state that she cannot articulate but definitely abhors. In other words, in an attempt to be helpful the therapist could accidentally turn his intervention into an additional experience of shark music for this mother.

Eliciting change in attachment-related caregiving behaviors requires us to help parents discover that their fences were erected to protect them from real and genuinely painful events in the past, many of which are no longer relevant to current life. First, however, it requires us to create a holding environment for the client. This means not only conveying interest in the parent's explicit concerns, as noted at the beginning of Chapter 7, but also offering a sense of safety for the parent's implicit, underlying fears.

Throughout this chapter we will be talking about nonconscious and unresolved fears in attachment relationships that seem to be shared by most of us. As children, it is not uncommon to become sensitized to particular struggles our caregivers had surrounding three central themes: separation, esteem, and safety. If, as we are building our view of the relational world, we experience Being-Without for risking autonomy (separation) or falling short of perfection (esteem) or expressing a need for boundaries with the parent (safety), we may begin to struggle precisely where we experienced a lack of Being-With. In our work we describe these struggles as "core sensitivities": separation sensitivity, esteem sensitivity, and safety sensitivity.

The mother who looks away from her fussy child might have felt the sting of rejection from her own mother whenever she showed a need for comfort. Today she carries into her own parenting procedural memories of having kept her mother nearby by stifling needs for soothing and showing how she could perform in a way that activated her mother's praise. Or maybe she has nonconscious memories of the grandfather who raised her, a domineering man whose imposition of an ever-shifting set of inviolable rules kept her off balance, on guard, and feeling both controlled and smothered. Now her young son's "demands" set off alarms that she'll be engulfed, and so she turns away from his need for her.

As to the father who seems uncomfortable both when his daughter goes off on her own and when she needs the comfort he asked her to seek, perhaps his mother kept a tight rein on him when he was young and inadvertently convinced him that people who choose to navigate their world, take charge, or act on their own behalf will be abandoned. Now he hears shark music when his daughter seeks to build self-reliance. Suddenly he feels like the helpless child his mother wanted him to be when he needs to take charge and be a safe haven for his daughter.

In COS parlance, the mother's behavior described above would have two options, either esteem sensitivity or safety sensitivity. The father's behavior just described is consistent with separation sensitivity. These are the three core sensitivities that can develop, like scar tissue, as a result of unmet childhood needs around the Circle.

The core sensitivities exist to some degree in everyone and often manifest in familiar personality traits. The reasons for the developing core sensitivities are familiar experiences to all of us. We are all sensitive to the experience of having our self-esteem honored adequately and at times struggle with our self-worth when we fail at a goal. We all are sensitive to abandonment, and even the threat of it can make us anxious. We are all sensitive to experiencing feelings of intrusion when someone we are close to pushes into our personal space even when we are sending signals to back off. The core sensitivities are about what happens when these everyday struggles become the norm and become woven into the core of implicit relational knowing.

Perhaps you have encountered esteem-sensitive individuals, who emphasize performance and perfection in themselves and others but seem to avoid the vulnerability of intimacy. Their procedural experience has taught them that they do not deserve love and intimacy just for who they are but rather for what they can achieve. They are driven largely by others' perceptions, seek affirmation of their worth by forming relationships with people who admire them, and may rage or withdraw in the face of criticism. Separation-sensitive adults are often people pleasers, who are preoccupied with their relationships and devote themselves to others' needs. They harbor such a strong fear of abandonment that they tend to avoid being alone. If they can't earn your company by being solicitous, they will try to get it by being helpless and always in need of support. Safety-sensitive individuals are uncomfortable with closeness because they believe that the cost of closeness is being controlled and losing the self. Where relationships are concerned, they are caught between a rock and a hard place. They may seem self-sufficient in the same way as the esteem-sensitive individual but, in contrast, do not like to be the center of attention. Their motto could be "To thine own self be true."

Understanding how parents manifest certain core sensitivities can prevent negative attribution in therapy. Understanding how parents act out these sensitivities can help clinicians recognize the forces behind shark music and how they shape caregiving behaviors. Both of these benefits can contribute to the creation of a therapeutic holding environment. Facilitating reflection is increasingly recognized as an important aspect of the change process (Fonagy & Bateman, 2007), often more effective than prescriptive advice. Helping parents learn to track their own process by enhancing their powers of reflection is at the heart of the COS methods. But without a safe haven to begin to tolerate the discomfort of shark music, and a secure base from which to explore their own internal process, parents cannot be expected to give up the self-protective strategies they have been relying on since their own childhood. A parent with few caregiving skills who can feel our support as he begins to recognize moments of positive connection with his child may, however, eventually function as a better caregiver than one with no such experience.

A holding environment precedes the capacity for reflection.
A capacity for reflection precedes the ability
to choose to be responsive.

The COS interactional assessment often provides clues about a parent's core sensitivity, but state of mind is revealed much more thoroughly through interviews, such as the enormously effective AAI (George, Kaplan, & Main, 1984). For clinical reasons we use our own interview, the COSI, detailed in Chapter 10. This interview, geared specifically for the COS intervention, explores parents' internal representations and feelings about their caregiving and their relationship with their child.

The goal of this chapter is to explain how core sensitivities enter into the story that has begun to take shape with the interactional assessment. It explores how each of the three sensitivities might manifest in different internal working models and corresponding attachment patterns and illustrates how integrating knowledge of a parent's core sensitivity into the treatment plan enhances outcomes. To understand how ingrained core sensitivities are, it helps to know something about object relations theory.

SPLITTING: THE FOUNDATION OF CORE SENSITIVITIES

In Chapter 4 we introduced the idea of a good face and a bad face, which infants associate with their parents. Within the conceptual world of object relations theory it is understood that infants are continually processing events in the context of three themes: an experience of the all-important caregiving "other," the developing self, and the affect resulting from the interaction between the two. When these interactions are positive, the child forms a positive or "good" sense of other and self, which results in a good feeling state. When these interactions don't go well, the child forms a negative or "bad" view of other and self, which results in a bad feeling state. When infants see the "good" parent before them, the "bad" parent does not exist.

This is a very simple way of describing the psychoanalytic concept known as "splitting," initially explored largely by Melanie Klein (1948) in the earlier part of the 20th century and later by Ronald Fairbairn (1952), Otto Kernberg (1975), James Masterson (1976), and other object relations theorists. Object relations theorists hypothesize that this sorting of experiences into either positive or negative categories represents the first step of organization for the developing child's mind. Dan Siegel (1999) refers to this as "state-dependent memory" (p. 105); it is the way infants and young children store procedural memories as unique and different working models of self, other, and feeling within different parts of the brain. Siegel describes these as "attachment-related contexts" (p. 106) that are then prone to being activated when similar experiences, even years later, evoke these hidden states of mind.

A major developmental goal is to integrate the good and bad self and other representations to form one accurate internal working model of self and other rather than keeping them split off within separate attachment-related contexts. Children begin to realize that they don't have an all-good parent and a separate all-bad parent but one parent who is neither all bad nor all good but something of a blend. "Good enough" parenting helps the baby regulate emotion and, through the process of rupture and repair described in Chapter 11, brings the "good" and "bad" objects (internal templates of the all-important other) together into an integrated whole often referred to as the capacity for whole object relations. The more a parent's caregiving falls short of this standard, however, the less likely that integration will occur. If ruptures are not repaired consistently, the split representations are not integrated and people keep the good object and the bad object separate, especially under stress, thus tending to reduce the rich texture and complexity of life to black-and-white generalizations. Three distinct configurations of these defensive strategies are spelled out in the three core sensitivities. How these strategies play out in close relationships for each sensitivity is summarized in Box 9.1.

The core sensitivities are closely related to attachment. If the good parent appears only when the baby expresses certain needs on the Circle and the bad parent appears when the baby expresses other needs, the baby will naturally begin to do what seems necessary to keep the bad parent away. Therefore a baby whose bids for comfort are rebuffed may start to stifle needs to be held and try to gain acceptance from her caregiver with exploration. This strategy is coded as avoidant attachment. Attachment classifications are based on the behavioral manifestation of the strategy, and core sensitivities are defined by the core beliefs behind those behaviors and strategies.

Developing a strategy to avoid the top or bottom of the Circle does not mean the child has given up hope. For example, a child selecting the split-off "good" parent who may show delight in his exploration is saying "If I can keep you close and loving by behaving in a way that you find tolerable, there is hope that I can keep becoming 'better' and eventually be loved."

The reality is that, without intervention, the parent who rebuffs bids for closeness will most likely continue to do so. Defensive strategies perpetuate themselves. Chances are this mother, whose cries for solace were ignored by her own mother, will experience the care seeking/caregiving arena as shark-infested waters. When her son cries in distress, she will react as any loving mother would whose child is approaching danger. She will try to steer him away from the sharks she has learned to avoid and toward exploration, where she remembers receiving acceptance. By unconsciously redirecting her son, she avoids the painful memories and feelings associated with requests for closeness or comfort.

By living in her procedural memory to protect herself and her son from sharks, she holds tightly to a view of herself as a "good" parent who is highly responsive. Because she has detached from her painful memories of both her unresponsive caregiver and her experiences of being rejected for seeking comfort, she is unable to recognize how the pain she dissociates from is the very pain she is inflicting on her child. Consequently, she is sowing the procedural seeds of a problematic core sensitivity in her son's psyche.

BOX 9.1. CORE SENSITIVITIES WITHIN CLOSE RELATIONSHIPS

Separation Sensitive

We feel we must focus on what others want, need, and feel, while not focusing on our own wants, needs, and feelings. We do this because we feel incapable of living life without feeling the continual availability of significant others. Our underlying fear is that if we focus on our own lives and our own capacity to do things well, we will be "bad" or "selfish" and eventually turned away from by those we need most. We believe our job is to focus on another's needs and appear to be helpless regarding our own.

- *Conclusion*: We attempt to control those close to us by taking care of them or getting them to take care of us; otherwise we're afraid they will leave us. Alternatively, we can often get upset when those close to us push us to take care of ourselves.
- *Common triggers*: We scan for signs that something is wrong *in the relationship* (thus keeping the relationship center stage, often within a state of upset and difficulty); we avoid taking a stand for fear it will lead to abandonment; we tend to be preoccupied with whether or not we are being loved enough.
- *What we might hear from others*: "You want too much from me." "You feel like you're clinging to me." "It's like you want me to threaten to leave and then dramatically decide to stay."
- *Unthought known-within-reflection*: "I think I once again wanted you to reassure me by staying close. (Because, just below the surface, I think you will leave me.)" "Whenever I don't focus on you and instead focus on me, I'm sure you'll turn and walk out. When I just said what I really believed, I was certain you were upset." "I think I just got helpless so you'd come near and take care of me."
- *Goal of treatment*: Recognition that our perceptions, opinions, and needs are healthy and essential; that to give these up is to deny who we actually are and thus to deny a deeper level of intimacy.

Esteem Sensitive

We believe that who we are, just as we are (unadorned, imperfect, flawed) is not enough to be valued. Therefore, to protect ourselves from criticism, judgment, and abandonment, we hide our genuine self and continually attempt to prove that we are worthy (i.e., unique, special, exceptional, anything but average) through performance and achievement.

- *Conclusion*: Perceptions of us feel all-important. We attempt to control perceptions—both what others think of us and what we think of ourselves. Our perception of what others are thinking is always somewhat fragile, so we seek reassurance and work at keeping our sense of self-esteem unrealistically high. We are often disappointed in others for not "getting us" or understanding us perfectly. We are vigilant about any view of us as having failed or being

(*continued*)

BOX 9.1. (*continued*)

inadequate. Some of us are conscious of this vigilance (often preemptively putting ourselves down for our imperfections so that others won't); some of us don't even want to imagine ourselves as "less than perfect" (causing those close to us to "walk on eggshells" in an attempt to make sure we don't experience any feeling of inadequacy or failure).

- *Common triggers*: We scan for positive and negative perceptions on the part of others; hair-trigger reaction to criticism, need to be right/need to *not* be wrong; desire to "be on the same page" with close others (to think alike and be in "full" agreement); any sign that our intimate relationship isn't "perfect" may be met with upset, blaming, or withdrawal. Vulnerability can feel excruciating.
- *What we might hear from others*: "It's not always about you." "It's just criticism, not the end of the world." "I'm not an extension of you." "I feel pressured to always be upbeat or only say nice things to you because if I don't you'll feel criticized."
- *Unthought known-within-reflection*: "I think I just asked you to make me feel special. (Because, just below the surface, I'm fairly certain that I'm not really worthy.)" "I wonder if I didn't just get mad at you to protect myself from feeling I was in the wrong." "I think I just withdrew because your disagreement upset my fantasy that we always think alike."
- *Goal of treatment*: Recognition that my genuine self is lovable, mistakes are inevitable, that differences are healthy, and that sharing our needs and our vulnerability can be fulfilling.

Safety Sensitive

We believe that the cost of being connected to significant others is giving up who we really are and what we really want, which inevitably leads to feeling controlled and/or intruded upon by "the other." Therefore, the only way to have an intact sense of ourselves is to remain somewhat hidden and quite self-sufficient. We want to be close, but we also want to protect ourselves by remaining somewhat isolated, while always dancing in a kind of compromise between intrusion/enslavement and isolation. This compromise keeps us unsatisfied (and those close to us frustrated) because we are neither fully in nor fully out of relationship.

- *Conclusion*: Managing physical and emotional distance is all-important. We attempt to be in control of closeness (when we get too close to another, our sense of safety is in doubt).
- *Common triggers*: Scanning for any sign of someone being dominant, manipulative, intrusive, or being "too close" ("too intimate," "too understanding," "too concerned"). Exposure (being seen) can feel excruciating.
- *What we might hear from others*: "I want more from you." "It's like you disappear on me." "Why do you go into hiding whenever I ask you about yourself?" "I don't want to control you; I just want to be close."

(*continued*)

BOX 9.1. (*continued*)

- **Unthought known-within-reflection**: "Once again, I just got frightened (anxious, uncomfortable) because it felt like we were getting too close." "I think I just retreated into my self-sufficient mode, sure that you were going to try to run things." "Maybe I just got kind of abrasive because I knew that would upset you and get you to back off." "At times like this I almost can't imagine someone willing to negotiate with me, instead of just taking over. I need to talk about this stuff and be sure you will really listen and not try to control the outcome of what we decide."
- **Goal of treatment**: Recognition that closeness doesn't necessarily mean enslavement; that bringing our self into relationship does not require being intruded upon, invaded, or controlled; that closeness and intimacy can be safe.

There is a difference between kicking a stone and kicking a dog.
The laws of physics can help us map a fairly certain trajectory
for a kicked stone, but physics fails us when we try to predict
exactly what will happen if we kick a dog.
—GREGORY BATESON (1972, p. 171)

When this stance [our internal experience and outside reality
are the same] is our default option, we're on automatic pilot
and, as such, all too constrained by outdated working models
and habitually structured patterns of thinking, feeling, and doing.
—DAVID WALLIN (2007, p. 136)

As Bonnie Badenoch put it, "Dis-integrated implicit memory can . . . take the form of *lying dormant in dissociated pockets and springing into action only when touched by internal or external experience*" (2011, p. 49, emphasis in original). This can become a multigenerational problem, sometimes of tragic proportions, due to the intransigent nature of the dissociation. "As tenacious as the brain is in integrating everything available to it," Badenoch says, "it is likely that *circuits that remain dissociated from the overall flow of the brain stay literally out of the loop of the default network*" (emphasis in original). Without a way to begin to make sense of how parents react nonconsciously to events that trigger implicit relational knowing, and to reflect upon it—without a way to integrate what has been split off—this pattern will likely persist into the next generation. Badenoch concludes that the role of psychotherapy is to create opportunities "for our brains to bring implicit neural circuits out of temporal isolation or dissociation . . . and enter the flow of our integrating brains" (p. 83).

IDENTIFYING CORE SENSITIVITIES TO ENHANCE
TREATMENT OUTCOME

The COS attempts to bring procedural memory into the flow of our integrating brains by facilitating reflective functioning within the context of the child's needs on the Circle. The success of this endeavor is enhanced by a differential diagnosis of the strengths and struggles specific to each dyad (discussed later in this chapter), as well as by evaluating parents' core sensitivities.

As attachment researchers were discovering that both children and parents can be classified within several distinct working models of attachment, object relations theorist James Masterson, on a parallel track, instituted a treatment methodology centered on the therapist's capacity to establish a clear differentiation between three specific personality disorders—borderline, narcissistic, and schizoid. Masterson determined that the vast majority of those seeking psychoanalytic treatment fall within the broad spectrum of one of these three character patterns. The capacity to accurately diagnose the particular themes of a given patient afforded the therapist a specificity of treatment that increases the likelihood of success. Although most people do not have a personality disorder, these character patterns can be usefully identified in a less rigid and pervasive form. To depathologize these themes, we created the term "core sensitivities" to encompass a wide range of intensity within these patterns (from mild to severe).

These object relations diagnostic categories do not coincide directly with those described in attachment theory, but rather add specificity to our understanding of the parents' internal working models of attachment. This specificity offers four advantages to treatment:

1. It helps us speak the language of the parents' underlying concerns.
2. It clarifies the goals of their defense.
3. It helps us avoid inadvertently triggering their defense.
4. It gives the therapist an empathic organization for defenses that at times can be quite difficult to manage.

For example, parents like the mother described above, whose child has an avoidant attachment, may have very different reasons for supporting avoidance. The separation-sensitive parent is staying away from the self-activation (autonomous self-assertion) required to manage her own feelings and respond to the child's distress. The esteem-sensitive parent is avoiding the memory of being humiliated for needing comfort. The safety-sensitive parent is avoiding being engulfed or enslaved by the child's need for closeness. Focusing on issues of humiliation with the parent who is separation sensitive or supporting more self-activation in the parent who is safety sensitive or assuring a parent who is esteem sensitive that her child will not smother her is clearly missing the mark. These poorly attuned interventions will leave the parent feeling misunderstood and unacknowledged.

The COS owes a major debt of gratitude to James Masterson and Ralph Klein for providing us with this critical tool. There are some differences in how we approach this work, notably in nomenclature. Our goal is to depathologize parents and view relational dysfunction as matter of degree along a continuum, with a dynamic tension always existing between "pathology" and "health." COS recognizes that all caregivers use some defensive strategies based on procedural memories and that these defenses often coalesce as core sensitivities. Ironically, the etymology of the word "pathology" itself normalizes the experience of emotional suffering in the context of insecurity. Although dictionaries define pathology as "something abnormal," the word has its root in the Greek word *pathologia*, which means "the study of human emotions"—everyday emotions—and pathology also gains definition from the word "pathos," which brings together "poignance" and "suffering." Emotional suffering can therefore be recognized as an essential aspect of being human, something we all have in common. This perspective steers us toward treating cases of relational dysfunction by diagnosing the specific patterns that parents use to defend against pain, not by diagnosing disorders.

It is important for the therapist to be aware that each of us struggles with issues involving the regulation of emotions about self-esteem and with the interplay of closeness and autonomy within relationships.

Working with a parent who regularly exhibits patterns of being abusive or neglectful (in dramatic or even subtle ways) can be very difficult and emotionally trying for the therapist. Applying a label like "borderline," "dependent personality," or "narcissistic personality disorder" can distance the therapist even further from the parent. The unfortunate and almost inevitable consequence is a "we/they" attitude within the therapist, which runs counter to creating a holding environment. And when we are dealing with even milder problems, such as the typical parent seeking therapy for a problem with a 2-year-old, these diagnostic labels often do not apply at all. Therefore, the COS approach substitutes "esteem sensitive," "safety sensitive," and "separation sensitive," terms that are more intuitively understandable and keep us focused on relational styles and on the affective quality of the shark music that organizes each style. In talking to parents, we do not use even these labels but simply help them reflect on the process that underlies their caregiving choices.

Flexible defenses	Rigid defenses
Esteem sensitive	*Narcissistic personality disorder*
Separation sensitive	*Borderline personality disorder*
Safety sensitive	*Schizoid personality disorder*

DIFFERENTIATING THE CORE SENSITIVITIES

Core sensitivities organize the internal defensive process manifested in caregivers' behavior, and yet trying to discern these sensitivities through the interactional assessment alone leaves the therapist doing a lot of guesswork. The underlying concerns of the parent are hidden—in this case *not* in plain sight. This is why the video record of the COSI is so helpful.

As noted in Chapter 8, the behavioral assessment inevitably raises questions. It is the core sensitivities that can explain some of the significant discrepancies observed among dyads who exhibit the same basic attachment pattern. The core sensitivities can be viewed as "rules to live by" regarding relationships—the protective strategies that are used throughout life to avoid "falling forever" in the words of Donald Winnicott (see Chapter 4)—that is, to avoid Being-Without.

> *A core sensitivity is an internal working model and particular way of splitting that has now become a moment-to-moment strategy:*
>
> 1. *"This is what I <u>must do</u> and what I <u>must not do</u> in order to stay connected."*
> 2. *"This is what I <u>must do</u> and what I <u>must not do</u> in order to stay away from 'Being-Without.'"*

Figure 9.1 gives examples of how each core sensitivity is typically expressed in caregiving relationships and also which treatment goals and interventions are often effective. The following descriptions sum up what you might see in the videos: signs of the typical fears, defensive fantasies, and linchpin themes associated with each of the core sensitivities and what the underlying concerns of the pattern could be.

Esteem Sensitivity

- What does it mean when a parent wants her/his child to be outstanding and "better than"?
- How does it feel to be considered "average"?
- Why would a parent feel threatened if his/her child does not think the way the parent does (one-minded)?
- Why is it that sometimes a parent is not comfortable letting her/his child fully experience the bottom half of the Circle?
- Why would a parent send her/his baby out to explore when the baby is clearly upset?

Esteem sensitivity involves the need to be seen as special, while always struggling with the fear of being exposed as imperfect and disappointing. Parents who prioritize performance and perfection, as noted earlier, are often "esteem sensitive." This parent tends to be more interested in what the child does than in who the child is. Thus relationship-for-the-sake-of-relationship will take a backseat to relationship-as-a-focus-on-achievement. Such a parent was likely raised in a performance-based environment where one's worth depended on accomplishment. When self-esteem is based primarily on performance, rather than on a secure base of mutual respect and delight, it tends to be fragile.

When children raised in such an environment become adults, they are overly focused on achievement/perfection and feel challenged and potentially criticized if you don't see things the way they do. They have a core belief, based on their caregiver's demands, that performance and one-mindedness are what maintains connection. Unless they question that core belief, they will ask the same of their offspring. Therefore they tend to be most comfortable on the top of the Circle and lack positive experience or expertise on the bottom of the Circle. Because of their fear of failure when they can't "solve the problem," their shark music is likely to play when their child expresses needs on the bottom of the Circle.

"I can go from feeling so content with my life as a parent to suddenly feeling like such a loser—almost in an instant. I know it has something to do with what other parents are thinking of me. I don't want anyone

FIGURE 9.1. Core sensitivities: Quick glance—Caregivers.

Sensitivity	Separation	Esteem	Safety
Caregiver's fear re: child	Child will go out to explore and never return; child will be more interested in the world than in caregiver.	Child will need comfort for feelings that trigger memories of rejection and humiliation in the caregiver.	Child will "need" too much and overwhelm/appropriate the caregiver's already limited experience of safety.
Caregiver's fear re: hands/taking charge	"Taking charge means that you'll get upset and leave me forever."	"Taking charge will force us to lose our one-mindedness and expose my vulnerability."	"Taking charge triggers your upset and you will overwhelm me. I don't want to enslave you."
Primary strategy to avoid shark music (common linchpin struggles)	Keep child focused on the relationship (bottom half of Circle) and/or make self indispensable to child on the top of the Circle; interfere with child's autonomy; avoid hierarchy (which requires self-activation) to keep child from getting angry and separating.	Keep child focused on exploration/performance/achievement (top half of Circle); dismiss child's requests for comfort and emotion regulation; see self and child as special; one-mindedness.	Keeping child focused away from the relationship (especially bottom half of Circle); promoting child's self-sufficiency to keep child from being too demanding or having unnecessary needs for closeness and connection.
Vigilance re: significant others	"Will you be enmeshed with me or will I be deserted?" Be enmeshed or abandoned	"Will you make me feel special or make me feel inadequate?" Be above or be below	"Will you intrude on me or will I be isolated?" Be isolated or be controlled
Defensive fantasies of child ("positive")	"Finally I have someone who will love me no matter what." (Ever-Available Other)	"I have the brightest/most special/most fragile child who I know perfectly and vice versa." (Perfect and Fused Other)	"My daughter really knows how to take care of herself in so many situations." (Self-Sufficient Other)

(continued)

FIGURE 9.1. (*continued*)

Sensitivity	Separation	Esteem	Safety
Defensive fantasies of child (negative)	"He throws such tantrums! He hates me already. He wants nothing to do with me." (Abandoning Other)	"She is so spoiled. All she ever wants is attention. Thank God for time-outs." (Critical/Demanding Other)	"I just wish he weren't so damn needy. For no reason he just keeps hanging on me." (Engulfing Other)
Target themes for video review and intervention	Work with shark music around hierarchy and competence of caregiver with child (e.g., interest in child's initiative and exploration on top half of Circle and separate experience, willingness to take charge when needed, clarity and firmness of purpose, clarity and directness of speech).	Work with shark music around attunement and positive experience of needs on bottom half of Circle (e.g., mutual gaze, tenderness and delight attending to child's feelings, willingness to negotiate, matching of child's tempo).	Work with shark music around closeness between caregiver and child, (e.g., mutual gaze, easy communication, seeing child's capacity for tenderness, successful negotiation of feelings and physical contact, seeing child's need for closeness as appropriate and time limited).
Range of negative self-representation from mild to severe in the face of unregulated affect	Incompetent, Guilty, Bad, Unwanted, Helpless/Hopeless, Abandoned	Disappointed, Vulnerable, Inadequate, Imperfect, Ashamed, Humiliated, Empty, Fragmented	Intruded on, Trapped, Enslaved, Appropriated,* Unable to Communicate, Futile, Complete Isolation*

*The safety-sensitive representations are split into two groups because the negative representations change depending on how close and involved or distant and removed they are from the relationship.

to think critical thoughts. So I have to be the best parent ever. My only value is the value that comes from standing out and being recognized as the greatest dad of all time."

This young parent is esteem sensitive. He could be giving a talk in front of a large audience, and when 200 people before him are enjoying the talk but 3 people in the back are snickering, he is devastated by the 3 in the back.

"I need to make sure you're continually impressed with my perfect parenting."

"By the way, no matter what I do, I will never be perfect."

The forces in the esteem-sensitive bind are: I need to be seen as perfect to be worthy; if I am seen as imperfect, I will be rejected; I am not perfect. The person who is esteem sensitive can never achieve perfection, so he keeps trying to stay one step ahead of the truth in a frantic attempt to stay out of the black hole of Being-Without. One of the ways to try to feel perfect is to have people see things exactly as he does and reflect that back to him.

Separation Sensitivity

- Why would a parent send her baby out to explore when he's not calm and then remind him he's still upset?
- What does it mean when a parent wants her child to stay little?
- Why would a parent feel distress letting her child fully experience the top half of the Circle when it is safe to do so?

Separation sensitivity involves the need to stay close, while always struggling with the fear of being abandoned. Caregivers who are separation sensitive were often raised in an environment where attempts to activate exploration and separation from the parent were met with disfavor. This caregiver, as a child, was expected to continually look to the parent as a resource without building an internal capacity for self-support. It is as if the parent was saying, "I need you to need me and not think about yourself." In other cases, the parent was so unavailable or preoccupied that the children riveted their focus on staying connected while forsaking any sense of knowing their own needs. Either way, for these children to initiate experience away from the parent or attempt to become competent at acting on their own behalf was to experience a loss of parental interest and availability—to be abandoned. As adults they tend to become overly caretaking, complying with the needs of others in return for the unspoken promise that these others will never leave. Parents who are separation sensitive focus on the desires, needs, and feelings of others, diminishing or even totally disavowing the importance of their own. As children they inhibited the desire for exploration and autonomy, and now they are afraid to make decisions or take charge. The internal pressure is to remain focused on the significant others in their life, at a considerable expense to their own competence and capacity.

These parents may push their children to the bottom of the Circle because their child is less likely to leave if distressed. At the same time caregivers who are separation sensitive often find it overwhelming to manage their children's needs on the bottom of the Circle because it requires too much autonomy and self-activation for them to manage their own emotions and focus on soothing or being in charge of their child. To protect themselves from feeling overwhelmed they might push the child into exploration and then cling to their child on the top by intruding or making themselves central in their child's play.

> "It just doesn't seem right that my mom would be mad at me for growing up and having my own baby. What's so bad about just trying to parent like I want to? I actually like my mom, at least some of the time. But she wants me to live close, call, text, always keep her in the loop. When I do something for myself, I start to feel guilty. Like right now, I feel like I'm being bad for even saying this out loud."

This is a classic separation-sensitive statement: I would like to have my own autonomy, but my caregivers aren't comfortable with my being on the top half of the Circle, so I need to focus on their comfort and forgo my need for separation. This young mother is starting to tell the truth, but then shark music shows up, reminding her that she always gets in trouble for considering herself as capable and competent. She felt the truth of wanting to do something on her own and then, in a split second, started to feel bad. "If I feel guilty," she says nonconsciously to herself, "I'll quit activating my move toward competence. By feeling guilty I maintain my lifelong preoccupation with my caregiver and can avoid memories of her turning away when I risked having a separate self."

> "Tell me what I need to do to guarantee you won't leave me."

> "P.S. I'll make sure I also do whatever it takes to drive you away."

These are the messages sent by the separation-sensitive person. The P.S. is engineered to keep the drama going, and the drama makes it impossible to leave—"I make you mad, you say you're going to leave, I apologize; we keep the drama going, and that means we're still here together, in relationship."

Safety Sensitivity

- What does it mean when a parent seems to constantly value self-sufficiency in his child over emotional closeness?
- Why would a parent avoid her child's strong emotions, both positive and negative?
- Why is it that sometimes a parent is tuned out or appears indifferent to where her child is on the Circle?

Safety sensitivity is our term for the schizoid personality issues initially developed by Ronald Fairbairn (1952), Harry Guntrip (1969), and Ralph Klein (1995). It involves the feeling, based upon splitting, that one has to choose between being close and intruded upon or being distant and isolated because there is nothing in between. Often, safety-sensitive parents, as children, felt they needed to protect their emerging sense of self from invasion by an overinvolved and misattuned parent. This need left them with an unsolvable dilemma: allow the intrusion and lose a sense of self or have a self, reject the intrusion, but live in isolation. In other cases, the caregiver who is safety sensitive may have been raised by an esteem-sensitive parent whose attempts at one-mindedness were experienced as intrusive or by a safety-sensitive parent where closeness was experienced as intrusion and self-sufficiency was considered the norm. Either way, safety-sensitive parents are seeking a compromise between emotional closeness and distance with their child. Seeking a way to experience attachment without losing autonomy, the safety-sensitive mother is likely to desire a relationship with her child yet remain vigilant for signs such as intense emotion that signal to her that she is about to be swallowed up by her child's needs. She may therefore keep her child at arm's length much of the time.

"To have a self I must remain alone."

"To be connected I must lose my sense of self."

"In grade school I never really fit in. My teachers all told my parents that I was a dreamer. I would just read for hours or lock myself away in my daydreams. I would think of being a father, but it was always in the distance. Now, when I'm at work I miss my daughter, but when I come home, I feel suffocated by her needs."

This father illustrates the struggle of safety sensitivity: When I am close, it feels too close and I want to be distant, and when I am distant,

I feel too isolated and I want to be close. No matter where I am, I remain unsatisfied.

"I need to keep you at a distance when you are close."

"But when you are not close, you are too far away."

CORE SENSITIVITIES IN THE CONTEXT OF ATTACHMENT PATTERNS

In the process of treating a troubled parent–child dyad, the importance of differential diagnosis cannot be overstated. One size does not fit all. The specific needs confronting the caregiver with esteem-sensitive issues vary significantly from those of a caregiver who is separation sensitive. Rather than having to intuit what might be useful with a particular parent, the therapist with a well-developed knowledge of the COS differential diagnosis can get specific in choosing interventions.

Differentiating the core sensitivities is, however, an exceedingly challenging task made even more complex by the fact that any behavior and any attachment pattern (avoidant or ambivalent) can be found with any of the sensitivities. To understand sensitivities you must look at the meaning behind the behavior rather than the behavior. The following descriptions represent the most common forms of working models but must not be considered comprehensive. Parent–child relationships are more complex than the maps we build to understand them.

Caregiver Core Sensitivities with a Child Who Has an Avoidant Attachment

The caregiver of an insecure avoidant child encourages independence at the cost of close physical and emotional contact. In the AAI these caregivers are considered "dismissing" of attachment needs on the bottom of the Circle, as stated earlier. They tend to be uncomfortable with direct emotional communication and appear uneasy with the expression of need. Over time, the child of such a parent learns to inhibit direct expression of wants or needs for the caregiver.

Hence it is not surprising that typically in the Strange Situation such a child shows little distress when the parent is absent, tends to turn away from the parent upon reunion, and has a relationship strategy intended to not rock the emotional boat. As attachment theorists explain, such a child expects his attachment needs to be dismissed. To avoid the pain of rejection associated with cuing needs on the bottom of the Circle, this child begins to build a pattern of creating distance and prioritizing exploration and/or achievement, which, not coincidentally, is what the child's parent emphasizes. Parents who emphasize achievement and exploration are often esteem sensitive and are usually comfortable on the top half while being dismissing of bottom-half opportunities.

Safety-sensitive parents are also dismissing of closeness and promote self-sufficiency in their child. They do this not because their self-esteem depends on achievement, but rather because they choose to have a certain emotional distance in the relationship as a way to protect the self from being engulfed or controlled. Because closeness to another person was not experienced as safe, a working model of relationship was established that systematically sacrificed intimacy to maintain distance. In its place, this person learned to prioritize self-sufficiency. As caregivers, even though they are genuinely interested in relationship, these adults tend to be very careful about showing it and remain vigilant concerning the intensity of the child's need for direct connection. An underlying fear of being emotionally smothered and a sense of being imprisoned by the child's needs remain salient themes in the caregiving relationship.

Sometimes we see a separation-sensitive parent foster an avoidant attachment with her child. In this case the parent promotes clinging behavior on the top of the Circle—for example, micromanaging the child's exploration—not to boost the child's achievement but so the child won't go too far away. This parent is not trying to support the child's exploration but is focused on the top of the Circle for the purpose of closeness. This parent also rejects or avoids the child's needs on the bottom of the Circle because they trigger painful memories and feelings. The autonomous self-regulation required to manage and ultimately put aside her own feelings so she can soothe her child is filled with shark music, so this mother distracts her child with toys. The separation-sensitive parent's need to be needed can be intrusive enough that the child learns to be avoidant to cope. This behavior can be particularly difficult for the separation-sensitive parent as it creates a relationship in which the parent feels abandoned, now having created her own worst nightmare.

Caregiver Core Sensitivities with a Child Who Has an Ambivalent Attachment

Another caregiver strategy is to engender anxiety about separation in the child. In the AAI this parent is categorized as "preoccupied" with relationship issues. Children raised within this context of caregiving tend to alternate between clinging and resisting closeness and therefore are not easily comforted, which keeps their attachment behavioral system activated for extended periods of time. These parents offer a distorted closeness in which the primary function is neither intimacy nor comfort. The distorted closeness tends to be enmeshment in separation sensitivity (emotionally entangled but of separate minds) and fusion (i.e., one-minded or "on the same page" in esteem sensitivity). Both the enmeshed parent and the fused parent tend to overuse the word "we" in their speech. Box 9.2 is useful to differentiate how the same word has different meanings depending on the core sensitivity.

As might be expected, during the SSP, children of preoccupied caregivers (separation sensitive and esteem sensitive) tend to be very upset about the initial separation from the parent. However, upon the caregiver's return, these children give mixed signals concerning reconnection. They cry, seek care, and when the care is given they resist, get angry, and throw tantrums.

The parents of these children can be alternately available (usually in the direction of intrusiveness) and exhausted/frustrated or embarrassed about the child's needs and requests. They tend to put the child down while the child is still obviously distressed, which maintains the drama of the child returning and demanding more. Hence the ambivalence on the part of the children is an accurate reflection of the context in which they find themselves.

Parents Who Are Esteem Sensitive within a Preoccupied/Ambivalent Attachment Bond

The "preoccupied/esteem-sensitive" caregiver, as a child, was punished or withdrawn from for differentiating from the parent. The caregivers in this

---

BOX 9.2. DIFFERENTIATING THE DEFENSIVE USE OF "WE"

Enmeshed (Separation Sensitive):
- "We" as a defense against being alone.
- "I don't need us to be the same; I just want you to stay with me. I will give up my uniqueness if necessary."

Fused (Esteem Sensitive):
- "We" as a defense against difference (separate).
- "I need us to be the same to feel stable."
- One-minded: "You, of course, think and feel like me."

category are preoccupied or overidentify with their children's needs. This vigilance about the child is, however, not brought about for the sake of the child, but rather to protect the parent's fragile sense of identity. As with the dismissing/esteem-sensitive caregiver, this parent is focused on perfection. However, rather than needing to personally exhibit perfect behavior, this parent seeks to fuse or be of one mind with a "perfect or special" child. Hence the child is seen by the parent to be "exquisitely fragile" and/or "uniquely perfect." Such a child is being held within the unreal context of being "too precious."

Parents Who Are Separation Sensitive/Preoccupied with a Child Who Has an Ambivalent Attachment

Parents who are separation sensitive seem preoccupied with the drama of relationship at the expense of a genuine relatedness. Often they will emphasize the child's need for them ("I'll bet you really missed me while I was gone") as a way to maintain dependence. Parents within this category have a hard time being in charge and establishing the hierarchy necessary for the child to feel secure within a context of known rules and limitations. So once again, the child adapts in whatever way possible, molding to the expectations of the caregiver: "If clinging, resistance, drama, worry, or enmeshment is what you need for me to stay connected, that is what you are going to get."

Caregiver Core Sensitivities with a Child Who Has a Disorganized Attachment

Again, the core sensitivity themes are common to all of us, whether our attachment bonds are secure or insecure. It is with a history of unresolved disorganized attachments, however, that the core sensitivities tend to be pervasive enough to approach the more severe and rigid side of the continuum of defensive strategies. All of the core sensitivities in their more severe and rigid forms coalesce as a way to manage the chaos of disorganization, and with adults these defensive strategies can at times form into the inflexibility and pervasiveness of a personality disorder.

> *Esteem sensitive:* When the child disappoints the parent, the parent feels humiliated and either gets enraged or completely withdraws, and the child is in a continual state of fear.
> *Safety sensitive:* The child experiences a caregiver who requires

self-sufficiency to such a degree that the child is forced to organize a parent who is experienced as neglectful.

Separation sensitive: The caregiver is so frightened of any self-activation (hierarchy) that might bring separation (perceived abandonment) that she pushes for role reversal and allows the child to be in charge.

DIFFERENTIAL DIAGNOSIS, DIFFERENTIATED TREATMENT

It becomes important to differentiate between caregiving strategies if we are to address the specific issues of the specific caregiver/child dyad before us. A caregiver who is dismissing of attachment with his child will require interventions that will encourage an increased willingness to negotiate closeness. If that parent is esteem sensitive, a specific doorway toward closeness can open when he realizes that the child is interested in him rather than in his performance-based persona. ("This little girl sure does enjoy you. She keeps looking at you in a way that says 'I'm so glad you are my dad.'") Central treatment themes for this caregiver would include addressing the shark music triggered by the vulnerability of attunement and positive "moments" of need between caregiver and child on the bottom of the Circle (e.g., mutual gaze, shared affect without having to do something about it, sincerity of affect, attending to the child's feelings, turn taking, willingness to negotiate, matching of the child's tempo).

If, on the other hand, the parent is safety sensitive, the therapist would emphasize the ways in which the child has no interest in overwhelming or controlling the caregiver. ("You see, she just smiled at you for a moment and then looked away. She really enjoys making contact and then spending a few moments by herself.") Treatment themes for this parent would thus focus on shark music that is triggered with safe closeness between caregiver and child on the bottom of the Circle (e.g., moments of face-to-face contact, mutual gaze that builds in length over time, comfortable give-and-take communication, recognition of the child's capacity for sensitive and tender contact).

Interventions for a separation-sensitive parent preoccupied with her child's needs would move in a different direction. Such a parent would be shown how her shark music interferes with building hierarchy within the relationship and supporting the child's natural desire for exploration and autonomy. This will support separation on the part of the child so the separation-sensitive parent needs to know that the child will go away but consistently return. ("Look at how she likes running away with that toy and then returning with something new to share with you.") Specific themes for treatment would include supporting the caregiver's competence with her child on the top of the Circle (e.g., willingness to take charge, focus on tasks, clarity and firmness of purpose, interest in her child's exploration and separate experience, frankness, clarity and directness of speech). Treatment would also seek to help the parent support competence in her child (e.g., completion of tasks, self-management, appropriate risk taking, experiences at a distance from the caregiver).

The preoccupied esteem-sensitive caregiver needs to manage shark music enough to find gradual comfort in her child's different ways of experiencing the world. ("This little guy really has a mind of his own. Look at how he is bringing you that truck. He seems to know you don't have one and wants to share his newfound pleasure with you. It's really nice when one of you can bring something new and different to the other.") Treatment themes for this parent focus on the caregiver's genuine attunement and would include the encouragement of increasing differentiation between parent and child, thus allowing the child's separate needs to be experienced as necessary and acceptable (e.g., recognizing the child's separate tempo and feelings, negotiation from separate minds, allowance of anger in both child and parent, sincerity of affect, frankness, clarity and directness of speech).

Factoring in the Parent's Capacity for Emotional Work

Caregivers exhibit a variety of attachment strategies and sensitivities. They also present themselves for therapy with differing capacities for emotional work. At one end of the continuum are parents who appear to be relatively secure in their parenting and demonstrate the ability to organize and talk about emotions. They come to treatment because they seek support for options that feel beyond their current caregiving repertoire. Many times these parents have recently read a book or article on the specifics of quality caregiving and seek help from a professional because of their conscientious commitment to healthy parenting. Much of what we present in this book can apply to these parents, albeit at a modified level of intensity and for fewer sessions.

At the other end of the continuum of a parent's capacity for psychotherapy are those caregivers who show little capacity to use the therapist as a secure base. They often have little history of a holding environment, their emotions are either detached or overwhelming, and often they demonstrate little reflective capacity. While likely showing signs of a disorganized attachment strategy, these parents will also present with a secondary strategy of being either dismissing or preoccupied. Predictability, providing safety, and being sensitive to their particular problems with affect regulation become central issues within the therapy. The focus needs to be on developing a safe therapeutic relationship rather than jumping into issues with their parenting.

AN EXPANSIVE CONTINUUM

Our task as therapists is to find a way to meet the needs specific to the family before us. To be of use to each family the therapist must be able to diagnose the caregiver strategy, the themes of dysfunction, the core sensitivity, and the parent's ability to address these issues. Many parents do not have either the willingness or the time to get to the underlying causes of their limitations and distortions concerning relatedness. Our ability to recognize what a family system can sustain, given current circumstances, is an essential feature of this work. It dare never be our goal to move these families to a predetermined point of relationship. "Success" will be within a context of many limitations, including those of the parent, the therapist, and the model of therapy being used. For this reason, it becomes important to see change as taking place along a broad continuum. This is, indeed, an expansive continuum, and we all, clients and therapists alike, find ourselves somewhere on it.

Within a context of keeping children's safety a central priority, our task is to genuinely appreciate each parent and each child as a person struggling to find the best way to meet her or his core needs to love and to work. It is a privilege to enter into these struggling lives. We are, each of us, consistently dealing with the pain of unmet needs and the joy experienced when these needs can finally be met. Gaining as full an understanding as possible of a parent's perceptions about caregiving and about the parent–child relationship is a major step toward helping parents realize their potential as caregivers.

10

The Parent Perception Assessment

Using the Circle of Security Interview
to Enhance Treatment Efficacy

> Sometimes questions are more important than answers.
> —NANCY WILLARD

After the interactional assessment we ask parents to participate in the COSI to help us track the interplay among core beliefs, feelings, behaviors, and perceptions. More specifically the COSI helps reveal the parents' capacities and the nature and meaning of their defensive strategy. This is essential information that is needed to design an effective, individualized treatment plan. The COSI illuminates the following elements:

- Coherence of the parents' narrative.
- Positive and negative attributions of the child and self.
- What parents value in relationships (e.g., intimacy vs. hierarchy).
- Ability to focus on their feelings and behaviors as well as the feelings and behaviors of others (reflective functioning).
- Empathy for self and others.
- Core sensitivities.

ASSESSING CAREGIVER CAPACITIES

In the COSI, Form 10.1 on pages 249–254, the capacities that each answer typically reveals are noted after each question. Following are some general points to keep in mind about these capacities and their possible treatment implications. How the answers to the COSI questions can be factored into treatment planning for a specific case is illustrated in the example that begins on page 227.

Narrative Coherence

In many therapies, including the COS, one goal is to help the client learn to build and maintain coherence in the face of difficult emotions. In this sense the COSI is like a stress test. We are trying to see whether the parent can provide a coherent narrative while responding to emotionally evocative questions. If not, where does the narrative break down and in what way? A central therapeutic tool of COS intervention is for parents to engage in reflective dialogue while reviewing videos of their child. It is necessary to achieve coherence while watching both moments of success and moments of struggle (shark music). The COSI is designed to provide valuable information about the level of coherence the parent can maintain so that therapists can pick video clips to match the level of intensity they think the parent can manage.

The importance of coherence to reflective functioning was introduced in Chapter 6. The AAI's (George et al., 1984; Main & Goldwyn, 1984; Main, Goldwyn, & Hesse, 2003) use of the term "coherence" is based on the work of Grice (1975), a linguistic philosopher who stated that cooperative discourse must meet the following conditions.

1. Quality: "Be truthful and have evidence for what you say."
2. Quantity: "Be succinct, and yet complete."
3. Relation: "Be relevant to the topic as presented."
4. Manner: "Be clear and orderly."

Severe lack of coherence typically violates all four of Grice's criteria and is often a marker for unresolved (disorganized/disoriented) attachment patterns in the AAI. Even though the COSI is not scientifically scored, the categories from the AAI can provide a useful clinical organization for treatment when reviewing the parents' answers to the COSI. As in the Parent Development Interview (PDI; Aber, Slade, Berger, Bresgi, & Kaplan, 1985), the COSI asks parents to pick words or phrases that describe their relationship with their child and then match them with a detailed memory of a specific episode in their relationship with that child (i.e., an episodic memory). How well the descriptive word or phrase matches the episodic memory reveals the parent's level of internal coherence. An example from our lab is a parent who used the adjective "fun" to describe her relationship with her child and when prompted for an episodic memory (detailed memory of a specific event) described a time when there was a fire in their house and the fire trucks came, and how much fun it was for them to have the fire trucks show up. Coherence comes into play in less extreme ways as well. For example, dismissing parents violate the criterion for quantity: they tend to be too succinct without offering the full relational nature of a memory; preoccupied parents tend to lack the capacity to relay a memory in a succinct manner, clarity often lost in a flood of irrelevant information.

Cognitive coherence is a complicated concept that cannot be addressed in depth here, but on the simplest level what the interviewer should be looking for across the COSI questions and answers is whether the interviewee's narrative creates a logical and progressive story. Does reasoning start to break down, with the parent going off on tangents or saying something that doesn't make sense? Are aspects of the story emotionally incongruous—for example, laughing while telling a story about her mother's death or describing delight with words but having a flat or nonresponsive face? In such moments you know that you will have to factor limited or lack of coherence (and possible disorganization) into the treatment for that parent.

Representations of the Child and Self

Parents hold a variety of perceptions about their child, on a continuum from positive to negative and from accurate to distorted. When parents are using splitting (see Chapter 9), they are unable to accurately evaluate the full continuum of positive and negative attributions and thus defensively see their child as "all good" (idealized) or "all bad" (pervasive negative attributions). A parent who can only see his child as flawless or fundamentally flawed will not experience the whole child, and the relationship will be stunted. It is a good sign when parents recognize the full range of their child's qualities, from positive to negative, yet all within the context of an underlying warmth and acceptance ("He's a great kid, and he can drive me nuts. But he's just so fun I really don't mind."). The child's need is to be known, accepted, and delighted in for who the child is. When the parent can do this, the child develops an accurate self-image ("I know who I am") and a high sense of self-esteem ("I know that I am worthy").

Dismissing/Preoccupied/Valuing Relationships

Adults who have a dismissive state of mind with regard to attachment focus more on function and less on feelings. A dismissing state of mind can show up as either directly negating the importance of relationship ("He's just so independent that I think he's someone who doesn't want to be all touchy-feeling-clingy") or having an idealizing description of the relationship without being able to corroborate the child's "perfection" with episodic memories. (For the word "competent" the parent responds, "She does everything well. I can't think of anything she isn't good at.")

Adults who have a preoccupied state of mind with regard to attachment tend to focus more on feelings and less on function. This parent tends to be preoccupied with the bottom of the Circle while discouraging competence, autonomy, and self-support ("He's just a mama's boy. He doesn't play much with other kids.").

Parents who have a balanced sense of relationships exhibit acceptance, understanding, and even warmth toward those they are remembering as the interview proceeds. Painful memories are experienced as memories rather than experienced as events or retraumatization. The parents have a way to make sense of other people's feelings and behaviors as well as their own. Blame and devaluation are noticeably absent ("I don't think I liked my dad much growing up. He worked all the time, and I took it personally. Only later did I realize he was holding down two jobs so that my brother and I could go to college. Even so, I wish we'd had more time together.").

If the parent is primarily valuing of attachment relationships with little or no dismissing or preoccupation, the therapist can be relatively at ease about how the parent will likely respond to the upcoming video reviews. Valuing of attachment relationships can be demonstrated by responses that seem to indicate that parents acknowledge and accept the need to at times rely on others and miss people they are close to during times of separation while still being able to manage their own lives. However, when parents are dismissing, the videos will likely focus on their tendency to limit the importance of the bottom of the Circle. For parents preoccupied with relationships, the videos may focus on hands or support for separation. Either way, the parents are being asked to see their preoccupation as a defense against the pain (shark music) evoked by their child's needs.

The Ability to Focus on the Self

"Let there be change in the world, and let it begin with you."

The capacity to focus on the self is basic to the process of psychotherapy. It implies the capacity for parents to focus on their own thoughts, feelings, and behaviors. It also implies the internal capacity to track moment-to-moment choices in the direction of either increased vulnerability or increased self-protection (defense). In this way the ability to focus on the self can be seen as a component of the larger domain of reflective functioning.

Focusing on the self can make parents feel much more vulnerable than focusing on the other (especially blaming). During treatment clients are asked to focus on their thoughts, feelings, and behaviors. Each person enters treatment with a different capacity to perform this crucial therapeutic function. We learn to be able to focus on ourselves during our own early development. For those who grow up in a highly insecure or disorganized family, survival is often contingent on focusing on others and anticipating either difficulty or danger. Under such conditions the capacity to focus on the self may well be impaired. This is why establishing a holding environment is so important to treatment outcomes. Clients who exhibit a lower capacity to focus on self often need the therapist's increased willingness to Be-With them. As they begin to trust that they can safely pay attention to their own thoughts and feelings within the caring presence of another, they can be more open and empathic to the thoughts and feelings of their child.

We were first introduced to this concept in the work of James Masterson. Looking over process notes from therapy sessions made it possible to determine how much time the client spends focusing on the self. It was eye-opening to see how little time many clients spent in therapy focusing on their own thoughts, behaviors, and feelings and how much time was spent defensively focusing on everyone else. A core goal in treatment is to help clients adjust this ratio so that a significant portion of the therapeutic time is spent focusing on the thoughts, feelings, behaviors, and memories of the self. An ability to focus on the self is critical to the COS intervention because the target for change is the parent. The parent has more freedom to change than the young child; just as we all have more freedom to change ourselves than to change another. Helping a parent shift away from focusing on all the things her partner does "wrong" that affect the child or all the things the child does wrong that affect the parent is empowering the parent to make change.

Reflective Functioning

We were introduced to reflective functioning (RF) by Howard and Miriam Steele, who were members of the team that created the concept and termed it RF (Steele & Steele, 2008). The Steeles provided us with generous support during the creation and early implementation of COS. Their influence helped us realize that increasing RF needed to be an important focus of our intervention. RF is clearly defined and measurable, and the research has confirmed that security of attachment of the child is associated with higher RF in the parent (Fonagy et al., 1991). For this reason enhancing RF became central to our theory of change.

Reflective functioning is the psychological capacity for understanding one's own thoughts, feelings, behavior, and intentions as well as those of the other. In other words, it includes the relationship capacity for parents to recognize how their feelings impact their behavior and how their behavior impacts others' feelings, which impact others' behaviors, which, in turn, starts the cycle over again.

Some of the questions about RF that can be answered by the COSI are:

1. Does the parent show awareness of the intergenerational transmission of knowledge or experience? For instance: "I am always a little hard on him when he says no to me. I guess I am a little like my father that way. He would not take no for an answer from me."

2. Is the parent interested in understanding the thoughts and feelings that motivate behavior in the child and in the self? For example: "When he's really throwing a tantrum, I will sometimes stop and wonder if I've been extra hard on him."

3. Does the parent appropriately recognize the developmental stage of the child and take that into consideration when explaining the child's behavior? For instance: "He says no to everything, but I know that's sort of a phase kids go through at this age."

4. Does the parent take into consideration the interviewer's perspective, as evidenced by correcting contradictions or confusing statements to make it easier for the interviewer to understand? For example: "I think I just went off topic when I started talking about my boss. What I am trying to say is that I don't like when I feel like my child is being demanding."

5. Does the parent ever step back and spontaneously make a reflective comment? For instance: "I know that it feels good when my child comforts me, but I don't want him to feel it is his job to do that."

6. When the parent discusses the internal motivations, thoughts, and

feelings of her child, does she make it clear that this is her interpretation of the child, versus acting like she absolutely knows what is inside of her child? For instance: "I worry that my child doesn't like me when I force her to do something" versus "My child doesn't like me when I force her to do something." This is especially important when parents have an inaccurate attribution about their child, such as "He is so manipulative" versus "When he acts that way, I feel so manipulated."

7. Does the parent show any indication that he is open to updating his internal working model regarding the child or self? For example: "I've been angry at him since he was in my belly. I thought he was kicking me on purpose. I know there is something off about that." When a parent lacks this capacity, it signifies that additional time may need to be spent building the option of a safe relationship. While our approach to treatment honors the caregiver's underlying positive intentionality toward her child, for many parents a history that may lack any experience of a holding environment can block access to this intention. A steady, caring presence committed to prioritizing Being-With rather than prioritizing "progress" can often allow the parent to update her view of others, including her child.

Knowing the parent's current capacity in each of the dimensions above helps establish the starting point for the intervention. If parents demonstrate adequate RF, the intervention begins with reflecting on the content of the COSI. Some parents report that just answering the questions gets them thinking about things they have never thought about, which they found useful. When there is no indication that the parent can reflect, the treatment will most likely be more challenging. Sometimes parents actively resist reflection. For example, a parent might indicate this by saying, "There is no reason to go digging around in the past and blaming my parents for stuff. Besides, I am doing just fine with my kids."

If parents have low RF, the initial phase is focused on building reflective capacity. Sometimes just inviting parents into reflective dialogue can make a significant change. Many parents, when asked what they think their child is feeling, have said, "No one has ever asked me that before." If they are resisting RF, the initial phase is designed to strengthen the holding environment to the point where the parent feels safe enough to enter into reflective dialogue.

Empathy

Empathy is learned during early development, and the ability to be empathic is associated with security of attachment (Sroufe, 1983; Kestenbaum, Farber, & Sroufe, 1989). We think of empathy as consisting of two parts: perspective taking and emotional resonance. Perspective taking involves the cognitive capacity to step inside the shoes of another and imagine the world from the other's point of view. This choice to take another's perspective helps us imagine what it might be like to be on the receiving end of our own behavior. It can also help clarify whether our intentions differ from another's experience of what we did.

The second aspect of empathy is emotional resonance. In the words of Carl Rogers, "To sense the client's private world as if it were your own, but without ever losing the 'as if' quality—this is empathy, and this seems essential to therapy" (1957, p. 98). It is important to help parents enhance their ability to resonate with what another person feels while simultaneously acknowledging that their experience of the other's experience may be distorted. For example, having feelings about their child's feelings can bias parents' understanding of their child's experience. It is also important to remind parents that they can only guess at another's feelings. Parents need to stay open to the possibility they may be wrong and that even their own children's feelings may differ radically from their own.

Parents' capacity to have empathy for themselves is also important. The most common defensive strategy for managing relationship conflict is to dismiss the conflict and blame the child or blame yourself. During the COSI we're hoping to get a glimpse of whether the parent demonstrates compassion regarding her own struggles versus self-blame. Empathy for the self is quite different from making excuses for one's behavior. Empathy for the self has the quality of acknowledging an error and at the same time maintaining a sense of self-worth and compassion for the self. A very common response to viewing the linchpin issue on video is for the parent to fall into a negative representation of herself and communicate self-blame to the therapist. As long as the parent is caught in blaming herself, her learning will be significantly impaired. Rather than talk her out of her pain and shame, this approach is designed to honor the parent's history and current feeling with empathy, support the parent's reflection on the defenses against the feelings, and help the parent create a choice of a nondefensive response that will better serve her and her child.

Many questions in the COSI focus on the parents' understanding of their child's experience. The early questions focus on both the parent's and the child's experience in the Strange Situation that they have just completed. These questions offer an opportunity to recognize whether caregivers are able to understand and identify with the needs and struggles of their child. For example, when asked about the child's experience of separation in the SSP, does the caregiver resonate with the child's distress? Does the caregiver recognize that the child needed comfort? Or does the caregiver deny this need, dismissing the vulnerability that is apparent in the child's tears? ("I think she was just tired. She missed her nap because we had to come here today. She normally doesn't cry like that.")

Sometimes the caregiver may focus only on a sense of blame and inadequacy. This can take the form of feeling blamed by the child ("I'm not sure what to do. I think she thinks I'm a terrible mother because I'm working again.") or self-blame ("When she was crying at the door, it's like she'd figured me out: 'Mom let me down again.' I just never know what to do.").

Looking at both the parent's descriptions in the COSI and the video from the interactional assessment allows you to contrast the parent's perception about the experience with the actual interactions. Doing this provides a window through which you can see the parent's capacity for empathy with the child. When a parent's capacity for empathy is low, the therapist will need to be on the lookout for the parent's vigilance concerning criticism and failure. Low empathy is often correlated with struggles on the bottom of the Circle. If genuine empathy is present, it can be used to support and motivate the parent and holds promise for a relatively straightforward journey through the video reflection process. If empathy is noticeably missing, especially if the parent seems dismissing of any need for comfort on the part of the child, the therapeutic process will need to include an artfully presented rationale for meeting needs on the bottom of the Circle. When empathy ceases being empathy and becomes overidentification with the child, therapy will most likely include helping the parent support her child's developing sense of autonomy.

Core Sensitivity

Identifying a parent's core sensitivity can be very challenging. In individual psychotherapy, the therapist has the luxury of discerning the core sensitivity of the client over time. In individual treatment the therapist has the distinct advantage of noticing specific interactional markers for a particular sensitivity and having the time to systematically ask questions about the meaning the client attributes to those markers. It is often the meaning behind the interactions that clarifies the core sensitivity, especially with clients who do not overtly exhibit a particular sensitivity.

At first we were not sure we could determine core sensitivity from a standardized interview and experimented with a good number of COSIs before we were confident that it was possible. The more flexible and adaptive a parent's defense is, the more difficult it is to determine the core sensitivity from the COSI. The more rigid and pervasive the defenses, the easier it is to determine the sensitivity. Fortunately, this corresponds to the relative significance of the core sensitivity in treatment planning: with highly defensive parents in particular, identifying the core sensitivity offers a roadmap for avoiding and/or responding to the parents' defensiveness. We find that understanding parents' core sensitivity also allows us to speak about their defenses in a manner that resonates with their experience. It provides a shortcut to making sense of their shark music and what is likely to trigger it. It clarifies what to do and, possibly more important, what not to do in treatment. The COSI case example presented later in this chapter illustrates how we obtain clues to a parent's core sensitivity from each question, and the detailed case examples in Chapters 13–15 illustrate how core sensitivities are factored into treatment planning and implementation.

It is essential, however, that therapists continue to evaluate parents' core sensitivities throughout the intervention to avoid falling prey to the tendency to make the parent fit the diagnosis rather than making the diagnosis fit the parent—or to limit the parent to a diagnosis. To paraphrase Alfred Korzybski,[1] core sensitivities are very useful maps but must always be seen as only a map and not the person the map represents.

THE CIRCLE OF SECURITY INTERVIEW

The COSI is not a research-based procedure like the AAI (George et al., 1984; Main & Goldwyn, 1984; Main et al., 2003), but rather a series of questions for clinical use in the development of treatment plans. The questions are, however, built on the groundbreaking work of the developers of the AAI, and two of the questions come from that interview. Three others come from the PDI (Aber et al., 1985). The remaining questions

---

[1] Scientist/philosopher Korzybski is credited with the idea that "the map is not the territory it represents" (1958, p. 58).

were influenced by the AAI and PDI, except those regarding the parents' response to the SSP that they have just completed. Those questions are unique to the COSI.

The COSI (Form 10.1, on pages 249–254) contains 25 questions. However, over the years we have changed the interview to suit various contexts in which it was being used, and we encourage clinicians to add or subtract questions as needed. To be sensitive to parents' fatigue and scheduling constraints, we designed the interview to last approximately 1 hour. Since it is a semistructured interview, the time required varies because of the brevity or length of the parent's responses.

ADMINISTERING THE CIRCLE OF SECURITY INTERVIEW

The COSI is administered by the interviewer with only the parent present. It is helpful to minimize distractions because it is a rather demanding process. The interview is filmed for later review, rather than recorded solely through transcripts as with the AAI, because we are interested in both verbal and nonverbal communication seen in tone, timing, and demeanor. The AAI is scored solely on the language reflected in the transcript of the interview, but having access to nonverbal as well as verbal communication helps identify dissonance between what is said and how it is said. Such dissonance can offer clues to unspoken meaning.

The video camera is placed on a tripod and is unattended during the interview. It is important not to zoom in so close that you can't see body postures or that slight movements take the person out of the frame. On the other hand, we don't want to have such a wide angle that it is hard to see facial expression. A good compromise is having the person's head and knees both in the picture. Using an external microphone will give much better sound quality than a microphone built into the camera. We also use a checklist (shown in Box 10.1) to make sure there is tape or adequate digital memory in the camera, the microphone and camera are turned on, the parent is in the picture, and so forth. It seems silly, but it is so easy to make mistakes in the rush and bother of the day.

Interviewers are encouraged to be very familiar with the interview so that questions can be asked in an engaging manner. We recommend checking off questions as they are asked and answered to avoid repeating or skipping questions. It is also important to stick to the script and not add questions or suggest answers. Adding (or deleting) questions alters the structure and rhythm of the questions, which are sequenced to increase and decrease

---

BOX 10.1. CHECKLIST FOR COSI INTERVIEWER

_____ Make certain microphone is on.

_____ Make certain that the camera is turned on.

_____ Make sure there is sufficient digital memory or place videotape in older-model cameras.

_____ Confirm positioning of parent in video screen. (Try to focus the picture on the face and upper half of parent's torso.)

_____ Press record button.

_____ Make certain "REC" image is on screen before beginning interview. Listen with earphone to be sure you have sound.

_____ Make tissues available.

_____ Have a copy of the final release form, with explanation.

_____ Have a black pen for signing.

---

the intensity in order to stress interviewees just enough to get data without flooding them with emotion.

The important data emerges from how the interviewee manages the discomfort evoked.

It is important to remember that this is a clinical interview and that some of the questions will evoke answers that are uncomfortable not just for the parent but also for the interviewer. It is common to be a bit nervous about setting up the video equipment, being recorded, keeping the questions straight, and so forth. Yet responses to uncomfortable material such as nervous laughter can influence the tone of the interview. It is the interviewer's job to Be-With the parent in a warmly engaged, interested, concerned, and respectful manner.

We recommend viewing the resulting video not just to assess the parent but also to evaluate your own effectiveness in Being-With the parent. Noticing how you respond to being emotionally activated can help you learn not to interfere with the parents' process. It is even more helpful to take turns watching videos with a colleague and talking about the ways you can each improve as interviewers.

The Importance of Timing

The timing of the questions is important. Too long a pause after an answer can confuse parents, make them feel their answer was inadequate, or imply that they are in a therapy session. On the other hand, asking questions in a rapid-fire manner suggests to parents that their answers need to be brief, which may inhibit responses that could provide valuable information. Some questions have multiple parts, and it is important to wait for an answer on each part before proceeding.

Getting Specifics

A key dimension derived from the AAI is to ask for episodic memories rather than general descriptions. There are three types of responses—episodic, pseudo-episodic, and generalized descriptions. It is important for the interviewer to be able to differentiate among them. Episodic memories are memories of an actual event, for example, "Last Wednesday, when we were at the park. . . . " Pseudo-episodic responses sound like "Every time we go to the park . . . ," and generalized responses take the form of "It is just always fun to be together." Episodic memories help clarify whether the initial answer is grounded in actual experience. An answer that cannot be backed up with an episodic memory may be highly filtered or may consist of hazy images of events or experiences that never actually occurred.

It's typical for participants' first response to be generalized memories, such as "My mother was loving because she used to read to me at night." When this happens, use questions and prompts to probe for a specific episode, such as "Please describe a recent incident when this happened" and "Can you think of a specific example?" If a parent uses "enjoyable" as an adjective to describe her relationship with her child and, when asked for an episodic memory, says, "We just have fun," the interviewer needs to prompt for a specific memory. If the person responds to the prompt by saying "We have fun all the time, playing, watching TV," a second prompt is needed, such as "Can you tell me about the last time you remember that happening?" If the interviewee says, "This past Wednesday" with no description, the interviewer needs to ask the parent to describe the experience.

Follow the script in terms of how many times to prompt, because parents' reluctance or inability to produce episodic memories is important information. When parents do not provide episodic memories, they expose a crack in their ability to talk coherently about emotion-laden issues. In a sense, analysis of those cracks sheds light on the parent's internal working model.

The prescribed prompts help guide the interviewer in situations where the parent is offering very little information. With some parents, however, it is difficult to hold their answers to the questions asked. When parents go on long tangents, it is sometimes necessary to provide some structure.

A pattern of long tangential answers gives us information, but once that pattern is established, if the interview is becoming excessively long, the interviewer may need to intervene (e.g., "Because we only have an hour, I may need to interrupt you sometimes so that we can get through all of the questions").

Effective assessment via the COSI takes practice and experience. After analyzing many COSIs, patterns that were initially hidden begin to emerge. Also, with experience and supervision, different questions begin to be asked. As curiosity matures it becomes clear that often questions are more useful than answers. We encourage therapists to team up with a colleague to gain insights from one another about what the COSI can—and cannot—reveal. Two sets of eyes often see more than twice as much as one set of eyes. We also hope that readers who intend to do this work on a regular basis will obtain additional training and supervision. In the meantime, though, the rules of thumb in Box 10.2 provide useful guidelines.

INTERPRETING THE CIRCLE OF SECURITY INTERVIEW

A great deal of information is embedded in parents' responses to questions on the COSI. The information can be found in everything from simple content to the interactional process in the interview. To retrieve the richness of the interview one must simultaneously ask what is being said, how is it being said, when is it being said, and why is it being said.

What is the parent saying?
How is the parent saying it?
When is the parent saying it?
Why is the parent saying it?

The "what" of a response is the content. Simple content can be useful, but in some ways it is the weakest source of information from the COSI. It can offer information such as the number and age of children, specific events, and so forth, but may not tell us what those things mean to the parent. Knowing that a parent had a miscarriage does not tell us whether the parent felt disappointed, relieved, sad, angry, or guilty. As you go through the interview you may find patterns in the content that contain useful cues or descriptions of themes such as intrusiveness, separation, criticism, and so on. Patterns are stronger information than single incidents. Any pattern that emerges may shed light on the parent's core sensitivity.

BOX 10.2. RULES OF THUMB FOR ADMINISTERING THE COSI

1. If asked if you observed the Strange Situation, answer truthfully. If not asked, don't volunteer that you did or did not see the parent's Strange Situation.

2. When a question asks the respondent to focus on her own experience (e.g., "What was that like for you?" or "How did that make you feel?") and she focuses on her child's experience (or another's experience, or on information), return to the question once more: "And how did that make you feel when [whatever the question focuses on] happened?"

3. When a question asks for specific information regarding an event and the respondent gives a general answer to the first probe, it can be uncomfortable to ask the second probe, but don't skip it.

4. If during an answer to one question the respondent inadvertently answers an upcoming question, ask the question anyway: "Can you say *anything else* about [the question already answered]?" or "You already gave some information about this, but the next question is _____."

5. When administering question 7 regarding the five words or phrases to describe the relationship with the child:
   - Tell the respondent that you will write the five words down and that you will then ask her some questions about her words. Be patient and encourage her to take the time to find five.
   - If, because of time constraints, you decide to follow up on only three of the words or phrases, after you have the five words, tell her you are now going to ask her about three of her words. Ask her about the first, third, and last word: "Your first [third, last] word was _____. Please describe a specific experience or incident that would explain why you chose _____." If she gives a general description, ask for a specific incident. If she gives a poorly elaborated specific incident, ask for another specific example. If after asking twice for specific episodic memories you do not gain them, go on to the next question.
   - If the second or fourth word is particularly different or informative, ask about that word and drop the least informative word from answer 1, 3, or 5.

6. Try to show empathy and understanding by sparingly using *nonverbal* responses (nods, smiles, "hmmm," etc.). Avoid making *comments* such as "That must have made you feel _____." Remember, many of the people you are interviewing are more adept at focusing their attention on what others want than on what they think and feel. We want them to fill in all the information from their own unique perspective. Offering our responses, opinions, and verbal encouragement may inadvertently invite them to follow our reactions to the material they are presenting.

7. When you ask a question and the respondent does not seem to be answering it, ask the question one more time.

8. When asked questions regarding her child's experience, if a parent does not offer an emotionally oriented description, ask: "And how did that make [name of child] feel?"

9. If an answer is too minimal (one or two words), ask once for more information: "Can you tell me more about _____?"

You will also notice that after each question we put themes in brackets that may emerge in the answer. For example, question 15 ("Does [name of child] ever get angry or frustrated with you?" [RF; empathy; emotion containment, positive vs. negative attribution]) is designed to shed light on the themes in the brackets. The answer, "Yes, and I wish I had a better way to respond, poor sweetheart, I tend to get as angry as he does" paints a very different picture of the parent than the answer, "Yeah, but it's not a problem for me. He's a brat and I just put him in his room until he decides to act his age." The first answer shows empathy and a positive attribution of the child (poor sweetheart), ability to reflect on the self ("I tend to get as angry . . . "), enough emotional containment to acknowledge the parent's part in the problem. The second answer shows a problem with reflective functions ("Yeah, but . . . "), a lack of empathy, a lack of emotional containment (dismissing), and a negative attribution ("it's not a problem. He's a brat . . . ").

How a parent responds in terms of demeanor (timid, aggressive, pleading, etc.) gives us building blocks to construct a complete picture. It is useful to look for clues to whether the parent is reporting information in a straightforward manner or there are elements present such as distancing, compliance, or devaluation that would shed light on the core sensitivity. Examples will be given in the case at the conclusion of this chapter.

To understand the salient issues of when a response is made, we must put the answer in the context of the current interaction. If the parent is responding to a perceived challenge, criticism, or intrusion, his response tells us something about his defensive style. For example, a parent who had just been asked to recall what he did as a child when he was upset looked at the interviewer with a suddenly harsh glance, pulled himself back into his chair, and said, "I turned up the sound on the TV the way my dad always did." The perceptible distance and modest aggression in his response helped us recognize how he was both currently committed to keeping a distance from anything to do with needs on the bottom of the Circle and hoping to maintain a defensive idealization of his father. This is consistent with esteem sensitivity and suggests the linchpin struggle in his relationship with his daughter would be on the bottom of the Circle.

Sometimes a response is just a response.

It is critical to keep in mind at all times that sometimes the only answer to why a parent said something is that it is a reflective, vulnerable, and accurate answer to a question. An important criterion for reflective vulnerability is that it not only includes descriptions of the child but also takes into consideration the parent's part in the interaction and does so without blaming the child or the parent. When describing his own history the parent can coherently share the emotional impact his own parent's actions had on him and sees his parent not only from the perspective of being a child but also now from the perspective of an adult without making excuses for his parent's actions. This is a high bar for vulnerability, and people fall at different points along a continuum from defensive to reflective and vulnerable. Connecting the transgenerational links from what they learned as a child to how they currently parent is also a good example of strong reflective vulnerability.

For example, it is not uncommon for a parent to imply that she didn't get exactly what she needed growing up when it came to comfort in times of distress. "My mom wasn't so great at picking me up and putting me on her lap. I struggle there too with Missy. Even though I know it is a problem for her, I still see myself avoiding picking her up." Such a parent isn't being defensive; she's telling the simple yet painful truth. She's clearly open to truth telling about how she is still struggling. The content might suggest safety sensitivity, but someone who was very safety sensitive would be unlikely to share that much information. The question is more a testament to how much access this parent has to her genuine self and how safe and open she feels in the process. The answer is not serving a defensive function. In contrast, the example cited above shows how the father's answer used aggression and distancing as a way to warn off the interviewer and stay away from the painful realization that his own father had never responded to his needs on the bottom of the Circle. Understanding how an answer functions in the relationship with the interviewer is very helpful.

The following are COSI answers from the mother in Chapter 8 who was used as an example in the interactional assessment. Each answer is followed by observations about the implications of the parent's perception, include several hypotheses regarding the meaning and the core sensitivity of this parent's answers. We find it useful to create competing explanations for the data and at the end resolve the conflicts to create one overarching organization. Sometimes one explanation becomes so unlikely that it is simply dropped. During trainings we often ask participants to explain a statement from the perspective of each of the three core sensitivities. This is not the complete COSI because, for brevity's sake, we selected the most salient questions and answers for use in a clinical (rather than a research) setting.

The first five questions of the COSI we call "reaction to the SSP." It is useful to ask these questions immediately after the SSP so the memory is fresh in the parent's mind.

Case Example

2. What was it like for you to participate in the experience you just completed with him/her?

I was a little worried about how he would do, and it felt good to see how well he managed it all and kept himself busy with the toys. There were a lot of toys that he liked in the box.

Implications of parent perception. This parent is showing concern, but we don't yet know if the concern is for herself or the child ("I was a little worried about how he would do"). We see both potential signs of empathy and a potential understanding of emotion regulation by her use of the words "managed it all" and might see this as a possible strength in terms of recognizing the importance of managing stressful experience. At issue is how this caregiver makes sense of her son's need at this point and her approach to the regulation of emotional difficulty.

Does her comment that she "felt good" about how her child kept "himself busy" with "toys he liked in the box" imply a sense of pride in his self-sufficiency and relief in his choice to not show he was vulnerable and missed her? Does her comment imply that she values his need for her while simultaneously welcoming his capacity to busy himself until her return? If the former, this would imply a need in treatment to focus on her tendency to dismiss needs on the bottom of the Circle. If the latter, it may speak to her valuing of his need for both self-regulation and shared regulation, implying a secure base and safe haven already being present in the relationship. It is important to pay attention to the fact that her assertion that she "felt good" could be masking disappointment that he didn't need her more. If this were the case, then it could imply her need to be needed, moving the potential intervention in the direction of issues regarding the top of the Circle.

3. You were asked to leave [name of child] in the room two times. What do you think that was like for him/her each time? (It is acceptable for parent to give a general description of both separations or be specific for each.) What was that like for you each time?

He seemed to do OK. The first time was easier because the stranger was there. On the second time he needed a little reassurance. He did really well handling it all. I think he is used to separations because I drop him off every day at child care.

Implications of parent perception. This parent is again showing signs of recognizing her child's need to self-regulate. We have no idea at this point if this is tending in the direction of her valuing his needs for both self- and coregulation (secure) or hoping he is self-sufficient with few, if any, needs on the bottom of the Circle (insecure/avoidant), or wanting him to require assurance, thus keeping his relationship with her central (insecure/ ambivalent).

"He did really well handling it all" can be a statement of recognition of his capacity to make sense of this current stress and work within the parameters of trust until she returns. Or it may mean that she is proud, disappointed, or relieved by his not needing another for self-regulation. If she feels proud, that could be consistent with esteem sensitivity. If she is relieved, this mother would likely begin to show signs of either esteem or safety sensitivity as the interview moves along. Disappointment is more likely to be seen with a mother who is separation sensitive. Proud, disappointed, or relieved cannot be differentiated by the content alone. Her demeanor and the contexts may offer clues. Also, we need to be very careful not to rule out the possibility that she is speaking from her genuine self.

4. Most parents have never had a chance to see their child from behind a one-way mirror.
   a. While you stood there watching [name of child] was there anything that stood out for you?

   I was impressed by his concentration playing with the toys. He was so absorbed in it that he did not really interact much with the stranger. I think being able to focus like that is a good thing.

Implications of parent perception. Yet again it is too early to decide what this response actually means. It shows that this caregiver is able to see her child's actions and make at least some sense of them. She doesn't connect his "concentration playing with the toy" as a means of self-soothing his distress at being left in the room with a stranger. This mom notices that he chose not to interact with the stranger and seems comfortable with this. Is she tracking his need to absorb himself with the toys as a way to manage the difficulty of the separation? If she sees that, we still don't yet know how she makes sense of this difficulty. Is it because she is gone? Is it because strangers aren't ever comfortable for him? Is this something she is proud of ("I was impressed by his concentration") and hence something she finds ways of encouraging in a way that values self-sufficiency over mutuality? Is this something she mentions as positive but actually feels slightly disappointed about? Can she welcome both self-regulation and mutual regulation?

> b. What do you think he/she needed during the time that you were watching him/her?
>
> *He didn't seem to need much of anything; if he did, I think he would have said something. The second time was probably a little stressful for him. He is not used to being left alone in a new situation like that.*

Implications of parent perception. Slight red flag: "He didn't seem to need much of anything." Having been left alone with a stranger in a strange room would understandably be stressful for a child. In addition, in separation one he asked her not to go, and she watched him play through the one-way glass with flat affect and looking sadly at the door. He did not appear to be having a good time. Her comment implies a potential dismissing of needs on the bottom of the Circle (protection, comfort, organization of feelings). The caregiver then brings her observation back toward a sense of balance: "The second time was probably a little stressful for him. He is not used to being left alone in a new situation like that." Recall that during the second separation he went to the door and called out for mom. So with a big cue like that she gets it and calls it a little stressful. Is she describing the simple clarity that goes with recognizing that he was somewhat stressed, but not overly stressed? (A reality check is inherent in the SSP because the evaluator can look at the video and decide how much distress the child is showing. If it is significant and the caregiver describes it as "a little stressful," this begins to look like a minimizing/dismissing of a bottom-half need. If on the other hand the child does in fact look only modestly distressed, we can increasingly trust this caregiver's perception of the child.) Her comment that "he is not used to being left alone in a new situation like that" may well be a clear and simple observation of what he is used to. It may also be a hint of how she works to make sure he doesn't experience too much aloneness, a kind of vigilance that may imply struggles on the top of the Circle.

5. You came back into the room two times:
   a. What do you think that was like for [name of child] each time?

   I think he was happy to see me. He didn't play much with the stranger.

Implications of parent perception. At the heart of the SSP is the reunion following each separation. The inevitable stress of being left behind by a primary attachment figure activates the attachment system in every child, including the full range of emotions that accompany being separated from the one the child relies on for the regulation of distress. Hence the child's response to the caregiver as well as the caregiver's response to the child (and the child's response to the caregiver's response) upon reunion is central to how attachment research has made sense of issues surrounding security and insecurity.

Part of how COS understands the parent's perception of the child upon reunion is that this particular time of reconnection stresses the parent in ways that may well highlight feelings and memories associated with his or her own history of emotion regulation and the level of support available in times of significant emotional need. The understanding is that the limitations in the caregiver's history may well repeat themselves (shark music and the subsequent nonconscious choice to stay away from painful feelings and memories) in the response to the child at this critical time in the SSP.

The brevity of this mother's response raises questions about her level of comfort regarding being needed on the bottom of the Circle. She states that he was happy to see her. Is this a way to not acknowledge his stress and just stay with all is good and happy, or is this a way to say her presence changed his feeling in a very positive way, implying she could see he wasn't happy when she was gone? The comment about the stranger could imply that she sees he acted in a manner indicating he was uncomfortable or she might be disappointed that he wasn't more social. However, even more than the specifics of her response the markedly succinct response to a moment of conscious (and likely nonconscious) distress in both of them says something about her potential to minimize his need on the bottom of the Circle.

When we put together her responses thus far about how she thought he handled the separation and reunion, we don't know quite what all this means. Does it mean that she is proud of him for not needing her (esteem sensitive) or that she is relieved that he doesn't demand too much of her (safety sensitive)? In either case, there is enough information to form a good question, such as whether she hears shark music when her child needs comfort. There is not enough information to make a judgment.

b. What was the reunion like for you each time?

I was a little uncomfortable that he might be upset and glad to see that he wasn't.

Implications of parent perception. What can we discern about her feeling and representations associated with her child's needs on the bottom of the circle? She indicates she is both uncomfortable in anticipating that he might be upset and glad he was not. Her anticipatory discomfort in this context combined with positive feeling that what she anticipated did not happen adds some weight to the question we are holding about whether she has shark music when he is on the bottom of the circle. What this means in terms of core sensitivity is still not clear.

In addition, we can see that this mother has a capacity for self-reflection, can focus on the self ("I was a little uncomfortable"), and is willing to share this with the interviewer. This is a powerful indicator that this caregiver may well be open to building a therapeutic alliance and to using the interviewer as a secure base. The willingness to share her emotional experience implies a nondefensive stance regarding how she may appear to another, a trait that is most commonly associated with safety sensitivity and insecurity or real self-expression and security. Secure parents often feel they have nothing to hide and thus simply describe what is actually happening. Safety-sensitive parents have an internal imperative to tell the truth, not because they welcome the exposure, but because they've come to believe that there must be some reference point that is trustworthy. Unable to trust others, they go out of their way to make of themselves this reference point of reliability.

c. In either of the reunions, did [name of child] show you that she/he needed comfort from you?

The first time I think he was happy to have me back so that he could play with me. The second time he needed a hug, so yes, he wanted a little comfort.

Implications of parent perception. Again, this mother can observe and make sense of her child's feelings (empathy) and also recognize his actual need, especially when his cue is clear and strong. In the first reunion he goes from somber to smiling after he places his hand on her leg. This is not exactly "happy." In the second reunion when he approaches her with a sad face and is subdued in his responses to her, she gets that he needs comfort and gives him a hug.

At the same time she, to some degree, minimizes that need by casting it as a desire to play with her. This may well begin to fit the "compromise" position of many safety-sensitive parents, who want to be there for their children while simultaneously hoping to keep some distance. To have a child who needs her "too much" might feel overwhelming, but to have a child who needs her to play with him can keep the level of need in a more manageable range.

Her second response again confirms her capacity to see need and a willingness to acknowledge and meet that need. Again, that need is ever so slightly minimized ("he wanted a little comfort"). Her response is not defensive and indicates that she may form an alliance that will support therapy and another hint in the direction of safety sensitivity and/or real self capacity.

The indicators for building an alliance are always important to note. This mother is now consistently offering her capacity to reflect *with* another in her presence and a capacity to share what she seems to actually be feeling, even when it is uncomfortable. These are very important indicators of potential success in the upcoming treatment.

   d. *Decision tree*:

1. [If he/she showed a need for comfort:]
   a. What did you do?

He came over to me and gave me that "give me a hug" look, and so I did.

Implications of parent perception. Again, she offers more reflection. She also clarifies that she can recognize his need regarding what her child was asking and respond to it. This response combined with the others seems to indicate that even if she is uncomfortable on the bottom of the Circle when her child cues her very directly, she can manage her own feelings and respond to his. Her commitment to her child and to meeting needs, despite discomfort, also speaks to the potential for an increasing capacity in the direction of meeting needs once she more fully understands how important they are and how her history may play a part in why she currently experiences discomfort.

With the differential for the core sensitivity leaning between esteem and safety, her capacity to offer vulnerable information about herself and lack of emphasis on performance takes the differential in the direction of safety sensitivity. While esteem-sensitive parents also struggle with needs on the bottom of the Circle, they are less likely to bluntly imply they are so limited in their capacity or even interest in meeting them. There is often a tendency to put a positive spin on each aspect of their interaction with their child. ("Oh, I think he may have been a bit uncomfortable, but he is so inquisitive that when I came in the room he wanted to make sure I saw that new toy.")

b. How did it feel when he needed comfort from you?

It felt fine. When he needs that, he lets me know, and he is not usually clingy or anything.

Implications of parent perception. "Fine" as a response says something about how need is acceptable, but not necessarily comfortable. Her choice of words to define what he didn't do ("clingy") lets us know what she is hoping to avoid and may well have taught her child not to express. That said, she has clearly not taught her child to deny that he has a need on the bottom of the Circle. He lets her know with a modest range of intensity, and she responds in kind. He may well need more, but clearly the job is getting done to some degree.

c. Is this the way he/she usually shows you he/she needs comfort?

Yes, this is pretty typical.

Implications of parent perception. This all seems to be par for the course. We may well have a fairly clear sense of their relationship regarding needs on the bottom of the Circle.

6. When you asked [name of child] to pick up the toys, could you describe what happened?
a. What do you think that was like for her/him?

He didn't want to do it, but that is typical. Once you get him going he does fine.

b. What was it like for you?

No big deal, something we do every day.

Implications of parent perception. This question asks the caregiver to reflect on how the child responds to hierarchy (hands). In this case the mother recognizes that her child isn't happy about needing to clean up, but she also recognizes that he knows she's the one in charge. No drama. No problem. ("No big deal, something we do every day.") In the SSP, when he resisted the cleanup she acknowledged his feelings that he didn't want to stop reading and shifted into taking charge in a firm and kind manner, and he complied. Her description here fits well with what happens.

Her perception that he responded well to her being in charge seems to be a positive aspect in their relationship. This is a clear example of a parent who doesn't feel helpless in the face of taking charge and doesn't experience a negative attribution when she needs to be.

8. What gives you the most joy in being [name of child]'s parent?

Watching him learn and grow and change.

Implications of parent perception. This question offers the caregiver an opportunity to explore the full range of delight in her/his child. There are no typical answers. This mother identifies her delight in the child's top half of the Circle capacities. Less focused on the relational closeness (understandable within the context of a growing perception of this caregiver as safety sensitive), her interest is in his capacity to learn and mature. These are clearly healthy goals and worthy of her delight.

a. Would you give an example?

I think it happens all the time. Every day he learns something new.

Implications of parent perception. This isn't an episodic memory. Rather it's a generalized summary. Hence the need for the interviewer to probe again.

Would you give me a recent example?

Well, let me see . . . it was just the other day he was eating a yogurt and after he finished he threw the container away. He just figured it out all by himself and I did not have to say a thing. That is so nice.

Implications of parent perception. Her answer is coherent and episodic within the context of the larger topic of learning and maturation. Of interest is why his capacity to learn greater autonomy and independence ("He just figured it out all by himself") brings joy to her. This can be both a sign of her support of his genuine security and/or a sign of her safety-sensitive need for self-sufficiency in her son.

b. What do you imagine he/she was thinking about you at that time?

This makes Mom happy. After he threw it away he looked at me and smiled and I told him that he did a good job.

Implications of parent perception. This may be an example of mutual miscuing or support for competence in learning. He seems to know that she likes his competence and, while important, it may be the centerpiece of their relationship. He knows what she wants and she rewards him for this knowing. While it is potentially positive for him to experience her approval of such a skill set, it can also suggest how they might share an unspoken agreement regarding her need for him to prioritize independence. So the question to hold is whether she overemphasizes self-reliance to protect herself from her discomfort with close intimate connection.

c. As you remember this example, what do you think about yourself?

I taught him how to think for himself, and it is working. I am doing OK.

Implications of parent perception. In terms of both parental hierarchy and the top of the Circle, this mother is very comfortable supporting this child's autonomy and capacity to work together. When considering that the SSP shows that this dyad is struggling on the bottom of the Circle, this mother's apparent agenda to view successful parenting as limited to the top of the Circle becomes clearer.

9. What gives you the most pain or difficulty in being [name of child]'s parent?

Well, it doesn't happen often, but sometimes he can get a bit whiny, and nothing seems to make him feel better.

Implications of parent perception. Once again, the theme surrounding struggles with comforting and some possible negative attribution ("whining") interfaces with the possible lack of organizing feelings on her part ("nothing seems to make him feel better"). The combination of a less than positive attribution with the sense that she is out of options is a common response for a caregiver who doesn't feel either capable or effective on the bottom half of the Circle. What she may be describing is her lack of options when it comes to offering herself as the source of emotion regulation for his emotional struggles. This is clearly a source of difficulty and pain for her.

a. Would you give an example?

I think mostly when he is tired or not feeling too well.

Implications of parent perception. This is not yet a full episodic memory. Does this mean that she is struggling with gaining coherence around this particular topic, and might this mean that this is where the focus of an intervention can be made? The interviewer probes further.

Would you give me a recent example?

It was not so recent, but over the holidays we had company and he was all wound up and excited, and one night he just melted down. I couldn't get him interested in anything, and later it was a struggle to get him to bed. Finally I ended up staying with him until he fell asleep. The next morning he was fine.

Implications of parent perception. She does land the memory in an episodic format. What she also makes clear is that her preferred technique for regulating his affective storm is to bring him further onto the top of the Circle ("get him interested in [something]"). Distraction and diversion can be helpful, but when used as the primary option during a time of emotional difficulty it shows how this mother struggles with the bottom of the Circle. This may well be in keeping with her potential safety sensitivity, actions that include a need to keep him somewhat distant and not "too close."

b. What do you imagine he/she was thinking about you at that time?

I am not sure, perhaps "Why can't you help me feel better?"

Implications of parent perception. This statement is significantly non-defensive and shows both reflective functioning (an ability to see how she isn't yet offering all of what her son needs) and empathy (the capacity to sense his own need and how it isn't being met). This level of awareness and the willingness to share it speaks to how she wants to find a way to be the parent he needs. It also speaks to her willingness to reveal vulnerable information about herself.

c. As you remember this example, what do you think about yourself?

When he gets wound up like that, it winds me up too, and I sometimes wonder if my reaction doesn't make it hard for him. I don't feel terrible about myself or anything, but I don't like it when I get all stressed out like that. When I feel that way, I just want a breather, and it is hard to get that until he settles down. It kind of feels like a catch-22: if I was calmer, I could help him more, but the only way I am going to get calmer is to not be around him, and then I wouldn't be there to help him. Does that make sense?

Implications of parent perception. Her response here is pure gold in terms of revealing the mother's understanding of her own struggle. The mother is now making it clear that she is significantly committed to helping her child manage difficult emotions and yet finds herself in a bind when it comes to managing the emotional stress this evokes in herself. Her willingness to be vulnerable, to self-reflect and recognize that it is her reaction to his distress that may well be the source of his difficulty, indicates a strong capacity to be successful in therapy. A capacity to focus on the self at this level virtually guarantees that this parent is more than willing to find another way and will respond positively to the new options made available within the COS approach to her struggles.

Her framing of the problem as a "catch-22" is a clear description of the safety-sensitive "dilemma" (Masterson & Klein, 1995, p. 63): "If I was calmer, I could help him more, but the only way I am going to get calmer is to not be around him." The safety-sensitive dilemma implies that to be too close is a problem and to be too distant is also a problem. She can't regulate herself adequately when he is too close, but when she goes away she's aware that they both lose out on what is needed. Neither closeness nor distance works; hence the catch-22. What's so poignant about her realization is that she ends it with her genuine compassion for her child, speaking about how the current situation doesn't allow her to "be there to help him." This mother is clearly looking to find a way beyond this dilemma.

13. Do you think [name of child] knows when you are upset or distressed?

Yes, I think he does.

Implications of parent perception. Her answer is a good sign that this parent can recognize her child's mind as attuned to hers without either seeing this as an exceptional capacity (esteem sensitivity) or much needed by the parent (separation sensitivity).

a. How does he/she know that you are upset or distressed?

I think he can just sense it; children know. I also try to let him know my feelings so that he doesn't have to guess what is going on. I mean obviously not all my feelings, but if I am having a bad day I will say so. If I am having a bad day, I don't want him to feel responsible or anything.

Implications of parent perception. Again, she is being clear and well balanced. She shows signs of being well aware of her mind as her own and her child's as his own, and aware that they need to be intentional about sharing rather than doing any kind of "mind reading," which can imply exceptional gifts and one-mindedness (esteem sensitivity) or wishful thinking and a kind of clinging to the child (separation sensitive). This mother, while appearing to land somewhere in the safety-sensitive range, is clearly secure enough in how she makes sense of her need to be intentional about sharing what is going on in her mind. She has clear boundaries ("[I don't share] all my feelings") and empathy for his need to not feel responsible for her experience ("I also try to let him know my feelings so that he doesn't have to guess what is going on . . . If I am having a bad day, I don't want him to feel responsible"). This clarity about separate minds is a sign of security and a support for the child to feel included in the parent's state of mind without being burdened by it. This is a significant strength and well worth acknowledging and helping this mother recognize as a strength once treatment has begun.

   b. Does he/she ever try to soothe you?
   Yes.

   Implications of parent perception. She is being clear and concise. This is precisely the clue the treating clinician will want to utilize as to how this mother will want to be approached. Be clear with her. No need to "teach" and imagine that empathy must be modeled in any way. Her empathy is fully intact. Her struggle has more to do with how to more fully trust that her empathy won't be swamped by the needs of another (her child or her therapist). Respecting her boundaries as she learns to more fully trust this is an important theme (shark music) that will allow her new options and choices with her child. She clearly wants what is best. Being available, more fully, is what will likely become the theme of her work.

   c. How does he/she do that?
   He will come over to me and touch me and say "You OK, you OK."

   Implications of parent perception. There is a shared empathy between them that is a wonderful strength. He wants her to be OK. He also may well be saying he needs more from her. Following treatment he may have greater access to her without her feeling potentially engulfed by his closeness.

   d. How does his/her soothing make you feel?
   I think it is sweet of him. It can make me smile.

   Implications of parent perception. She is saying she is fine with this level of closeness. It isn't too much. This calibrates for the clinician that she has real capacity in this area. She may want to expand beyond this, but that will be her choice. We're not looking at psychopathology in this dyad. That said, new ground can be covered; new options in the direction of closeness may be available.

e. When he/she soothes you, what do you imagine he/she is feeling?

I think it makes him feel good that he can soothe me, but it also is probably upsetting to see me that way. I don't want him to feel like it is a burden, like his job or anything.

Implications of parent perception. This is what we would hope to hear from all parents. Children need to know they can have a positive impact on their parents, even the distress of their parents. But they don't need to feel they are responsible. This mother recognizes the difference and this, again, is a significant strength, showing that she has moderate to strong reflective functioning. At the same time, her word "burden" may imply her own experience in close relationships—possibly feeling responsible in ways that aren't/weren't helpful. Remembering this word and using it at the appropriate moment in therapy may well be very useful.

14. All parents have moments of irritation or anger with their young children.
    a. What's that like for you?

I really hate it when I get angry at him.

Implications of parent perception. We're not sure yet what she means by "angry at him," but we know she is upset that she moves in that direction. We also know that she doesn't try to hide what may be seen as a liability or imperfection by the interviewer.

b. If you had to guess, what is he/she thinking about you at these times?

Oh, probably "What did I do to make her so angry?"

Implications of parent perception. This is how most, if not all, children feel when their parents get angry. It's powerful to see that she can empathize with this dilemma for her son. It may also give us a hint about how she felt as a child. Her clarity about his potential experience may tell us something about her own.

c. What are you thinking about yourself?

I don't like myself when I subject him to my anger. He's just a little kid and doesn't deserve all this.

Implications of parent perception. Her concern for her child is a good sign. We don't know what level of anger she is describing here. This will be worthy of focus during treatment, as will the level of anger she may have experienced from her caregivers in her own childhood.

> d. Does he/she ever get scared of you?
>
> *I think there are times he does, and that is just what I don't want to do.*

Implications of parent perception. This tells us more, but it still remains to be determined just what she is describing. It is possible that her own behavior is excessive. It is also (very) possible that her memories about scary behavior are impacting her assessment of her current behavior. All of this becomes grist for the mill (gradually, tentatively, carefully introduced) once therapy begins.

> e. How can you tell?
>
> *He has cried when I get angry.*

Implications of parent perception. This may well mean her behavior is intense. It may also mean that she signals him of her distress and that he is upset by her distress about her anger. This will simply need to be explored in treatment. Either way, this seems to be a topic worthy of focus and one she is likely open to addressing.

> f. What does she/he do at those times?
>
> *He is upset, and then I have to find a way to put my anger aside and help him calm down.*

Implications of parent perception. Her empathy, capacity to focus on the self, and willingness to offer emotion regulation on the bottom of the Circle are on display here. When she knows he is in significant need, she can offer the bottom of the Circle (comfort and organization of feelings). If our earlier observations are correct, it may be that when he isn't so upset she struggles, which may imply that the simple, moment-to-moment filling of his emotional cup may be difficult. If so, this could be the by-product of her safety sensitivity, a tendency to keep a consistent distance that the child will sense and not choose to travel beyond unless deeply distressed. Offering this mother access to how this steady-state distance may be a "burden" for her child might offer another option for him and a place of shared searching with her therapist during treatment.

23. Is there something that you learned from the way you were parented that you would like to pass on to [name of child]?

    My parents were into puzzles and encouraged me to figure them out, and it really helped me think for myself, and I hope he learns that.

Implications of parent perception. We are seeing signs of self-sufficiency passed along from generation to generation. Staying on the top of the Circle is considered a high priority, as it was by her parents. She has no doubt about this as important. If it were balanced well with the bottom of the Circle, she would be accurate. Without this balance, her child is out of balance.

24. Is there something in the way you were raised that you don't want to repeat with [name of child]?

    I had pretty good parents, but they were terribly busy, and sometimes I felt kind of alone, and I hope he doesn't end up feeling that way. I knew they were there if I needed them, but I would feel like I don't want to bother them when they had so much to do.

Implications of parent perception. This may well be the confirmation of what we have been looking at throughout the interview. She did have parents who had limited or no focus on the bottom of the Circle. Her internal experience was that she felt "alone." She exhibits her empathic hope that her child doesn't have to endure that same aloneness. To ask for needs on the bottom of the Circle is to be a "bother." She is trying to make sense of this, but without a roadmap and some clarity within a safe relational setting, this may not happen. With the support and nonintrusive sensitivity on the part of a well-thought-through treatment plan, this mother can potentially broaden the relational options with her son.

COMPLETING THE TREATMENT PLAN

The treatment plan is now ready to complete. We know from Chapter 8 that the "job gets done," and when his attachment system is activated the little boy seeks comfort, uses Mom to calm, and returns to exploration.

There is some struggle evidenced by her pushing him from the bottom of the Circle to the top of the Circle when he is still distressed and his cup is not full, and when he is more subtle about his distress she doesn't quite see it. Her struggle on the bottom of the Circle is the linchpin issue. From this observation the assumption is made that her shark music is about offering herself to soothe her son's feelings of distress. From the COSI it is now possible to know more about the meaning and significance of her shark music.

The mother explains that her shark music has to do with how she gets wound up when she is called on to be with her son when he is distressed. She is not able to self-soothe unless she can be away and have breathing room, as if being with another and managing her own emotions are incompatible. This is procedural memory in action and forms the foundation of her safety sensitivity, which is an internal working model where autonomy and relatedness are incompatible and if you pick one you lose the other. Since you want both, you end up dancing back and forth between the two, trying to find the best of both worlds and ending up with a compromise in which you don't really have either. For this mother the challenge will be to remain emotionally available even if it makes her anxious and to learn to see her son's need for her as good and not a threat that will emotionally overwhelm her. To facilitate this treatment the implicit will need to be made explicit so she will have language to describe her linchpin struggle.

The good news is that this mother already has many strengths that can help her take this risk to find a new way. She is very reflective and willing to be vulnerable. She is not blaming of her son or herself and can see that her reactions are a key part of her struggle to be with him when he needs comfort. She also demonstrates a strong level of empathy for his experience. All signs are for a positive outcome.

The therapist has a green light to go forward with the linchpin and a yellow light in terms of her anxiety about her current capacity to stay in the relationship and manage intense emotions. She is not someone who should be pushed in any way to reveal emotions, as this will back her into a corner and the only solution she would have would be to create distance from the therapist. No matter how sensitive the therapist is to this issue, inevitably she will feel that too much emotional material is coming up as she processes her video. Noticing these moments as ruptures in the closeness and intensity of the therapeutic relationship and finding ways to repair is essential to building safety in the relationship. It is very important to let her set the distance and intensity of the therapeutic encounter while remaining steady and available during a completely nonjudgmental conversation about her need to manage how close and how far she is at any given moment. Her therapist should be more invested in whether they can have a conversation about this than in how close or intense the therapy is.

The therapist should not expect this client to be pleased with clips that show how much her son needs her unless the therapist notes that once his cup is full he will naturally shift into exploration. This will give her a sense of relief that intense emotional moments with her son are time limited. Even though this feels like too much in her current relationship with her child, we are trying to help her know that her feelings are procedural (shark music) and not an accurate indicator of what really happens and thus there is light at the end of the tunnel.

The basic therapeutic story from the interactional assessment was:

"My child needs me for comfort when upset. When my child needs comfort, there are times when he miscues me by acting like he wants to play, and after a while he cues me for comfort. When I respond to his need for comfort, there comes a point when I try to get him to explore before he lets me know his cup is full and he is ready to explore. I do this as a way to manage my shark music about staying with him in his distress until he cues me he is ready to go."

This story can now be enhanced with the knowledge from her core sensitivity to form the following, more complete story:

"My child needs me for comfort when upset. When my child needs comfort, there are times when he miscues me by acting like he wants to play, and after a while he cues me for comfort. When he comes to me for comfort, I want to respond, and the intensity of his distress can also wind me up so much that I want to get away and have a breather to help myself calm down. At this moment I feel in a real bind: if I withdraw, I will feel calmer, but he does not get the comfort he needs; if I stay with him, he has me, but I am so wound up I don't know how to calm myself. To manage this I try to find something in between these two extremes by miscuing and pushing him to be interested in exploration so that I can find a way to be there and not feel like it is too much for me."

It is now possible to complete the treatment plan (see Figure 10.1). With a completed assessment the linchpin can be selected from the interaction in the SSP, and you can use the COSI to help organize a treatment approach with the parent while taking into consideration the parent's strengths and struggles within his or her own internal working model. We find the combination of the two helps maximize the possibility for negotiating a therapeutic secure base relationship and success in helping the dyad find a more secure relational style.

FIGURE 10.1. Completed Circle of Security Assessment and Treatment Plan Organizer.

1. **List the strengths and struggles on each part of the Circle.**
   - Hands
     - Follow: *Many examples of confident presence and coregulation of emotion.*
     - Misattune: *Some pressure to be on top of Circle when child is on bottom. Some pressure to be self-sufficient.*
     - Take charge: *Takes charge with confidence and without evoking fear.*
     - Abdicate: *No signs of abdicating. Mother organized the relationship.*
     - Shifting/competing strategies: *No signs.*

   - Top
     - Support for exploration: *Mom smiles as her son makes the decision to go out and explore. She has a positive attitude as he selects the toys he is interested in.*
     - Watch over me: *Mom watches him as he starts to play with the puzzle box and the doctor kit.*
     - Delight in me: *She seems to enjoy his exploration, but she is limited in expressing delight.*
     - Help me: *He asks for help with the puzzle box and blood pressure gauge.*
     - Enjoy with me: *The mutual smiling as they engage with the toys.*

   - Bottom
     - Welcome my coming to you: *In the first reunion when she smiles and he comes to her and in the second reunion when she holds out her arms and offers a hug.*
     - Protect me: *Only example was when stranger came in but Mom did not read his anxiety at that moment and he did not directly cue her that he needed protection. So no clear example. (This is not unusual in the SSP.)*
     - Comfort me: *When he had his back to her and focused on the toy it was a miscue. Mom miscued him when she pressured him to go out to explore before his cup was full. She holds out her arms, and he gets up onto her lap and calms, so she can do this.*
     - Delight in me: *Closest to delight was the reading, but still limited.*
     - Organize my feelings: *When he was standing in front of her looking sad in the second reunion, she took charge and said you need a hug and brought him in.*

(continued)

FIGURE 10.1. (*continued*)

- Of the above struggles, which is the "linchpin struggle"? *Comfort me: Mom can do this but overuses distraction to explore and rushes him to finish with comfort before he is ready. A secondary goal would be to help Mom express more delight.*

2. **What is the sensitivity?** ❑ Esteem ☑ Safety ❑ Separation

   - How does the sensitivity inform an understanding of the linchpin struggle? *His distress becomes too much for her, and she needs distance to self-soothe. She looks for a compromise of not too emotionally close and not too distant, and the compromise is to be with him in exploration.*

   - How might the sensitivity inform the presentation of the linchpin struggle?

   Give examples of how to frame the issues or approach the caregiver regarding the linchpin struggle: *Help her see that when she is with him a little more he calms and wants to explore on his own. His desire is not to control or overwhelm her with his emotions but to be with her so that he can develop and grow. Be mindful that she will want to set the distance and intensity of the therapy. Don't pursue her and don't withdraw.*

   Give examples of how **not** to frame or approach the caregiver regarding the linchpin struggle: *Don't emphasize how wonderful it is that he needs her so much and she should just embrace his emotions. Don't pressure her for feelings.*

3. **Rate reflective function.**
   A. Low: evasion and/or generalized statements to questions that ask for reflection
   B. Medium: a number of instances of reflective functioning
   C. High: reflective functioning is clear throughout the interview

   Comments: *High in reflective functioning. Here are two good examples: It kind of feels like a catch-22: if I was calmer, I could help him more, but the only way I am going to get calmer is to not be around him, and then I wouldn't be there to help him.*

   When he/she soothes you, what do you imagine he/she is feeling?
   I think it makes him feel good that he can soothe me, but it also is probably upsetting to see me that way. I don't want him to feel like it is a burden, like his job or anything.

4. **Rate empathy on two dimensions.**
   A. Rate perspective taking
      a. Low: lacks and/or evades perspective taking
      b. Medium: a number of instances of perspective taking
      c. High: perspective taking is clear throughout the interview

FIGURE 10.1. (*continued*)

Comments: *Medium to High: she can see things through his perspective and she also minimizes and comes in and out of seeing his need of her.*

When asked what he needed when alone: *He didn't seem to need much of anything.*

B. Rate affective resonance
   a. Low: lacks resonance
   b. Medium: limited resonance with certain affective states
   c. High: capacity for resonance across broad range of affect

   Comments: *She has medium capacity to resonate with his emotions. The more intense his affect, the less capacity she has to resonate with him because she gets lost in her own inner chaos.*

5. **Rate capacity to focus on the self.**
   A. Low: avoids or seems unable to focus on self
   B. Medium: limited focus on the self
   C. High: can focus on self when appropriate

   Comments: *High capacity to describe her thoughts and feelings. Examples:*
   When he gets wound up like that, it winds me up too, and I sometimes wonder if my reaction doesn't make it hard for him. I was a little uncomfortable that he might be upset.

6. **What do you want this caregiver to learn? (Mini-story for shark music)**
   Create step-by-step learning goals. (You may need to do this twice with some complex dyads where you have two linchpin goals.) [This is the version with the additional information from the COSI.]

   - Learning Goal One (My child needs me for *X* on the Circle) "Linchpin Need": *My child needs me for comfort when upset.*

   - Learning Goal Two (When child needs *X* s/he miscues by doing *Y*) "Child Linchpin Miscue": *When my child needs comfort, there are times when he miscues me by acting like he wants to play.*

   - Learning Goal Three (When my child needs *X*, I miscue by doing *Z*) "Parental Linchpin Diversion": *When he needs comfort, I encourage his exploration. When I respond to his need for comfort, there comes a point when I feel wound up, and so to manage my shark music I try to get him to explore before he is finished and he lets me know his cup is full and he is ready to explore.*

   - Learning Goal Four (I do *Z* as a way of managing my [name affect if possible]) "Shark Music": *I miscue him and encourage exploration when he*

(*continued*)

FIGURE 10.1. (*continued*)

needs comfort as a way to manage my shark music. My shark music is about how his intense emotions wind me up so much that the only way I know how to calm is to be alone. If I am alone, then so is he, and he needs my help, so I am caught between a rock and a hard place.

- Learning Goal Five (I have the capacity to respond to need X and manage my shark music as exemplified by . . .) "Underused Linchpin Capacity": *When my child is upset and comes to me (reunion 2), I offer to pick him up and comfort him. When I do this, he calms and is interested in exploration.*

FORM 10.1.

Circle of Security Interview

Hello. My name is _____. For the next hour or so, I'll be asking you a variety of questions about how it is for you to be a parent. I'd like to begin by briefly getting to know something about you and [name of child]. Then I'd like to find out your response to the experience the two of you just had together. Then I'll ask you several questions about your relationship with [name of child] and we'll close with a few questions about your life while you were growing up and your relationship with your parents.

1. To help me get to know about you and [name of child], can you briefly tell me something about your life together:
   a. When was he/she born?
   b. Do you have other children and if so, how many, and what are their names and ages?
   c. Are there other people in your life who you consider to be helpful in the raising of [name of child], and if there are can you briefly describe who they are and how they are helpful? [A general description here is acceptable.] [These questions offer an opportunity for the interviewer to join with the parent, give a general orientation to the interview, and allow the parent to both reflect on and potentially access his or her support system as the interview unfolds.]

Thank you. I'm now going to ask you several questions about the experience that you and [name of child] just had together in the room (upstairs, downstairs, down the hall, etc.).

2. What was it like for you to participate in the experience you just completed with him/her? [This gives a beginning glimpse at the parent's reflective functioning (RF) and the parent's approach to recognizing and regulating emotions in the child and him/herself, and a way to begin making sense of the parent's representations regarding self and other.]

3. You were asked to leave [name of child] in the room two times. What do you think that was like for him/her each time? [It is acceptable for parent to give a general description of both separations or be specific for each.] [RF; parent's current experience of empathy, recognition of needs, and approach to recognizing and

regulating emotions] What was that like for you each time? [RF; empathy regarding self; capacity to recognize and regulate personal emotions]

4. Most parents have never had a chance to see their child from behind a one-way mirror.
   a. While you stood there watching [name of child], was there anything that stood out for you? [RF; empathy; need recognition and emotion recognition and regulation]
   b. What do you think he/she needed during the time that you were watching him/her? [RF; emotion recognition and regulation; empathy for self]

5. You came back into the room two times:
   a. What do you think that was like for [name of child] each time? [It is acceptable for parent to give a general description of both reunions or be specific for each.] [RF; need recognition; emotion recognition and regulation; empathy]
   b. What was the reunion like for you each time? [Same rules apply as above.] [RF; emotion recognition; empathy for self]
   c. In either of the reunions, did [name of child] show you that she/he needed comfort from you? [RF; need recognition; emotion recognition and regulation; empathy]
   d. *Decision tree:*
      1. [If he/she showed a need for comfort:]
         a. What did you do? [RF; need recognition; emotion recognition and regulation; empathy]
         b. How did it feel when he needed comfort from you? [RF; need acknowledgment; capacity for self-regulation in context of need and emotional intensity]
         c. Is this the way he/she usually shows you he/she needs comfort? [RF; issues of congruence and coherence regarding vulnerable information]

   Or:
      2. [If he/she didn't seem to require comfort:]
         a. How does [name of child] show you when he/she needs comfort from you? [RF; need recognition; emotion recognition and regulation]
         b. What is it like for you when she/he shows you that he needs comfort from you? [RF; self-regulation in context of need and emotional intensity; congruence and coherence regarding vulnerable information]

6. When you asked [name of child] to pick up the toys, could you describe what happened? [Capacity for appropriate hierarchy; regulation of self and other in context of emotional intensity]
   a. What do you think that was like for her/him? [RF; empathy]
   b. What was it like for you? [RF; empathy; coherence in context of intensity]

Now I'd like to ask you some questions about your day-to-day relationship with [name of child].

7. I'd like to ask you to choose five words or phrases that describe *your relationship* with [name of child]. I know this may take a bit of time, so go ahead and think for a minute, and then I'll write down each word or phrase you give me. [RF; coherence/congruence]

   [For words 1, 3, and 5:] You used the word _____ to describe your relationship with [name of child]. Please give me a specific example or incident that comes to mind that shows what you mean by _____.

   [Ask the question for a specific memory up to two times if necessary to get an episodic memory. The same applies to all questions asking for episodic memories.]

8. What gives you the most joy in being [name of child]'s parent? [RF; emotion regulation; capacity for positive affect and pleasure]

   a. Would you give an example? [Coherence/congruence] [If necessary, probe for a specific recent example.]

   b. What do you imagine he/she was thinking about you at that time? [RF; projection/representation of other]

   c. As you remember this example, what do you think about yourself? [RF; self representation]

9. What gives you the most pain or difficulty in being [name of child]'s parent? [RF; emotion regulation; emotion containment; positive vs. negative attribution, openness regarding vulnerable information.]

   a. Would you give an example? [Coherence/congruence] [If necessary, probe for a recent example.]

   b. What do you imagine he/she was thinking about you at that time? [RF; projection/negative vs. positive attribution regarding other]

   c. As you remember this example, what do you think about yourself? [RF; self representation; empathy regarding self]

10. What is your greatest fear as [name of child]'s parent? [RF; congruence and coherence in context of painful information; capacity for containment of emotion]

11. Does [name of child] ever get silent or pull away from you? [RF; need recognition; emotion regulation in context of intensity; negative vs. positive attributions; empathy]

    [If yes:]

    a. What do you think he/she is feeling at those times? [RF; negative vs. positive attribution; emotion recognition and regulation]

    b. Why do you think he/she does that? [RF; empathy]

   c. How do you feel when he/she acts that way? [RF; congruence and coherence in context of intensity; empathy for self]

   d. What do you do? [RF; emotion regulation; understanding of repair]

12. Does he/she ever get clingy, pouty, or act younger than his/her age? [RF; need recognition; emotion recognition and regulation]

   [If yes:]

   a. What do you think he/she is feeling at those times? [RF; need recognition; empathy]

   b. Why do you think he/she acts that way? [RF; need recognition; negative vs. positive attribution]

   c. How do you feel when he/she acts that way? [RF; congruence and coherence in context of intensity; empathy for self]

   d. What do you do at those moments? [RF; congruence and coherence; need recognition regarding autonomy and comfort]

13. Do you think [name of child] knows when you are upset or distressed?

   [If yes:]

   a. How does he/she know that you are upset or distressed? [Understanding of child's age-appropriate emotional capacity; implications for idealization or role reversal; emotion regulation themes]

   b. Does he/she ever try to soothe you? [Implications for idealization or role reversal; emotion regulation]

   c. How does he/she do that?

   d. How does his/her soothing make you feel? [RF; emotion regulation; idealization or role reversal]

   e. When he/she soothes you, what do you imagine he/she is feeling? [RF; idealization or role reversal, empathy for child]

14. All parents have moments of irritation or anger with their young children.

   a. What's that like for you? [RF; coherence/congruence]

   b. If you had to guess, what is he/she thinking about you at these times? [RF; positive vs. negative attributions]

   c. What are you thinking about yourself? [RF; self representation; empathy]

   d. Does he/she ever get scared of you?

   [If yes:]

   e. How can you tell? [RF; congruence and coherence in context of intensity; empathy]

   f. What does she/he do at those times? [RF; congruence and coherence; need recognition]

15. Does [name of child] ever get angry or frustrated with you? [RF; empathy; emotion containment; positive vs. negative attribution]
    a. What's that like for you? [Coherence/congruence; empathy for self]
    b. If you had to guess, what is your child thinking about you when he/she is angry and irritated? [RF; positive vs. negative attribution; empathy]
    c. What are you thinking about yourself? [RF; empathy for self]
    d. Are there ever times when he/she is irritated or angry with you that it's frightening for you? [RF; congruence and coherence; role reversal]
    [If yes:]
    e. Can you tell me something about that? [RF; emotion regulation; congruence and coherence]
    f. What do you do at those times? [RF; congruence and coherence]

16. Sometimes young children want to do things their own way, a way that is very different from what their parents may want. [RF; need recognition; empathy]
    a. Does this ever happen between you and [name of child]?
    b. [If yes:] Please describe a recent incident when this happened. [Coherence/congruence]
    c. Did you work it out? If so, what happened? [i.e., What did he/she do and what did you do?] [Congruence and coherence; capacity for repair; positive vs. negative attribution; empathy]
    d. If not, what happened? [RF; empathy; need recognition; capacity for repair; emotion regulation]

17. Can you describe a time when it felt like [name of child] was being "impossible"? [RF; emotion regulation; empathy for child and self; positive vs. negative attribution]
    [If yes:]
    What did you do to make things better? [Congruence and coherence; capacity for repair; empathy for child and self]

18. If you could change one aspect of *your relationship* with [name of child] what would that be? [If the answer focuses only on the parent or the child and doesn't focus on *the relationship*, probe further.] [RF; congruence and coherence; focus on the self; real relationship vs. idealized relationship goals]

19. Some parents tell us that they believe their child came into their life for a particular reason.
    a. Have you ever had such thoughts about [name of child]? [Focus on the self; real relationship vs. idealized relationship]
    b. If so, can you briefly tell me the reason you think that [name of child] is in your life? [RF; idealized representation/emotion regulating function of the child; parent's expectation of child; self and other representation; empathy for child]

Now I'd like to ask you a few questions about your own experience growing up as a child in your family.

20. Who was primarily responsible for raising you? [Needs to be limited to one or two people.]

21. Earlier we talked about what your child does when he/she is upset or needs comforting from you. Now I'd like to ask you:

    a. As a young child, as far back as you can remember, what did you do when you were upset or distressed? [RF; congruence and coherence; emotion regulation history; empathy for self]

    b. What did your [primary caregiver] do? [If two primary caregivers, ask question for each.] [RF; congruence and coherence; emotion regulation; empathy for self and caregivers]

    c. Do you remember being held at these times? [RF; congruence and coherence; need and emotion regulation history; empathy for self]

22. All children, as they are growing up, have times when they want to do things their own way. Think back as far as you can remember and tell me about a time when you wanted to do something your own way. [RF; need and emotion regulation history regarding autonomy]

    a. How did your [primary caregiver] react? [If two primary caregivers, ask question for each.] [RF; congruence and coherence]

    b. How did that make you feel? [RF; need and emotion regulation; empathy for self]

    c. How old were you?

23. Is there something you learned from the way you were parented that you would like to pass on to [name of child]? [RF; congruence and coherence; positive vs. negative attributions; idealized vs. realistic goals; need and emotion regulation goals as basis for treatment plan and contract]

24. Is there something in the way you were raised that you don't want to repeat with [name of child]? [RF; congruence and coherence; positive vs. negative attributions; idealized vs. realistic goals; need and emotion regulation goals as basis for treatment plan and contract]

25. I have one final question. What do you hope [name of child] learns from his/her experiences of being parented by you? [RF; congruence and coherence; idealized vs. realistic goals; need and emotion regulation goals as basis for treatment plan and contract]

11

Treatment Principles and Planning

> In blocking off what hurts us, we think we are walling ourselves off from pain. But in the long run the wall, which prevents growth, hurts us more than the pain, which, if we will only bear it, soon passes over us. Washes over us and is gone. Long will we remember pain, but the pain itself, as it was at the point of intensity that made us feel as if we must die of it, eventually vanishes. Our memory of it becomes its only trace. Walls remain. They grow moss. They are difficult barriers to cross, to get to others, to get to closed-down parts of ourselves.
> —ALICE WALKER (1990)

At the heart of the COS approach is the intent to help parents and other primary caregivers bear some of the pain of problematic childhood attachments, pain from which they have walled themselves off via self-protective strategies triggered by shark music. Our intervention was created using principles from psychoanalytic defense analysis. James Masterson viewed the therapeutic process as a struggle between the "false defensive self" and the "real self" of the client, with the therapist interpreting or confronting the negative consequences of the defenses used and supporting and offering relational space for the emerging real self (Masterson, 1985; Masterson & Klein, 1989). By "real self" Masterson meant something like the potential, or innate, self, with "false" meaning that the defensive self is an impaired version of the true self within all of us. Within the theoretical construct underlying the COS approach we use the term "protective self" or simply "defensive self." The real self is hidden in plain sight, and it is our job to keep our eye on the real self during therapy, to keep supporting the real self. It is critical to this approach that we aim our intervention at the *person* in treatment, not behaviors. Since the COS intervention is highly specific to the development of secure caregiving, the full array of real-self capacities is not addressed in this book or in the relatively brief COS intervention. Knowing the capacities of the real self, however, helps us differentiate the struggle of the real self from the protective confines of core sensitivities, so one list of these capacities is presented in Box 11.1.

The parent's core sensitivity is a protective/defensive self-organization that can and will interfere with the flexibility to respond to the child's needs all around the Circle. Taking risks to act outside of the defensive limits imposed by shark music will require the parent to access one if not many of the real-self capacities.

Children develop a false defensive self to manage parents' habitual use of their defensive strategies. Unfortunately, it is easy for this to occur because we all tend to overuse what we know and believe to be protective even if the situation does not call for it. The defense was learned procedurally and is now employed automatically. We are not good at reevaluating our defenses and saying "Since I am safe now, I no longer need to use this defense that once helped me survive." We don't really know anymore what we are defending ourselves against or even that what we are doing is trying to protect ourselves from pain. So when we experience anything that is associated with a dysregulated emotional state from the past, we experience fear or discomfort with regard to that need. This is, of course, where shark music shows up. To manage the perceived danger we immediately shift into a defense to protect ourselves.

The COS is designed to give the real self a chance to reemerge by making the implicit defensive process explicit. Using video clips from the interactional assessment, we help parents see their implicit defense *in action* in response to children's needs that present no real threat. Parents are able to see how their unnecessary internal strategies and protective actions compromise secure attachment. Parents also end up seeing that in turn they themselves miss out on the experience of intimacy that can come from providing a safe haven/secure base for their child. Being able to name and track this process gives parents a choice: rather than simply heeding the shark music, they can meet the needs of their child.

It is important to note that this recognition does not automatically lead

---

BOX 11.1. THE CAPACITIES OF THE REAL SELF

- The capacity to experience deeply a wide range of feeling, both pleasant and unpleasant
- The capacity to expect appropriate entitlements, such as experience of mastery and pleasure
- The capacity for self-activation and self-assertion, including the ability to identify one's own unique individuality, wishes, dreams, and goals and to be assertive in expressing them autonomously
- The capacity for the acknowledgment of self-esteem, because one cannot always depend on others to shore up one's self-esteem
- The ability to self-soothe
- The ability to make and follow through with commitments despite obstacles or setbacks
- The capacity for creativity, the ability to be creative in altering old, familiar patterns of living and replacing them with new and more successful ones
- The capacity for intimacy, which requires the capability of entering into a close and open relationship with another person with a minimal experience of abandonment or engulfment
- The ability to be alone without feeling abandoned
- Continuity of self, the capacity to recognize that the real self persists over time and circumstances
- Reflective functioning, the capacity to imagine and recognize the reality of separate minds

---

From Roberts and Roberts (2007). Copyright 2007 by Jason Aronson. Reprinted with permission.

---

to different behavior, because the parent is left with a difficult choice. The parent will need to hold her uncomfortable feelings long enough to recognize and reassure herself that her feelings are based on shark music. When in highly charged affective states, the ability simply to ask the question "Is my reaction more about the past than the present?" is a watershed distinction that allows parents to choose security for their child. Learning to ask the question creates opportunity for change in the interstices of habitual responses. Parents don't always have an immediate answer to the question "Is it safe?" but pausing to reflect heads off a significant proportion of hair-trigger responses to shark music.

Because the therapist may be providing the first setting for an experience of safe reflection, he or she is playing an important role in helping parents choose real-self versus protective-self responses. To clarify and help therapists remember their role, the COS intervention uses the acronym RAR: relationship, affect, reflection.

AFFECT: HELPING PARENTS ACCEPT AND HOLD PAINFUL EMOTIONAL STATES

Affect is at the center of the defensive process. If it were not for uncomfortable emotions triggered by a child's need, choosing to act from the real self would be straightforward. However, when parents make the decision to disregard their shark music, they are exposed to the very affect that necessitated the defense in the first place. Helping clients accept and hold painful emotional states is therefore a core goal in COS work. To build the capacity of making real-self choices, parents need someone to Be-With them as they face emotions that have always been frightening. You cannot conquer a fear of water by walking around the pool with a better understanding of the principles of swimming. It is getting into the water and learning that you are safe in the face of your fear that makes the difference. Defensive procedures are enacted while experiencing an emotional state, and clients need to practice alternative procedures when they are in that feeling state. It is a lot easier to talk about managing your anger when you are calm than to actually manage it when you are fuming, but it is learning to choose alternative behavior in the moment of anger that creates real change. Because unregulated affective states are the heart of the original struggle, it is essential that we offer parents the resource of regulating presence as they begin to consider another option. This is especially true at moments during reflection when the parent is feeling some of the original affect that led to the onset of shark music. Our choice to Be-With parents during their brief return to memories of Being-Without often leads to new options for parents with their children.

RELATIONSHIP: CREATING A SAFE HAVEN/SECURE BASE FOR CLIENTS

A key principle of the COS intervention is that parents' relationship capacities are best enhanced when they themselves are operating within a secure base relationship. However, when providing supervision, we find Being-With is difficult for many therapists. When their clients have negatively charged feelings, therapists often jump in and reassure, offer advice, or engage in a cognitive discussion that pulls the client out of the affect versus Being-With the client in the affect. As mentioned above, a significant part of therapy is allowing the client to experience the feared affect as something that can be shared, tolerated, and explored so that when the person comes out the other side he feels the affective state is less frightening and ultimately more manageable than he had imagined.

The imagery used by COS for parents is the parent's hands holding the child, and the image for therapists is the therapist's hands holding the parent. Winnicott's description of the holding environment parents can provide for their children could apply equally to the one that therapists can create for clients. For example, merely substitute "parent" for "infant" in this statement: "Being reliably present and consistent to ourselves we provide the stability which is not rigid but which is alive and human, and this makes the infant feel secure" (Winnicott, 1994, p. 89). The secure base/safe haven concept operationalizes holding into a clear relational process that can be observed and ultimately measured, not just in the parent–child relationship but in the parent–therapist relationship as well. Karlen Lyons-Ruth makes the argument that historically attachment has focused on the more observable forms of protection, but emerging neuroscience is showing that "social affiliation reduces stress hormones such as cortisol and enhances hormones of well-being such as oxytocin" (Lyons-Ruth, 2007) and thus creates a buffer for children from the immediate effects of "toxic stress" (Shonkoff, Boyce, & McEwen, 2009) and the negative developmental consequences. It is important to note that the sharing of positive emotions such as delight and joy is part of a protective secure base. In fact Being-With during positive emotional states is just as important to stress regulation and secure attachment as Being-With during painful emotional states, again in therapy just as much as in parent–child dyads.

It is important to note that in the COS intervention we do not pressure parents to feel or to feel more. As they participate they will naturally feel, and we want the therapist to be available during those moments to Be-With the parent in his experience and to allow the parent, not the therapist, to be the one who initiates the emotional process. The therapist will often need to Be-With the parent in the same manner that the parent needs to Be-With his child. In other words, sometimes a fearful collapsing parent needs the therapist to be strong and not treat her as fragile, thus sending a message of competency that the therapist sees as an unrecognized strength. With another parent, the therapist may need to support the parent's willingness to be vulnerable to feelings of sadness or fear.

> *The COS is based on the "do unto others as you*
> *would want them to do unto others" approach.*
> —JEREE H. PAWL AND MARIA ST. JOHN (1998, p. 7)

The therapist's need to experience with the parent is the same empathic shift that we want the parent to make toward her child—a shift toward Being-With. This shift comes from the parent gaining a greater understanding of the child's needs around the Circle and honoring the particular need the child is currently experiencing. (The language we use to explain the needs around the Circle is illustrated throughout Chapter 12.) In parallel, to be optimally effective in eliciting change the therapist needs to gain a greater understanding of the parent's needs around the Circle and how that parent's core sensitivity affects the choice to either explore or defend against those needs. Therefore, taking core sensitivities into account is a key component of establishing a therapeutic relationship with each parent (see page 265 for more on treatment planning). The core sensitivities also give the therapist a way to frame struggles so that the parent can more accurately recognize and reflect on exactly where and when her shark music begins to show up.

REFLECTION: INCREASING PARENTS' OBSERVATIONAL AND INFERENTIAL SKILLS

We have described reflective functioning in several places so far in this book, especially in Chapter 6. In a few words, the goal of the COS is to increase parents' reflective functioning by creating a therapeutic relationship that allows them to accept, hold, and name emotions they tend to defend against. Containing their defensive reaction long enough to observe their child's attachment and exploratory behavior helps parents make more accurate inferences about their child's needs and feelings. Accurate inferences lead to sensitively attuned responses.

Seeing versus Guessing

Seeing versus guessing has also been discussed earlier in this book. The review of the video clips from the interactional assessment (the SSP) is key to helping parents develop observational skills. Often when parents are asked to describe what they see in the first video clip of their child, they jump to inferences (e.g., "He is acting angry" or "He's trying to get my attention by crying") rather than making behavioral observations. It is the therapist's task to help parents see the distinction between seeing and guessing: seeing is marked by a behavioral description, such as "He is walking around the room, picking up toys and then putting them down." Guessing is virtually everything else, such as "He's upset and doesn't know what to do with himself" or even "He doesn't like the toys he's picking up." Any description that implies the parent knows the child's internal motivations, beliefs, thoughts, or expectations is a guess.

Even guesses based on observation can be inaccurate, but without careful observation guesses are typically based more on the parent's projection than on the child's experience. In such cases, the gap between what can be observed and what the parent concludes is usually quite wide. Yet parents make the leap because procedural memory tells them their inference is fact. Learning to see accurately and use that as a base for guessing helps parents distinguish their shark music from the truth of children's needs. The first step in creating new caregiving options is for parents to adroitly separate seeing from guessing.

In helping parents make this shift we have found it effective to encourage them to be curious rather than try to draw conclusions—to create questions rather than statements. When we show parents a little bit of video, we ask them to make a behavioral description before they give their first interpretations, then ask them to tell us what they are seeing that supports their interpretation and then to make a case for alternate interpretations.

Ultimately the goal for the seeing and guessing exercise is for the parents in the COS treatment to be able to observe *and* infer with greater accuracy than before—to be able to answer all of these questions while watching a recorded interaction:

- "What is your child doing?" (observation)
- "What do you think your child is needing?" (inference)
- "What do you think your child is feeling?" (inference)
- "What are you doing?" (observation)
- "What are you feeling?" (self-reflection)
- "What are you needing in this moment?" (self-reflection)
- "What are you thinking about yourself as you watch this?" (self-reflection)

All of this observation and inference, as well as the self-reflection (which represents access to one's own internal organization), adds up to RF. It is procedures like these that the COS uses to enhance parents' ability to reflect while feeling within the context of a safe relationship with the therapist. Then the hope is that the parent will be able to take this enhanced capacity into the day-to-day world of raising a child.

AN OVERVIEW OF RAR IN THE CIRCLE OF SECURITY INTERVENTION

As mentioned earlier, the COS intervention is tailored to each dyad's specific needs. The data gathered during the interactional and parent perception assessments are put to constructive use in the 20-week program. The first two sessions are devoted to teaching parents about their child's needs around the Circle. They begin the process of learning to recognize those needs by practicing seeing before guessing with filmed parent–child interactions.

When parents demonstrate discomfort with what they see, we apply what we have learned about their core sensitivities, their ability for reflective function, their empathy, and their capacity to focus on themselves (see the treatment organizer introduced in Chapter 8 and continued in Chapter 10). As stated above, the goal is not to alleviate parents' discomfort, which only perpetuates the status quo, but to use that discomfort and their defenses against it as a guide to uncover their innate capacity—underused strength—that is hidden by the discomfort and defense. In this way, the COS is very much a strengths-based intervention. Holding the expectation that parents can bear their discomfort for the purpose of developing important caregiving capacities is a powerful competency message about the parents' strength and potential. Evidence for this potential may be subtle, such as a mother who keeps herself emotionally distant from her child reaching over and touching her child when the stranger comes into the room or letting her child lean against her leg until her child seems more comfortable. Recognizing and reflecting on these tiny cracks in caregivers' defensive strategies allows the parents' positive intentionality to emerge.

In this early phase of the treatment, creating a holding environment might mean:

1. *Recognizing the positive intention and hope of each parent to do her best for her child.* The therapist's statement might be something like "In spite of the difficulties that you faced growing up, you're here to offer the best care possible for your child. Despite your own mistakes, you are here to find new options for a more secure future."
2. *Honoring how difficult it is to make a commitment to a program that asks for regular and ongoing attendance.* It's important to allow parents to acknowledge both the difficulty and the commitment.

3. *Acknowledging your commitment to making the group a positive and fulfilling experience.*

4. *Talking about how important this work is to the child and reassuring the parent that the COS protocol is based on almost 50 years of research.*

5. *Acknowledging that participation may well include some anxiety about the group.* Offer parents a chance to name their anxiety and to see that they are not alone in their apprehension about the experience.

6. *Using the Circle to guide you in your response to the parent.* We often find it useful to ask ourselves, "Where is this parent on the Circle at this time?" Even when a parent is experiencing palpable emotional pain, that parent may be on the top of the Circle, exploring memories and feelings. This is a "watch over me" moment, not a "comfort me" moment, on the Circle. The therapist must have a sense of warmth and empathy while Being-With the parent, but offering comfort at this time will short-circuit the parent's exploration. However, when parents become defensive, overwhelmed, flooded, or are simply ready to move on, it becomes an "organize my feelings" moment. The therapist may be called on to coregulate the parent's emotions. Often parents are oscillating between the top and bottom of the Circle during this work, and often, either on the top or bottom of the Circle, it is the therapist's presence, rather than words, that helps parents most. Think of it as putting a floor under the parents' feelings so that they do not plummet into the darkness of Being-Without (see Chapter 3).

Silently Being-With can be the most valuable thing the therapist offers.

In weeks 3–8, the group watches Phase One video clips from one parent's SSP each week. The clips have been chosen and edited by the therapist to illustrate both strengths (successes with the linchpin struggle) and struggles (clarifying that there is more work to do). The therapist models Being-With the parent in the video review. When it is appropriate, the rest of the group members are given an opportunity to share their insights, including seeing and guessing in a supportive manner that fortifies the holding environment.

In week 9, parents are introduced to shark music and the Circles of Limited Security (ambivalence, avoidance, and disorganization). Noting that we all have our own shark music, the therapist normalizes the fears or pain that create insecure caregiving choices.

One goal of the first video review is to prepare parents to focus on the linchpin struggle during the second video review (weeks 10–15). As in the first round of video reviews, during the second round the group watches carefully chosen video clips of one parent per week. These clips focus directly on the linchpin struggle. Watching video of themselves not meeting their children's needs is obviously an emotional experience for many parents. Here the therapist's abilities to Be-With the parents, during this challenging phase of the group, is paramount.

The 16th session is a time for recording the dyads in a modified SSP, which the therapist then edits for review during the third phase of video reviews (weeks 17–19, two parents each week). Parents are certainly encouraged to notice and celebrate positive changes. However, our experience is that parents' enhanced abilities in seeing and guessing make them aware of the continued struggles captured in these videos. Often parents are eager to make use of this video review to further their work. In week 20 the group celebrates its accomplishments.

CUSTOMIZED TREATMENT PLANNING

The interactional and parent perception assessments described in Chapters 8 and 10 provide the information needed to fill out sections 1–5 of the treatment organizer shown in those chapters. Section 6 is a good place to record the goals of treatment based on an understanding of the caregiver's unique vulnerabilities and needs, as shown in Chapter 10. Before treatment begins, video clips are selected to reach those goals. Record data regarding the clips in section 7. (See the section "Guide for Finding Video Clips in the Strange Situation Video" in Chapter 8 for suggestions for finding video clips. The treatment organizer shown in Chapter 10 does not illustrate this section filled out because that information would be meaningless without the video for the case example used there.)

NEGOTIATING THE THERAPEUTIC CONTRACT

The therapeutic contract is not a series of symptom-oriented checkmarks but a dynamic process that evolves over time. During intake the framework of the therapeutic contract that will guide the treatment process is established. For example, explaining how the assessments and video reviews can help meet the parent's goals by improving the parent–child relationship, the therapist acknowledges and normalizes the fact that relational change is needed. The therapist is negotiating with the parent for a critical commitment toward change in relationship versus simply changing the child's behavior. Over time, this contract will become more sophisticated and focused because assessment per se continues well past the so-called assessment phase. Therapists must always be reviewing treatment goals and plans as new information unfolds during treatment. In the goal-corrected partnership between the therapist and the parent, the parent's goals for being in treatment and the role that the therapist plays in helping the parent meet those goals are continually clarified.

THE ROLE OF CORE SENSITIVITIES IN TREATMENT PLANNING

Understanding the core sensitivity of the parent facilitates the negotiation of a therapeutic alliance. When available, this understanding gives the therapist an important roadmap, offering specific themes for treatment and particular avenues that can be pursued or that are best avoided in the service of joining with the parent. The therapist uses this understanding to communicate empathy with the implicit relational knowledge of the parent. Even though this knowledge is outside the awareness of the parent, the therapist's attunement enhances the parent's experience of being known without judgment. The therapist is not reading the parent's mind, which would be intrusive and potentially dysregulating, but demonstrating empathy. From a place of understanding and empathy, the therapist can help parents see that the defensive organization being used to protect the self is, in fact, impairing their real self and limiting their relationship with their child.

The ability to differentially diagnose core sensitivity can take *some* of the guesswork out of how to approach treatment. Take the goal of developing the real-self capacity to experience a broad range of emotions, both negative and positive, as an example. Having this capacity is essential for meeting the needs of a distressed child. Each person's core sensitivity offers an understanding of why he or she would limit the capacity to experience emotion. An esteem-sensitive person will equate negative vulnerable feelings with failure and potential shame if exposed publicly, so she will deny them. A separation-sensitive person will equate painful feeling with being alone and abandoned and will seek someone to take care of him.

A safety-sensitive person will fear that experiencing strong emotions will expose her to intrusion as she manages her pain, and so she will isolate herself. The same real-self capacity has three very different meanings and evokes three different defensive reactions.

Not only do core sensitivities affect parents' capacity to meet children's needs, but they play a role in forming parents' goals for their child. The defensive goals for an esteem-sensitive, separation-sensitive, or safety-sensitive parent vary significantly. For example, three parents, all apparently focusing on developing their child's academic skill of mastering numbers, may have very different underlying goals. The esteem-sensitive parent may well be feeling an internal pressure to have her child appear to others as highly skilled and above average ("Tammy, show the lady how quickly you can do the number puzzle"). The separation-sensitive parent may become anxious and encourage the child's return each time his baby starts to walk away to find a new toy ("Look, Jennifer, come back and finish our number puzzle"). The safety-sensitive parent may find a variety of ways to keep her child focused on learning as a means of maintaining an acceptable level of distance from the child ("Johnny, there is a number puzzle over there for you to work on"). To compliment the esteem-sensitive parent on her child's precocious competence merely exacerbates that dyad's tendency to remain on the top of the Circle. To focus on the separation-sensitive parent's warmth and caregiving skills may well send the message that keeping his child dependent is a good thing. To offer the safety-sensitive parent support for how competently her child plays on his own would only add more fuel to an already well-established defensive system being lived out in their relationship. The three core sensitivities can arise during treatment in many varied ways, so it is always important to integrate them into planning and to be alert for their underlying presence in working with clients.

In addition, as can be recognized in the examples above, it is important to remember that core sensitivity isn't found within behavior. Rather, it can be made sense of as we come to understand the meaning behind a parent's behavior. The exact same statement from a caregiver ("Look at that number puzzle") will have a different meaning for each of the core sensitivities.

Separation Sensitivity

The most common defensive orientation of separation-sensitive people is helplessness. This involves seeking others to solve their problems and take care of them. Acting on their own behalf, especially in times of adversity (taking charge of experiences requiring self-assertion), is often a significant struggle, as they fear this will drive others away and lead to their being alone and ultimately abandoned. A key to providing therapeutic support is therefore to expect competency and challenge helplessness while continuing to Be-With the parent. It is almost always counterproductive to give advice or tell them what to do. This only rewards incompetence and maintains their defensive perception of being helpless.

When parents act helpless, therapists tend to want to be helpful by giving advice and directives and even taking over doing things directly for the client. For example, at the end of the interactional assessment the parent may be struggling to have a child pick up the toys, and it can be tempting for the therapist to step in and help get the cleanup done. When the parent is asked to reflect on her experience and seems confused and unable to do so, it is tempting for therapists to start to fill in the blanks. The therapist might start to tell the parent how she may be feeling, how she might be thinking, and what kind of conclusions she should be reaching. It is essential to maintain the distinction between challenging a parent's helplessness with a positive expectation to use an emerging capacity for reflection and taking over and doing it for her by telling her how she might think and feel.

Parents whose defense is helplessness against feelings and memories of abandonment will always struggle with situations that challenge them to be more competent. Parents who are separation sensitive are typically much better at avoiding self-activation than the therapist is at maintaining the challenge. Often therapists feel guilty and unreasonable for challenging parents' helplessness and succumb to what is presented as a perfectly reasonable claim that they don't know how to do it. While it is true that these parents may lack specific skills to perform some parenting tasks well, trying to teach them skills when their primary defense is helplessness is like pouring water into a sieve. Helping parents see that a need to act on their own behalf (and that of their child) triggers their shark music and then challenging them to bear the discomfort and risk a new level of parenting competence will be much more effective than focusing on skill building.

The theme of rupture and repair within relationships becomes central in all of COS treatment. Parents within each core sensitivity have unique themes that lead them to fear that their tentative hold on relationship has been broken. For the caregiver who is separation sensitive, this anxiety centers around the certainty that any act of autonomy will lead to abandonment. It is not uncommon for a parent who is separation sensitive to become upset with a clinician's belief that the parent is more capable than she currently chooses to be. Hoping to induce guilt and a retraction of the therapist's belief in her capacity, the parent may become upset, implying that the therapist is uncaring. Rather than believing this bid to "repair" what has actually never been broken, the therapist needs to calmly honor the intensity of pain while pointing out that there is no danger of a break in the relationship (with either the therapist or the child) and that autonomy can, in fact, always include a sense of supportive relationship (autonomy-within-relatedness).

Since COS treatment is focused on parent–child relationships, the helplessness that is challenged is often highly focused on the parent taking charge in the relationship. The taking charge tends to be in two major areas: (1) directing, scaffolding, and/or setting limits (such as getting the child to clean up the toys, especially when the child resists); and (2) being proactive when the child is distressed (for example, taking charge of the situation and comforting or organizing the child's feelings). It is common for parents who are separation sensitive to express resentment, anger, or confusion regarding either of these demands placed on them by the child. Addressing this as fear about the self-activation needed to meet these demands rather than trying to reduce the demands on the parent will move the therapy much further.

Therapists can get into trouble with parents who are separation sensitive by slowly becoming more and more accommodating and taking care of them. When the therapist inevitably begins to resent the constant demands, she may shift her approach and "confront" the parent from a place of pent-up anger and resentment. This precipitates the parent's acting out, for which the therapist then feels responsible and guilty. So the therapist goes back to taking care of the parent, and the cycle starts over. We have learned through many failures that the best response to feeling guilty or angry with a parent who is separation sensitive is to be quiet and organize your own feelings until you can return to a place of compassionate clarity. When effectively placing the defensive strategy before the parent, there is always a sense of empathy and warmth.

To be successful, confrontation must include kindness.

Confrontation has nothing to do with creating conflict or discord. Rather, it has to do with carefully naming the caregiver's defensive choices in such a way that he can begin to recognize the impact they have on him and his child. In this way, should you begin feeling angry at the parent, always consider that your experience of anger may be part of a process in which you are being cast as a character in the parent's internal representational "movie" that defensively guides him. Feeling the pull to be angry and rejecting provides important insight, but acting out the pull sabotages the therapy. When you feel the pull, ask yourself why now, at this moment in the treatment, you feel like being harsh. Is it because your own shark music has been activated, or is the parent shaping you into the rejecting person he defensively anticipated? This is where supervision is crucial, to provide the therapist with a safe haven and a secure base to sort out such emotionally challenging questions.

> *The therapist needs to answer the basic question "How much of this*
> *is about me and how much of this is about the client?"*
> *before the therapist's feeling states can be integrated into treatment.*

Being pulled into acting out a role, either positive or negative, is part of all treatment, and the therapist's capacity to reflect on this process is essential to the quality of the emerging therapeutic relationship. In brief work such as the COS intervention, we do not recommend that therapists interpret their feeling states to the parent. Instead, use the experience to increase empathy for the parents' internal world.

Shana, a 23-year-old mother of two, found it difficult to express why she had signed up for the group. "I don't know, I mean, it is sort of like I need somebody that knows what to do about my kids. My mom was lost, and now so am I." While this offers some insight into her history, more significant was the fact that Shana was immediately telegraphing her "helplessness" and her sense of needing someone else to do the "heavy lifting."

Afraid to take charge (self-activate for the sake of her children), Shana continually appeared unable to say "no" to her 2-year-old daughter, who was now clearly in control of the relationship. When it came time to view her "shark music" video, Shana called early to say she had a headache and couldn't make it. Her therapist, fully aware of her separation-sensitive struggles, simply challenged her choice to not view a video clip that might change the tide of the relationship. "Shana, your headache sounds tough to be sure. At the same time, I think the idea of seeing what Marcy needs from you triggers your shark music and to protect yourself you let your headache keep you from group."

Challenged in a caring way, without being told what to do, Shana chose to show up. The video clearly showed that her daughter was "running the show" and that Shana had no semblance of being "bigger, stronger, wiser, and kind" but rather displayed an abundance of "weak." Shana recognized that she was acting the way her mother had acted toward her and was struck by a wave of horrible memories and feelings. Rather than being overwhelmed by the experience, she was motivated and empowered.

The following week she demonstrated a different sense of herself. When asked what she had learned from the video review the week before, she replied in a clear, determined voice, "I'm not lost. I'm not weak. I'm not my mom. I am not going down that road anymore."

Less than a month later a staff member working with Marcy said that she almost couldn't recognize Marcy as the same child. "She doesn't try to run the classroom or me. It's like she's a little girl for the first time in her life."

Esteem Sensitivity

Parents who are esteem sensitive have come to believe that who they are, just as they are (imperfect, average, inevitably flawed), is not enough to be valued. Conversely, to feel valued, they must be vigilant about any implication of having failed or being inadequate as parents or having others not see their child as special (either especially good, especially bad, or having unique special needs, as long as it helps them maintain the image of being a truly remarkable parent). Therefore, one challenge for therapists working with parents who are esteem sensitive is to give feedback to the parents without the parents feeling like failures and thus needing to defend themselves.

Learning something new requires managing the vulnerability of not knowing something and potentially being seen as doing something in a less than optimal way. If this vulnerability is associated with feeling like a failure, the process of learning can be colored with negative emotions. This is especially true if the learning is about something so fundamental as how to parent.

Central to positive therapeutic outcomes is the parents' ability to manage the vulnerability of staying focused on the self while exploring areas of struggle. When parents who are esteem sensitive feel vulnerable, they are already struggling with feeling as if they have failed and are thus quick to misinterpret the therapist's comments as an assault and either launch a counterattack or fall into shame. The therapeutic process is often one of rupture and repair. The rupture and repair that is so critical to developing a secure attachment between parent and child was introduced in Chapters 3 and 4. In the therapeutic relationship, Kohut was the first to identify the rupture/repair process in working with narcissistic patients. He theorized that through repeated repairs of ruptures in the transference relationship with the therapist the patient develops a more secure internal state ("transmuting internalization," Kohut, 1977, p. 32). This concept is illustrated in Chapter 12 in the details of negotiating treatment progress.

What helps parents who are esteem sensitive feel stable is feeling understood by someone Being-With them. The therapist who realizes that esteem sensitivity requires a central focus on communicating empathy for the parent's experience aids this process. No matter how hard the therapist tries to offer empathic feedback, ruptures will inevitably happen, which, fortunately, creates an opportunity for repair. Repair is about the therapist empathically acknowledging the experience of the parent from the parent's perspective. This will often include the therapist openly, and without defensiveness, considering how what he has done has likely caused the pain currently being experienced.

Sometimes it can feel like threading a needle to both hold the integrity of the feedback and hold and communicate the empathy needed for the parent to learn about an area of insecurity with the child. This is where knowing and communicating the positive intentionality of the parent is very useful. By honoring the parent's positive intentionality, the therapist helps the parent feel valued and thus more able to manage the vulnerability of imperfection. Masterson called this kind of intervention a "mirroring interpretation" (1993, p. 76) because mirroring (understanding and honoring) the patient's experience precedes the interpretation of the defense. ("It can be so painful to imagine we've done something that isn't best for our child. I know you want what's best for Brian. I think that's why you're beginning to look at what just happened in a new way.") This maximizes the chance of the parent's experiencing the intervention as useful rather than an attack.

As explained in Chapter 9, individuals who are esteem sensitive feel stable in relationships where they have a sense of "one-mindedness" with the other. Having differences is experienced as a threat, as if one person has to be right and thus the other wrong. If parents who are esteem sensitive feel "one-minded" with the therapist, an idealizing transference forms in the therapeutic relationship. It is not being suggested here that the therapist strives to be "one-minded" with the parent, but without an initial idealizing transference, it is difficult to eventually move to a genuine therapeutic alliance.

A therapeutic alliance is different from "one-mindedness." In fact it is almost the opposite of "one-mindedness" in that it requires that parents trust the therapist enough to show their real self rather than demand that the therapist mirror and protect the protective self. This is a slow process in which the parent often takes two steps forward and one back.

For many therapists the esteem-sensitive parent's idealization feels uncomfortable, and they attempt to have the parent see them in more realistic ways. ("You're the best therapist I've ever met. You know so much more than those other people I've tried.") Attempts to undo this perception, no matter how difficult it is to experience, will usually cause problems in the treatment. The parent's idealization helps him feel safer and thus provides a pathway for the therapist to explore struggles with less danger of ruptures. It is only in long-term in-depth therapy that this idealization would ever be openly explored with the client. This means that therapists have to deal with their own countertransference feelings about idealization so that they don't disrupt the view of a parent who strives to think he is fully understood without risk of disappointment.

> Darcy was both excited to be joining the group and obviously nervous about the level of vulnerability that was implied within the first week's session. "I've done a lot of these groups," she said, "and I've read a ton of books. It's not like I'm just a beginner when it comes to figuring out how to be a good parent."
>
> Darcy's son Jacob, age 4, showed very little capacity to play with other children, and his continual need to look for approval before any exploration mixed with his inability to ask for comfort when he was clearly anxious had his teachers very concerned. Darcy initially didn't sense any problem with these issues. "For one, he's a shy kid," she explained. "Second, he's so smart he doesn't really want to play with kids that aren't as bright as he is. Plus he's learning to be independent."
>
> Video reviews showed clips to help Darcy recognize both Jacob's clear reticence regarding exploration without permission from Darcy and his significant "shyness" about approaching her following the separation in the SSP. To help her manage her vulnerability, the therapist held the focus on the child by asking, "What do you think he might be feeling here when he starts to approach you and then turns toward that toy?"
>
> Now 14 weeks into the process, Darcy clearly recognizes her son's lack of play and listlessness when she's out of the room. "I think he really does miss me." Upon seeing him come close and then move past her, she quickly claims what she had previously felt too afraid to admit: "He's miscuing me. It's like he hears my shark music and it's now playing in his ears." Tears that might have seemed impossible several months ago are now on her face. "I don't want to do this to him. He clearly needs his cup filled, and I haven't been offering it to him. That's my job, not his."

Safety Sensitivity

Parents who are safety sensitive believe that the cost of being close with their child is being controlled and/or intruded upon. Therefore, they believe that the only way to keep a safe and intact sense of self is to be self-sufficient and to expect self-sufficiency from their child.

The therapist's job is to balance two critical dimensions: to have sufficient emotional engagement with the parent for the therapeutic process to take place, while secondarily maintaining sufficient emotional distance so that the parent does not feel intruded upon or controlled. Obviously, these two goals can often be at odds. If you are too quiet and don't invite engagement, the parent can view you as indifferent. If you pursue the parent with too much teaching or too many assumptions about her motivations, you will be experienced as intrusive. Even too much empathy or warmth can be experienced as intrusive as it can feel to someone who is safety sensitive like you are getting inside of her mind without her permission. The initial goal is to help the parent negotiate enough connection with the therapist to engage emotionally in the learning process without being overwhelmed. Describing and then talking about the struggle between the need for both closeness and distance can be very helpful if done in a way that respects the parent's need to manage the intensity of the therapeutic relationship.

Since there is no way to keep just the right distance all the time, not too close or too far, the relationship will inevitably have ruptures. So again rupture and repair becomes critical for the success of the therapy. Repair is about the therapist acknowledging that she has likely moved too close or kept too far away and then recommitting to being stable and open while allowing the parent to set the distance and intensity of the process. When the parents who are safety sensitive feel in control of titrating the distance in the therapeutic relationship, they feel safer and may then be willing to take more risks.

A common way to get into difficulty, however, is to pursue parents who are withdrawing because they feel intruded upon. Pursuing this parent with more questions or suggestions can make the parent want to withdraw even further or feel trapped and forced to answer the questions. The more the therapist pursues under these circumstances, the less safe the parent feels, which may precipitate the parent's withdrawal from treatment to get the needed distance.

The central therapeutic theme in treatment is the management of the safety-sensitive dilemma. Although it may be deeply hidden, the parent wants to have close intimate relations, especially with her child, but to act on this yearning exposes her to the fear of being controlled, smothered, and overwhelmed. To protect herself the parent starts to seek distance and disengagement. Once she has successfully negotiated enough distance, she begins to feel isolated and disconnected and so begins to yearn for connection, which, once pursued, starts the cycle again.

The most common way to defensively manage the "dilemma" is to create "the compromise" (Klein, 1995), which is a way to be half in and half out of important relationships. The therapist will see this process in the interaction with the child and likely see the same process in the therapeutic interaction. For example, the parent leaves child care without hugging her child good-bye and then lingers at the window, where she can watch her child without being seen. Or she doesn't hug her child good night but then, after her child is asleep, lies down next to her as a way to feel close.

As in all successful treatment, timing is crucial. Often the rhythm of the conversation with parents who are safety sensitive is slower and has more conversational pauses than with the other core sensitivities. Therapists can feel compelled to fill all the spaces with questions, interpretations, or teaching due to their own discomfort with silence. A critical part of working with parents who are safety sensitive is attuning to their rhythm, not too fast and not too slow. As much as possible, let them lead the interactional dance. If the process ever gets awkward or tense, slow down and make room, but don't go away.

It can help the parent feel safe to know where the therapist is coming from. Offering a "position statement" is a way to clarify this issue (Klein, 1995). Even if what the therapist has to say is difficult to hear, parents would rather know what the therapist is thinking than not know and fill in the blanks with memories of the anticipated other. This is quite different from parents who are esteem sensitive because, especially under stress, they want to hear things that confirm their sense of being "one-minded" and enhance their self-esteem. Once the parents who are safety sensitive know the therapist is committed to remaining consistent and reliable, they can set a distance that feels safe. A position statement is usually not a complex statement but more of a simple matter-of-fact self-report by the therapist about the therapist's own experience. The parent may think the therapist is indifferent to her struggle, so clarification that the therapist is feeling interested and concerned rather than indifferent is often enough. It is best to select words that are warm but not too warm. Statements such as "I feel like hugging you" or "I am feeling deep affection for you" by their nature would be too much and defeat the very purpose of offering a position statement in the first place.

> Adrienne clearly loved her 3-year-old son, Brian. But she simply couldn't let herself admit it. Her focus was consistently on how he was upsetting her: "He goes out of his way to demand, demand, demand. It's like he does it on purpose to upset me."
>
> Unable to recognize that her anger was actually a way to maintain a "safe distance" from Brian, Adrienne began the group with the certainty that her child was "a monster." And, in spite of the obvious difficulties caused by such negative attributions, Adrienne and Brian shared a lot of affection during exploration in the SSP. However, when it came time for her to exit the room, Brian "went ballistic, demanding that I stay. I could only leave by prying him from my side." The video confirmed that she did use some degree of force to extricate herself from his presence.
>
> During the second video review, Adrienne is offered an opportunity to see Brian crying for her at the door. Upon entry, she quickly takes his hands, which he has pushed toward her, and shoves them away from her. With nothing said on the part of the group facilitator, Adrienne sees her miscue and says, "He really needed more from me." She then recounts a story from the day before when he had "acted out" by tearing up a family book and she had noticed a similar need. "He was asking for me. He wasn't trying to be mean. He just wanted more on the bottom of the Circle."
>
> Within 6 weeks of this observation Adrienne was describing her relationship with Brian in markedly different terms. "He's no angel. But he's no devil either. He's a little kid who wants his mom. I do struggle there. I think I always will. But that's not his fault. I need to keep finding ways to fill his cup."

PROCEDURAL EMPATHY AND THE PARENT'S PROCEDURAL CHALLENGE

Understanding the dynamics of core sensitivities can help enhance procedural empathy on the part of the therapist. Having empathy for another's struggles within implicit relational knowing is often not immediately intuitive because it requires stepping inside the internal working model of another and seeing the world filtered through the lens of a core sensitivity. To do this well it can be helpful for therapists to have some understanding of which core sensitivity seems to fit their own procedural struggles. While not definitive, it can be useful to recognize the defensive strategies that organize our own perceptions. To this end, discussing our defensive patterns with a colleague, within therapy or supervision, is highly recommended. Knowing your own relational tendencies and seeing yourself through the lens of another's core sensitivity clarifies how your best intentions can so easily be misperceived and lead to a rupture. When ruptures happen, core sensitivities suggest potential meaning for the rupture and pathways for repair. The value of knowing about core sensitivities is not about diagnosing or finding rote therapeutic techniques but creating an attuned state of mind in the therapist.

Parents' innate caregiving system creates a powerful pull to meet children's needs. Yet procedural memories and the learned patterns that have been used to defend against them can trump parents' innate caregiving wisdom. Wise therapists respect both the power of shark music and the power of the genuine self. When parents are given a clear choice between the two, typically their positive intentionality and innate wisdom rise to the surface. One definition of courage is to do what needs to be done in spite of fear, which is exactly what we are asking of our clients. Parents in treatment will often take risks for their child that they would not take solely for themselves. This is why Selma Fraiberg stated that working with babies and parents is like having God as a copilot (Emde, 1987, p. xix).

12

The Circle of Security Intervention Protocol

> We do not treat our patients to cure them of something done to them in the past; rather we are trying to cure them of what they still do to themselves and to others in order to cope with what was done to them in the past.
> —PHILIP M. BROMBERG (1998)

After assessment and planning are completed, the more formal therapy process begins. COS is being implemented in clinical (inpatient and outpatient), residential, community, and in-home settings, with families and/or in individual formats. Because group therapy has the advantage of offering parents the support and insights of other parents, and it is the format that we have evaluated in research, this chapter focuses on the group intervention. Adaptation of the intervention for other modalities is discussed at the end of this chapter. The logistics of holding group sessions and filming the (ideally) six dyads for the reviews may be impractical in some clinical settings, but extensive clinical experience indicates that the same steps can be equally effective in individual, couple, and family therapy formats. In this chapter we include handouts that we use in groups and model the language we have found effective in talking to parents.

As described in Chapter 11, the quality of the relationship that the therapist negotiates with the caregiver is crucial throughout the COS protocol. In each phase of the treatment, caregivers are invited to gradually increase their vulnerability by delving into progressively more sensitive material. At first they are asked to make observations and conclusions about their child's needs and feelings based on the Circle paradigm; then they are asked to focus on their own experience, especially times they experience distress regarding their child's attachment needs. Video often exposes procedural scripts that are outside the caregivers' awareness. It is not uncommon for caregivers to experience distress when they realize they are not responding to their child as sensitively as they wished. When the participants in the intervention become upset, it is essential that they experience the therapist as a holding environment with whom they can share, process, and begin to make sense of new thinking and emerging emotions.

Participants are encouraged to feel successful if they can reflect on what needs their child may have and how they are behaving, thinking, and feeling about their child's needs. Even though security or insecurity of attachment is measured by behavior change, the emphasis in treatment is on the capacity to reflect, to feel, and to share. Behavioral prescriptions for caregivers are rarely if ever given.

The COS addresses the relationship, not the behavior.

WEEKS 1–2: CREATING A HOLDING ENVIRONMENT AND PROVIDING PSYCHOEDUCATION

As we have explained, the theory of change in COS is based on the belief that parents have the capacity and desire to respond to their child's needs. However, well-established defenses against painful affects associated with their own developmental histories prevent them from seeing and responding to their child's basic attachment cues (Fraiberg, Adelson, & Shapiro, 1975). In our view, these key defenses are part of implicit relational knowing and as such they are active within the relationship even though they are outside the awareness of the parent. In developing the COS protocol, a key challenge was how to help caregivers understand and address such an emotionally entrenched and complex construct in a relatively brief intervention model without overwhelming them. Therefore we devote the first two sessions of the protocol to critical psychoeducation and the establishment of a holding environment to prevent parents from feeling intellectually or emotionally overwhelmed.

Week 1

Having participants feel valued, respected, emotionally engaged, and intrigued is crucial during the first group meeting. It is the beginning of creating a holding environment for all of them. Parents don't know what to expect and tend to think that this will be a didactic class like other experiences they have had. Since they were videoed and know you will be showing them clips of the parents with their child, many expect to see things they are doing wrong. The AAI has been described as "surprising [to] the unconscious" mind (George et al., 1996, p. 3). In our protocol we want to surprise the unconscious of the parents in a positive and emotionally engaging way with a message that we value them and that this experience is likely going to be different from other experiences they may have encountered regarding parenting.

We accomplish this, after introductions and after reviewing and explaining the "Outline of 20 Weeks" (Box 12.1), by playing an edited video from the relationship assessment that is a compilation of three or four brief positive interaction clips for each parent with the soundtrack of a song that expresses children's deep need and love for their parents (such as "You Are So Beautiful" by Joe Cocker). In a humorous fashion we state that we asked all their children what song they would like to sing to their caregivers and they unanimously selected this one. (We have come to call these clips "the beautiful tapes.") After the video is over, there is usually silence in the room. No one knows what to say. Several parents will be working hard not to cry. When the parents are asked what it was like for them to watch the video, it is common that little discussion evolves. The

---

BOX 12.1. OUTLINE OF 20 WEEKS

- Week 1: Introduction
- Week 2: The Theory behind the Circle
- Weeks 3–8: Phase One review of videos edited from the assessment SSP
- Week 9: Introduction of new information: shark music and limited circles
- Weeks 10–15: Phase Two review to look at new clips edited from the assessment SSP
- Week 16: Open session for group process and preparing to film a modified SSP
- Weeks 17–19: Phase Three review to look at clips edited from the modified SSP
- Final session: Celebration and graduation

one question they often have is whether they can have a copy of the video. Of course the answer is yes.

Next we introduce the formula for security (shown in Figure 2.3, page 33), which can be used as a handout. This is an important handout. It needs to be explained and explored with the parents. Some parents can be bigger only at the expense of being kind, and others can be kind only at the expense of abdicating parental function (bigger and stronger). "Whenever possible, follow the child's lead" is loaded with information. The idea that a child can cue a parent for his needs and that a parent can respond is news to many parents. This theme of following a child's cue will become central in the weeks to come.

The last idea is "when necessary, take charge," which says that the parent needs to have a clear reason to take over. If a parent is taking charge, what is the reason or need that is being addressed? So many insecure parents take charge or interfere with the child's needs on the Circle when they could be following—for instance, taking over and directing the play—yet, when the child needs a parent who is willing to take charge, that parent follows with abdication and allows the child to control the process. Following when possible and taking charge when necessary are critical dimensions and will be used countless times as parents' videos are reviewed.

The next "surprise" is that we have the parents learn about the basic rhythm of their children going out and coming back into the Circle by showing them clips of their children already doing it. So we are not so much teaching them something new as having them discover "Circle moments," something their children are already accomplished at doing. We have one "Circle moment" per parent prepared, each lasting anywhere from 10 to 30 seconds. The first moment is played without any theory. Parents are asked to describe what they see, and the therapist helps them learn the difference between seeing and guessing (see Chapter 11). The ability to separate seeing from guessing is, as already stressed throughout this book, a foundation in COS that enables the parent to explore all the video to come.

After a few clips are processed, it will become obvious that what the parents are watching is children following one of two sequences: (1) exploring, touching base with the parent, and going back to exploration or (2) being in close with the parent, going out to explore, and coming back to reconnect. Once the basics of this rhythm have been "discovered," Figure 12.1 is handed out and explained as a way to organize what they see is already happening. The remaining clips are explored using the Circle as a reference point, asking parents whether the child is on the top, meaning going out to explore, or on the bottom, meaning coming back in to touch base. At this point only the basic rhythm of going out and coming in is highlighted. In week 2 the specific needs will be explored more thoroughly.

The following is how we explain the Circle to the group.[1]

"Let's use the idea of Secure Base as a starting point for taking a tour around the Circle of Security [Figure 12.1]. We will start with what we call the top half of the Circle. When children feel safe and secure, their curiosity kicks in and they want to learn about the world. However, before they set off to explore, children need a sense that their parent is supporting that exploration (see 'Support My Exploration' on the Circle). 'Support My Exploration' is one of the two transition needs on the Circle. Even young children watch their parents very carefully to figure out what is safe and what is dangerous. Since they depend so much on their parents to protect them while they explore, young children also watch to see if their parent is paying attention to them for that protection. Young children don't actually think about this— remember, they are wired to do this automatically! Over time, they remember what parents have indicated is safe and what is dangerous. Support for exploration is often a combination of the history of that parent's support for exploration, as well as an immediate cue of safety.

"With support from their parent, children head out for grand adventures. They may wander across the room or behind the couch. As they get older, they can travel farther and stay away longer. And here's one of the most important points—as they are exploring, children need their parent just as much as they do when they are in their parent's lap. Even though what children need from their parent changes as they travel around the Circle, it is important to remember that children need their parent all the way around the Circle.

"When the child is exploring, it is usually the parent's job to watch out for danger or be there in case something happens (see 'Watch over me' on the Circle). Although the parent may be barely aware of this, and the child may seem preoccupied with play, if the parent becomes unavailable, the child's exploration will end.

---

[1] All modeled therapist explanations in this chapter are reprinted or adapted from Cooper, Hoffman, and Powell (2009b COS-P Manual).

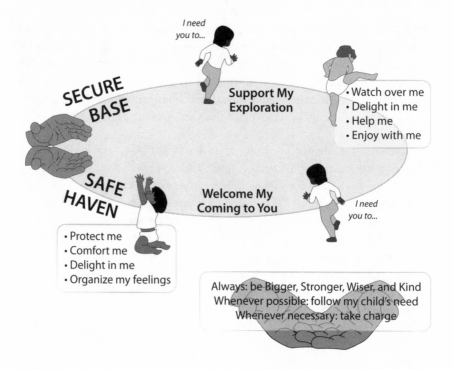

FIGURE 12.1. Circle of Security: Parent attending to the child's needs. Copyright 1998 by Cooper, Hoffman, Marvin, and Powell.

"Sometimes children need more than having the parent watch over them. At times children need help exploring (see 'Help me' on the Circle). This requires the caregiver to provide the necessary help without taking over (children need just enough help to do it by themselves). This is called 'scaffolding' and usually requires the parent to continue to follow the child's need rather than taking charge.

"At other times, children simply want their caregiver to enjoy with them (see 'Enjoy with me' on the Circle). These shared moments provide children with a sense that the caregiver is attentive, available, and attuned. They also make children feel they are worthy of such attention.

"At all times, children need to know that no matter what they are doing, their parent finds delight in them, for no other reason than their simply being alive. Hence, during moments of exploration—moments that often have to do with building autonomy and mastery—a child will look back just to make sure the parent is delighted ('Delight in me'). This delight doesn't have to do with 'what I just did' but 'that I just am.' Such moments do much to build a well-ingrained sense of self-worth in the child.

"When children have explored long enough or become tired, frightened, or uncomfortable, they are no longer interested in exploring. Or if children get into an unsafe situation, parents need to take charge and end the exploration. Either way children suddenly have a new set of needs that require a response from their parent.

"We are now talking about the bottom half of the Circle. Unless they are very frightened, the first thing children need on the bottom half of the Circle is a sign from the parent that they are welcome to come back to the parent. 'Welcome My Coming to You' is the second transition need on the Circle. (See 'Welcome My Coming to You' on the Circle.) Like support for exploration, children's sense that they are welcome to come back is a combination of a history of support and an immediate cue.

"Children sometimes cue their parents for protection (see 'Protect me' on the Circle). Providing protection from clear and immediate danger is a basic part of parenting that we clearly understand. However, children are sometimes frightened and need to be soothed even when you know there's no danger.

"Sometimes the child is not in danger but needs comfort (see 'Comfort me' on the Circle). Although most parents understand the idea of comfort, not all parents have experience with either comforting or being comforted, and so they struggle giving comfort to their children.

"Sometimes children need help organizing an internal experience that feels overwhelming (see 'Organize my feelings' on the Circle). Most parents understand that their children need help organizing their external world or their behavior, but for many parents, it is a new idea that children need help organizing their internal world. Children's need for internal organization may come from being tired, hungry, disappointed, startled, sad, frustrated, and so forth. Whatever the cause, children need their parent's help because they are still too young to do it alone. It is through the repeated process of parents helping their children organize internally that children learn how to manage feelings both by themselves and in relationship. When the needs on the bottom of the Circle are met and children feel safe and secure, their curiosity kicks in and the Circle continues."

Parents are told that children who know they can negotiate the needs on the Circle are secure because they have a secure base and safe haven. We hand out and go over the list of benefits introduced in Chapter 1 and provided for reproduction in Box 12.2.

We know that all parents want their children to feel secure, and we have found that wanting this is necessary but not sufficient. We give them the handout "The Path to Secure Attachment" (see Figure 12.2) and explain the three steps that we have found to increase the likelihood that their child will feel secure. These three steps will be the backbone of the parents' experience during the 20 weeks the group is together.

At the end of the first session parents are asked to observe and discover "Circle moments" that happen during the next week so they can share them at the beginning of session 2. The group should end with parents feeling valued, successful, positively challenged, and curious about what will come in future meetings.

Week 2

Week 2 starts with the sharing of Circle stories, which are episodic memories of times the parents in the group saw the Circle in action with their children. It helps to take time and explore each parent's story. As

---

BOX 12.2. THE DIFFERENCE THAT MAKES A DIFFERENCE

After 50 years of research we know that the more secure children are, the more they are able to:

- Enjoy more happiness with their parents.
- Feel less anger at their parents.
- Turn to their parents for help when in trouble.
- Solve problems on their own.
- Get along better with friends.
- Have lasting friendships.
- Solve problems with friends.
- Have better relationships with brothers and sisters.
- Have higher self-esteem.
- Know that most problems will have an answer.
- Trust that good things will come their way.
- Trust the people they love.
- Know how to be kind to those around them.

Copyright 1999 by Cooper, Hoffman, Marvin, & Powell.

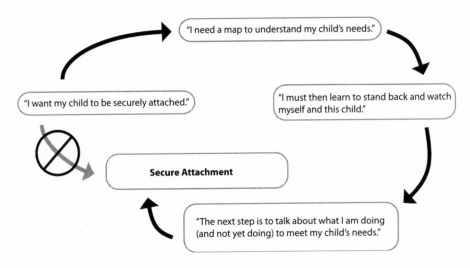

FIGURE 12.2. The path to secure attachment. Copyright 2004 by Cooper, Hoffman, and Powell.

parents' stories are processed there will be ample opportunities to review the Circle.

Explaining Affect Regulation

The need on the Circle that is often the most difficult for parents to understand is "organize my feelings." This is understandable because it stands for the rather large topic of affect regulation. The theory behind this need was covered in Chapter 2; in practice the challenge is to explain the concept in a clear, easy-to-understand manner to parents.

You can use Figure 12.3 to illustrate that very early in life the parent is organizing the emotional experiences of the infant and that slowly the infant begins to manage with the help of the caregiver. You can see this in the first 4 months of life. As the child manages emotion with the help of the caregiver, there are moments when the infant is overstimulated with positive or negative emotion, turns away for a moment, and then comes back and reengages with the caregiver. These moments of going away for a second are the beginnings of the infant learning to self-manage emotions. So it is within the safe relationship with the parent that the child learns both how to use the parent and how to use the self to manage the whole range of emotions we are all capable of feeling.

FIGURE 12.3. Learning to manage emotions. Copyright 2001 by Cooper, Hoffman, and Powell.

Therapists who have completed the training to be licensed to use the COS-P DVD (Cooper, Hoffman, & Powell, 2009a; for more information go to *www.circleofsecurity.net*), as well as the training to use the 20-week model, often show segments from the DVD here and in other key places in weeks 1, 2, and 9. We use Figure 12.4 to depict how Being-With allows parents to coregulate their baby or toddler's emotions, with the following explanation:

"Some very important research is finding that our choice to understand and share the feelings our children have is one of the most essential gifts we have to offer. We call this gift 'Being-With.' Our willingness to Be-With children and feel some of what they feel gives them an experience of being safe and connected as they learn about emotions.

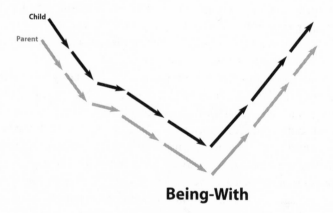

Being-With

FIGURE 12.4. Resonance with and attunement to negative feeling. Copyright 2009 by Cooper, Hoffman, and Powell.

For many of us it's easier to Be-With our children when they're feeling happy. It's when they are struggling emotionally that we find it more difficult. We often want to get them back to feeling happy by distracting them or trying to talk them out of their upset. Interestingly, what helps children the most is having us with them in their emotions rather than having us try to stop them from feeling what they feel.

"To help visualize what children need from us, imagine the black arrows are your child's feelings of distress. The gray arrows represent your holding and organizing this experience of upset. As you stay with your child's increasing distress, your child experiences you Being-With him or her. Knowing someone is there makes the feeling less overwhelming and allows your child to come up the other side. Having confidence that we do not have to be alone when we are upset is at the heart of feeling emotionally secure."

The therapist can ask group members about experiences they have had when someone was willing to Be-With them by understanding and accepting their feelings.

Being-Without, the opposite of Being-With, often looks like Figure 12.5. When a child shows a feeling, the caregiver pushes against the feeling and tries to get the child to feel something else. When you watch a parent and child interact this way, it looks like an emotional struggle with the parent pushing for one thing and the child reacting and becoming more distressed. Imagine coming home after a very painful experience, mentioning

Being-Without

FIGURE 12.5. Child being pushed to conform to parental shark music. Copyright 2009 by Cooper, Hoffman, and Powell.

it to your partner, and having your partner immediately say, "Oh, come on now, cheer up—and let's do something fun like watch television." How would you feel? The therapist can invite parents to talk about times they wanted someone to Be-With them and the person would not.

At this point we acknowledge to the group that, *of course in the real world of our busy lives, we often distract or redirect our children away from feelings.* This is not a problem unless this is the primary way the parent helps his child manage emotion. The child needs to know that the parent can Be-With every emotional experience some of the time, but it is not necessary for the parent to Be-With every feeling every time it occurs. The powerful take-home message for the baby is "No matter what you feel, I can and often will be there with you." It is important to remember that frequently Being-With is the most efficient way to move children into a more positive affective state, and attempts at distraction, redirection, and pressuring children to feel what they are not feeling can actually prolong the period of distress.

Next we say:

"Also, sometimes our children need us to take charge so that we can get done what needs to be done. Remember one part of being bigger, stronger, wiser, and kind is, whenever possible, follow your child's need, but the other part is, whenever necessary, take charge. There are many times every day that taking charge wins out over focusing on feelings.

"We don't want to teach our children that the whole world stops every time they have a feeling, but it is important for our children to know at their core that every feeling they have can be shared when the time is right. Only then can they trust that there is no feeling that they have to experience all alone. With that in place, distraction and redirection can often be helpful. Here is some reassuring information: If you are able to Be-With and hold your child's feelings more often than not, that seems to be good enough."

In addition, it may be helpful to emphasize that Being-With isn't a technique, but rather a state of mind. It's helpful for parents to realize that they can't suddenly begin to coregulate feelings and expect immediate results. At times children will respond quickly to having a caregiver meet their needs rather than force an agenda. But it is also common for a child to take time to adjust to a caregiver who is now willing to respond in this new way. It will be helpful to clarify with the parents that they will need to give their children time to adjust to this new approach to caregiving. Being-With is about building the quality of relationship over time versus getting an immediate result.

Helping Parents Learn to "Name That Need"

The next part of the session is focused on parents learning to describe behavior and infer where the children are on the Circle; in other words, name the need. This is very important, because describing what they see and then guessing where their child is on the Circle promotes reflective capacity in the parent. From the assessment footage you need to select one moment of each parent and child successfully negotiating one of the needs on the Circle (see Figure 12.6, "Name That Need"). Make sure to have several examples from the top of the Circle and several from the bottom. With high-risk dyads it can be challenging to find "Comfort me" and "Organize My Feelings" clips. This is where training and supervision can be invaluable in training the eye to recognize brief moments of success precisely where struggle seems prominent. COS calls this finding underutilized strengths (see Chapter 7), and it takes trained eyes to see brief moments of capacity in a sea of insecurity or disorganization.

In addition to naming the need, parents need to decide whether this is a follow or take-charge (lead) moment. It is always useful to include one take-charge moment in this exercise. The most common example of taking charge can be found in cleanup. Whether it is a "Help me" moment or an "Organize My Feelings" moment, the parent often needs to take charge. As the program progresses, a capacity for reflecting about when and why they either take charge or do not take charge becomes central for abdicating parents to reevaluate their behavior.

It is important to pick clips in which the parent is successful at meeting the need. The chosen clips need to allow the group to agree on what they are seeing. However, guessing the right need has little to do with what this is about. Choosing clips in which one need shifts to another or two needs are simultaneously present (e.g., enjoy and delight) engages parents in reflective dialogue. Learning to sequence their observations and create multiple hypotheses about the child's need is far better than having the group come to a quick conclusion. A secondary benefit to naming the need is that the therapist can observe whether parents struggle in differentiating top-half from bottom-half moments. If a parent cannot see needs on one half of the Circle, it is important to note and remember that struggle.

In the process of describing what a child and parent are doing, it's important to focus on the behaviors you actually see. We all tend to guess how people are feeling or thinking and include that in our descriptions of what we're seeing. When someone is smiling, for example, we tend to think that we can see he is happy and thinking pleasant thoughts. But some people smile when they're nervous; thinking they are happy would be a mistake. As noted in Chapter 11, reviewing the videos is a good way to learn to separate what we see from what we guess.

Say to the parents in the group:

> "An important developmental learning for children is the capacity to identify and communicate needs. Parents are in the position of having to guess a child's needs based on the child's actions. The Circle of Security is about an essential set of needs children have regarding their relationship with parents. Using the Circle of Security as a map, guess which needs are being demonstrated in each video vignette."

After each clip, ask the parents:

1. *What did you see [name of child] doing?* Help the parents learn to describe behavior and separate that from conclusions, labels, and guesses. At first parents will respond with conclusions or guesses like "he is acting angry or controlling." You can ask them what color "controlling" is, a question that emphasizes that the answer needs to be what they see, not what they think. Another question that gets at the same issue is "What is he/she doing that leads you to the conclusion that he/she is angry?"

2. *What do you think the child needs?* The parents will be choosing from the needs identified on the COS.

3. *What do you imagine the child is feeling?* Parents may need help in increasing their vocabulary of potential feelings that a child might experience. After all parents have contributed, sometimes it will be necessary to add some feeling alternatives. The COS protocol focuses on six key emotions: anger, sadness, joy, fear, curiosity, and shame. Helping parents begin to track these six emotions offers them clear themes to look for with their children.

4. *Is this a follow or take-charge (lead) moment?* Follow your child's cues unless there is a reason to take charge. If the parent is taking charge, what is the reason? As stated earlier, many parents take charge when they

do not need to and don't take charge when it is needed. Often with disordered dyads this will be a central issue in their shark music session. You will be laying the initial groundwork for that here.

Figure 12.6 lists all the needs around the Circle and provides room for parents to check what need they see for up to six video vignettes.

Central to providing secure parenting is the ability to identify the needs of your child. Often, parents feel they have to guess what their child needs. The *Circle of Security* is designed to help you identify both the specific need that your child is experiencing in a particular moment and whether you need to follow your child or take charge.

Using the *Circle of Security* as a map, identify the specific need being shown in each video example.

Video Examples	1	2	3	4	5	6
Support My Exploration by…	Following Taking Charge	Following Taking Charge	Following Taking Charge	Following Taking Charge	Following Taking Charge	Following Taking Charge
Watch over Me by…	Following Taking Charge	Following Taking Charge	Following Taking Charge	Following Taking Charge	Following Taking Charge	Following Taking Charge
Enjoy with Me by…	Following Taking Charge	Following Taking Charge	Following Taking Charge	Following Taking Charge	Following Taking Charge	Following Taking Charge
Help Me by…	Following Taking Charge	Following Taking Charge	Following Taking Charge	Following Taking Charge	Following Taking Charge	Following Taking Charge
Comfort Me by…	Following Taking Charge	Following Taking Charge	Following Taking Charge	Following Taking Charge	Following Taking Charge	Following Taking Charge
Protect Me by…	Following Taking Charge	Following Taking Charge	Following Taking Charge	Following Taking Charge	Following Taking Charge	Following Taking Charge
Organize My Feelings by…	Following Taking Charge	Following Taking Charge	Following Taking Charge	Following Taking Charge	Following Taking Charge	Following Taking Charge
Delight in Me by….	Following Taking Charge	Following Taking Charge	Following Taking Charge	Following Taking Charge	Following Taking Charge	Following Taking Charge

- *Always*: be BIGGER, STRONGER, WISER, and KIND.
  - *Whenever possible*: follow my child's need.
    - *Whenever necessary*: take charge.

FIGURE 12.6. Name That Need. Copyright 2001 by Cooper, Hoffman, Marvin, & Powell.

Introducing Rupture and Repair

The session ends on the topic of rupture and repair. The bad news for parents is that no one gets needs right all the time and the good news is that security is about finding ways to repair the relationship when it ruptures. We define rupture in the parent–child relationship in a very specific way: when the parent steps off the Circle, the relationship is ruptured. If you think of the hands on the COS graphic Figure 12.1 as representing the parent, then a rupture is the parents taking their hands off the Circle. Sometimes parents rupture the relationship by taking both hands off the Circle, but at other times they rupture it by taking only one hand off the Circle. If you think of one hand representing a secure base from which to explore and the other hand representing a safe haven to which to return, you can understand ambivalent (top hand) and avoidant (bottom hand) attachment as the parent taking one hand off the Circle.

When a parent persistently takes the safe haven off the Circle, the child will likely become avoidant. When the secure base is consistently unavailable, the child often becomes ambivalent. However, all parents sometimes take a hand off the Circle. Imagine being tired and hot and your child, sticky from eating an ice cream bar, cries and reaches to be picked up. You might well distract or redirect him, which is in effect a minor rupture. On the other hand (pun intended), imagine your child climbing on the jungle gym. Although he is perfectly safe, you find yourself getting more and more anxious the higher he gets. Suddenly you find yourself scooping him up and saying, "Hey, let's go swing together." Again, this is a minor rupture in the relationship.

When a parent takes both hands off the Circle (when the caregiver becomes mean, weak, or gone), the child experiences a more intense level of rupture. All parents have times when they lose balance and move from bigger and stronger into mean, or try to be kind in a way that bypasses being in charge, becoming weak. Or the parent steps away from the relationship in such a way that the child feels all alone and without a trustworthy resource. These ruptures, when recognized, named, and repaired, become a source of shared coherence within the relationship. When these ruptures happen, especially on a consistent basis, and go without repair, the child begins losing trust in this all-important relationship as a resource for security.

Repair is talked about as a process of the caregiver getting back on the Circle. First the parent has to collect herself, then she has to help soothe and organize her child's feeling so everyone is calm enough to go to the next step. The reflecting part of repair cannot be done if the child is still calming on the bottom of the Circle. After sensing the parent's recommitment to Being-With, the child will move to the top of the Circle, and then parent and child can explore what happened with each taking responsibility for his or her part. Then they can make the emotional repair by getting on each other's side. The last step is to consider new options for how to do it differently next time.

Figure 12.7, on repairing relationships with a "time-in," (Weininger, 1998, p. 21) helps parents learn more about the process of repair.

I'm Upset and My Child Is Upset

When necessary, I start with a *"Time-Out"* (for me, for my child, or for both of us) until I get back on the circle by:

Realizing that I am Bigger, Stronger, Wiser, and Kind.

Reminding myself that no matter how I feel, my child needs me.

*A *"Time-Out"* can be helpful as a first step, but not as a punishment.

I'm Calm (Enough) and My Child Is Upset

We can build a safe "repair routine" together (remember: the first 1,000 times are the hardest!).

I take charge so my child is not too out of control.

We can change location. Go to a neutral place that is our "Time-In" spot, where we sit together and let feelings begin to change.

I maintain a calm tone of voice (firm, reassuring, and kind).

We can do something different (for several minutes): read, or look out the window, or attend to a chore together.

I help my child bring words to her/his feelings. ("It looks like this is hard for you" "Are you mad/sad/afraid?").

I talk about my feelings about what just happened. ("When you did that, I felt...").

I stay with my child until s/he is calm enough. (It may take a while for a child to calm down from overwhelming and unorganized feelings. Rule of thumb: Stay in charge, and stay sympathetic.)

I'm Calm (Enough) and My Child Is Calm (Enough)

I use the following to support our repair and to make repair easier in the future:

I help my child use words for the needs and feelings that s/he is struggling with by listening and talking together. (Remember KISS - Keep It Short and Sweet.)

I help my child take responsibility for her/his part and I can take responsibility for my part. (Rule of thumb: No blaming allowed.)

We talk about new ways of dealing with the problem in the future. (Even for very young children, talking out loud about new options will establish a pattern and a feeling that can be repeated through the years.)

FIGURE 12.7. Repairing relationships with a "time-in." Copyright 2001 by Cassidy, Cooper, Hoffman, and Powell.

At the end of the session, encourage the parents to come to the next group with a new "Circle story" and talk about the upcoming series of video reviews. One parent's video will be reviewed each week; be prepared to say whose video will be reviewed which week. It is best to start with the parent you see as the easiest to work with in terms of being most reflective and least defensive. It is important to have the first review go well, because it sets the stage for all reviews that will follow. All the parents will be wondering and watching this first video review to see how the process works.

PHASE ONE: REVIEWING VIDEO CLIPS TO DISCOVER UNDERUSED PARENTING CAPACITIES

The first round of video reviews in the COS protocol is called Phase One; it begins in week 3 of the treatment and continues until each parent has had a turn. With a group of six, Phase One would end in week 8. Each week, edited video clips from one parent's SSP are processed with the parent and the group. Phase One video reviews focus on parents demonstrating success with underdeveloped parenting capacities (e.g., a parent who is dismissing sharing a moment of emotional connection) with a preview of the work that will be done in the Phase Two video reviews. The Phase Two video review will focus on the defensive process that blocks the parent from fully using her underdeveloped capacities. During the video review, the other parents are given a worksheet to enhance their observational skills and are invited to share insights and support for the parent whose video is being reviewed.

Although Phase One videos show parents' struggles and focus on the part of the Circle that the parent finds least comfortable, parents are not formally introduced to insecure attachments until week 9. During all group meetings, caregivers' struggles are normalized, and consequently the group becomes a safer place for participants to explore and acknowledge which half of the Circle is less comfortable for them. Phase One video review is designed to help the parent become familiar and feel safe with reflective dialogue as each parent reviews his or her video. It is also intended to set the stage for the more challenging Phase Two video review, which addresses the linchpin struggle that was selected for each dyad during the assessment phase.

Before Phase One, the therapist selects four or five clips of approximately 10 to 30 seconds each:

- The first clip is a very positive clip that evokes the parent's caregiving and has a "softening" effect. It could be a sweet moment with shared touch or eye contact from the reading or play. Often, but not always, it is a clip that shows the child longing for the parent during the separation.

• The second clip will show an underutilized strength that is selected based on the linchpin struggle that will be addressed. So, for instance, if you are working with a parent whose linchpin is unavailability on the bottom of the Circle, an underutilized strength would be illustrated by a clip that shows the parent responding to a bottom-half need, even if it's only for a few seconds. For a parent whose linchpin is hands, such as abdicating parental authority, an underutilized strength might be a moment in the cleanup in which the parent took charge, even for a moment. (If such a moment is rare, it may be best to save this clip to be used as an underutilized strength in Phase Two.) Often finding these moments is a challenge; they tend to be of brief duration and may take careful editing or a willingness to keep the clip very short in order to present. Over the years we have found that there are almost always underutilized strengths hidden in each video.

• The third clip is referred to as "shark music minor" because it presents the linchpin struggle at a very manageable level of intensity. This tests the waters to see how defensive or open the parent will be when asked to process something that has some emotional difficulty involved. The parent's response to the vulnerability helps the therapist predict how ambitious to be in selecting the intensity of the shark music clip used in Phase Two. This is the first moment in the protocol where the therapist asks this parent to dialogue about an observed struggle. The clip can show something as simple as a child cuing the parent to follow and the parent taking charge and leading when it was not necessary. Typically, the shark music minor clip addresses the same issue, with less intensity, as the shark music major clip.

• The last clip is a celebration of success regarding the linchpin struggle and the parent–child relationship. We want the parent to leave the group feeling challenged but also hopeful. The last clip is sometimes described as anything that moves the group to say, "Awwww." A tender moment of closeness or a shared gaze or smile might do the job. The more the clip can be tied into the overall story, the better.

As each parent takes a turn to do the Phase One review the therapist must help the group be a safe enough environment in which to be vulnerable. Typically the holding environment and the fact that every parent knows he will have a turn forms a code of mutual support. It is amazing how strong the mutual support tends to be. However, sometimes parents do act out, and in those cases the therapist needs to protect the parent who is on "the hot seat" for that day. If a group member gets uncomfortable and defends herself by utilizing criticism and says something harsh like "You really blew that," the therapist must interact with the group member and briefly help that parent with her defensive criticism by inviting her to focus on her own feelings. Exploration may move in the direction of wondering if the clip touched something in her own experience (past or present) and inviting her to talk about it. Even if she doesn't explore her own feelings, it quickly stops the critical process in a way that is both firm and kind while simultaneously introducing the group to the nature of defense. All of this must be brief, however, because the therapist does not want to take time away from the video review at hand.

The group members also may offer comfort or reassurance in a manner that sabotages the parent's work. In this case the therapist can interpret the nature of the group's defense and ask the parent if she wants to be rescued. Parents virtually always say no, and so the therapist can quickly negotiate with the group about their bearing their discomfort. If a parent did say yes, the therapist could then respond openly about the parent's need. If the group has a parent who is consistently disruptive or defensive, it becomes necessary to set a boundary and limit the parent's involvement as kindly as possible until a conversation can be arranged to discuss this issue outside of group time.

The hope is to avoid embarrassing the critical or protective group member while protecting the parent who is viewing her video. It can sometimes be helpful to say, "I see that you have a lot of important feelings about this particular issue, and we can explore them during your video review." At this point the therapist simply turns the focus back toward the parent who is viewing her video. The remote control is a powerful tool. Saying to the group, "Let's watch the clip again" and pushing the play button ends the interaction.

WEEK 9: ENTER SHARK MUSIC

In week 9 parents are asked to share how the first video reviews went for all of them by describing the most difficult and best moments in the process. Prior to the introduction of shark music, parent struggles are normalized, with the group reading out loud the handout "Welcome to the Club" (see Form 12.1).

The handout emphasizes that all parents struggle. As parents receive permission to experience struggles as common, even inevitable, they begin to relax. To help caregivers explore their relative comfort with the needs on the Circle, we suggest they reflect on their own histories, including where their own parents experienced strengths and struggles on the Circle. As the group begins to discuss their own experience of growing up, they are increasingly willing to reflect on what they are currently passing on to their children. We consistently emphasize that we have no interest in blaming their parents, but rather find that reflecting on their own history makes it less likely that they will pass struggles on to their children.

To help parents understand how state of mind influences our feelings, beliefs, and defenses, we use a two-part audio/video clip. Part one opens with a beautiful ocean view from atop a bluff. As explained in Chapter 5, this clip is set to Pachelbel's Canon in D major. The video clip is taken from the viewpoint of someone strolling down a forested path leading to the ocean. This 50-second clip, which ends on the beach looking out to the water, tends to elicit a calm, pleasant, safe feeling. The second part of the clip uses the exact same beach scene, but this time the background music is set to a musical composition that suggests the well-known cello theme from the movie *Jaws*. This clip tends to evoke quite different feelings. Suddenly, the stroll through the calm forested path is transformed into an eerie trek among looming trees and undergrowth teeming with hidden danger. The final approach to the beach evokes a sense of foreboding and a strong desire to flee from the water.

Parents have an immediate visceral experience, and within several minutes they grasp that the background music dramatically shifts the mood of these two identical visual experiences. We explain that a state of mind is like music we play in our head. Music is an excellent metaphor for state of mind in that it colors or even defines our subjective experience, is emotionally evocative, and is not based on language.

The type of music evoked by each of our children's attachment and exploratory behaviors depends on our history with these behaviors. As explained in Chapter 5, if our history of exploration and autonomy or our requests for closeness and comfort are associated with distress, then our children's needs on that part of the Circle may evoke a similar distress. It is important to clarify that shark music is a fearful response to something that is actually safe.

Although current research suggests that the brain is immensely more

complex (Pessora, 2008), and the parts of the brain react in a more simultaneous than sequential manner, we teach caregivers to differentiate between
"limbic system alerts" and "prefrontal lobe assessments." In this presentation to parents, we assert that limbic system alerts are faster than they
are accurate, and prefrontally mediated interpretations are slower but
more likely to be accurate. By helping parents understand that they can be
"hijacked" (Goleman, 1995) by a "shark music" response from their limbic
system, we lay the groundwork to create a "choice point."

A choice point is created when caregivers realize that their amygdala
(part of the "feeling brain") is designed to give an immediate alert based
on their "library" of things associated with danger in the past. Because the
amygdala is designed to be faster than accurate, false positives abound.
Many experiences feel frightening but are not dangerous. The choice is
to continue to defend against nonexistent sharks or to reflect and engage
the prefrontal lobe (referred to with parents as the "thinking brain"). By
bringing the feeling brain and thinking brain into dialogue, caregivers can
develop a response based on a more accurate assessment of the current
situation.

When working with parents, we use this formula: When my child
does X, I hear shark music, but rather than protecting myself by doing Y,
I choose to bear the emotional discomfort and reflect on the current situation so that I can respond appropriately to my child's need. In summary,
when a parent risks experiencing and reflecting on, rather than defending against, the feelings evoked by shark music, previously unexplored and
unregulated negative affective states can be brought within a safe context
of reflective dialogue, allowing a therapeutic shift to occur.

Beyond normalizing caregiver struggles, the underlying goal of this
exercise is to outline specific struggles that caregivers can expect to see.
Caregivers are told that struggles may well show up regarding hands issues,
top-half issues, bottom-half issues, or a combination of the three. At the
same time, these struggles are described as understandable given the power
of shark music to keep painful experiences outside awareness. In addition,
the "Welcome to the Club" handout honors the positive intentionality of all
parents. Thus, a context of "no blame" is established, deepening the parent's sense of trust in the positive intentionality of the group therapist and,
by implication, the group process.

After "Welcome to the Club," parents are introduced to insecure
attachment first by understanding how state of mind affects perception
with the use of shark music and then with the Limited Circle graphics

shown in Figures 12.8 and 12.9. The therapist can introduce the limited Circles this way:

> "Let's look at how our shark music teaches our children to miscue. We'll begin with the 'limited top of the Circle.' For some of us, letting our children separate is difficult, so when they go out to explore, our shark music gets triggered. This teaches our children to say, 'I need you to support my exploration, but that makes us uncomfortable.' Why do they say this? Because when *we're* uncomfortable, they're uncomfortable. But when our children want to explore, they know our shark music is coming, so they avoid it and they act like they want comfort or protection. This is called a *miscue*. You can think about it as your child saying 'I need support for exploration, but that makes us uncomfortable, so I miscue you and act like I need comfort or protection.'"

> "The 'limited bottom of the Circle' comes from our being uncomfortable with closeness. So when our children need to be welcomed in, our shark music is triggered. This teaches our children to say, 'I need you to welcome my coming to you, but that makes us uncomfortable, so I miscue you by acting like I want to explore or be distant.'"

These graphics are an oversimplification of avoidant and ambivalent attachments but serve the function of illustrating the constructs to parents. We then present the idea that we all tend to be more comfortable on either

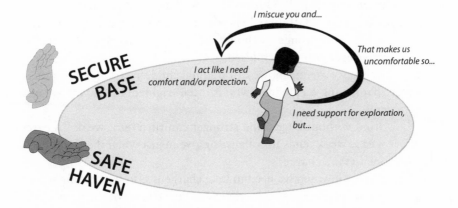

FIGURE 12.8. Limited top of the Circle: Child miscuing—responding to caregiver's needs. Copyright 1999 by Cooper, Hoffman, Marvin, and Powell.

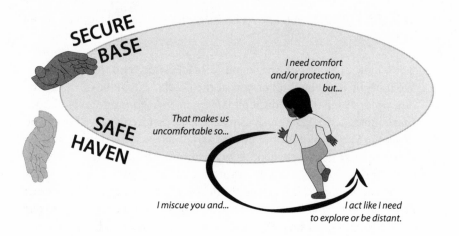

FIGURE 12.9. Limited bottom of the Circle: Child miscuing—responding to caregiver's needs. Copyright 1999 by Cooper, Hoffman, Marvin, and Powell.

the top half or the bottom half of the Circle. If we don't attend to the half of the Circle that we are less comfortable with, we are in danger of missing our children's cues and inadvertently teaching them to miscue about their needs on that half of the Circle. In this way, our initial miscuing becomes the theme for their miscue of us.

> "To understand limited hands [see Figure 12.10], first, let's review what we learned about hands. Our children need us to balance bigger, stronger, wiser, and kind. 'Limited Hands' show up in three different ways.
>
> "Bigger and stronger without kind can turn into mean. Our being unkind is never good for children.
>
> "When we are mean, we can frighten children, and the research is clear that having a caregiver who is often frightening leads to serious problems.
>
> "Kind without bigger and stronger can turn into 'weak.' A caregiver who is weak tends to collapse or give in just when the child needs someone to take charge.
>
> "Giving in when we need to take charge is also frightening to our children. If we are not strong enough to take charge of them, our children fear that we are not strong enough to protect them.
>
> "The third way we can have limited hands is by being 'gone.' Being gone is different from coming and going. We all have times when we're

FIGURE 12.10. Limited hands: Losing the wisdom to stay in balance. Copyright 2009 by Cooper, Hoffman, and Powell.

away from our children, times when we go to work, spend the evening out, or just answer the telephone. Being 'gone' as hands is when we're repeatedly absent in a way that leaves our child living in fear with no one to turn to.

"Alcohol or substance abuse, choosing romantic partners over the needs of our children, and neglect all are examples of our being gone, which leaves our child feeling confused, abandoned, and unable to cope. When a child has repeated experiences of a caregiver who is gone, even when the caregiver returns, it takes time and hard work before the child can fully trust that someone will stay."

The last topic for the group to explore has to do with choosing security (see Figure 12.11). This is a hopeful message clarifying that even though we all have moments of choosing and not choosing security, it is a choice. With reflection and practice parents can enhance their ability to choose security for their children. This new awareness turns shark music away from a potentially negative event into a warning system that when paid attention to allows for the new possibility of choice.

After the figure is processed, the session ends with the therapist telling the parents that the Phase Two video reviews will focus on understanding shark music and choosing security.

PHASE TWO: REVIEWING VIDEO CLIPS TO IDENTIFY THE LINCHPIN AND RECOGNIZE THE CAPACITY FOR MORE SECURE STRATEGIES

During weeks 10–15 parents participate in Phase Two video reviews. The focus is on helping parents identify their linchpin struggle and the associated shark music affect. As in prior reviews, one parent a week is presented with video clips that have been reedited from her preintervention

Your Child's Need:

When your child's *need* requires a response that is not comfortable for you . . .

Shark Music:

You suddenly *feel* uncomfortable . . . (e.g., lonely, unsafe, rejected, abandoned, angry, controlled)

Choice Point:

- You can *respond* to your child's need (in spite of the discomfort it causes you),

OR

- You can *protect* yourself from further pain by overriding your child's need (limiting or avoiding a response). If you protect yourself from uncomfortable feelings, your child's need will go unmet. Over time s/he will begin to express that need indirectly, causing both of you difficulty.

All parents hear shark music with some of their child's needs. The parents of secure children *recognize* their shark music. Often (not always) they *choose* to find a way to meet their child's need, in spite of the temporary pain it causes them.

Steps to Security:

1. Recognize the discomfort ("Here's my shark music again.").
2. Honor the discomfort ("I hurt now because this particular need triggers my shark music.").
3. Respond to your child's need.

FIGURE 12.11. Choosing security. Copyright 2001 by Cooper, Hoffman, Marvin, & Powell.

assessment. The goal in Phase Two video reviews is to help parents recognize that they already have the capacity to meet their child's needs (as seen in the underutilized strengths clip), but their shark music makes meeting their children's needs feel frightening even though it is safe. This allows them to make a conscious choice to utilize more secure strategies when their child's needs trigger shark music.

The video clips have the same themes as Phase One reviews but are shown in a different order. The shark music major clip is shown immediately after the softening clip and is often more intense and direct in the presentation of the core linchpin struggle. By now the holding environment of the group is intact, and the parent has more skills and experience to be able to manage the increase in vulnerability.

Each parent will experience vulnerable feelings during this review, and some will show their feelings more than others. It is not uncommon for parents to cry as they realize they have been fostering insecurity in their child. Although it is not helpful to push for more affect for affect's sake, it is often helpful to allow enough silence for the parent to spontaneously reflect on how this particular insecurity is an aspect of his own upbringing. Having an interested, concerned, and caring therapist and group to share the pain with helps make the feelings less frightening and more manageable. It also increases reflective capacity and helps establish a choice point where there previously had not been one. Until the implicit is made explicit and procedural memory is given language, chronic patterns of insecure interaction remain hidden and hence outside the realm of choice.

When a parent becomes emotionally vulnerable and shares intense feelings, the therapist's primary goal in that moment is to Be-With the parent. Teaching of any kind is always secondary to the parent's experience of having her pain witnessed and held. It is not uncommon for the affective intensity in the room to trigger the therapist's shark music. Often therapists respond by "overteaching" in a nonconscious attempt to dampen the intensity in the room. A more useful approach includes direct yet noninvasive eye contact with the parent and a willingness to stay focused on the pain, often without words. Often what parents need most is the space to slowly, in their own way, explore this uncharted territory while being held on the Circle.

The goal isn't resolution or even understanding of past pain; rather the goal is to Be-With the parent, both as a healing presence and as a model of bigger, stronger, wiser, and kind. When parents realize that their pain is not unspeakable, it feels safer to override their shark music. We also hope that experiencing firsthand the power of Being-With will make the parent more able to offer this to his child.

A common defensive reaction to seeing the shark music clip is to blame the self and fall into a negative self-representation of "I am a bad parent." It's very useful for the therapist to see this as a defense. This defense has different meanings and functions depending on the parent's core sensitivity. In general, the moral defense, discussed in Chapter 4, is in play. In other words, "If I can blame myself and conclude that I am a bad person, then I do not have to see the complexity nor have compassion for how I have learned to be this way." The idea of being bad is a conclusion that was and continues to be reached with a sense of very limited resources in a moment of Being-Without. It is a conclusion made through the eyes of a child who desperately needs to make sense of things that don't make sense and preserves some childlike sense of hope that at least if the child is bad then he can try to be better and his "good" parents will treat him kindly. The defense needs to be explored and normalized as a familiar way to make sense of problems in relationships by believing that the reason the relationship is in trouble is that the child is bad. This helps the parent's underlying pain and the legitimacy of how certain needs have gone unmet remain central in the therapy.

The third video shown is the underutilized strength clip. The strongest video example of underutilized strength regarding the linchpin struggle is saved for this moment. It reaffirms that the parent has the capacity to meet the child's needs when she chooses to override shark music. For example, for an abdicating, disorganized parent, the shark music will show a moment of collapse. The underutilized strength clip will show a moment of *taking charge*. This is a competency statement to empower parents with the knowledge that they have the capacity, but they need to override their shark music. As previously stated, it may be difficult to find an example of an underused capacity because, by definition, it is underused. In all likelihood the moment will be brief; however, there is almost always something hidden within the SSP to use for this purpose.

In the final clip, the goal, as in the Phase One review, is to end with a celebration of success. It is always useful to leave some time at the end of video reviews to ask the parent how the review went for her and to make room for the group to talk about their experience. Often the support the parents give each other at the end of each group session makes a significant difference.

WEEK 16: RECORDING A MODIFIED STRANGE SITUATION FOR THE FINAL REVIEWS

Around week 16, the parents are filmed in a modified Strange Situation. Parents should not be filmed until they have completed their second video review. The dyad is asked to start with 4 minutes of blowing bubbles together. This often creates sweet moments to use in the next video review. Then the bubble toy is removed, and the parent and child play with toys for 3 minutes. The parent then leaves for a separation of up to 3 minutes. The parent returns for a reunion that lasts 3 minutes. The taping ends with 3 minutes of reading and then a cleanup.

PHASE THREE: CELEBRATING POSITIVE CHANGES
AND SEEING SHARK MUSIC IN ACTION

This new filming allows the parents to use all they have learned thus far. It is wonderful when parents are successful in overcoming their linchpin struggles, but it is more common for parents to make the same mistakes they did in the initial SSP. What is different in this filming is that parents know about their shark music and their child's needs. When they fail to meet their child's needs, they are often shocked. They suddenly have a whole new appreciation for the power of shark music. They are primed and ready to take on their struggle in the Phase Three video review.

For example, a mother watching her third video review said, "My daughter is being me, and I am being my mom. That is just what my mom would do. That is just what I didn't want to do in this taping. I really need to look at my shark music." The pain of that insight, linked with what she knew about shark music, had a profound effect on her. Her postintervention SSP was coded secure.

The modified SSP videos are edited for Phase Three reviews that take place during weeks 17–19. We originally thought this video review would be a straightforward celebration of success, and so to complete the groups before the end of the Head Start school year (during which we were conducting our early groups), we scheduled two video reviews each week. This is a design flaw since Phase Three video reviews are often the most intense and productive of all. When possible, therefore, it is better to extend the group for 3 weeks and do one review per week.

Week 20 is reserved for the graduation celebration. Each parent receives a "Certificate of Graduation." A new music video is created using some of the clips that the parents reviewed during the group to music we select to celebrate their learning. The parents are encouraged to share their experience of participating in the protocol. If the group is being used for research purposes, final arrangements are made for the postintervention assessments. At the end of the group or after the final assessment for groups involved in research, the parents are given a copy of the clips used in their video reviews.

THE CIRCLE OF SECURITY IN DIFFERENT
TREATMENT MODALITIES

People often ask whether it is better to work with parents together, with only the primary attachment figure, or with each parent separately, and which treatment modality (group, individual, or family) is best. The question can be extended to any coparenting team. Sometimes a grandparent, significant other, stepparent, or other person is the primary support person for a parent, and therefore the question of their involvement in the intervention arises. This is a quick review of some of the pros and cons of each combination.

To begin with, it is important to know that any therapeutic intervention is essentially a family therapy intervention. We all have multiple families: our family of origin, our current support system, and the family that continues to "live" inside of us in the form of internal representations and procedural memories. Families can be usefully conceived of as systems, and since changing any element changes the entire system, effective interventions, even with individuals, have rippling effects throughout our current relationships and our experience of past relationships. Expanding the conceptualization of the issue from the individual to dyads to triads is challenging. However, putting blinders on to avoid the complexity of couple and family dynamics does not make the issues go away or lessen the influence they have on children. Even when you are working with individuals, it is useful to think in terms of families.

However, the underlying therapeutic approach does change in important ways depending on who is in the room. When working with an individual, the relationship between the therapist and the client is central and immediate, and this allows work within the transference to play a crucial role. Transference, within the COS model, is the experience of past significant relationships (including relationship patterns and struggles) that now manifests within current significant relationships. For this reason it is assumed that a parent will likely experience the therapist as having qualities that may trigger past memories and feelings regarding those in authority. When working with two people, the focus tends to become the interactions between the two people (partners, parent/child, etc.). When working in family therapy, thinking and working with at least triadic interactions is essential. In group therapy, it is important to manage the group process and attend to the developing alignments and coalitions.

One of the first things to consider in deciding which modality to use is your level of expertise in each area. If you are not confident in a certain modality, but you would like to develop your skills, finding supervision is essential. The next line of questioning is to examine the pros and cons of each modality for a specific person.

Individual Therapy

Working with an individual often allows the therapist to pace the intervention to meet the client's needs rather than maintain a schedule for the group. If time permits, the therapist can do more in-depth work with defenses and family of origin issues. Individual therapy may also be a good approach for parents who are uncomfortable or feel too vulnerable in group settings, a circumstance that may become clear during the intake. Also, parents whose esteem sensitivity is so rigid and pervasive that they act out in ways that become toxic to the group (devaluing or displaying grandiosity) are better served individually.

On the downside, without other parents involved, the individual client misses out on vicarious learning from group members, group support, and the normalization of parenting struggles. Also, if you strictly adapted the group protocol for individual work, the intervention would be completed in six sessions (two sessions for introduction, two sessions of video review, one session to introduce new material, one session for third video reviews and wrap-up). The parent would have seen only one family (his or her own) and would have had very little time to build observational and inferential skills. Slowing the process down and going into more depth can help with this. For example, a parent who shows signs of being defensive about even the hint of having a struggle may well need several sessions prior to launching into video review. Taking time to walk through the implications of this parent's COSI—with time spent exploring what it was like in her own family of origin—can be helpful. Slowing the pace down becomes central, with the primary goal remaining focused on providing a context of Being-With, especially when beginning to explore vulnerable themes. As the parent begins to trust the clinician, it may become safe enough to risk exploring struggles that previously would not have been available for shared reflection.

The COS-P DVD

For the clinician, it is often much easier to organize individual work than to organize a group. In fact the group setup with its video requirements may be prohibitive for some clinical settings. In this case, it can be helpful to integrate the COS-P DVD into individual work. The DVD shows other parents openly discussing their struggles and their shark music and shows practice clips for the viewer to use to practice with the material.

*The COS-P DVD (Cooper et al., 2009a) was designed to
offer the key components of the original COS approach within
a brief, 8-week parenting program. The protocol presents
stock video footage of secure and problematic parent–child
interaction, observational skill training, and approaches to
support reflective functioning. It includes many of the original
COS components, such as "Name That Need," struggles
around the Circle, and shark music. It is designed to be
delivered in a step-by-step process for use in groups, home
visitation, and individual counseling.
The DVD is available as part of the COS-P training.*

Couple Therapy

One important advantage of working with parenting partners together
is having access to how the couple's dynamics contribute to meeting or
not meeting the child's needs. It is not unusual for problems in the dyad
to manifest as parenting problems. This is true for romantic partners as
well as grandparent/parent or other coparenting arrangements. Also, the
complementarity (the shared dance in which each partner triggers and
maintains a particular defensive strategy) of the couple can be leveraged
for therapeutic purposes. For example, if one parent is more comfortable
with being bigger and stronger and the other more comfortable with being
kind, typically they fall into a deviation-amplifying feedback loop. In other
words, one parent focuses more on kindness to try to make up for how
strict the other parent is being, but the second parent is being strict in an
attempt to make up for how permissive the first parent is acting. In trying
to compensate for each other's overused strength they move further apart
and create a mean versus weak scenario. The therapist can help couples
reverse this feedback loop by having them learn from each other's strength
to develop their underused capacity.

The downside in working with couples is that the couple's dynamic
may be so conflicted that it derails the work. It is difficult to risk focusing
on the self in a vulnerable manner when your partner is attacking you. In
relationships in which one partner is dominated by the other, the dominated partner's becoming bigger, stronger, wiser, and kind may threaten
the dominant partner. This is, of course, true whether the partner is in the
room or not, but the partner may sabotage the process of therapy. Also,
the same problems with lack of group support and vicarious learning that
affect individual therapy apply to couple work. The COS-P DVD can be

useful for couples as well by offering the vicarious vulnerability and reflection of the parents in the DVD.

Couples whose relationship is strong enough for them to learn from and support each other in the learning process are good candidates for couple work or group work together. Also, couples who are struggling in their relationship but are amenable to treatment can get an extra benefit from couple work. When couples are so conflicted as to derail their learning, the therapist must decide whether to work on the couple issues before approaching the COS material or perhaps have the couple work separately either in group or individually.

Family Therapy

In the first case in which we collaborated to apply attachment principles to treatment, we worked with a couple and their youngest child. We alternated between filming family sessions one week and reviewing the video with the parents the next week. This gave us access to the triadic interactions as well as the couple dynamics. Typically we would include the entire family, but we chose not to include the other children for simplicity's sake. This process illustrated how closely integrated attachment issues are with the whole range of family interactions. Much like a Rubik's cube, families are richly cross-joined so that you can't change one facet without affecting the whole system.

Having access to the family offers many advantages in tracking and intervening in the family structure. For example, children sometimes try to support a struggling couple by drawing attention either toward or away from themselves in either positive or negative ways. If the couple has a common cause (caring for a troubled child) or a common enemy (dealing with a problem child), the focus is temporarily diverted from the problems in the couple's relationship. Sometimes children sacrifice meeting their own needs to take a burden off the couple (e.g., controlling caregiving children). Rigid coalitions, incongruent triangles, and distortion in the family hierarchy can all contribute to a child not getting needs met on the Circle.

The downside to working with families is that it is difficult to track the complex interactions without training and supervision. Also, the same problems with lack of group support and learning are present.

Families whose children span a wide age range are good candidates for family therapy because the attachment issues of children who are too old for the Strange Situation can be addressed. For multiproblem families, the attachment work can be integrated into working on other issues more easily in a family setting.

Group Therapy

This entire chapter has been focused on the group intervention that we have studied in research, but a few specific points about the group modality's advantages and disadvantages are worth making here. We have found in COS groups that the level of vicarious learning, normalizing parental struggles, and group support is quite profound. Our initial concerns that parents would act out toward each other in destructive ways has not been borne out by our experience. In fact, the focus on Being-With, empathy, creating a holding environment, and the therapist being the "hands" has proven to be effective in creating support. This support often continues after the group has ended as parents continue to stay involved with each other.

Working with triadic issues in group is, however, difficult. In the 20-week group format it is difficult to resolve problems in parents' relationship with their coparent. Even if the coparent is in the group, there is no time to work with interpersonal issues in depth and stay on schedule with video reviews. Structuring the group to accommodate video reviews restricts the amount of processing that can be done on emerging issues. You always have one eye on the process and one eye on the clock. Ongoing groups such as the ones we have done in the prison system, school settings, residential treatment, day treatment, and so on allow more time to process than the 20-week model.

Parents who act out in ways that are destructive to group cohesion are not good candidates. Conversely, parents whose discomfort with groups or social situations is strong enough to derail their work are not good candidates. Single parents or parents who are isolated from other parents can find groups especially helpful. We have found that working with groups of fathers provides support and encouragement from other men that many fathers lack. Other groups organized around shared situations, such as recovering parents, stepparents, foster parents, and so on, can offer a great deal of support.

In terms of group structure and facilitation, there is a therapeutic commitment for the groups to start and end on time so that parents can rely on the constancy of the experience, which helps create a secure base. This is a very difficult issue for therapists learning to do this work. Many therapists tend to work beyond the allotted time in an attempt to resolve the review more fully for the parent. This can lead to participants in the group feeling caught between staying to support the parent and their own schedule conflicts, often with regard to their children. It also creates uncertainty: once you open up emotionally, there is no clearly defined end.

What are the core sensitivity implications for each parent's experience of an ending time that depends on the intensity of their emotion? The separation-sensitive parent may prolong endings to be taken care of and avoid separation, the safety-sensitive parent is likely to feel trapped, and the esteem-sensitive parent may be dancing between potential shame and one-mindedness with the therapist and the group. Given all the possibilities, ending roughly on time in a nonrigid way is by far the safest and most solid way to build the therapeutic experience. If it appears to be an emergency, the therapist can invite the parent to talk one on one after the group is over.

CONCLUSION

Regardless of the treatment modality, the more that parents feel held by the therapist, the more support they will feel to choose courage over fear and give their child a new level of security. Ultimately this act changes not only their child's attachment with them, but also their own internal sense of security. They may still hear shark music, but the volume has been turned down. The fear that has limited their thoughts and actions becomes manageable, and they have greater confidence in themselves as individuals and as caregivers. Foreboding has been replaced with hope for a more secure future.

FORM 12.1.

Welcome to the Club

Being a parent may just be *the* most difficult job on the planet. Every day, parents—the world over—want the best for their children. And every day, parents—the world over—fail to meet some of the needs of their children. "Help me" moments go unseen. "Watch over me" moments get interrupted. "Comfort me" and "Organize my feelings" moments end up being pushed away or lost in the rush and stress of everyday life.

Welcome to the club.

Of course, it's hard to know that we make mistakes. The good news is that, as parents, we all have an inner wisdom that helps us work with these mistakes. No matter who we are, if we listen to ourselves there is always something inside us that asks us to keep trying. No matter what our history, if we pay attention, there is a place in our hearts that wants to meet the needs of our children.

All parents have wisdom.

The best news is that parenting can be *the* most wonderful job on the planet. And one of the most wonderful parts of being a parent is knowing that we can add to our wisdom. We can recognize our weaknesses, learn from our mistakes, and find new ways to meet the very real needs of our children.

All parents struggle.

Please know that mistakes in parenting are inevitable. Every parent in this room wishes this weren't so. Each parent in this room is trying very hard to make sure that the needs of her or his child are being met. That's why you have taken the time and energy to be here, week after week. After so much work, to realize that there are things that aren't going right for your child can be upsetting.

Our greatest hope lies in beginning to realize that our weaknesses as a parent tend to be in a particular area on the Circle of Security. Every parent on the planet has an overused side and an underused side on this *Circle*. That isn't the problem. The problem begins when we don't realize that we have a stronger side and a weaker side. The problem gets bigger when we try to overuse our stronger side to make up for underusing our weaker side. The problem continues, one generation after another, when we don't find a way to deal with what it is within us, and in our history, that keeps that side weak.

It's hard to give what we weren't given.

It's hard to give what we weren't given. For example, it gets hard to give as much comfort as our child requires when it wasn't much a part of our own childhood. There will be times when our child cues us, asking for tenderness, and we hurt a little. At those times we may pull back and self-protect without even knowing it. We may get busy or ask our child to focus on a toy—cuing her/him in a subtle way to not make a direct request for comfort—because every time our child asks for the gentle holding we went without, it reminds us of a lack we carry within us, and that causes pain. Understandably, then, we will find ways to avoid those moments. Little ways. Unfortunately, our child will begin to realize this and eventually try to help us out by asking for fewer and fewer of these moments.

Or, maybe our parents weren't so good at letting us go out and explore the world. They kept us close, often too close. Now, as parents ourselves, we tend to feel uneasy when our child steps further away from us into the Circle. We aren't sure, just like our parents weren't sure, that it really is a circle and that our child will soon come running back to our waiting arms.

Sensitive to pain.

But, if we can know that we are sensitive to pain on one side of the Circle we can begin to change our behavior. We can step back and watch ourselves ("There I go again."). We can watch ourselves, but not with judgment, and not with criticism. We can learn to stand back and observe our behavior with kindness. Really. We can honor how hard it is to give something to our child that we may have gone without when we were young. ("Of course this is difficult for me.")

And, we can know that while it is hard, it is not impossible. Our wisdom and our genuine desire to meet our child's needs, all the way around the Circle, make it possible for new doors to open. We can come to realize that while it is difficult, if we can just recognize and admit our discomfort for a while (sometimes 15–30 seconds of additional closeness—or distance—is all that our child wants), our child's need will be met. If we can provide that closeness or distance an extra five or six times a day, everyone—child and parent—will be happier and feel more secure.

It just may be that the best part of parenting is being with our child as those real needs are being met . . . all the way around the Circle.

Welcome to the club.

PART III

CASE EXAMPLES

13

Laura and Ashley

Laura is 27 years old and married to Tom, age 29. They have one child, Ashley, age 3. Laura works in the field of biotechnology. Laura initially sought help from our family practice, seeking "parenting tips" because, while she felt she was already an "excellent mother," she thought it would be valuable to meet with "someone who is an expert in parenting."

INTAKE

In her first interview Laura cited the numerous books she had read about parenting. Only later in the same interview did she mention that Ashley's preschool teacher thought Ashley needed help because she was hitting other children. Laura quickly described this as "the teacher's problem" because Laura was convinced that other children were actually hitting Ashley and that she was only fighting back in self-defense. When the therapist directly wondered about the possibility that Ashley might potentially have struggles of her own, Laura was quick to defend her daughter and imply that the problem was centered in the other children and the teacher.

In the same interview, Laura described her own childhood as difficult. Her father was an active alcoholic, and her mother made excuses for him when he was verbally abusive. She said her mother was very busy throughout Laura's years growing up and would occasionally blow up at her and slap her. She said she was committed to doing a much better job at parenting than either of her parents had done. Laura was clearly intelligent and

---

Part of this case example was introduced elsewhere in this book, starting with one segment of the Strange Situation depicted at the beginning of Chapter 1.

was noticeably proud of her current and past accomplishments in school. A touching moment occurred about 30 minutes into this interview when she was able to describe a teacher in the fourth grade who had taken a special interest in her and supported her belief that she could be a good student. Her appreciation of this teacher spoke to Laura's capacity for gratitude, warmth, and a willingness to experience the importance of another's support.

It was proposed that Laura join a 20-week COS group that was scheduled to begin in the community within the next several weeks. Wondering if she needed such an extensive program, Laura nonetheless accepted this invitation, guided by her somewhat hidden yet clearly strong motivation to find an answer to her daughter's aggression. Laura's husband was not able to attend the evening sessions because of a tight work schedule; however, Laura stated that he would be very supportive.

INTERACTIONAL ASSESSMENT: THE STRANGE SITUATION PROCEDURE

When Ashley was on the top half of the Circle exploring the toys provided, Laura would intervene by pressuring her to complete the task and saying "Come on, I know you can do better." For instance, when she used the stacking ring toy, Laura asked her to name the colors, get the order of the rings correct, and so forth. When Ashley lost interest in this toy and focused on another, Laura asked her to go back to the ring toy and complete the task so that the toy was left properly assembled. Whatever toy Ashley became interested in, Laura focused on instructing her to competently complete the task. Ashley had few opportunities to simply explore her environment and follow her own curiosity. There were several times when she was struggling with the puzzle but not asking for help, and Laura jumped into Ashley's play and gave instructions. At one point she quizzed her 3-year-old with the question "Where's the chartreuse one?"

Laura's behavior appeared to indicate she believed acting like a teacher with Ashley was the best way to help in her development. From the perspective of the COS approach, there isn't a problem when parents teach a child and offer help in making sense of a particular task. Rather, it's that problems arise when the parent has a pattern of pressuring the child to achieve for *the sake of the parent*. A child who learns to focus primarily on the parent's needs is seen to be on the path to compliance rather than healthy autonomy, a less secure experience of both self and other.

In this case Laura constantly interfered with her child's natural curiosity and interest in exploring. Within the context of attachment research secure parents are able to scaffold their child's exploration (see Box 3.5, page 54).

When the stranger came into the room, Ashley quickly looked to her mother for reassurance. As her mother turned away from her and started talking with the stranger, Ashley grew quiet for a few moments and then appeared to put a forced smile on her face and attempted to reengage her mom with a toy her mother had given her. From a COS perspective, when Ashley was anxious and on the bottom of the Circle and needing comfort, she recognized her mother's miscue of turning away and responded in kind, miscuing her mother by acting like all she needed was support for exploration. Throughout the initial 6 minutes of the SSP, Laura and Ashley maintained a kind of tag-team performance with encouragement to perform from Laura and a willingness to comply by appearing bright and competent from Ashley.

During the first separation Laura got down on the floor, touched Ashley to get her attention, and told her she was going to go and that Ashley should stay and play with the toys. Ashley did not protest when Laura left the room and stayed focused on playing with the toys. Ashley interacted with the stranger about the toys and appeared not to be affected by her mother's absence. In the second separation Laura did much the same as in the first, and when she told Ashley she was leaving, the little girl immediately asked for help with a toy. It is of note that Ashley miscued her mother and chose to ask her mother for teaching as a way to keep her in the room to manage her discomfort with the separation. This is a strategy that had a high likelihood of success given her mother's interest in teaching. Laura told Ashley that she would help her when she got back, but that for now she should stay and play and Mom would be right back. She left, and a few moments later Ashley tried to leave the room, and the stranger had to go to the door and reassure her that her mother would be right back. When the stranger said, "Your mommy will be back in a minute," Ashley replied, "I want to go too." The second separation showed that Ashley was upset, and her attachment behavioral system had been activated. After the stranger intervened and then left, she called out for her mother, but seeing that Mom wasn't going to return immediately, she began to sing softly to herself and went back to playing, albeit with a solemn face. Interestingly, she chose to play with the exact toy her mother had previously offered her, staying with it the entire time her mother was gone.

In the first reunion Ashley gave Laura a toy, and within seconds Laura was teaching Ashley how to use the toy. The two engaged in using the medical kit, and after about 30 seconds Laura tried to get Ashley to explore other toys. Each time Ashley came in to play with Laura during this first reunion she directed Ashley out to play with another toy. From Ashley's perspective, each time she tried to come in to her mom on the bottom of the Circle she was sent out. The behavior of pushing a child out when her attachment is activated is an example of rejecting of attachment behavior and pressuring to be on the top of the Circle. The second reunion was similar to the first. Laura spent most of the time miscuing Ashley by keeping her on the top of the Circle and pressuring her to learn how to complete the puzzles that were in the toy box. Ashley continued to miscue by acting as if all she needed was support for exploration, as if her distress over being left alone had never arisen.

Some of the most tender moments happened during the reading, in which they sat side by side on the couch and talked about the book. After the reading Laura had no trouble taking charge and getting Ashley to clean up the toys.

At the end of the SSP it was clear that Ashley was not able to come to Laura when distressed, get her emotional cup filled, and then return to exploration on her own. Instead when she was distressed and on the bottom of the Circle she miscued and acted as if all she needed was help in exploration, and Mom reinforced this with an almost constant pressure to be on the top of the Circle and excel. Laura had no trouble taking charge, and so the key struggle was the bottom of the Circle.

Ashley's attachment strategy was scored insecure avoidant.

THE PARENT PERCEPTION ASSESSMENT: THE CIRCLE OF SECURITY INTERVIEW

In the COSI, conducted immediately after the Strange Situation assessment, Laura conveyed that she did not see Ashley as needing comfort at any time during the SSP. Even when seeing Ashley's distress from behind the one-way mirror, including attempts to join her mother upon separation, Laura described her behavior this way: "The time she was with that lady it didn't bother her at all. Sure, she didn't want to be with that lady, but as long as she gets to be the center of attention not much else bothers her. The second time I left I think she just wanted to do what her mom was doing, so she tried to be good and keep herself occupied." When asked directly whether Ashley needed comfort, she stated, "No." When she was asked what it was like to return to the room, Laura said, "I was proud of her for being good and not trying to get into mischief when she thought nobody was looking." As for Ashley, she said, "I am sure [the reunion] was a relief, but she's never been the type of kid that goes, 'Oh, good, you're home now.' She is more like 'OK, you're here; that's cool.'"

When asked what was it like for her to watch Ashley from behind the one-way glass, she said, "She behaved the way I thought she would. She's kinda bossy and likes to make deals with people, you know, a sort of 'You're going to do this before I do that' kind of thing." What stood out was how all Laura could see was her daughter's need for "attention" and how proud Laura was that Ashley could play by herself or with the stranger. For Laura not to recognize Ashley's distress, even when it had led her to try so hard to get out of the room, implied that Laura needed to defensively exclude seeing Ashley's distress. This is what Dan Siegel describes as being "mind-blind" and what we see as an inability to recognize needs on the Circle.

Laura's mind-blindness to her daughter's need for comfort seemed understandable as we began to make sense of her own background. When Laura was asked who was responsible for raising her, she answered "me." She reported that her father was usually home but often either yelling at her or passed out after another bout of drinking through the day. She described her relationship with her father as verbally abusive. She also recalled many times when he chided her for getting upset. "He'd always call me a baby if I cried. I learned real fast not to ever go there." Her primary source of comfort was a choice to go to her room alone, read a book, and get away from all the screaming and upset that defined her family.

Laura described a particular memory from when she was 12 years old. Laura's 8-year-old brother struggled with a learning disability that significantly impacted his capacity to read. When he was in the third and fourth grade, the teachers asked Laura's parents to do reading exercises with him to help him keep up with his class. The parents didn't follow through, and Laura remembers secretly doing those exercises with her brother. She didn't let her parents know she was doing this out of fear that she would be punished. She stated that both her parents were very quick to anger and if she didn't do things their way they "berated you for hours and then found ways to bring it up again sarcastically, out of the blue, when it had nothing to do with what was going on right then. I felt totally trapped there and would brood about my little brother ending up feeling the same way."

When Laura was asked if there was anything she had learned from her parents that she would like to pass on to Ashley, she said, "No, I do everything I can to do the exact opposite" and "I hope no one could even tell I was raised by them."

Before Laura became pregnant, she and her husband had been in a band, and every time the band practiced they drank all night. When they learned they were going to become parents, they decided to change their lives and immediately stopped using alcohol, quit the band, and changed their lives completely. "I wonder where we'd be today if we hadn't had Ashley," Laura speculated.

Laura is like many of the parents who participate in Circle of Security. She had a noticeably insecure relationship with her parents. She did not want to re-create the frightening atmosphere or pass along memories of the negative events she had grown up with. In fact Laura wanted to do the opposite of how her parents had treated her in her parenting of Ashley. This desire to offer protection from previous difficulty is a common theme with almost all parents who have painful histories. Sadly, knowing what not to do does not offer a sufficient roadmap for what to do. It is a lot like trying to find your way from Kansas City to San Francisco with the only information available being "Never go east." Laura consistently read parenting books, watched DVDs on how to raise children, and came to the conclusion that focusing her energy on Ashley's cognitive and behavioral skills was the key to success. "She's a smart kid, just like I was. But nobody helped me. You'd better believe she's not going to feel that way about me when she grows up."

Because the COSI revealed that Laura viewed herself as never having had a safe haven as a child, it is not surprising that she would not be able to see her own daughter's need for comfort and safety. To see Ashley's need for comfort and respond to it would, of course, evoke procedural memories, long hidden from conscious awareness, about what she had missed as a child. Ashley's needs on the bottom of the Circle would activate Laura's shark music, and so not seeing that need effectively protected Laura from distressing feelings and memories. What she could see was what she felt had made the important difference while she was growing up: focus on exploration and competence. This skill set was how Laura had learned to protect herself from danger and all the feelings associated with the loss of a deeply needed safe and soothing relationship. In this light, it makes sense that Laura thought teaching Ashley to explore was actually soothing. As is almost always the case, parents offer their children the very best they know how to offer, given the limited lens they were offered to make sense of offering care.

The COSI is used not only to understand parents' representations of their child and of their self regarding the needs on the Circle but also to learn about the parents' core sensitivities. The following are some of Laura's answers that helped identify her core sensitivity.

When asked what gave her the most pain in her relationship with Ashley, Laura mentioned that school was stressful for her as a parent. "They just don't recognize how incredibly smart she is." When asked what gave her the most joy, Laura stated, "When I see her do something well that I taught her." When asked if she would like to change one aspect of their relationship, she answered, "I would like to be all knowing. I would know exactly what to say when she's being stubborn. Sometimes I have to figure out what's the right thing. There's always like a magic key if I say it just the right way." After a pause of a few seconds she added, "Usually I know what to do."

The theme that emerged was that Laura often interpreted interaction through the lens of performance and perfection. Laura had learned to manage the pain of her empty and abusive childhood by performing well and then experiencing her success through acknowledgment by others as her primary source of comfort. It is important for all of us to feel good about our successes. However, Laura had learned to skew this process to the point that success at tasks was now her central ingredient for maintaining a sense of stability in her emotional life. Her momentary good feelings about success (whether her own or Ashley's), coupled with the way that success required intense focus, allowed Laura to blunt and keep outside of awareness a far more fundamental experience of feeling profoundly unimportant and ultimately alone. Were it not for the encouragement of adults other than her parents, especially her fourth-grade teacher, Laura might have had nothing positive to reach for as a way to stay away from her emotional pain.

Laura's core sensitivity was identified as esteem sensitivity.

A common theme within esteem sensitivity is the perceived stability that results when those close to us are thought to be "one-minded." In addition, an experience of being "perfectly understood" by an idealized other who can make perfect sense of things offers protective assurance of not having to reexperience the painful dysregulation associated with the past.

For Laura, the experience of closeness had a lot to do with those near her "being on the same page." It therefore made sense that Laura treasured moments with Ashley when she mirrored her experience in such a way that Laura felt like "that little girl really gets me." When Laura talked about what gave her the most joy in her relationship with Ashley, she emphasized that "when she does things that I do that are good, especially something that I taught her. . . . She knows me better than anybody else and gets the little nuances of my personality." Laura went on to emphasize how special it was to her that Ashley got her jokes like no one else could and then concluded, "We are always on the same wavelength." During the interview Laura would light up emotionally whenever she talked about how Ashley's experience was exactly like her own. When she perceived that Ashley was not on the same page with her, Laura would describe her daughter with more negative attributions: "She wants to be the center of everyone's world and have everything go her way." But, for the most part, Laura painted an idealized picture of a special and talented child who was almost always perfectly attuned and fully synchronized with her mother.

Given Laura's painful background and her esteem sensitivity, this mother showed a noticeable capacity to reflect on her experience. In addition, she offered a somewhat surprising willingness to be vulnerable while not idealizing a painful past. Even though she did use defensive devaluing of others when she was upset (the teacher), overall Laura communicated a desire to learn and the capacity to tolerate (for her child's sake) moments of openness to her pain. One of the most inspiring aspects of this work is seeing how children can call forth a hidden potential from their parents to respond in ways that are incompatible with long-established defensive patterns.

In terms of making sense of the differential diagnosis, Laura seemed to be too self-sufficient and dismissing of attachment to fit within the theme of separation sensitivity. Her primary defensive motivation was focused on perfection (in herself and in her child) and maintaining a "one-minded" experience of being continually "in sync" with Ashley. These themes are quite the opposite of an individual considered to be safety sensitive. Those who fit the safety-sensitive category are not concerned with specialness, are less focused on perfection (although they may be focused on *precision,* which is oriented toward ensuring a predictable, safe world), and are likely to run in the opposite direction from anything that appears to be one-minded. Laura's focus on perfect behavior, perfect understanding, specialness through performance, and sameness were all themes considered to be consistent with esteem sensitivity. In addition, while using devaluation as a way to manage her vulnerability, Laura showed a genuine strength in her capacity to admit imperfection and pain in relation to her childhood experience. When she did report vulnerable feelings about herself regarding Ashley, they were often in the category of feeling bad for not being a more perfect parent. When asked what she wanted to change about her relationship with Ashley, she stated she would like to always know just the right thing to do. Finding her way to perfection seemed to be the best possible exit from her shark music.

THE LINCHPIN

Laura provided basic hands on the Circle and organized Ashley's experience without being frightened or frightening. She did not show the disorganized caregiving behaviors associated with "mean, weak, or gone" (COS interactional assessment, Chapter 7). In addition, when Ashley was on the bottom of the Circle she did not display the kinds of controlling behaviors associated with a disorganized attachment. Laura provided her daughter with enough structure to be appropriately in charge. During the reunions she organized the process, as opposed to her child taking care of and organizing her. Even though the two of them were limited on the bottom of the Circle, the process was coherent and predictable, and Ashley had a clearly avoidant defensive strategy that worked well enough that they could focus on exploration and remain stable. For these reasons, the linchpin was to help Laura focus on the miscues the two of them shared on the bottom of the Circle. Ashley's need for comfort, during both the separation and the reunion, appeared to be central. It was believed that if Laura could offer herself as a safe haven when Ashley was upset, Ashley would have the chance to be far more secure in her relationship with her mother. A secondary goal was set focusing on offering Laura a chance to reevaluate how much time she spent pressuring her daughter to achieve. These two goals overlapped because Laura not only used pressuring to achieve when Ashley was on the top of the Circle but also used pressuring to achieve when she was on the bottom of the Circle, a miscue on the part of Laura unconsciously intended to protect herself from a lifetime of shark music.

Once the linchpin was selected, the Strange Situation was reviewed carefully in search of moments of underutilized capacity. For Laura an underutilized strength would be any moment when she was emotionally available or welcoming Ashley to come to her and any moments when she was simply enjoying Ashley and was not pressuring her to be more competent. Imagine what a mistake it would be to emphasize Laura's strength in trying to get her child to learn more. Without assessment and a clear treatment plan, a "strength-based" approach might offer encouragement and positive feedback for Laura's teaching and Ashley's precocious intelligence and capacity beyond her years and would, of course, only reinforce the problem they already have.

As described in Chapter 12, the Strange Situation video clips chosen for the Phase One video review provide the foundation for treatment and focus primarily on underutilized strengths, with one clip chosen to expose the parent to limited vulnerability by having her watch a modest struggle that foreshadows processing the linchpin issue in the next review. How the parent responds to watching and reflecting on the initial clip offers valuable information on the parent's reflective and relationship capacity for processing the linchpin issue, which will make her much more vulnerable.

PHASE ONE VIDEO REVIEW

Laura's first video review started with clips that emphasized shared enjoyment and delight. Emphasis was placed on how important shared delight is for a child to feel deeply valued. The second separation was used to emphasize that when Laura started to leave she must have sensed some need for reassurance on Ashley's part because she got down on the floor to Ashley's level, made eye contact, and touched her. Placing emphasis on this moment of offering some comfort rather than on its limited nature, the therapist used this as an opportunity to honor this mother's genuine intention and potential capacity to meet her child's need on the bottom of the Circle.

At the moment in the separation when Ashley increased her protest as her mother was walking out the door, Laura shifted gears and tried to get her daughter refocused on the top half of the Circle by drawing her attention to several toys. Distracting children when they are upset is a common and often useful strategy. But when children seem to need more than that, parents of secure children will often cease attempting to distract and focus on the child's emotional experience, offering a moment of Being-With before returning to encouraging exploration as they proceed to leave the room. Aside from the brief moments of gently touching Ashley or saying she would be right back, Laura focused primarily on distraction via exploration. Laura's engaging and then offering distraction demonstrated that she knew Ashley needed some form of reassurance upon the separation. As

Laura watched the video she stated she could see Ashley did not want her to go and that she needed some help organizing her feelings. She smiled, realizing that she had offered a moment of concern, which softened her next realization that she had quickly focused on distraction. Laura was almost amazed to see the way her daughter had cued her to stay and play with her in an attempt to keep her mother in the room. "I hadn't seen that. I hadn't noticed that. I was so focused on leaving." This was an excellent indicator of Laura's capacity to manage vulnerable information, much of which implied that she had been less than perfect in that moment. Rather than quickly denying the importance of what she had just seen, Laura was able to see Ashley's distress and need for comfort. She was also able to utilize the group and the therapist as a safe enough resource to hold her emerging vulnerability.

The next phase of the review focused on Ashley needing her mother, especially when her mother was absent during separations. At first, Ashley tried to leave the room, and when she could not go she managed her feelings by playing with a toy her mother had offered her (a common theme that we have come to call "Mommy dust"). She then began singing to herself. As is true for all parents involved with the Circle video reviews, what was new for Laura was slowing the relationship down, looking at it from enough distance, all within the now familiar vocabulary and roadmap associated with the Circle. Laura was seeing her daughter as having a real need for comfort on the bottom of the Circle shared by all children and finding ways to self-soothe while alone. Implied in this growing awareness, especially when shared by parents in a group setting, is an honoring of each specific need on the Circle as appropriate. This recognition and shared acceptance often undoes the negative programming that has resulted from a lifetime of having that particular need framed in a negative light in one's family of origin.

Laura was gaining a very new lens through which to see Ashley's experience and began to see that her distraction in the direction of "play" was not addressing Ashley's needs on the bottom of the Circle. As is always the case, the contextualizing protocol of teaching parents how to make sense of a child's need upon the parent's leaving during the SSP helps each parent make new sense of old behavior. Letting parents learn that "all children feel distress upon separation" normalizes the child's need, offers a way for the built-in empathy in the parent to come forth, and provides a simple vocabulary to make sense of what is happening and not yet happening. With the two words "cue" and "miscue" a parent can now watch her behavior and the behaviors of the child and have a series of "aha" moments, minimizing the need to defend. This work is based on the assumption that a parent's hardwiring to experience empathy is stronger than the need to defend against mistakes in parenting. Through the years we have, fortunately, seen this to be the case most of the time.

For Laura, what was most prominent in the Phase One video review was that her daughter was, in fact, distressed and in need of comfort and organizing her feelings on the bottom of the Circle. The question on the table was how Laura would help her daughter negotiate these needs upon her return from this separation. The part of the first review that made Laura most vulnerable—and in many ways was most valuable—was showing Laura the first reunion. What became immediately apparent is that Ashley did not show her mother the distress she had demonstrated when she was alone. During the first 30 seconds of the reunion she miscued her mother by initially turning sideways and keeping her back to her mother as she entered the room. She then engaged her mother by walking toward her with a doctor's kit and at one point getting close enough to look in her ear. Unable to notice her needs at the time of the original SSP, Laura went along with Ashley's miscues of turning away and appearing as if all she wanted to do was play. At this point Laura was shown only the first part of the reunion, emphasizing Ashley valuing and seeking her out. The second part of the reunion in which Laura miscued Ashley by repeatedly sending her out was the linchpin for the Phase Two video review.

The Phase One video review had thus delivered the essential building blocks of the intervention: Laura was able to realize that Ashley didn't want her mother to go, that she was upset and needed her mother when she was gone, and that Ashley did not directly show her distress and need for comfort upon her mother's return but engaged her mom through the use of toys.

Clinically, the therapist had to work within this mother's struggle with being esteem sensitive. It was important to keep in mind that she would be susceptible to feeling criticized and experiencing herself as a failure if she viewed clips that suggested she might be making significant mistakes as a parent. Hence "struggles with some success" were highlighted rather than sheer struggles. The therapist said, for example, "You must in some way have sensed Ashley was on the bottom of the Circle, because otherwise you would not feel the need to offer her reassurance by touching her as you left." It is important for all interventions to honor a parent's needs for safety and recognize how any exploration of limitations in the all-important area of parenting creates a profound vulnerability in every caregiver.

This particular review ended on a positive note, showing the two of them enjoying reading and laughing together. When Laura was asked at the end of the session what the process had been like for her, she stated that Ashley was "cute" and she liked seeing all the details that she would normally not see. Immediately after this, she acknowledged that there were things she hadn't seen. She then said, "I like trying to read everything she is doing. I think I am pretty good at this." When she was vulnerable and admitted that she hadn't seen everything, she immediately had to balance the scales by protectively emphasizing how capable she was as a parent. This process of hair-trigger "damage control" is most commonly seen within those who are esteem sensitive. Not doing something perfectly, or even "good enough," immediately feels like failure. A central therapeutic goal when working with a parent who may be esteem sensitive is to help that person tolerate modest and growing experiences of being vulnerable. As these are regulated together within the therapeutic context, a person can begin to learn something about herself without being flooded with shame and falling into a negative experience of the self as a failure. Little, if anything, can be learned from the perspective "I am perfect," and little, if anything, can be learned from the opposite perspective of "I am a complete failure." Sadly, the more esteem sensitive someone is, the more these are the only two perspectives available. Laura was giving indications of having the capacity to focus on herself and manage some vulnerability, a good sign for her potential to learn and more fully utilize the COS intervention.

PHASE TWO VIDEO REVIEW

The task at hand in Laura's second video review was the process of facing her shark music and recognizing the specifics of how she had been teaching Ashley to be avoidant. Helping Laura see precisely how she pressured her daughter to stay away from her need for comfort and rely solely on exploration as a way to manage distress was the linchpin theme. To prepare her to engage in this linchpin issue, several vignettes were selected that were used in the Phase One video review that reminded her of how much her child needed her for comfort and how valuable she was to her daughter. When she watched Ashley alone in the Strange Situation as she was trying to leave the room, Laura stated, "Originally I just thought all she needed was something to do." It was important news for Laura that what Ashley really needed was her. She was reminded of Ashley's strategy of miscuing her when she was on the bottom of the Circle by acting like she needed support for exploration.

The therapist emphasized how many things Laura did well with her and then told her that Ashley's being on the bottom of the Circle and needing comfort seemed to be an area in which Laura had a blind spot. The therapist stated, "In the moments when she needs you on the bottom of the Circle, the two of you have gotten into this groove that you both shift into exploration."

The linchpin clip was the second half of reunion one, in which Ashley kept trying to seek contact with her and Laura kept turning her out to go explore. Laura's Phase Two video review was during week 12, and by this point in the program her ability to observe and analyze interaction had increased significantly. Laura knew the COS vocabulary, she knew the Circle roadmap, and she had come to trust her therapist and the other group members to a significant degree. As she watched the clip, her face became more and more somber and pained. When the clip was over, she was overwhelmed with negative feelings about herself and started to cry, stating that "I wasted all that time pushing her away when all she wanted to do was cuddle with me." After a long pause in which she withdrew into herself, looked down, and tried to control her tears, she said, "I thought that I always wanted to play with her, to be with her. I didn't think that I ever told her no when she needed to do stuff with me, when she needed something. I thought of myself as a mom who would stop whatever I was doing. And I thought I always did that. I thought I was really good at that, and I always yell at my husband for not doing that. I guess I don't do it either. It shows how many times she stood there and said, 'I want to play with you' and I didn't listen to her."

Upon seeing herself struggle, she went from being an all-good (perfect) mother to being one who was all bad (failure)—a core struggle with esteem sensitivity, as mentioned earlier. The therapist chose a path of Being-With in the moments that followed. At first he simply sat there in the group as Laura began to express her pain. He allowed her the opportunity and the time to feel it rather than leaping in to reassure her or divert her attention. He waited until it was obvious that she was going to protectively refocus her pain in the direction of how bad a mother she was. He then focused on trying to help Laura remember and know all the good she did for her daughter while openly acknowledging that mistakes were in fact a part of what was going on: "As we say in these groups every week, welcome to the club. You, like everyone, have some shark music. I think your shark music happens right here, precisely at the moment when you see Ashley needs comfort because she's starting to feel upset, and so to manage all this you encourage her to explore. I also think that you have every right to have this shark music, because I'm quite sure that no one ever offered you comfort when you felt upset and alone." Laura acknowledged this and slowly backed away from the intensity of the shame she had just been experiencing. She also looked around the room that included parents sitting silently, almost reverently, some with tears in their eyes.

The goal of this work is not to take away a parent's pain but to help her experience her pain within a safe and caring relationship. This helps increase the possibility of being able to be in pain without self-attack. In Laura's case, when she is attacking herself, she is actually experiencing a lesser pain, one that is difficult to be sure, but one that defends her against the deeper pain of being alone without any support on the bottom of the Circle. It is this underlying pain that drives her behavior of avoidance and her dismissing of the need for comfort and the regulation of sadness and fear and anger—in herself and in her daughter. Self-attack is a procedural memory, one Laura remembered seeing in her father and one she developed to motivate herself to do better while growing up in a family that offered little or no support.

"Laura," the therapist said, "I've got some good news and I've got some bad news. The bad news is that your shark music was learned early and you have begun teaching it to your daughter. The good news is that it's not too late. In fact it's still early in Ashley's life to learn something you didn't have a chance to learn until now. And I've got some very good news. If you look at this video, you'll see that Ashley is remarkably persistent in seeking you out. I've been at this for a long time, and when I see that I see a child with some expectation that you'll respond—a child who hasn't in any way given up hope that you'll get it." The therapist further emphasized, "Sometimes you respond to her and sometimes you don't. If you simply didn't respond to her, she would've given up long ago on trying so hard. You don't keep knocking at the door that is never answered. I think your comfort zone is encouraging exploration and now you see that what she wants is not a toy—that what she really wants is you."

Esteem-sensitive parents often think the value they have with their child lies in the things that they do. It is news for them to see that their children value them simply for who they are. When asked what it was like to talk about this, Laura stated, "Awful. I mean it's good because I want to do those things for her, but I always felt that I did do those things for her.

I stayed home with my daughter for the first 2 years of her life, and all I did was do what I thought she needed. I became a different person, a better person. Instead of drinking all night with the band, I just stayed home and read and learned about being a good mother. I read everything I could find online and bought tons of books and magazines. I did everything that seemed like the right thing to do. I bought all the right toys. I did all the right things. All Ashley wanted was to sit on my lap, and I pushed her away. All I've ever tried to do is stuff that she needed, and I wasn't even looking at what she really wanted."

The therapist responds by reemphasizing that "sometimes you do this and sometimes you don't, and now you know this is your cutting edge. Even though this is very painful to watch, knowing this will help you figure out how to make a choice about responding to her need for comfort. What comes across is how much you want to do this—you really want to do this. You changed your life, and you have done a tremendous amount for her, and this is looking at one piece of it, and it's your growing edge and it's something you never got. As I said a few minutes ago, you didn't get this. When you needed comfort, there was no one there." Laura looked relieved and said, "I know." It's important to note here that the terms "cutting edge" and "growing edge" were deliberate choices on the part of the therapist as a way to appeal to Laura's esteem-sensitive perspective. These words imply growth and learning and therefore may have made her more receptive to the message.

The ending clip was a segment of the reading episode, which was highly interactive and not focused on just completing the task. The emphasis on this last clip is about the dyad's ability to connect and Laura being available to Ashley during this activity. She was not able to enjoy this clip the way she enjoyed seeing their reading in the Phase One video review because she was under the sway of feeling like she may have failed. Her success with the reading seemed too small to her to make up for the much larger "mistake" of pushing Ashley away. She stated, "Of course I can do reading." The session ended on a reasonably acceptable note, and it was clear that Laura left the session struggling to maintain any positive sense of herself in the face of acknowledging her shark music and her core struggle.

PHASE THREE VIDEO REVIEW

A few weeks after the Phase Two video review, Laura and Ashley participated in making a new video of their interaction. The filming started with the two of them blowing bubbles together, followed by a modified Strange Situation (no stranger), one separation/reunion, book reading, and cleanup. The purpose of the filming is to give parents a chance to use their new knowledge so that the therapist and the group can celebrate each parent's success and continue to acknowledge struggles in the final video review.

Laura and Ashley had fun with the bubbles, and Laura delighted in her with little of the prior pressure to achieve. During the separation Ashley was clearly distressed. In the reunion Ashley behaved similarly to her behavior in the first video, miscuing her need for comfort by acting like what she needed was support for exploration. The big difference was that Laura knew that her daughter was on the bottom half of the Circle and in need of comfort. This can be an awkward process for parents. Now they want to comfort their children, but the children are still operating out of a well-established pattern of miscuing. Parents can't force the child to seek comfort but must look for opportunities to respond and communicate that they are available. Sometimes parents will try to hold their child and the child will remain within his defensive pattern and try to get away. When this happens, the parent can feel rejected and discouraged. During the reunion Laura immediately went to Ashley and gave her a kiss on the cheek, and Ashley pulled her head away. Laura then sat on the floor facing Ashley and responded to her interest in the toys. As Laura played with a pretend camera, Ashley asked her for the camera so that she could take a picture. As Laura gave her the camera, Ashley slipped and knocked her knee against the toy box. Laura used this as an opportunity to kiss her "owie." Ashley allowed the kiss but seemed somewhat reserved. Laura then invited her into her lap, and she willingly accepted for the purpose of the pretend photo shoot together. Ashley soon wanted to go out and get other toys. At first the initiative to connect came from Mom. After Laura stopped trying, Ashley's initiative to seek Mom started and Ashley came to her to "play" with the doctor's kit. This is of course reminiscent of the first filming, but this time Laura remained responsive and not pressuring to achieve and the process appeared enjoyable for both of them. With the doctor's kit Ashley was able to touch her mom and be close to her.

At the beginning of this last video review, Laura joked with the group about how she had "sobbed" the whole time during her last video review. "I was mean when she wanted me, and I was horrible." The group tried to reassure her, while the therapist simply reminded her that all parents struggle and that he was grateful that she had been willing to be so vulnerable and see that struggles happen in her relationship with Ashley. "Once we know our shark music, so much can happen that couldn't happen before. But then, I'm getting ahead of myself. I think you'll see exactly what I'm talking about in a few minutes." And then the video review began.

The first clip was the two of them playing with the bubbles, and Laura saw the delight. She showed how vulnerable she felt by saying that if she was not able to see the "delight in me" moment she would have to take the whole course all over again. She indicated she was waiting to see a clip that made her feel bad like last time.

Much of the session was about helping her see herself in a positive light even if she was not a perfect parent. After seeing the reunion she could see Ashley needed comfort and was miscuing with exploration. Laura was very relieved to see that she did not push Ashley away when she came to her, and she was able to relax knowing that she would not have to see herself pushing her daughter away again. At the end she said this review was much better than last time.

During the last group session Laura was asked, "What was the most rewarding and most difficult part in participating in the group?" Laura thought the most rewarding was knowing how much Ashley needed her even if she acted so independent. The most difficult was seeing herself push Ashley away during times when it was now obvious that she was needed.

In the postintervention Strange Situation
Ashley was scored secure.

During the play episode and in all episodes Laura did not pressure Ashley to do more or better. Laura did offer a few moments of teaching at Ashley's request for help. On reunions Ashley would move a little closer, but Laura struggled with being patient while waiting for her to come in and so would come to her with a kiss or a hug that was a little too fast for Ashley. Ashley seemed to be in the midst of slowly changing from avoidance to the utilization of her mother as a safe haven. When Laura moved in too quickly, Ashley miscued her mom by pointing out a toy and moving away to explore. Laura was trying to do the right thing, and when Ashley did not reciprocate Laura would wait and make room for Ashley to come in. This was a difficult transition period in which Laura knew how it "should" work and yet had to be attuned enough to move at Ashley's pace. Overall Ashley was able to use her mother as a safe haven when she was upset and as a secure base to explore and thus was scored secure. Laura showed far more pleasure in her interaction with her and followed her interests with very little pressure to achieve.

POSTINTERVENTION CIRCLE OF SECURITY INTERVIEW

In the postintervention COSI Laura stated that when she watched her from behind one-way glass she could see that what Ashley needed was for Laura to be with her. She could see Ashley's distress and her need for her mom. When asked if she thought Ashley needed comfort, she said, "Yes, but only because I've taken the class. Now I'm better able to read her cues. Before I just thought she wanted to play, and now I know she just wanted me to be with her and kind of organize her feelings and be down there with her. Before, I would've just thought she didn't have a problem with me being gone."

When asked, "How do you think participating in the Circle of Security project has had an impact on you and your child in either a positive or a negative way?" Laura stated, "I think it's mostly been positive, and it's helped me read some of her miscues, and she miscues a lot. It also has helped me understand some things about why I act the way I do sometimes. It was really hard for me. I'm very critical of myself, and when I saw things on the videos that weren't positive I got critical. I still am beating myself up about it. I still have a really hard time dealing with those things. . . . It was really hard for me. But, overall, it was a very positive experience."

14

Ana and Sam

Ana is a single mother who works long hours at a minimum-wage job. Her 3-year-old son, Sam, was diagnosed with cerebral palsy and had significant problems with gross and fine motor skills as well as speech. Sam could crawl but not walk without assistance and had very limited verbal skills. Ana joined the COS program out of interest in learning more about parenting.

INTAKE

During the initial interview Ana stated that Sam participated in weekly physical therapy and speech therapy. He also attended Head Start daily. Sam was born premature and was in the neonatal intensive care unit for 2 months after his birth. During the first year of life he had several surgeries that required long stays in the hospital. Ana reported that for a long time she was uncertain whether Sam would live or die.

Sam's physical and emotional needs are very demanding for Ana. She is very dedicated and determined to take care of Sam's medical needs and manages to get him to every scheduled appointment, multiple times a week, with little complaint.

INTERACTIONAL ASSESSMENT: THE STRANGE SITUATION PROCEDURE

Ana entered the room first, and right behind her Sam crawled into the room and moved rapidly to the box of toys in the center of the floor. Ana placed her purse and Sam's jacket on the couch and sat in an adjacent chair. Sam made a beeline to the jacket and took it off the couch. Ana asked in a somewhat flat tone if he wanted to have the jacket with him. Sam said yes, looking at his mother, and Ana briefly looked away and said, "OK." As soon as Ana looked back toward Sam, he quickly looked away. Nothing to conclude this early into the assessment, but initially we could say this might be a way in which the two avoided making eye contact.

Sam went back to the toys without his jacket. As Sam explored, Ana seemed attentive, but she maintained a flat affect with minimal responsiveness whenever he gestured in her direction. She appeared to be studying her child from a somewhat detached place, almost as if she were looking at him from behind the one-way mirror. When Sam finished taking all the rings off the stacking toy, Ana asked him with a slight edge to her voice, "Now what are you going to do? Do you think you can put them back on?" As Sam did so, Ana counted the rings. When Sam finished, she moved to him, clapped his hands, and said, "Yeah," and for the first time since entering the room she smiled briefly, clapping her hands with his. Their shared focus on his play continued throughout the first episode and ended with Sam picking up a play stethoscope from a doctor kit and initiating physical contact with his mother for the first time. As he placed the stethoscope on her heart, Sam and Ana had their first warm exchange, laughing and sharing a delighted gaze. Only 3 minutes into the assessment, there appeared to be a combination of strengths and struggles in this dyad: Ana's comfort zone regarding emotional availability appeared limited, while Sam was clearly tentative about physically approaching his mother. At the same time, they clearly were capable of shared affection.

When it came time for Ana to leave, Sam appeared to accept the separation with no protest and continued to explore, almost as if his mother hadn't left the room. He briefly interacted with the stranger about the toy he was playing with and showed no visible signs of emotional distress. Given the number of times per week that Sam was in the care of professionals who were helping him, he was likely to be acclimated to being left with alternative caregivers.

During the reunion Ana greeted Sam, saying "Hi," and offered him a smile. He quickly responded with an enthusiastic smile and said "Hi" in return. When Ana asked if he had had fun during her absence, Sam didn't answer but quickly turned his back to her and focused on a toy box. Ana appeared to be unhappy as he turned away. Sam then placed a baby doll under a larger toy. Ana asked him what he had done to the baby. As they talked about the doll, Sam suddenly changed the subject and pointed to an "owie" on his own leg. Ana moved closer to look, while Sam picked at it. Ana chided him by saying "Leave it alone" with modest irritation in her voice. Sam looked at Ana and continued to hold his leg. Ana then bent toward Sam and kissed his "owie," asking if it was better now. Sam immediately started to pick at it again. Ana said, "I think you should leave it alone," but Sam continued to pick. Ana blurted, "Stop" and abruptly pulled his arm away so he couldn't continue to pick at his leg. Sam looked at his mom and once again began to pick at his sore. Again Ana said, "Stop it," pulling his hand away from his leg, and Sam looked directly at her and said, "No." Ana smiled at him, Sam folded his arms, and then Ana imitated him and playfully folded her arms. Sam grunted a "No," and Ana grunted a "No." Ana asked if Sam was mad, and Sam said "No" and then picked at his sore again. Once again Ana said, "Stop it," while Sam indicated he was not going to stop by picking at the sore again. Ana then reached playfully toward his stomach and tickled him while simultaneously diverting him to another toy.

The reunion started with a quick greeting, without any comfort seeking on the part of Sam, who quickly turned his back on his mother and focused on exploration. Then their interaction slowly escalated into a struggle in which Sam became more and more oppositional and Ana seemed to both dislike and welcome it, ending with a kind of bantering game in which they imitated each other saying "No" and then found a way to get out of the escalation by moving on to another focus.

The second separation was much like the first, with Sam accepting the separation with no comment or gaze at Ana as she left. He continued with his exploration except for one moment after about 2 minutes of being alone in which he stopped playing, stroked his hair repeatedly, and looked at the door through which his mother had exited with a distressed, longing look.

When Ana came in for the second reunion, Sam was looking out the window while on his hands and knees. Ana went over to Sam, stood right behind him, and asked, "What do you see?" They talked for a moment about what Sam was looking at, and as Sam turned toward the room, Ana began to walk away, while turning her head toward him briefly, and for a few seconds they made eye contact. Ana sat in the chair and asked if he was having fun. Sam said, "No." Ana asked, "What do you want to do?" and Sam indicated that he wanted to leave by saying "bye-bye." Ana said, "We are not going bye-bye now. I want you to play with the toys." Sam again said, "No," Ana smiled, and Sam protested by saying "No" again several times. Ana told him with a teasing voice that he was a "faker." Sam made a dash for a toy and vigorously engaged with it while looking directly at Ana. Sam's disability was making it hard for him to use the toy properly, and he struggled with moving some of the moving parts. Ana oscillated between trying to help Sam and watching him with the flat, detached facial expression she had exhibited earlier. When Ana turned the toy around in an attempt to make it easier for him to use, Sam immediately crawled and reoriented himself so he was exactly in the same position relative to the toy that he had been in before Ana moved it, as if to say "I don't need your help." At no time during this interaction did Sam indicate to Ana that he wanted her assistance.

Sam's attachment strategy was scored insecure avoidant.

At this point the Strange Situation was officially over. What we observed was that Sam showed little apparent distress at separation, allowing his distress to emerge enough to be seen for only a few brief moments while alone. During reunions Sam miscued and focused on exploration and did not go to Ana for comfort, even though his emotional cup was not filled. This is, of course, consistent with an avoidant attachment. What made the avoidance unusual was the slow escalation between Sam and his mother in which he became mildly oppositional and Ana smiled and teased him at a time when his attachment needs were activated. Also what stood out was how Ana seemed to go away emotionally, appearing emotionally flat and gone, and then suddenly intervene when Sam appeared to be struggling with using a toy.

The linchpin struggle was that when Sam's attachment was activated he miscued by acting like all he wanted and needed to do was explore. This is again consistent with avoidant attachment. In addition Sam ended up acting oppositional, with Ana sending mixed messages regarding his opposition. Sam's oppositional behavior was not controlling, and Ana was clearly in charge, so the pattern did not meet the criteria for disorganized attachment. At the same time, this was a troubling pattern that had the potential to create distance and conflict in their relationship.

As described in Chapter 8, the COS interactional assessment adds a reading and a cleanup episode to the SSP. When Ana asked Sam if he wanted her to sit by him and read, Sam quickly said, "Yes." They were about 10 feet away from the couch, and Ana offered to help Sam walk to the couch. They both stood, with Ana holding Sam's hand, and slowly, with awkward, halting, and barely coordinated steps, Sam crossed the room as Ana gently held his hands and encouraged him to walk. There was something noticeably tender about this interaction, enough so that it brought tears to the eyes of many in the group. When Sam and Ana reached the couch, Ana asked her son if wanted to sit by her or on her lap, and Sam simply replied, "Yeah." Sam sat by Ana, and they read *Where the Wild Things Are* as Sam slowly snuggled into Ana. They negotiated a process in which Ana read and Sam turned the page. At one point Sam got ahead of Ana's reading by turning pages too fast, and Ana had to ask him to go back and turn the pages more slowly. This time no escalation or opposition occurred. At the end of the story they looked at each other with noticeable affection, and Sam said, "All done," to which Ana warmly replied, "Yes, all done; the end." Sam closed the book, looked at Ana's face with a big smile, and said, "Yes, the end."

During the cleanup episode Sam mildly said, "No" at first, Ana took charge, and after some struggle Sam shifted into cooperating with Ana and put the toys away. Ana came across as warm and firm and scaffolded Sam's efforts to put some toys back together before they went into the toy box.

The challenge now for the therapist was to make sense of all this. Ana could be quite affectionate and warm and also detached and somewhat "gone." She was capable of taking charge with warmth and authority and was quite skilled at scaffolding Sam's efforts. She was also quite focused on Sam being competent on the top of the Circle and did not seem to address the bottom of the Circle with any noticeable ease. When taking into account Sam's physical struggles, all of this took on another layer of complexity. Ana was surrounded by many professionals telling her how best to help Sam progress with fine and gross motor skills as well as with speech and cognitive development. One question that needed to be asked had to do with how much of what we were seeing with Ana in the Strange Situation was a manifestation of Ana's original and now Sam's current implicit relational knowing and how much their shared behavior was the effect of coaching by other professionals. The one thing that could be known for sure was that Sam was not faking his avoidance, and the escalation between the two of them was clearly an aspect of how they currently knew how to negotiate the tension between closeness and autonomy. It could be assumed that if these current patterns continued, Sam would not be able to use his mother as an emotional safe haven, and he would increasingly have to make sense of complex emotions with limited help from his mother. If a pattern of escalated conflict continued as a way to negotiate contact, this

shared miscuing could easily develop into Sam being increasingly oppositional in his relationship with Ana.

THE PARENT PERCEPTION ASSESSMENT:
THE CIRCLE OF SECURITY INTERVIEW

When Ana was asked what she thought it was like for Sam when Ana
left him in the SSP, she said, "I think he was fine. I don't want to make a
big deal out of it. He knows that I will be right back." She paused briefly,
then added, "I am surprised that he didn't care that much." Ana seemed to
be saying that separations were no big deal and he was OK. But she also
revealed an underlying concern that she wasn't needed. Even though clearly
unrecognized on any conscious level, was she letting us know that while
she was procedurally predisposed to his maintaining some level of distance
from her on the top of the Circle, her own unattended needs on the bottom
of the Circle were also being triggered? Which is to say, did she have mixed
feelings, wanting him to be independent while also experiencing his independence as too distant and a sign of not caring? When asked what it was
like for her to leave, she stated that "It wasn't bad . . . I like watching him
do stuff." When asked what she thought Sam needed when she was watching him from behind the one-way mirror, Ana stated, "I don't think he
really needed anything." Ana seemed not to see Sam's needs on the bottom
of the Circle and, except for the brief indication of some reticence about his
wanting too much distance, claimed to like it best when she was watching
him be active on top of the Circle.

When Ana was asked what was it like for her when Sam needed comfort, she said, "Sometimes I don't know—it's probably because he has special needs—sometimes it's hard for me because he needs comfort for the
things he can't do, like running. He wants to and then gets upset about that
kind of stuff: he will stand up and try to hold on to stuff and walk and falls
down, and he wants comfort like when he hurts himself. It is not a long fall,
but because he's frustrated and his feelings are a little hurt because he can't
do stuff like that, he needs comfort. It's just that it is really hard for me to
watch him struggle like that. Comforting him when it is not his disability
seems easier. With issues around his disability there is nothing that I can
really do for that. It's hard to think about stuff that could have been different, like before he was born so premature and there is stuff I could have
done before. I still have a lot of . . . I have a hard time with that."

Ana struggles with comforting Sam when it comes to his disability because she feels helpless to do anything to help him with it, activating unresolved feelings of guilt that she may have caused some of Sam's problems by her own behaviors during the pregnancy. Later, when asked what gave her the most pain in her relationship with Sam, she stated, "Watching him struggle more than other kids his age." And she told a story about going to a park where other children were playing. While Sam was playing with the other children, he was crawling and they were running around, and some of the kids became impatient with how slow he was because they were waiting for him to finish so they could take a turn going through a large plastic tunnel. As Ana was trying to decide whether it was safe to let Sam continue to play and whether there was anything she could do to help Sam, another parent came up to her and told her Sam was too old to be crawling. Rather than confront this person's insensitivity, which made her quite angry, Ana focused on safety for Sam and decided it was too dangerous. She tried to get Sam to disengage from the toys, and Sam became very upset. Ana felt terrible because Sam did not understand why he couldn't play and was just mad at his mom for ending his fun. "And once again I think of the stuff I could have done different because he was so premature," Ana concluded.

Managing feelings about a child's physical limitations would understandably be a struggle for any parent. But when her feelings regarding his physical struggles were combined with her lack of resolution about the role she may have had in his premature birth and how his cerebral palsy came to be, the level of struggle increased. Added were a procedurally learned tendency on her part to avoid the comfort and closeness on the bottom of the Circle and the problems implicit in her multiple reasons for choosing some level of emotional withdrawal from her son—something of a recipe for ongoing difficulty for both of them. Even without her propensity to avoid needs on the bottom of the Circle, Ana was struggling with a process that is hard for parents with children who have significant disabilities: (1) mourning the loss of the child that could have been, (2) accepting the child who is, and (3) adequately resolving feelings of self-blame and/or shame.

As the COSI interview progressed we were able to confirm that Ana was struggling with more than unresolved feelings regarding Sam's disability. As was noticeable throughout the SSP, her implicit relational knowing regarding needs on the bottom of the Circle organized her way of being in the world so that she was compulsively self-sufficient and did not rely on others for emotional support, and she was now in the process of teaching her child procedurally to do the same.

When asked what she did when she needed comfort as a child, she recalled a history of no one comforting her and of those she relied on getting mad when she showed any need for comfort. Her father was abusive. Her mother left when she was 5, and she lived with her father for a few years and then returned to her mother, who was preoccupied with boyfriends and vacillated between being emotionally dismissing and completely unavailable. Ana learned to be self-sufficient at a very early age, which included taking care of all household chores and doing the cooking by the time she was seven. When she wanted attention and didn't get it, she remembers being angry. Eventually she learned not to expect or even want attention. She went into foster care when she was 9 years old because Child Protective Services deemed her mother to be negligent. She lived in several foster homes and described hating the way she was treated. She ran away from foster care at age 14, living on the streets and "couch surfing" with friends until, at age 17, she became pregnant with Sam.

Ana's early attachment experiences were of either an unavailable or a frightening/abusive caregiver. At the same time, as evidenced through the SSP, Ana's capacity to stay in charge of the relationship with Sam without any noticeable signs of role reversal/distortion made it clear that she had developed enough internal coherence to avoid being considered disorganized.

Discerning the specific themes of whatever defensive strategy Ana had used through her life to blunt a painful childhood would be an important step in accessing the themes and needs that she was still trying to keep at a distance. Therefore identifying her core sensitivity was critical.

The most obvious strategy observed in the SSP was her tendency to maintain and support a high level of self-sufficiency. Given the nature of her childhood attachment relationships, it was clear that she had learned not to expect affection and to dismiss the needs on the bottom of the Circle. Ana's self-sufficiency, avoidance of dependency, and noticeable acceptance of separation were clearly not pointing in the direction of separation sensitivity. The more common options for a parent who is unwilling to offer emotional availability for needs on the bottom of the Circle would be either esteem or safety sensitivity.

Ana did not spend any time trying to impress the interviewer during the COSI, and at no time did she appear focused on specialness regarding herself or her son. She didn't show signs of being vigilant regarding Sam's rejecting of her and, given her willingness during the COSI to openly expose her struggles as a parent, didn't appear to be concerned about being a perfect parent. Ana did not self-protectively devalue Sam when they dis-agreed during the SSP, nor did she do so when discussing her parents dur-ing several moments of the COSI when she was clearly vulnerable. She did not seem to be vigilant about how she appeared to others—the incident at the park being a good example—and thus esteem sensitivity was also eliminated.

Safety sensitivity began to make the most sense. She seemed to fit this particular core sensitivity with her orientation toward avoidance, her com-pulsive self-sufficiency, and her primary defense of emotionally distancing and then reengaging with Sam during the SSP. Also, the way she would alternate between sharing and hiding her warmth from Sam was indicative of the dance between closeness and distance that is common for some-one who is safety sensitive. In addition, the therapist's countertransfer-ence became an important clue: he kept noticing that he was protective of her boundaries and cautious about being intrusive or "too much" for her. Countertransference can be a powerful indicator of a core sensitivity once a therapist has calibrated his emotional reactions to each of the core sensi-tivities. The themes regarding intrusion and protecting her from too much intensity fit the safety-sensitive category.

Ana's core sensitivity was identified as safety sensitivity.

THE LINCHPIN

The overarching linchpin was their avoidant relationship and how Sam was not using Ana as a safe haven, a bottom-half-of-the-Circle goal. The oppo-sitional teasing/escalation was included in the linchpin and thought of as a protective miscue on the part of Ana, a substitution for connecting directly, especially when Sam's attachment was activated and his emotional cup was not full. To accomplish this goal, first Ana had to see the genuine nature of her son's attachment needs for her on the bottom of the Circle. Second, she needed to contrast her two ways of being with Sam and their impact on him: warm and emotionally available versus detached when Sam was strug-gling with the limits of his disability and with his need for her following the separation. Noticing how she responded to his need for her with mixed signals was seen as a central theme of the upcoming intervention.

These goals fit with Ana's internal working model of safety sensitivity. She was much more comfortable with closeness when she had a physical function to perform and avoided moments that were close and emotionally intense whenever she didn't have a defined function. This was most notice-able when Sam was upset following the reunion and she couldn't do some-thing to solve a specific "problem" and make Sam's pain go away. To be with Sam's pain and not have a well-delineated solution reintroduced Ana to her shark music, memories and feelings associated with lack of caregiver support when she had needs for comfort and protection. She had survived her childhood by learning to be compulsively self-sufficient and not count-ing on others. When children are upset, there are moments for all caregivers when they are unable to make the pain disappear. These are moments when the caregiver is genuinely helpless to solve the problem and must tolerate a certain kind of emotional powerlessness, having only the capacity to Be-With the child in his or her pain. Managing feelings of vulnerability and helplessness is built into the job description of every parent. Because of Sam's disabilities, Ana had to manage significantly more of these feelings than many parents. Add to this her history of abuse and neglect and it's very understandable that she would not want to return to feelings of help-lessness in the face of emotional need.

Ana also seemed to be cautious with her positive feelings. Many people who view relationships through the lens of safety sensitivity feel that the expression and experience of intense emotions, especially those associated with an experience of closeness, are "too much." Because of this they work to titrate any experience of potential intimacy and the associated feelings by maintaining distance, physically and/or emotionally, as a way to man-age the perceived risk involved. This is part of the half-in-and-half-out compromise that protects Ana from her core dilemma: to be close is to be too close, triggering memories and feelings of intrusion, danger, and being controlled; to be distant is to be too distant, triggering a history that included experiences of intolerable isolation, with no hope of connection. Ana genuinely wants to be connected with her son, not only for his well-being but for hers. Her wanting this is built into the innate health and posi-tive intentionality that motivates her as a parent. But, as is always the case, shark music evolves from the painful experiences in our history.

For Ana, shark music is synonymous with the risks associated with closeness, which includes a history of how poorly her caregivers managed her needs whenever she was on the bottom of the Circle. Memories of an abusive father and a mother who leaned on Ana, demanding to be taken care of, make up the "too much" that Ana was now seeking to avoid in the closeness experienced with Sam. In addition, when Sam needed closeness as a way to regulate his experience of helplessness, Ana was likely flooded with the forgotten needs (and the longing associated with them) that went unmet throughout her childhood. So the linchpin goal of encouraging Ana to Be-With Sam in both positive and negative emotional states on the bottom of the Circle (delight, comfort, organization of feelings) would challenge her implicit relational history and require her to understand and hopefully manage her shark music in a new way.

PHASE ONE VIDEO REVIEW

Ana was the second parent in the group to review her video and thus had a modest familiarity with the process. The review started with a clip that showed the two of them cooperating and enjoying reading together. The clip ended on the moment when they looked into each other's eyes, smiled, and Sam said "the end." Ana focused on how she was working to keep Sam engaged and cooperative and interested in the activity of reading. As the therapist pointed out the shared delight, Ana grew pensive, moving inward and becoming noticeably thoughtful. There was clearly something about emphasizing her warmth that made her pull back, almost disengaging from the conversation. Given her history of intrusive parents who likely shared few if any such moments of delight with Ana, it was appropriate not to pursue this any further at this early point in the intervention. To have done so would clearly have been "too much" and triggered further withdrawal on Ana's part. The importance of this initial introduction of shared delight and a simultaneous reading of Ana's cues that this topic was laden with pain is twofold. First, it honors the innate sweetness that Ana and Sam shared, an underlying shared delight that was at the heart of their relationship. Second, it honors the cues that the parent is giving the therapist. To recognize that this theme is important while also recognizing that Ana was needing to go slowly is part of how a therapeutic alliance is built.

The next clip showed Ana kissing Sam's "owie" during the reunion. The kiss was interpreted as a positive engagement by Ana, and then the struggle that ensued about picking the sore was explored briefly. Ana saw Sam's opposition and said she herself had a bad temper and had to take herself away to calm down whenever Sam made her angry. Sam's behavior was labeled "feisty" by the therapist, and Ana was asked if she liked her son being feisty. She smiled and acknowledged that she did. She then told stories of Sam fighting as an infant to survive his surgical operations and disabilities. She really needed a son who fought against the odds and without conscious awareness had clearly reinforced Sam's opposition in their relationship. "Sam has always been a fighter and it helped him survive." Ana was beginning to show her capacity for reflection. In addition, she was letting the therapist know that her innate sense of empathy was very much at work in her relationship with Sam. "I think he often makes me mad, but he's not really being bad. It's almost like he wants to connect with me." Assigning a positive attribution to behavior that can often be seen as negative was another very good sign for the future of this mother and her son. The key question at this point: Would she also be able to see her own motivations as positive as she explored her part in insecure aspects of their relationship?

The next clip showed a contrast between Ana being engaged and her flatness/detachment as Sam struggled with one of the toys. A moment on the video in which Sam couldn't figure out how to use the toy was emphasized, and Ana said she really hated it whenever she saw that happen. "I hate to see him struggle with his disability." The moment on the video when Sam seemed to be struggling the most was the moment when Ana became the most disengaged. Her reaction was framed as a way to manage her own pain when seeing Sam struggle so hard. She accepted the interpretation but did not engage emotionally with either the therapist or the group, clearly choosing to back away from this opportunity to further explore the pain she likely felt every day of her life. At this point in her work she was reflective and cognitively engaging while also keeping an emotional distance from the therapist and the intensity of the story being told with the video. Given that this was the first time she was talking about experiences that she historically had learned to manage so much by herself, she was taking significant risks and showing remarkable courage by allowing this tableau to unfold in the presence of others. Yet again, it was assumed that she was paying close attention to how sensitive the therapist would be regarding issues of pushing her too fast and too far. His understanding of her safety sensitivity and the central role of honoring anything surrounding an implication of intrusion was a helpful safeguard in titrating how the intervention was to unfold.

The last clip was of Ana helping Sam walk to the couch to read. Immediately after seeing the clip she said, "Sometimes he is so sweet." Unbidden, the therapist was suddenly aware of having tears in his eyes. Ana was also fighting back tears as she was allowing herself to feel more at this moment in the group process. As she looked away, the therapist worried about her reaction should she look toward him, recognizing their shared sadness. His momentary dilemma: "If she sees my tears, I may be experienced as too much for her. If I look away, I may trigger yet another memory of someone who is unavailable and who won't honor her need for safe connection." Ana resolved the dilemma by maintaining a distance from the therapist and not looking at him or anyone else. It can be assumed that, procedurally, she was living out what she had learned as a way to manage pain: "I'm on my own, so I need to go away and figure it out by myself."

After about 30 seconds the therapist broke the silence by saying "I think you may be working to manage your own pain while you offer your son the support he needs and help him do things like walk." Her tears increased. The room sat in silence until she began to talk a minute later. "It took me a long time to accept his disability. That he may not walk, that he may never run." She cried while looking away and said she didn't want to talk about it. Holding her head in her hands, she cried silently for about 30 seconds. She then looked up and said, with tears, "Sam looks so happy in that clip. But he's had such horrible things happen in his life." Ana then turned away from everyone again and hid her face and cried. Waiting until her tears had subsided, the therapist said that it was clear that she was really helping her son. Ana said she felt lucky that Sam was doing as well as he was. She then apologized to the group for her tears. Several in the group immediately jumped in and said, "Don't apologize." One of the mothers who was clearly separation sensitive immediately jumped up and gave Ana a big hug. The therapist couldn't see Ana's face but was worried that her safety sensitivity could influence her experience of the hug as an intrusion, if not a kind of smothering flowing from the other parent's need to offer a hug. After the hug ended Ana was looking away, did not say anything to the mother who hugged her, and got out of her chair to walk across the room to get a tissue to wipe her tears. Not surprisingly, her back was to the group as they continued to make supportive comments to her. She came back to her chair and listened while looking away. The hug had increased her need to go away and, understandably, had not helped her feel safe and engaged.

All of the parents were profoundly moved by Ana's commitment to her son and the pain she had to manage every day. One parent said it really touched her that Ana could see the goodness of her child even when he was experiencing such difficulty. This mother went on to say, "We take so much for granted. And it's so easy to see our kids as bad when they're just trying to deal with how tough things can be. I feel bad that I think my girl should know better when she probably is just trying to figure stuff out." Ana silently absorbed the supportive comments. The support evoked a comment about her wish that Sam's father was more involved and could see Sam the way the group saw him. "He only comes around about once a year."

The session ended with the therapist acknowledging that Ana's ability to manage her pain and her working to find a way to support Sam were so important. Ana listened while looking away, then took a deep breath and sighed. Time had run out, and there was no space to explore how Ana had experienced the session and how it was to be so open with her pain. It was hard to know whether more discussion would have been experienced as helpful or too much.

At the very end Ana was given a picture of Sam sitting with her at the end of the reading, a moment when they were looking at each other with smiles on their faces. This offering of a picture at the end of the video review is built into the protocol and is intended as a way to have the parent leave with an image that reminds her of the essence of the therapeutic message, which in this case had to do with how much emotional engagement matters. Ana acknowledged the gift but did not choose to hang around afterward and made a quick exit.

PHASE TWO VIDEO REVIEW

The second video review starts with a clip of Ana and Sam mutually enjoying playing with a number puzzle. It was a moment of shared positive emotion in which the two of them worked well together. The group saw Sam's need on the Circle and labeled it an "enjoy with me" moment. When asked whether she remembered what she was feeling at the time, Ana said she was impressed with her son's ability to do the puzzle. The therapist commented that she looked comfortable as she supported Sam's exploration. Ana said that helping him in this way was comfortable.

The next clip showed the separation, and the first thing Ana mentioned was that Sam didn't seem to care that she was gone. This inaccurate representation of her son as not caring about her absence was part of Ana's procedural memory associated with countless experiences of no one caring and no one being there for her. Finding a way to zero in on this misperception of Sam's emotional state and offer a cautious yet direct challenge was now key. From a clinical point of view, Sam clearly needed her during their time of separation. To clarify this need, the entire 3 minutes of Sam being alone was shown and explored moment by moment. It was important that Ana see through the playing with toys and begin to discern his underlying distress. She watched Sam alone in the room and observed that his play was not as joyful or expansive as it had been prior to her leaving the room. Ana initially thought he was frustrated and maybe a little nervous. The therapist asked Ana to contrast Sam's emotional tone while playing when Ana was not there with that when Ana was there. "Ana, ask yourself this question: Is he exploring for the fun of it or exploring to distract himself from feelings of being left alone and without you?"

When Sam looked at the one-way mirror, the video was paused and Ana was asked what she saw in his face. Ana said he looked lost and remembered being behind the glass with Sam looking right at her. She noticed that Sam was stroking his hair and thought this might be a way for him to self-soothe; that it might even be that Sam was distressed. She commented that he really didn't care about the toys and just took a toy out and put it back over and over. After a pause of several seconds, the therapist added, "I had the thought that Sam is looking for you." Several said they thought Sam needed comfort from Ana. Ana remained silent and appeared to be thinking as Sam's need for her was emphasized.

The next clip was the second reunion in which they briefly made eye contact. At first viewing Ana thought once again that Sam did not care that she had returned. Going over the video and watching their eye contact, Ana was able to see that there was a brief moment of connection. Ana said she actually remembered this moment and wanted to pick him up and then decided not to because she did not want to "baby him." This was, of course, good news for her therapeutic work. She would not have the urge to pick him up if she did not think Sam needed some form of comfort. So bottom-of-the-Circle caregiving options were operating below the surface but quickly (and procedurally) dismissed as harmful to Sam. This is central to what Masterson described as the "triad" (Masterson & Lieberman, 2004, p. 32). An experience of genuine need (and activation of the self on behalf of that need) leads to painful memories, which quickly lead to an established pattern of defense. For Ana self-activation would require engaging in meeting Sam's need on the bottom of the Circle and tolerating the feelings associated with how her own needs for closeness had historically gone unmet and even been dangerous. The moment she felt the urge to honor Sam's need for her active care, her shark music was activated and she returned to a well-established form of self-protection—dismissing her intentions as harmful to Sam. This is always understood to be happening outside of conscious awareness on the part of the parent. Within the context of the therapy, the gradual recognition of this three-step process (acknowledging need, triggering shark music, triggering defensive strategy) gradually becomes available for shared reflection.

This was the linchpin to the entire intervention, because as long as this process went on outside of her awareness it would stop Ana from responding to Sam's need for comfort, which is seen to be the central issue in her avoidance. This was the key to her shark music. The therapist asked her to reconsider her concerns about babying her son and how she may be on to something with her initial instinct. Ana then shared another concern: "I'm worried that hugging Sam might be more for me than for Sam, and I don't want to do something like that."

Ana laughed as she viewed the part of the video where she asked Sam if he was having a good time and he said "No" and "I want to go bye-bye now." The whole group was enjoying Sam's directness about how he felt, and Ana was watching with laughter and affection for how direct he was about his need. But she was also watching with her new eyes, the ones now capable of making sense of her shark music. Having seen his need, which included his capacity to speak directly about being uncomfortable, Ana watched herself call Sam a "faker," at which point Sam became somewhat upset and then oppositional. As is true within every intervention regarding the Circle, the underlying assumption is that children don't create difficulty because they want to. They become "difficult" because their genuine need somewhere on the Circle is not being recognized and responded to. The therapist then said, "Sam needs you, and this is turning into a feisty interaction with you enjoying his feistiness. He'll settle for being feisty, but he is miscuing you with his feistiness because what he really needs from you is comfort." Ana was suddenly pensive and quiet. She said she could see that happens sometimes. She then looked away, sounding thoughtful and maintaining an emotional reserve.

The next clip, which had been used in her Phase One video review, showed the avoidance and opposition regarding the "owie" from reunion one. This was used as another example of Sam miscuing with feistiness when he needed comfort. Ana saw it and felt bad she did not comfort him, and she began to reflect on all the times she might have comforted him in the past. The therapist said, "I think you have a conflict about all this. You don't want to smother or baby him, and at the same time you have this instinct that says to you 'Pick him up and hug him.'"

At this point Ana had a kind of "aha" moment. She commented on how she had thought she was being more comforting than she really was being and she began to feel bad about it. Recognizing that she could have been spiraling into self-blame, the therapist focused on her positive intentions regarding Sam's feistiness. "For a lot of reasons like his disability and your own conflicts about all this, I think you are more comfortable on the top of the Circle, as we're beginning to see in these moments on the video when Sam needs comfort on the bottom of the Circle. You appreciate feisty because you want Sam to be a fighter. Feistiness toward exploration will help him in life, but being encouraged to be feisty and potentially oppositional when he needs comfort will be a problem for him and for you." Ana responded thoughtfully, "This seems all so true, and I really thought I was more comforting. I think I do the same thing with my dad. We pick on each other: I say he is fat, and he says I have a big nose, and we tease each other as a way to make contact, and we never show affection directly." Teasing with underlying affection has a quality of engaging someone while at the same time keeping a distance, which can be the chosen compromise for someone who is safety sensitive. Ana was beginning to put another puzzle together, this time with the support of the therapist and the group. She was seeing how she keeps a certain distance with those she loves.

The next clip showed the stranger coming in and Sam clearly turning toward Ana. When Sam reached out with his hand, Ana reached out and gave her hand to him, and this gave Sam a sense of connection and safety. This is a part of the COS protocol where the clinician seeks to find a video clip that emphasizes an underutilized competency. In this case, even though Ana was uncomfortable on the bottom of the Circle, her positive intentionality as a parent momentarily overrode her shark music and she offered comfort. This is, of course, the very thing she wasn't able to do during the reunions, likely because the intensity was so much higher at those moments. This was used not only as a positive message that Ana had the capacity to provide comfort but also as a challenge, implying that her well-established avoidance was not about lack of skill, because she was already capable of doing it. Therefore the reason she so often stopped herself from offering comfort was that it evoked shark music. To stop the emotional chaos, she protected herself from her pain by not responding to Sam's need and focusing her attention on the top of the Circle. It was very impressive that she was being vulnerable enough to remember and share the eye contact moment from the reunion and had the reflective capacity to explore the meaning behind her behavior.

The final clip was focused on the cleanup, where Ana took charge in a firm but kind manner and Sam worked with her cooperatively. The success was explored from the perspective that Sam needed help organizing his behavior and his feelings.

At the end of the session Ana was asked what it was like for her to have learned and shared in this way. She responded, "It sucked. I thought I was doing these things." The therapist said, "I hope you do not take home with you the conclusion that you are not available. You are remarkably available, and you have this conflict about how much availability is safe and about how much to engage. I think it's possible that you lean on exploration and worry that if you comfort Sam too much you will smother him. You have good instincts, and you can feel a wanting to give comfort, and this evokes a conflict in you. But you have this right-on instinct." Ana wondered whether it was OK to go with her instinct. The therapist said he trusted that if she was thinking Sam was upset and needed her comfort or a hug then that instinct was a good one. Ana went inward for a few moments, looking at the floor and appearing thoughtful. The group ended after other parents talked about their experience that day.

PHASE THREE VIDEO REVIEW

The third video review is based on a new recording of parent and child interacting in a modified Strange Situation using blowing bubbles together as the first activity. The video is created to give parents a chance to see themselves beginning to make important changes in their way of reacting to their child's Circle needs. The review has the quality of celebrating change and acknowledging ongoing struggles.

Ana looked rested and calm on this video. As she watched the video, her facial expression shifted between joy and concern when Sam struggled with using the bubble wand. In this video Ana was so much more animated and not flat at all. Ana stated that this part was fun. The therapist explored how she seemed more available in this video than in the last video when Sam was playing with the bead toy. She was reminded that we had talked about how that flat look on her face was about her feelings of watching Sam have so much trouble with a toy, and she agreed that this was true. The therapist said, "In this video Sam had some trouble with the bubbles, and you seem more at ease with helping him and letting him struggle." Ana attributed the change to the fact that the activity of bubbles was more fun. This was true and also masked the fact that Ana was so much more animated and available with her positive emotions.

The next clip was of a separation, and Ana went to the door without looking back. As Ana left with her back to Sam, he showed his need for Ana by slowly turning and looking at Ana's departure with a sad expression. When Ana saw this during the video review, she said at the time she didn't think Sam cared if she left and she didn't know he had done that. She said she doesn't look back during separations because "if Sam doesn't care, I am bummed, and if he does care, I am also bummed, because I have to leave him when he is upset." This means that by protecting herself from painful feelings during separations she also didn't see Sam's need for her, which perpetuated her inaccurate representation that Sam did not need her and kept alive a representation of herself as not needed. The therapist did not say anything about these themes to her and in retrospect wished he had.

Sam rocked himself when alone after the separation, and Ana could see how he was self-soothing. The recording was made with a camera person in the room because the videos were made at Head Start. When he was alone with the male camera operator, he called him Dada, and when Ana came back into the room he brought up Dada. As Ana watched this, she indicated this was a painful topic for her because she felt bad that Sam did not have a father who was involved in his life. During this clip, when Sam became mildly oppositional, Ana did not smile, looked more serious, and did not engage in the escalation. Ana said she had been working on giving Sam more firm structure.

At the end of the review she was given a picture of them blowing bubbles with mutual joy, and she smiled at the picture. The therapist said, "You give him a lot." Ana said, "I try to." The therapist said, "You appear more available in this video." Ana confirmed that this was so and mentioned that since watching the earlier videos she had tried to be more available.

CONCLUSION

The final review process, including thoughts about the past months of learning within the group, was hard for Ana because it offered direct access to what she was doing and not yet able to do regarding Sam's needs on the bottom of the Circle. Ana had thought she was being available to Sam and more available than her parents had been with her. She had thought that when Sam was in need of her he could come to her. "But I watched myself when he needed me, and I seemed cold." "I was really shocked and disappointed in myself when I saw that there were so many times Sam probably needed a hug or needed reassurance and I didn't do it. I feel deeply all those things . . . and so I have worked on that a lot, and I went through days of feeling really bad and evaluating what I was doing. I still catch myself doing those things, but I really try to make sure that I am available and open, and I didn't used to let myself be mad at him or let myself be upset with him or let myself be happy, and now I do." The therapist made it clear that her new effort came across in the video and that it looked like she had made a decision to be more available. She replied, "I think I am better at the practical part of stuff. I think I am a really good protector and provider and the other parts are hard." Asked about the "comfort me" part, Ana said yes, that was hard. "For regular things the 'comfort me' is strange to me, but if he has to have surgery I am great; I go into autopilot. I am good at taking care of the technicalities of everything."

Ana ended her last review on a powerful note of understanding how she had lived on the top of the Circle, avoiding the bottom, and that her strong suit was doing what needed to be done and putting aside her own and Sam's emotional needs. Behind the scenes she had really been working on all this and had not shared the intensity of her struggle until this last video review. She had turned away and appeared thoughtful so many times during prior group sessions, and her comments were a sample of what she had been working through silently. Her relationship with the therapist mirrored the nature of her struggle, as is often the case in therapeutic relationships. She both reached out to the therapist and, as it became too much, created distance by going into herself and processing much of the painful material alone. She enacted the safety-sensitive dilemma throughout the process by having one foot in the therapeutic relationship and one foot out as she processed her videos. For her to have shared as much as she did during the group challenged the very nature of her procedural knowledge. It is also interesting to think about how she developed such a strong capacity for reflection. Her courage and commitment were remarkable. She, on the other hand, probably had only a fleeting glimpse into how remarkable she actually was.

On the postintervention SSP Ana did not appear flat and detached at any point. On the first separation Ana turned as she walked toward the door and looked at Sam as she left, and Sam asked for reassurance by asking if she would be right back. Ana confirmed that she would. During this interaction they made eye contact. On the first reunion Sam looked up at Ana and said "Mama," and Ana smiled, made eye contact, and said "Hi, Sam." After the initial greeting Ana got down on the floor with Sam, who once again started to engage Ana by putting toys in his mouth with Ana saying "Don't put them in your mouth" and Sam doing the old dance of putting them in his mouth and looking at Ana, who once again said "No." Ana tried to be more serious as she set the limit, but the old smile was still there. This undercurrent of opposition when Sam's attachment needs were activated, met quickly by Ana's smile, remained a work-in-progress. While it had lessened noticeably, it was still active.

On the second separation Ana negotiated with Sam to leave, and when she did they made eye contact just before the door closed. Sam's need for Ana was more evident in this separation as he tried to open the door and get out of the room. On the second reunion Sam was standing right by the door, and as Ana opened the door Sam said, "Come in" as the two of them made eye contact. Sam reached for Ana's hand, and Ana held his hand, reached for the other, helped him stand, and then picked him up with both of them smiling. They talked, and then Ana and Sam hugged and Ana sat down with Sam in her lap. After about a minute Sam indicated he wanted to get down to play with a toy. During the entire episode there was no escalation or opposition, which supports the theory that when Sam's cup was full he didn't need to engage in a less fulfilling and miscuing way.

Even though some of the old struggle remained, the change was significant, especially in the second reunion, in which Sam sought contact with his mom, maintained and used the contact until his cup was full, and then indicated he was ready to go explore. These are the basic ingredients of security.

In the postintervention Strange Situation
Sam was scored secure.

POSTINTERVENTION CIRCLE OF SECURITY INTERVIEW

During the postintervention COSI the last question was "You have just completed 20 weeks with the Circle of Security Project. How would you say that your belonging to this project has had an impact upon you and your child, in either a positive or negative way?"

Ana's answer was:

"It consumed my thoughts 24 hours after every meeting, and I remember thinking 'I am a pretty good parent.' . . . Then I remember watching the first video, and there were lots of times on that first video that I probably should have comforted Sam or talked to Sam. He was struggling with that bead toy, and I got blank or angry, and you could see it, and I thought that I was better than that. I was angry afterwards and pretty down on myself, not sure if I wanted to go back to the class. . . . Then I took it and evaluated every little thing about our day-to-day life for days afterwards, and I keep catching myself doing things like ignoring him or getting angry and not hearing what he was saying. All the things that I didn't want to do. Then I decided I was going to change it and be more available. . . . In the next movie we made I changed and I could see I was better, and I was proud of myself for making the change. I know I will probably have to work on it for a long time because this is what I have lived up until now and it is like a total change. . . .

"It helped to know that I was not the only parent and that we all struggled. I liked that in our meetings I didn't hide anything and I talked about everything openly, and I think everyone else did too. I have friends who have children, and we talk about how our kids make us mad, how our kids make us happy and what they did today, but this was so different. . . . We talked about our strengths and weaknesses as parents. When Sam has to have surgery, I am a trooper. I do all the technicalities, I talk to the doctors, I get everything in order, I am real supportive of him and tell him things are going to be OK. I am a good provider and really protective. I tell him I love him and show him I love him. I am nurturing to all my friends. I am nurturing to everybody. But I feel too close to my kid, and when he hurts I hurt so bad it kills me, so I think that I detach myself a little bit because I don't want to hurt and I don't want him to hurt either.

"I thought I had gotten past my childhood and I was a different person and I wasn't as angry anymore and that my kid was happy and I was doing the right thing. You never want to think that you are falling in the same patterns that I never wanted to do. I was bitter about it for a while. Everything else was positive and great. . . . I hear Sam now a little more, a lot more probably . . . I think it would be beneficial for all parents to step back and take a look through the one-way mirror."

15

Shelly and Jacob

Shelly is a single mother, age 22, whose 3½-year-old son, Jacob, was referred to the COS intervention program by the lead administrator at his child care facility. Jacob had been behaving aggressively toward other children and several teachers in the classroom. When this was raised as a concern, Shelly acknowledged that his anger and outbursts were also a problem at home.

INTAKE

During the initial interview Shelly revealed that Jacob's father had disappeared after Jacob's birth and could not be located. Shelly described feeling helpless in addressing Jacob's behavior problems. Her demeanor and presenting attitude concerning Jacob betrayed a sense of helplessness and powerlessness in the role of parenting. "I want to be a good mom. I try. But he's just so difficult. He's always had a temper, almost like he wants to make things difficult." At the same time, Shelly was both eager and a bit nervous about having a chance to participate in a program where she might learn more about how to be an effective parent. Beyond that, she showed noticeable signs of reflective capacity during the brief 20-minute intake. "I know my mom made a bunch of mistakes, and I just don't want to repeat

---

Another version of this case originally appeared in *Attachment Theory in Clinical Work with Children: Bridging the Gap between Research and Practice*, edited by David Oppenheim and Douglas F. Goldsmith. Copyright 2011 by The Guilford Press. Adapted by permission.

those. But I don't know what to do. I try and try, but nothing I do seems to work. I'd like to think it's all Jacob's fault, but I know it isn't." When told that she would be a good fit for the upcoming 20-week group, she was very interested. The thought of meeting regularly with five other parents to discuss both the struggles and possible new options within parenting seemed to be a good fit for her.

INTERACTIONAL ASSESSMENT: THE STRANGE SITUATION PROCEDURE

As Shelly and Jacob entered the room, Jacob immediately moved toward the box of toys in the center. Less than 10 seconds into his interest in a rubber dinosaur Shelly interrupted his play by asking him what he was doing. He seemed to disregard her question and kept playing. Looking somewhat despondent, Shelly waited another 10 seconds and repeated her question, this time wondering, "Do you want me to play with you?" He said no without hesitation, and in response she looked down, shrugged her shoulders, and looked like she was about to cry. After a few moments she spoke in an almost childlike tone, whispering "OK." Another 5 seconds passed, and she suddenly interjected in an overbright tone completely the opposite of the dejected sadness she had just projected, "I'm fine. Maybe you just want me to sit here and watch you play." Jacob agreed, and Shelly said "OK" with the same overbright demeanor. Within 6 seconds she suddenly said, "Do you want to read a book?" Again he said no, and again she replied with an overbright tone, apparently designed to deny her pain, "I'll just let you play."

Jacob then began a monologue narrating his play. Although it was obvious that he was not speaking to her, Shelly took his narration as an opportunity to interact with Jacob, and within 20 seconds she had joined him on the floor and was trying to join in his play. As Shelly pursued her son, he responded by turning his back to her. For the rest of their interaction the two seemed to be having a kind of tug of war, with Jacob continually fighting to assert his independence and Shelly fighting to be included. Shelly would ask Jacob a question to get involved, and he would either grunt a quick response or completely ignore her as he tried to play alone.

As he persisted in exploring on his own, Shelly would intensify her look of discomfort at being left out and would sigh loudly, once again trying to join his play. Occasionally Jacob would play with her for a few moments but would quickly return to ignoring her and then go back to his agenda. Shelly clearly did not offer Jacob an opportunity to explore on the top of the Circle. Noticeably lacking was any apparent capacity to offer him support for the autonomy he craved while also simultaneously remaining involved by offering her delight in and enjoyment of his initiative from a distance. Shelly's vacillating glances toward the ceiling, then toward Jacob, then back to the ceiling were clear signs of distress. Her voice, alternating between dejection and an odd, cheery "I'm just fine with whatever you do," also spoke to a level of upset that both she and her son were continually required to manage. What was abundantly clear was that her pursuit of him while he was exploring and her noticeable disappointment when he would deny her requests were part of a problem that the upcoming intervention would need to address.

When Shelly left the room during the separation phase, Jacob seemed to remain fully involved in his play. At the same time, he would make brief (half-second) glances toward the door where she had exited, then quickly return to the toys. He was clearly doing his best to maintain a facade, one that implied he was fine and busy with the toys. Clearly he had learned to minimize showing his distress. There were also subtle shifts from a more animated play when his mother was in the room to a listless play and flat affect after she had left. The most revealing indication that he was actually distressed by his mother's absence was the brief but significant moment when he looked again toward the door, then began searching the one-way glass behind which his mother was standing. The look on his face was one of sadness, almost longing. He apparently didn't know what to do when his mom was in the room. Even more, he didn't know what to do when she was gone.

As noted earlier in this book, the manner in which a parent and child verbally and nonverbally negotiate their "interactional dance" in the first few moments of a reunion reveals their core caregiving/attachment strategy. When Shelly returned to the room for the second reunion, her first words were "What are you doing?" Jacob kept his back to her and did not answer until she prompted him by repeating the question, at which point he shrugged and said, "Nothing." Shelly then sat down on the floor next to her son and with a noticeable anxiety in her voice said, "What does that thing do? Show me," and touched the toy. With a stern face Jacob said "No, stop it." Shelly, appearing frightened, immediately responded, "OK, I'll just watch." But after a couple of seconds she tried to join in again, asking, "Can I do this one?" When Jacob again told her "No!" she said, "OK, I'll leave you alone" with the same overbright tone she had been using whenever she pretended to accept his need for distance. With that, she started to move toward the chair.

Suddenly Jacob directed her by saying, "Do this one." Shelly quickly moved back to him and followed his directions. When he did not engage her in the play, she gave up and went back to sit in the chair. After a few seconds Jacob moved closer to her. At a distance of about 36 inches he continued his play at her feet while keeping his back turned to her.

At the point of making an evaluation this dyad's attachment strategy was not clear-cut. During the reunions, Jacob showed both avoidance, acting as if he did not need his mother, and rejection. His rejection of her had a resistant/ambivalent tone: both pulling her in closer and pushing her away. There were also noticeable signs of role reversal: at several points, most noticeably during the second reunion, he started directing his mother, acting controlling and angry. This would be a time, within the context of a secure attachment, where his caregiver would be expected to help him with the distress caused by their separation. Instead, Shelly allowed him to be in charge of the reunion, accommodating to his angry direction and control. Throughout the SSP, especially at the emotionally laden point of return following the separation, Shelly appeared to be the child and Jacob seemed to be the one in charge.

Shelly's caregiving strategy was also mixed. She showed clear signs of struggling with both the top and bottom of the Circle. She could neither support Jacob's autonomous play (continually interfering) nor offer comfort when he appeared distressed during the reunion (asking questions and almost begging to be included in his play). This latter theme was the key data showing that the linchpin issue was that Shelly had both hands off the Circle. At the point of reunion, when the child needs the caregiver to function as someone who is "bigger, stronger, wiser, and kind"—offering to be capable, in charge, and caring—Shelly was unable to provide this function for her son. Instead, as noted above, it was Jacob who was given the role of taking care of his mother's distress—a task he struggled to accomplish through a combination of distancing gestures and punitive commands.

Jacob's attachment strategy was scored insecure-other.

No single pattern was predominant. Jacob showed signs of avoidance, ambivalence, and controlling punitive, and thus he was scored insecure-other. In the Cassidy–Marvin Preschool Attachment Classification System, this classification indicates a mixture of contradictory, nonnormative attachment patterns and for research purposes is regarded as a disturbed pattern with the same, if not more troubling, developmental trajectory as those scored with disorganized attachment.

THE PARENT PERCEPTION ASSESSMENT: THE CIRCLE OF SECURITY INTERVIEW

During the COSI, Shelly seemed confused by the questions, particularly those regarding herself and her own thoughts and feelings, often answering with "I don't know." She said she did not think Jacob needed her at any point during the SSP. At multiple times during the interview she would seem overwhelmed by a question and ask the interviewer to repeat the question. Only later would it make sense to the clinician involved that this fit a lifelong pattern of utilizing perceived helplessness as a bid to have another take charge.

While talking about Jacob's potential distress, Shelly described having been worried when asked to leave the room. The source of her anxiety was Jacob's potential to be upset: "He could throw a big old tantrum." Noticeably focused on how his distress would cause her distress, this mother's inability to maintain awareness of her child's need was now coming into clear view.

At another point she revealed that when Jacob recently told her he loved her, "It was a huge boost to me. I felt like someone actually loved me." This statement poignantly revealed her profound insecurity about feeling cared for, her view of emotional bonds as fragile, and the power she had given her child to be the arbiter of her emotional support system.

This mindset was reinforced by Shelly's answer to the question about what gave her the most pain in her relationship with Jacob. She said "discipline" and then described how she felt when she refused to give Jacob candy for breakfast: "I got mad at myself because I had just made my son hate me, because I didn't give him what he wanted. I knew it would be downhill from there." To Shelly, if her son got upset or disapproved of her, his love for her was at stake, and if he did not love her, he would abandon her. Jacob's availability thus was an essential ingredient in Shelly's perceived emotional stability, establishing the role reversal that threatened both her sense of security and his.

What Shelly said next, however, showed that she had access to at least moderate levels of reflective functioning: "But then I realize if I give him everything he wants, when he isn't given what he wants he'll act out. If that keeps up, who knows what he could do?" Her capacity to recognize the potential consequences of her actions—that giving her son what he wanted in the moment would ultimately harm him—was clearly a hidden strength. This was a moment in the assessment process that showed that pursuing the intervention could likely be fruitful for Shelly and her son.

Another promising sign was that even though Shelly had no way to currently make sense of her shark music, she recognized that she had anxious feelings when she tried to take charge. At the moment the only option that seemed to make sense as a way to manage these painful feelings (and memories) was accommodation to her son's demands. And yet hidden in that brief observation was the awareness of and the desire to find another way. Even when brief, such signs of reflection and hope offer the beginning building blocks for both a therapeutic alliance and a successful treatment plan.

Even though it takes going through the entire COSI to form a hypothesis regarding the parent's core sensitivity, the preceding information is sufficient to formulate an initial impression. A person who is safety sensitive tends to keep the child focused away from the relationship and seeks to promote self-sufficiency, most often by encouraging the child to stay interested on the top of the Circle. This was clearly not the case for Shelly. Parents who are safety sensitive are not likely to continually request to be included in a child's play. There would be no discernible undercurrent pulling the child toward the parent, as is the case here. Most certainly the wording and body language signifying that Shelly was almost desperate to keep her son focused on her needs would not be seen on the part of a safety-sensitive parent. Hence, safety sensitivity was ruled out.

We are left with two other options: esteem and separation sensitivity. In each case it is possible to have a parent who is focused on a discernible sense of connection. Separation-sensitive parents tend to have an enmeshed "I'm afraid of being abandoned and don't want to live without you" undertone in how they cling to their child. The focus is on keeping the child close and, for as long as possible, maintaining the illusion of mutual dependence.

Most esteem-sensitive parents keep their child focused on the top of the Circle, wanting their child to perform or build skills that will move them in the direction of achievement. But a subset of esteem-sensitive parents are focused on how special the relationship is, implying a perfection that is to be found in how "perfectly close" (fused or one-minded) the relationship appears to be. (Note the word "appears" because the perception of others is central for those who are esteem sensitive.) Esteem sensitivity, in this case, is built around the perception of an adored child in a wonderful relationship, implying a perfect parent.

Shelly, while almost entirely focused on remaining as close to Jacob as possible, did not seem at all concerned with how wonderful or perfect he might be or how special their relationship was. Above all else, she seemed to want him near (no matter how perfect or imperfect he might be), with the underlying hope that she wouldn't be abandoned.

The final conclusion regarding Shelly's core sensitivity was reached by analyzing her responses on the COSI (Form 10.1, Chapter 10, pages 249–254). Beyond the issues described above, the clinical team asked themselves specific differential questions while watching the video of the COSI. The following are several additional questions that were asked:

- When Jacob acts as if he does not need his mother, why does this have such emotional power for her?
  - Does it make her feel alone, helpless, panicky, and abandoned (separation sensitive)?
  - Does it make her feel rejected and like a failure as a less than perfect parent (esteem sensitive)?
  - Note: There is no corollary option for safety-sensitive parents. It would be exceedingly rare to find a safety-sensitive parent who is deeply troubled by a child's distance followed by continual requests to be allowed into the child's play.
- What is the meaning behind Shelly's intrusion into her son's exploration?
  - Is she interfering to teach him to perform better so that she will appear and feel successful as a parent? Does she feel so identified (one-minded) with Jacob that she can't discern the difference between his interests and her own (esteem sensitive)?
  - Is she replaying the intrusion she experienced in her own play, a kind of "taking over" that she knew from her parent (safety sensitive)?
  - Is she threatened by his autonomy on the top of the Circle because he will no longer need her and she will feel painfully alone and unwanted (separation sensitive)?
- During the reunion, what is the meaning of her not providing comfort on the bottom of the Circle?

□ Does she dismiss the need for comfort, seeing it as exposing her unnecessarily to vulnerability and as something that will keep him off the path that leads to success? Upon return, does she want to be included in his play as a way to use shared performance to reconstitute their shared perfection (esteem sensitive)?

□ Does she quietly appreciate her child's apparent independence, noting it as an acceptable distance, especially during a time of intense need (safety sensitive)?

□ Does she fill his cup inadequately on the bottom of the Circle to keep him in need in the hope that he won't leave (separation sensitive)?

Shelly's core sensitivity was identified as separation sensitivity.

For Shelly, Jacob's initiating autonomy was perceived as the first step in his likely, almost inevitable abandonment of her. Depressed, emotionally neglected, and often alone as a child, as revealed by Shelly's COSI, this mother had given birth to Jacob hoping for the experience of one person who would love her unconditionally and protect her from needing to revisit the pain of her past. When asked if she felt Jacob had come into her life for a reason, she said that prior to becoming pregnant she had been so depressed that she did not want to go on, and Jacob had given her a reason to live. Later she said there was nothing she had learned from her mother that she wanted to repeat with Jacob because she did not feel "cared for or wanted" during her childhood.

Shelly's defensive management of her shark music led her to "give up" when her son needed her to take charge.

Shelly was unaware of her part in Jacob's anger and rejection of her, and the painful reenactment of being unwanted triggered a visceral sense of being an unwanted, unloved, and unlovable child: "If I tried to do anything on my own, she would be angry at me unless I did it her way." Shelly's experience of the Circle wasn't positive on either the top or the bottom. Doing something on her own, activating in the direction of the top of the Circle, meant guaranteed loss of connection. Self-assertion and autonomy became associated with painful feelings of rejection, abandonment, and being left alone.

Hence Shelly experienced the same fear when claiming her parental role of providing guidance for her son. To activate on her behalf and Jacob's behalf would trigger her shark music, the painful memories and feelings associated with autonomous actions that were never supported by her mother. To take charge she had to rely on her own internal resources, which procedurally were associated with feelings of abandonment. As a child she had learned that helplessness and collapse had actually gotten her some semblance of connection. Unaware that she was involved in a painful repeat from her past, Shelly had returned to being helpless and "giving up" as a way to manage her fear of abandonment by having "the other" (originally her mother and now her son) step in and be the one in charge. In the way that shark music typically distorts our perception, Shelly had learned to block painful affect by abdicating her parental authority, clinging to her son, and asking him to take care of her.

Of course, Shelly had no sense of how this was happening. The power of this work is that once parents are given a way to see the painful patterns that are being reenacted, most of the time they work hard to make the necessary change.

THE LINCHPIN

Parents with children classified as insecure-other are often more challenging to help than parents who have children classified as disorganized. Because multiple insecure patterns are used, a single insecure pattern sometimes cannot be selected as the linchpin for intervention. Thus, several linchpins must be addressed, which in turn tends to make the treatment more complex. However, what was learned in the assessment of Shelly and Jacob clearly pointed to a linchpin centered on Shelly taking charge—being the hands on the Circle.

When the time came for Shelly to get Jacob to pick up the toys during the SSP, she started out with timid requests and then shifted to pleading when he ignored them. But there was one crucial moment that stood in contradiction to all others. When Shelly told Jacob, in a firm adult tone, to take a toy out of his mouth, he promptly complied. This moment demonstrated what we call an "underused strength." A parent who can do it once obviously *already* has the skill (albeit underused) and potential to do it again. But the caregiver avoids using this capacity because it evokes a feeling state (shark music) that she does not want to reexperience. In this case this makes the central focus of the intervention—the linchpin struggle—helping Shelly reevaluate her state of mind when Jacob needs her to take charge and learn how she protects herself from painful emotions by abdicating her parental "in charge" role.

PHASE ONE VIDEO REVIEW

The following goals were chosen for Shelly's Phase One video review:

- To help Shelly see that her son needed her *all* the way around the Circle—while exploring and when hurt and distressed. This ran counter to her procedural beliefs about Jacob's need for her, a view of the inevitably abandoning "other" that had haunted her since early childhood. Through the intervention she would be challenged to reevaluate her conviction that he did not need her. Knowing this was contrary to her belief that Jacob's need for her was provisional and depended on whether she was "good" (dependent on his approval) or "bad" (standing on her convictions). For Shelly to know that she was indispensable would challenge her internal working model and thus create a necessary state of emotional disequilibrium for her. This could actually feel like good news to her, because it could free her from the sense that Jacob's connection with her was conditional and that he could leave at any moment.

- To help Shelly acknowledge that being excluded from playing with Jacob was painful. Talking about her pain could help prepare her for the next, more challenging video review, where she would face the disorganizing ways she managed her pain and the increasing insecurity it created for herself and her son.

- To assist Shelly in seeing that she could in fact take charge, as evidenced by the moments when she acted "bigger, stronger, wiser, and kind" by using a direct, strong voice with her son. When she asserted her parental role, her son followed her lead. For her to see this in a video clip would challenge her false representation of herself as incompetent and serve as an illustration of her underutilized take-charge strength. This key moment, in which she told her son, "Take that out of your mouth" would become a cornerstone that would stand in sharp contrast to the way she usually pleaded with him.

Shelly seemed nervous when the first video review started, but she had seen other members of the group go through the process and support each other. As she prepared to watch her clips, she shared a recent memory of almost coming to tears when Jacob told her he missed her. The other parents in the group reinforced her importance to her son.

The first set of clips showed rare moments of Jacob successfully using his mother to explore his environment, revealing that he needed her even when he was exploring. Interestingly, Shelly felt valued as she saw their interaction. Many parents in high-risk populations did not feel valued during their own development, and so they often project negative attributions onto their child's expression of need ("He just wants attention"; "She doesn't like me"), which can end up organizing their experience of their child's needs at any point on the Circle. It was a good sign that Shelly could see and accept his need for her. It implied that she was open to a positive shift in her relationship with Jacob and that she welcomed the opportunity to feel good about herself and their relationship.

The next clip showed Shelly appearing hurt when Jacob wanted to play on the top of the Circle. She clearly had experienced this cue from him as negative: "I think he always wants to do things without me." At first she was defensive when one of the other parents asked her to talk about the look of upset on her face when Jacob had refused to play with her. The therapist then commented, "What comes across is it looks like you felt hurt." She softened and said, "Yeah, it does hurt." After having identified the many ways Jacob needed her, the therapist explored her feelings of rejection and wondered if she knew just how important she was to him. Shelly softened further and acknowledged that sometimes when he wants to play alone she feels unimportant to him. Shelly's willingness to talk about the vulnerable feeling of "not being wanted" associated with her son's exploration demonstrated yet another indication of her capacity for change and her intention to find a new kind of relationship with Jacob.

The final clip reviewed was of the moment in the cleanup when Shelly told her son to take the toy out of his mouth. At first she had trouble seeing her strength, but the other mothers talked about Shelly's competence in a positive manner, and upon a second viewing of the clip Shelly was finally able to see the difference in her tone. The therapist named this firm, take-charge tone "The Voice," and Shelly used this as a metaphor for having confidence in herself and knowing her importance as a parent. This awareness would help her apply a much-underused capacity that she currently possessed. The COS approach isn't about learning a new skill set. In fact, no newly learned parenting skill would make a difference as long as her state of mind told her that she wasn't needed and that her child was always on the verge of abandoning her. Recognizing that she had a central importance in Jacob's life and that he was waiting for even more opportunities to experience her as "bigger, stronger, wiser, and kind" allowed her to tap into her positive intentionality as a parent and look for new places to use "The Voice."

At the end of this first video review, Shelly said she had never thought about how Jacob's cues and miscues affected her and that she liked these discoveries—yet another indicator of her willingness to make changes for the sake of her son. Thanks to the power of specifically chosen video clips, Shelly was beginning to see for the first time how her history was being repeated in her relationship with her son.

Over the next 6 weeks (Phase One), Shelly shared "Circle stories" about using "The Voice," which she described as working sometimes and failing at others. This caused her to vacillate between feeling strong and feeling helpless.

PHASE TWO VIDEO REVIEW

Shelly's second video review was designed to focus on how, during moments when her son was angry, she collapsed just when he needed her to take charge as a means of helping him organize his feelings. She described a recent incident in which she did not know how to manage her son when he was angry. The therapist said, "For some reason when your son is upset he doesn't know how to use you to calm down. Do you know what's going on that when he is upset he wants to push you away, even when you want to help him?" Shelly appeared hurt as she nodded her head in agreement and said, "That is what I do with my mom. When I'm flipping out, I push her away." As is true for many COS parents, Shelly was beginning to recognize the transgenerational connection between the caregiving she had received growing up and her current attempts at caregiving. With her statement, Shelly was expanding her reflective capacity and beginning the process of establishing a "choice point," the conscious decision to look at feelings and then alter behavior. Until the implicit is made explicit and procedural memory is given language, chronic patterns of insecure interaction remain hidden and therefore outside the realm of choice.

Shelly continued, "This makes me feel bad. When he wants me to leave, it hurts. I am trying to comfort him, and he's telling me to go away. He's saying 'I don't want you to be here.'" Shelly said she wanted to help Jacob calm, but he would not allow her to do so. This exposed her linchpin issue of allowing Jacob to be in charge of the relationship as a way to avoid her own fear of being abandoned by him. Yet again, feelings and memories associated with acting autonomously by exercising her right to choose what was best triggered memories of how this had always led to her mother's withdrawal. Without knowing it, Shelly then blocked access to what would be healthiest for herself and her son.

Sensing her anxiety, the therapist decided to modify the typical COS protocol by giving Shelly the central message of the video review *before* she watched the video. Once she understood where the session was going, she might be able to calm her fear of being exposed as a bad parent and become more accessible to the learning process: "I think that when he needs you, he gets controlling. And when you allow yourself to be controlled, it scares him." Shelly began to cry, closed her eyes, and tried to gain control of her feelings. She did not speak until she had contained her feelings. In the intensity of the moment, Shelly had gone inward, closing off from the relationships available in the room, and thus revealed her procedural memory of not reaching out to others when she was overwhelmed with feeling.

> SHELLY: I know he is very controlling and becomes more and more controlling every day.
>
> THERAPIST: That is what I want to help you with.
>
> SHELLY: I know I am supposed to be the one who is in control, but I am not. He is the one who controls me . . .
>
> THERAPIST: When he is being this little controlling guy, I think he is afraid. He's the one who is really afraid, and you are the person he needs. He needs you to be bigger, stronger, wiser, and kind because he's the scared one. If you can remember that, I think it might help a lot.

Shelly's tears had lessened, and the group members explored the idea that behind a child's angry controlling behavior is fear and the need for a strong caregiver. Shelly's struggle touched all the parents, and they talked about their own struggles with their children. When the time came to watch her video, she indicated that she was ready.

The initial goal for the session was for Shelly to review how important she was to her son. Video clips were chosen to help Shelly see his cues and miscues—the change in his affect when she left the room and, most significantly, a creatively edited single video frame of Jacob's face gazing with longing at the door his mother had exited. As that image was projected on the television screen the therapist asked, "What does this say to you?" Shelly softened and said, "Where is my mom?" Shelly saw and, even more important, acknowledged the truth of his need and her importance to him.

Shelly was now caught in an emotional dilemma: If she accepted her importance, she felt needed and cared for but was also exposed to the painful knowledge that this positive feeling had been rare and missing for her during much of her life. For Shelly to admit her importance to Jacob meant that she would have to face some of the pain she had been avoiding. The therapist gently challenged her limited way of seeing her son, and group members joined in supporting the idea of her value and his need for her. With her fragile insight about her value to Jacob, she was as ready as she was likely to be in this session to confront her shark music.

Shelly's linchpin clip was the second reunion in the SSP, when Jacob kept his back to her upon her return. She had tried to play with him, and he had taken control by turning her down and telling her what to do several times. When she had withdrawn and started to move away, he cued her about his actual fear and need by calling her back to his side and immediately miscued her by taking control and told her what to do again.

During her Phase Two video review Shelly was able to say that Jacob kept his back to her when she reentered the room because he was hurt. This new depiction of Jacob implied that she was able to hold her image of him as small and hurt instead of her more defensive image of him as big, powerful, and rejecting. The therapist said, "When he needs you, he manages his feelings by turning away from you, becoming rejecting and taking control." Shelly answered, "It's kind of hurtful because I want to play with him. I want to play with him and he doesn't want me to, and so I just give up." In this statement, Shelly disclosed her linchpin problem. When she felt rejected and unwanted, she gave up, and this left Jacob without a mother who was available to provide him with care and stability. When Shelly collapsed, it frightened Jacob and he managed his fear by becoming more angry and controlling. His anger frightened Shelly, and she typically collapsed even further. The therapist said, "You are so hurt, and having to deal with your own pain of rejection makes it hard for you to be bigger, stronger, wiser, and kind. But Jacob needs you, and the last person in the world he wants to get rid of is you. But he can't show you, he can't risk it. If he did and you collapsed again, where would he be? So he acts like he doesn't need you just when he needs you most! He is saying he missed you and he doesn't know how to show you his need, so what he shows you is his control. It's like he's saying 'Someone has to be in charge here.'" There was a long pause, and then the therapist spoke again: "What is it like to think about Jacob this way?" Shelly responded, "It's a relief that what he actually needs is me. I am not giving him what he needs, but in a way, I did not know. But now I do."

Shelly's face revealed both positive feelings and pain as she talked. The session ended with watching the clip with "The Voice" from the Phase One video review again and reminding Shelly of her competency. Shelly felt threatened by the challenge the clip represented and stated she had tried to use "The Voice" but that it didn't work. The therapist said, "When you speak with 'The Voice' and are also expecting to be hurt by Jacob's rejection, you end up needing acceptance from him, and that turns everything around. He then has more power than you. He has power with his rejection. But it is a power you can't give him because it will frighten him and it hurts both of you. You mean everything to him, and it's very important that you know this." Shelly said, "It is hard" and began to cry.

As she cried, the therapist asked her if there was anything she needed. She covered her face and withdrew emotionally. After a few minutes, the therapist decided to comment on her way of managing her emotions by saying, "I can see that you are used to sorting things out alone, and today is an important step because you are sorting this out with us." Group members spontaneously gave her support and offered to be available to Shelly outside of group when she needed to talk about her feelings.

At the end of the session, Shelly admitted that she still felt she had done something wrong "to make him feel so angry." Because her learning would cease if this defensive pattern of thinking of herself as bad succeeded, the therapist focused at the end of the session on helping Shelly consider that she had done nothing wrong, was not to blame, and in fact was supporting herself and doing something right by looking so directly at her shark music in her relationship with her son.

Since time was virtually up, the therapist told her a story about a dream he had been told as a way to briefly address the intensity of her self-blame. In the dream this person was angry at himself because of mistakes he had made in his life. When he looked up, he saw his father standing in front of him and realized it was his father's fault because his father had been emotionally unavailable and rejecting to him, so he started to yell at his father. As he was yelling at his father he looked over his father's shoulder and saw his grandfather standing there and realized that he was actually angry at his grandfather, because his grandfather had taught his father to be this way. After he raged at his grandfather for a while, he looked over his grandfather's shoulder and saw his great-grandfather and great-great-grandfather, stretching out forever. All of a sudden his anger was gone and he understood that he was the product of generations. He then knew his anger and blame were really about grieving for what he had needed and not received. He also knew that now was his time to learn something new for himself and for his family's future generations.

The therapist then said, "I think the goal for every parent is to take what is good from where we came from and leave what didn't work behind and to do something a little bit better. Shelly, my question to you is, Are you 'bad' right now, as you are working so hard to find new ways to be with your son?" Other group members jumped in and were supportive of Shelly, and the group ended for the day with her oscillating between mildly smiling with the group's support and looking somber and sad.

PHASE THREE VIDEO REVIEW

Shelly showed progress in taking charge with Jacob in several episodes on the new video created in week 15 of the protocol and used for the last video review. When playing with the bubbles, Jacob started frantically popping the bubbles and waving his bubble wand so wildly that Shelly had to set limits. She was able to take charge and help Jacob slow down while keeping the play enjoyable. When it was time to put the toys away, her approach went from a plea of "Can you help me?" to a modest directive of "Let's pick up the toys" and successfully ended with the take-charge position of "Put that toy away." Shelly was revealing both her new capacity and her ongoing struggle. Jacob was much more cooperative with her throughout the filming.

When Shelly left Jacob during the separation, he showed distress but then acted like all he needed was help with a toy when she returned. With the new insight she had gained Shelly was able to remain emotionally even in her responsiveness to him rather than "giving up" when he appeared frustrated. A significant goal of this last video review was to give Shelly support for maintaining the change that had been set in motion. This was particularly important because children will often go through a transitional phase, a time when the child does not provide immediate reinforcement for the parent's new approach.

Shelly appeared less anxious and more available during her final video review. When she reviewed the vignette of her coming back into the room and Jacob miscuing her, she said she did not think of him as needing her when she returned—in the heat of the moment her shark music had kept her from recognizing her value to her son. But she was now able to feel good about her importance to Jacob when reminded of it. Likewise, when she first observed the toy cleanup, she was unable to see her increased firmness with Jacob. Even after playing the video twice and with feedback from the group, she barely saw that she was taking charge. Even though Shelly had started to behave differently, she continued to struggle with seeing herself in a new and positive light. Yet again, seeing her son's need and seeing her new capacity meant facing additional pain. To go against the grain of her history and risk another path would mean passing through shark-infested waters, even if the sharks were only in her memory.

During the postintervention SSP, Shelly acted less tentative, more supportive of Jacob's exploration and did not give up when Jacob acted resistant or controlling. Jacob sought contact with his mother during the reunions but miscued her by showing some resistance to her care.

In the postintervention Strange Situation
Jacob was scored secure.

The preschool scoring manual describes the B-4 category, the score Jacob received, in the following way: "The behavior of children in this group is generally secure, but elements of immature, dependent, ambivalent, or resistant behavior are also present." (Cassidy, & Marvin, 1992, p. 29) Jacob had begun to use his mother as a secure base and as a safe haven and showed mild miscuing (resistance) as he did so. In the postintervention SSP, Shelly followed Jacob's exploration and did not intrude in his interests. With Shelly less intrusive, Jacob was less aggressive. Shelly appeared more confident during the reunions and Jacob far less controlling. When he was controlling, Shelly maintained her position as the "bigger, stronger, wiser, and kind" parent, and Jacob appeared almost to be pretending in his controlling behavior. In the first few moments of the second reunion, Jacob maintained sustained eye contact with Shelly as he greeted and talked to her. During the preintervention reunions, Jacob had hardly looked at his mother at all. He could now increasingly turn to his mother, seeking help with his emotions and support for his exploration. His anticipated developmental trajectory with his newfound secure attachment to his mother was substantially more positive.

POSTINTERVENTION CIRCLE OF SECURITY INTERVIEW

In the postintervention COSI, Shelly demonstrated her understanding that Jacob needed her when she was out of the room: "When he was alone, he looked around for me," and he was "excited to have me come back. . . . I

knew he wanted and missed me." Shelly was still oscillating between thinking of herself as "good" and seeing herself as "bad." Because her internalized relationship with herself is far more entrenched, representing a lifetime of experience, this was understandable. Each time she saw that Jacob
needed her to take charge, a crisis was set off within her internal working
model. Shelly immediately remembered and then anticipated rejection and
abandonment. Her ongoing resolution of this internal conflict between feeling positive about and threatened by her son's need for her was central to
lasting change.

Later in the COSI, when asked what had given her the most difficulty
in her relationship with Jacob, Shelly cited exactly the same issue as in
her initial COSI: discipline. She then told the same story of Jacob once
more demanding candy for breakfast. This time she said, "You've got to
learn someday you can't have candy for breakfast . . . then we switched to
eggs." When asked how she thought Jacob was thinking about her in this
incident, she replied, "He didn't like me because I didn't let him have what
he wants." When asked how she thought about herself in this incident, she
replied, "Good, I guess. I didn't give in and let him have the candy." When
describing this conflict in the initial COSI, she had feared her son would
hate her if she took charge. Her newfound capacity to hold a positive image
of herself as she appropriately took charge, especially in the face of her son's
rejection, was seen as crucial progress.

At the end of the interview, she was asked how participation in the
project had affected her relationship with her son. She stated with positive
emotion, "He cues [me] when he needs something like a hug when I come
into the room. . . . When I pick him up from day care, he is excited to see
me, and he never used to do that before. . . . He is all happy to see me!"
For her son to show her his need so openly when previously he did not
indicate his need for her makes it clear that he has changed and that she has
changed. The key for their future security was now centered around Shelly
holding on to her reflective capacity, remembering her value to Jacob, and
maintaining the supportive network she had formed within the group. As
she continued to risk further exploration of her newfound capacities she
had a very good chance of giving Jacob the security she had not received.

One year later parents from the group were interviewed about their
experience of participating in COS. The children of the parents had
remained enrolled in Head Start for 1 more year after the intervention, and
the parents had continued to interact with each other as part of participating in the program. During the meeting the parents were very supportive

and laughed with each other as they recalled their experiences. One parent said that Shelly had seemed so reserved at the beginning of the program. Shelly recalled that when she started the group she was very afraid of opening up to people she didn't know, and over the course of time "I blossomed." The whole group enjoyed her comment, and they all laughed together. When asked what had helped her do that, she stated that it was the support and feedback from everybody in the group. As she said this, the other parents said in a very positive way that her relationship with her son was now so different than it had been. One parent asked what had helped her the most, and she recalled the video clip where she took charge and learned that she had a "mom voice." She stated that before this she used to plead with Jacob so he wouldn't get mad and acted more like a friend than a mom. She now feels more like a mom.

References

Aber, J. L., Slade, A., Berger, B., Bresgi, I., & Kaplan, M. (1985). *The Parent Development Interview.* Unpublished manuscript.

Ahnert, L., Lamb, M. E., & Seltenheim, K. (2000). Infant-care provider attachments in contrasting child care settings: Pt 1. Group-oriented care before German reunification. *Infant Behavior and Development, 23,* 197–209.

Ainsworth, M., Blehar, M., Waters, E., & Wall, S. (1978). *Patterns of attachment: A psychology study of the Strange Situation.* Hillsdale, NJ: Erlbaum.

Badenoch, B. (2011). *The brain-savvy therapist's workbook.* New York: Norton.

Bateson, G. (1972). *Steps to an ecology of mind: Collected essays in anthropology, psychiatry, evolution, and epistemology.* Northvale, NJ: Jason Aronson.

Baumrind, D. (1967). Child care practices anteceding three patterns of preschool behavior. *Genetic Psychology Monographs, 75*(1), 43–88.

Beebe, B., Jaffe, J., Markese, S., Buck, K., Chen, H., Cohen, P., et al. (2010). The origins of 12-month attachment: A microanalysis of 4-month mother–infant interaction. *Attachment and human development, 12*(1–2), 3–141.

Beebe, B., Knoblauch, S., Rustin, J., & Sorter, D. (2005). *Forms of intersubjectivity in infant research and adult treatment.* New York: Other Press.

Blum, D. (2002). *Love at goon park: Harry Harlow and the science of affection.* Cambridge, MA: Perseus.

Bollas, C. (1987). *The shadow of the object: Psychoanalysis of the unthought known.* New York: Columbia University Press.

Bowlby, J. (1944). Forty-four juvenile thieves: Their characters and home-life. *International Journal of Psycho-Analysis, 25,* 19–53.

Bowlby, J. (1988). *A secure base: Parent–child attachment and healthy human development.* London: Basic Books.

Bowlby, J., & Ainsworth, M. D. S. (1951). *Maternal care and mental health.* Geneva, Switzerland: World Health Organization.

Bretherton, I. (1992). The origins of attachment theory: John Bowlby and Mary Ainsworth. *Developmental Psychology, 28,* 759–775.

Britner, P. A., Marvin, R. S., & Pianta, R. C. (2005). Development and preliminary validation of the caregiving behavior system: Association with child attachment classification in the preschool strange situation. *Attachment and Human Development, 7*(1), 83–102.

Bromberg, P. M. (1998). *Standing in the spaces: Essays on clinical process, trauma, and dissociation.* London: Analytic Press.

Bronfenbrenner, U. (1977). Toward an experimental ecology of human development. *American Psychologist, 32,* 513–531.

Carlson, E. A., & Sroufe, L. A. (1995). Contributions of attachment theory to developmental psychopathology. In D. Cicchetti & D. J. Cohen (Eds.), *Developmental psychopathology* (Vol. 1, pp. 581–617). New York: Wiley.

Cassidy, J. (1994). Emotion regulation: Influences of attachment relationships. In N. Fox (Ed.), *The development of emotion regulation.* Monographs of the Society for Research in Child Development (Vol. 59).

Cassidy, J. (2008). The nature of the child's ties. In J. Cassidy & P. R. Shaver (Eds.), *Handbook of attachment: Theory, research, and clinical applications* (2nd ed., pp. 3–22). New York: Guilford Press.

Cassidy, J., & Berlin, L. (1994). The insecure/ambivalent pattern of attachment: Theory and research. *Child Development, 65,* 971–991.

Cassidy, J., & Marvin, B., with the MacArthur Attachment Working Group. (1992). *Attachment organization in preschool children: Coding guidelines* (4th ed.). Unpublished manuscript, University of Virginia.

Cassidy, J., & Mohr, J. (2001). Unsolvable fear, trauma, and psychopathology: Theory, research, and clinical considerations related to disorganized attachment across the life span. *Clinical Psychology: Science and Practice, 8*(3), 275–298.

Cassidy, J., & Shaver, P. R. (Eds.). (2008). *Handbook of attachment: Theory, research, and clinical applications* (2nd ed.). New York: Guilford Press.

Cassidy, J., Woodhouse, S., Sherman, L., Stupica, B., & Lejuez, C. (2011). Enhancing infant attachment security: An examination of treatment efficacy and differential susceptibility. *Journal of Development and Psychopathology, 23,* 131–148.

Cassidy, J., Ziv, Y., Stupica, B., Sherman, L. J., Butler, H., Karfgin, A., et al. (2010). Enhancing maternal sensitivity and attachment security in the infants of women in a jail-diversion program. In J. Cassidy, J. Poehlmann, & P. R. Shaver (Eds.), Incarcerated individuals and their children viewed from the perspective of attachment theory [Special issue]. *Attachment and Human Development, 12,* 333–353.

Cooper, G., Hoffman, K. T., & Powell, B. (2000). Marycliff Perinatal Circle of Security Protocol. Unpublished manuscript. Spokane, WA.

Cooper, G., Hoffman, K., Marvin, B., & Powell, B. (2000). Circle of Security Facilitator's Manual. Unpublished manuscript.

Cooper, G., Hoffman, K., & Powell, B. (2009a). *Circle of Security Parenting: A relationship based parenting program* (DVD). Information available at *http://circleof-security.net.*

Cooper, G., Hoffman, K., & Powell, B. (2009b). *Circle of Security Parenting Manual* (for use with COS-P DVD). Unpublished manuscript distributed as part of COS-P training.

Coulton, G. (Ed. & Trans.). (1906). On Frederick II. In *St. Francis to Dante.* London: David Nutt. Retrieved from *www.fordham.edu/halsall/source/salimbene.1.html.*

Emde, R. N. (1987). Foreword. In L. Fraiberg (Ed.), *Selected writings of Selma Fraiberg.* Columbus, OH: Ohio State University Press.

Fairbairn, W. R. D. (1952). *Psychoanalytic studies of the personality.* Tavistock Publications Limited in collaboration with Routledge & Kegan Paul, London.

Feldman, R., Greenbaum, C. W., & Yirmiya, N. (1999). Mother–infant affect synchrony as an antecedent of the emergence of self-control. *Developmental Psychology, 35*(1), 223–231.

Felitti, V. J., Anda, R. F., Nordenberg, D., Williamson, D. F., Spitz, A. M., Edwards, V., et al. (1998). Relationship of childhood abuse and household dysfunction to many of the leading causes of death in adults: The adverse childhood experiences (ACE) study. *American Journal of Preventive Medicine, 14*(4), 245–258.

Fonagy, P., & Bateman, A. W. (2007). Mentalizing and borderline personality disorder. *Journal of Mental Health, 16*(1), 83–101.

Fonagy, P., Gergely, G., Jurist, E., & Target, M. (Eds.). (2002). *Affect regulation, mentalization, and the development of the self.* New York: Other Press.

Fonagy, P., Steele, H., Moran, G., Steele, M., & Higgitt, A. (1991). The capacity for understanding mental states: The reflective self in parent and child and its significance for security of attachment. *Infant Mental Health Journal, 13,* 200–217.

Fonagy, P., Steele, H., & Steele, M. (1991). Maternal representations of attachment during pregnancy predict the organization of infant–mother attachment at one year of age. *Child Development, 62,* 891–905.

Fonagy, P., Steele, M., Steele, H., Higgitt, A., & Target, M. (1994). The Emmanuel Miller Memorial Lecture 1992: The theory and practice of resilience. *Journal of Child Psychology and Psychiatry and Allied Disciplines, 35,* 231–257.

Fonagy, P., Steele, M., Steele, H., & Target, M. (1997). *Reflective-functioning manual, version 4.1, for application to Adult Attachment Interviews.* Unpublished coding manual, University of London.

Fraiberg, S. (1980). *Clinical studies in infant mental health: The first year of life.* New York: Basic Books.

Fraiberg, S., Adelson, E., & Shapiro, V. (1975). Ghosts in the nursery: A psychoanalytic approach to the problems of impaired infant–mother relationships. *Journal of the American Academy of Child and Adolescent Psychiatry, 14*(3), 387–421.

George, C., Kaplan, N., & Main, M. (1984). *Adult Attachment Interview.* Unpublished document, Department of Psychology, University of California, Berkeley.

George, C., & Solomon, J. (2008). The caregiving system: A behavioral systems approach to parenting. In J. Cassidy & P. R. Shaver (Eds.), *The handbook of attachment: Theory, research, and clinical applications* (2nd ed., pp. 833–856). New York: Guilford Press.

Gillath, O., Selcuk, E., & Shaver, P. R. (2008). Moving toward a secure attachment style: Can repeated security priming help? *Social and Personality Psychology Compass, 2*(4), 1651–1666.

Goleman, D. (1995). *Emotional intelligence: Why it can matter more than IQ.* New York: Bantam Books.

Goleman, D. (2006). *Social intelligence: The new science of human relationships.* New York: Bantam Books.

Greenberg, M. T., Speltz, M. L., & DeKlyen, M. (1993). The role of attachment in the early development of disruptive behavior problems. *Development and Psychopathology, 5*, 191–213.

Greenberg, M. T., Speltz, M. L., DeKlyen, M., & Jones, K. (2001). Correlates of clinic referral for early conduct problems: Variable- and person-oriented approaches. *Development and Psychopathology, 13*, 255–276.

Grice, H. P. (1975). Logic and conversation. In P. Cole & J. L. Morgan (Eds.), *Syntax and semantics: Speech acts* (Vol. 3, pp. 41–58). New York: Academic Press.

Guntrip, H. (1969). *Schizoid phenomena, object relations and the self.* New York: International Universities Press.

Hesse, E. (1999). The Adult Attachment Interview: Historical and current perspectives. In J. Cassidy & P. R. Shaver (Eds.), *Handbook of attachment: Theory, research, and clinical applications* (pp. 395–433). New York: Guilford Press.

Hoffman, K., Marvin, R., Cooper, G., & Powell, B. (2006). Changing toddlers' and preschoolers' attachment classifications: The Circle of Security Intervention. *Journal of Consulting and Clinical Psychology, 74*, 1017–1026.

Hoffman, K. (1997). *Seeing with Joey.* Unpublished Manuscript. Circle of Security International.

Holmes, J. (1999). Defensive and creative uses of narrative in psychotherapy: An attachment perspective. In G. Roberts & J. Holmes (Eds.), *Healing stories: Narrative in psychiatry and psychotherapy* (pp. 49–66). New York: Oxford University Press.

Huber, A. (2012, April). Understanding my own and my child's mind: Examining the role of caregiver reflective function in transforming relationships using Circle of Security. Symposium conducted at the meeting of the World Association for Infant Mental Health World Congress, Cape Town, South Africa.

Karen, R. (1990, February). Becoming attached. *The Atlantic.* Retrieved from *www.theatlantic.com.*

Karen, R. (1994). *Becoming attached: First relationships and how they shape our capacity to love.* New York: Oxford University Press.

Keller, T. E., Spieker, S. J., & Gilchrist, L. (2005). Patterns of risk and trajectories of preschool problem behaviors: A person-oriented analysis of attachment in context. *Development and Psychopathology, 17*, 349–384.

Kernberg, O. F. (1975). *Borderline conditions and pathological narcissism.* New York: Jason Aronson.

Kestenbaum, R., Farber, E. A., & Sroufe, L. A. (1989). Individual differences in empathy among preschoolers: Relation to attachment history. In N. Eisenberg (Ed.), *New directions for child and adolescent development: No. 44. Empathy and related emotional responses* (pp. 51–64). San Francisco, CA: Jossey-Bass.

Klein, M. (1948). *Contributions to psycho-analysis.* London: Hogarth Press.

Klein, R. (1995). The self in exile: A developmental, self, and object relations approach to the schizoid disorders of the self. In J. F. Masterson & R. Klein (Eds.), *Disorders of the self: New therapeutic horizons: The Masterson approach* (pp. 3–142). New York: Brunner/Mazel.

Kohut, H. (1977). *The restoration of the self.* New York: International Universities Press.

Korzybski, A. (1958). *Science and sanity: An introduction to non-Aristotelian systems and general semantics.* Forest Hills, NY: Institute of General Semantics.

Lichtenberg, J. D., & Slap, J. W. (1973). Notes on the concept of splitting and the defense mechanism of the splitting of representations. *Journal of the American Psychoanalytic Association, 21,* 772–787.

Lieberman, A. F., Padrón, E., Van Horn, P., & Harris, W. W. (2005). Angels in the nursery: The intergenerational transmission of benevolent parental influences. *Infant Mental Health Journal, 26*(6), 504–520.

Lieberman, M. D., Eisenberger, N. I., Crockett, M. J., Tom, S. M., Pfeifer, J. H., & Way, B. M. (2007). Putting feelings into words: Affect labeling disrupts amygdala activity in response to affective stimuli. *Psychological Science, 18*(5), 421–428.

Lyons-Ruth, K. (2007). The interface between attachment and intersubjectivity: Perspective from the longitudinal study of disorganized attachment. *Psychoanalytic Inquiry: A Topical Journal for Mental Health Professionals, 26*(4), 595–616.

Lyons-Ruth, K., the Process of Change Study Group. (1998). Implicit relational knowing: Its role in development and psychoanalytic treatment. *Infant Mental Health Journal, 19*(3), 282–289.

Main, M. (1981). Avoidance in the service of attachment: A working paper. In K. Immelman, G. Barlow, M. Main, & L. Petrinovitch (Eds.), *Behavioral development: The Bielefeld Interdisciplinary Project* (pp. 651–693). Cambridge, UK: Press Syndicate of the University of Cambridge.

Main, M., & Goldwyn, R. (1984). *Adult attachment scoring and classification system.* Unpublished manuscript, University of California, Berkeley.

Main, M., Goldwyn, R., & Hesse, E. (2003). *Adult attachment scoring and classification system.* Unpublished manuscript, University of California, Berkeley.

Main, M., & Hesse, E. (1990). Parents' unresolved traumatic experiences are related to infant disorganized attachment status: Is frightened and/or frightening parenting behavior the linking mechanism? In M. T. Greenberg, D. Cicchetti, & E. M. Cummings (Eds.), *Attachment in the preschool years* (pp. 161–182). Chicago: University of Chicago Press.

Main, M., Kaplan, N., & Cassidy, J. (1985). Security in infancy, childhood, and adulthood: A move to the level of representation. In I. Bretherton & E. Waters (Eds.), *Growing points of attachment theory and research* (pp. 66–104). Monographs of the Society for Research in Child Development, Vol. 50 (1–2, Serial No. 209). Chicago: University of Chicago Press.

Main, M., & Solomon, J. (1986). Discovery of an insecure-disorganized/disoriented attachment pattern. In *Affective development in infancy* (pp. 95–124). Westport, CT: Ablex.

Main, M., & Solomon, J. (1990). Procedures for identifying infants as disorganized/disoriented during the Ainsworth Strange Situation. In T. B. Brazelton & M. Yogman (Eds.), *Attachment in the preschool years: Theory, research, and intervention* (pp. 121–160). Chicago: University of Chicago Press.

Masterson, J. F. (1976). *Psychotherapy of the borderline adult.* New York: Brunner/Mazel.

Masterson, J. F. (1985). *The real self: A developmental, self, and object relations approach.* New York: Brunner/Mazel.

Masterson, J. F. (1993). *The emerging self.* New York: Brunner/Mazel.

Masterson, J. F., & Klein, R. (Eds.). (1995). *Disorders of the self.* New York: Brunner/Mazel.

Masterson, J. F., & Lieberman, A. R. (2004). A therapist's guide to the personality disorders. Phoenix, AZ: Zeig, Tucker, & Theisen, Inc.

Meins, E., Fernyhough, C., Wainwright, R., Das Gupta, M., Fradley, E., & Tuckery, M. (2002). Maternal mind-mindedness and attachment security as predictors of theory of mind understanding. *Child Development, 73*(6), 1715–1726.

Miga, E. M., Hare, A., Allen, J. P., & Manning, N. (2010). The relation of insecure attachment states of mind and romantic attachment styles to adolescent aggression in romantic relationships. *Attachment and Human Development, 12*(5), 463–481.

Mikulincer, M., & Florian, V. (1998). The relationship between adult attachment styles and emotional and cognitive reactions to stressful events. In J. A. Simpson & W. S. Rholes (Eds.), *Attachment theory and close relationships* (pp. 143–165). New York: Guilford Press.

Minuchin, S. (1980). Philadelphia Child Guidance Clinic, summer practicum.

Oppenheim, D., & Goldsmith, D. F. (Eds.). (2011). *Attachment theory in clinical work with children: Bridging the gap between research and practice.* New York: Guilford Press.

Pawl, J. H., & St. John, M. (1998). *How you are is as important as what you do.* Washington, DC: Zero to Three.

Perry, B. D., Pollard, R. A., Blakley, T. L., Baker, W. L., & Vigilante, D. (1995). Childhood trauma, the neurobiology of adaptation and "use-dependent" development of the brain: How "states" become "traits." *Infant Mental Health Journal, 16,* 271–291.

Pessora, L. (2008). On the relationship between emotion and cognition. *Nature Reviews Neuroscience, 9*(2), 148–158.

Polan, H. J., & Hofer, M. A. (2008). Psychobiological orgins of infant attachment and its role in development. In J. Cassidy & P. R. Shaver (Eds.), *The handbook of attachment: Theory, research, and clinical applications* (2nd ed., pp. 158–172). New York: Guilford Press.

Premack, D., & Woodruff, G. (1978). Does the chimpanzee have a 'theory of mind'? *Behavioral and Brain Sciences, 4,* 515–526.

Ramachandran, V. S. (2009, November). TED talk. Retrieved from *www.youtube. com/watch?v=w7lXYwcRppI.*

Reid, C. (Ed.). (2008). *Letters of Ted Hughes.* New York: Farrar, Straus & Giroux.

Riem, M. M., Bakermans-Kranenburg, M. J., van IJzendoorn, M. H., Out, D., & Rombouts, S. A. (2012). Attachment in the brain: adult attachment representations predict amygdala and behavioral responses to infant crying. *Attachment & Human Development, 14*(6), 533–551.

Roberts, D., & Roberts, D. A. (2007). *Another chance to be real: Attachment and object relations treatment of borderline personality disorder.* New York: Jason Aronson.

Rogers, C. R. (1957). The necessary and sufficient conditions of therapeutic personality change. *Journal of Consulting Psychology, 21*(2), 95–103.

Schore, A. N. (1996). The experience-dependent maturation of a regulatory system in the orbital prefrontal cortex and the origin of developmental psychopathology. *Development and Psychopathology, 8*(1), 59–87.

Schore, A. N. (2002). Dysregulation of the right brain: A fundamental mechanism of traumatic attachment and the psychopathogenesis of posttraumatic stress disorder. *Australian and New Zealand Journal of Psychiatry, 36*(1), 9–30.

Shanker, S. (2004). The roots of mindblindness. *Theory and Psychology, 14*(5), 685–703.

Shonkoff, J., Boyce, W., Cameron, J., Duncan, G., Fox, N., Gunnar, M., et al. (2005). *Excessive stress disrupts the architecture of the developing brain* (Working Paper No. 3, pp. 1–11). Cambridge, MA: National Scientific Council on the Developing Mind, Harvard University.

Shonkoff, J. P., Boyce, W. T., & McEwen, B. S. (2009). Neuroscience, molecular biology, and the childhood roots of health disparities. *Journal of the American Medical Association, 301*(21), 2252–2259.

Shonkoff, J. P., & Phillips, D. A. (Eds.). (2000). From neurons to neighborhoods: The science of early childhood development. Washington, DC: National Academy Press.

Siegel, D. (1999). *The developing mind: How relationships and the brain interact to shape who we are.* New York: Guilford Press.

Siegel, D., & Hartzell, M. (2004). *Parenting from the inside out: How a deeper self-understanding can help you raise children who thrive.* New York: Penguin.

Slade, A. (2008). The implications of attachment theory and research for adult psychotherapy: Research and clinical perspectives. In J. Cassidy & P. R. Shaver (Eds.), *The handbook of attachment: Theory, research, and clinical applications* (2nd ed., pp. 762–782). New York: Guilford Press.

Solomon, J., & George, C. (1999). The place of disorganization in attachment theory: Linking classic observations with contemporary findings. In J. Solomon & C. George (Eds.), *Attachment disorganization* (pp. 3–32). New York: Guilford Press.

Solomon, J., & George, C. (2008). The measurement of attachment security and related constructs in infancy and early childhood. In J. Cassidy & P. R. Shaver (Eds.), *Handbook of attachment: Theory, research, and clinical applications* (2nd ed., pp. 383–416). New York: Guilford Press.

Solomon, J., & George, C. (Eds.). (2011). *Disorganized attachment and caregiving.* New York: Guilford Press.

Sroufe, L. A. (1983). Infant–caregiver attachment and patterns of adaptation in preschool. In M. Perlmutter (Ed.), *Minnesota Symposia on Child Psychology: Vol.16. The roots of maladaptation and competence* (pp. 129–135). Hillsdale, NJ: Erlbaum.

Sroufe, L. A. (1995). *Emotional development: The organization of emotional life in the early years.* New York: Cambridge University Press.

Sroufe, L. A., Carlson, E., Levy, A. K., & Egeland, B. (1999). Implications of attachment theory for developmental psychopathology. *Development and Psychopathology, 11,* 1–13.

Sroufe, L. A., Egeland, B., Carlson, E. A., & Collins, A. W. (2005). *The development of the person: The Minnesota study of risk and adaptation from birth to adulthood.* New York: Guilford Press.

Sroufe, L. A., & Waters, E. (1977). Heart-rate as a convergent measure in clinical developmental research. *Merrill-Palmer Quarterly, 23*(1), 3–27.

Steele, H., & Steele, M. (2008). On the origins of reflective functioning. In F. Busch (Ed.), *Mentalization: Theoretical considerations, research findings, and clinical implications* (pp. 133–156). New York: Analytic Press.

Stern, D. (1985). *The interpersonal world of the infant: A view from psychoanalysis and developmental psychology.* New York: Basic Books.

Stern, D. (1995). *The motherhood constellation: A unified view of parent–infant psychotherapy.* New York: Basic Books.

van IJzendoorn, M. (1995). Adult attachment representation, parental responsiveness, and infant attachment: A meta-analysis on the predictive validity of the AAI. *Psychological Bulletin, 117,* 387–403.

van IJzendoorn, M., Schuengel, C., & Bakermans-Kranenburg, M. (1999). Disorganized attachment in early childhood: Meta-analysis of precursors, concomitants, and sequelae. *Development and Psychopathology, 11,* 225–249.

Viorst, J. (1986). *Necessary losses: The loves, illusions, dependencies, and impossible expectations that all of us have to give up in order to grow.* New York: Fireside.

Walker, A. (1990). *The temple of my familiar.* Boston: Mariner Books

Wallin, D. (2007). *Attachment in psychotherapy.* New York: Guilford Press.

Weininger, O. (1998). Time-in parenting strategies. Binghamton, NY: Esf Publishers.

Winnicott, D. W. (1965a). The capacity to be alone. In *The maturational processes and the facilitating environment* (pp. 29–36). New York: International Universities Press.

Winnicott, D. W. (1965b). The theory of the parent–infant relationship. In *The maturational processes and the facilitating environment* (pp. 37–55). New York: International Universities Press.

Winnicott, D. W. (1971). *Playing and reality.* London: Tavistock.

Winnicott, D. W. (1974). Fear of breakdown. *International Review of Psycho-Analysis, 1,* 103–107.

Winnicott, D. W. (1994). *Talking to parents.* New York: Da Capo Press.

Zeanah, C. H., Larrieu, J. A., Heller, S. S., & Valliere, J. (2000). Infant–parent relationship assessment. In C. H. Zeanah (Ed.), *Handbook of infant mental health* (2nd ed., pp. 222–235). New York: Guilford Press.

Index

The letter *f* following a page number indicates figure.

396 Index

Treatment (*continued*)
parent's capacity for emotional work and, 208–209
phase one in the COS protocol, 294–296
phase two in the COS protocol, 301–304
phase three in the COS protocol, 305
RAR acronym (relationship, affect, reflection), 262–264
recording a modified SSP, 304
reflection and, 260–261
relationship and, 258–260
shark music and, 296–301, 299f, 300f, 301f, 302f
video review, 294–296
weeks 1-2, 278–294, 282f, 285f, 286f, 287f, 291f, 293f
week 9, 296–301, 299f, 300f, 301f, 302f
week 16, 304
Welcome to the Club form, 312–313
Treatment planning. *See also* Goals
Circle of Security Assessment and Treatment Plan Organizer, 163, 179, 180f, 182–184, 245f–248f
Circle of Security Interview (COSI) and, 219–220
core sensitivities and, 265–275
customized, 264
example of, 245f–248f
overview, 241–244, 255–257
Triggers, 192
Trust
assessing caregiver behavior and, 144–145
attachment and, 20–21
Being-With and, 38–39
Circle of Security (COS) and, 24–25, 24f
disorganized state of mind and, 103
expectations and, 49–51
Tuning, 141–160, 142f. *See also* Attunement

U

Unavailability of attachment figures, 28
Unpredictability, 103
Unresolved/disorganized behavior, 95–96

V

Video use. *See also* Filming technology
case example, 326–334, 346–354, 367–374
celebrating changes in the modified SSP, 305
Circle of Security Assessment and Treatment Plan Organizer, 183
Circle of Security (COS) and, 15–16
Circle of Security Interview (COSI) and, 220–221
core sensitivities and, 196–197, 199f
guide for finding video clips in the Strange Situation, 165–169
identifying the linchpin, 301–304
overview, 256
phase one in the COS protocol, 294–296
phase two in the COS protocol, 301–304
phase three in the COS protocol, 305
recording a modified SSP, 304
shark music and, 89–90
therapeutic contract and, 265
treatment and, 263
video review, 294–296
video review and, 301–304
weeks 1-2, 278–294, 282f, 285f, 286f, 287f, 291f
week 16, 304
Vigilance, 198f
Vulnerability, 225–226

W

Warning signs. *See* Shark music
Weakness
assessing caregiver behavior and, 154–156, 157
introducing shark music to parents, 301f, 302f
rupture/repair process and, 292
Welcome to the Club form, 312–313
Winnicott, Donald, 39, 60–61
Woodhouse, Susan, 59, 138, 162
Working models of attachment, 194–196

Z

Zero to Three organization and, 5